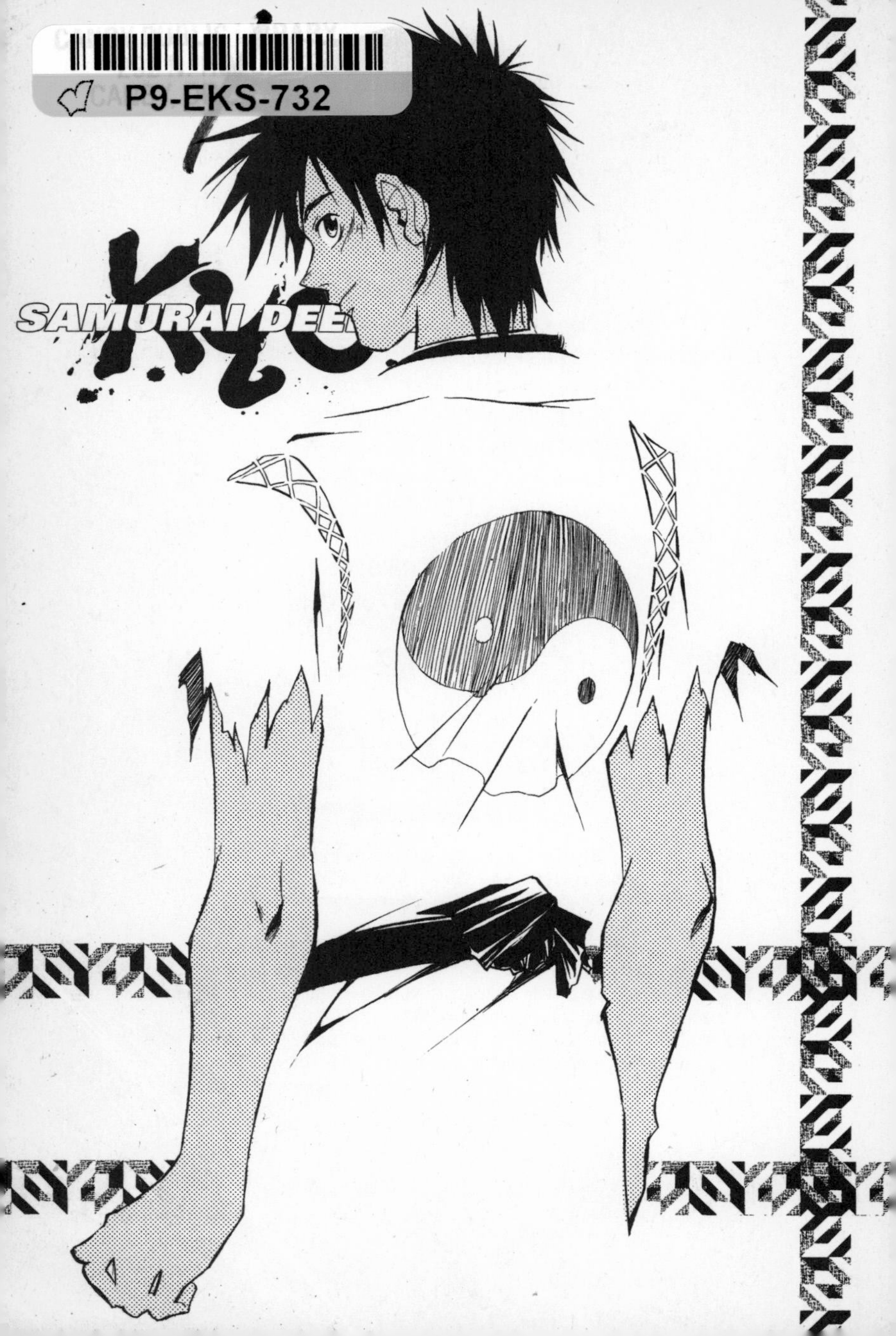
SAMURAI DEE
KYO

Translator - Alexander O. Smith
Script Editor - Rich Amtower
Copy Editor - Carol Fox
Retouch and Lettering - Miyuki Ishihara
Cover Design - Raymond Makowski
Graphic Designer - James Lee

Editor - Jake Forbes
Managing Editor - Jill Freshney
Production Coordinator - Antonio DePietro
Production Managers - Jennifer Miller, Mutsumi Miyazaki
Art Director - Matt Alford
Editorial Director - Jeremy Ross
VP of Production - Ron Klamert
President & C.O.O. - John Parker
Publisher & C.E.O. - Stuart Levy

Email: editor@TOKYOPOP.com
Come visit us online at www.TOKYOPOP.com

A TOKYOPOP® Manga

TOKYOPOP Inc.
5900 Wilshire Blvd. Suite 2000
Los Angeles, CA 90036

Samurai Deeper Kyo Vol. 5

ISBN: 1-59182-541-5

First TOKYOPOP printing: February 2004

10 9 8 7 6 5 4 3 2 1
Printed in the USA

SAMURAI DEEPER Kyo

Vol. 5

by Akimine Kamijyo

Los Angeles • Tokyo • London

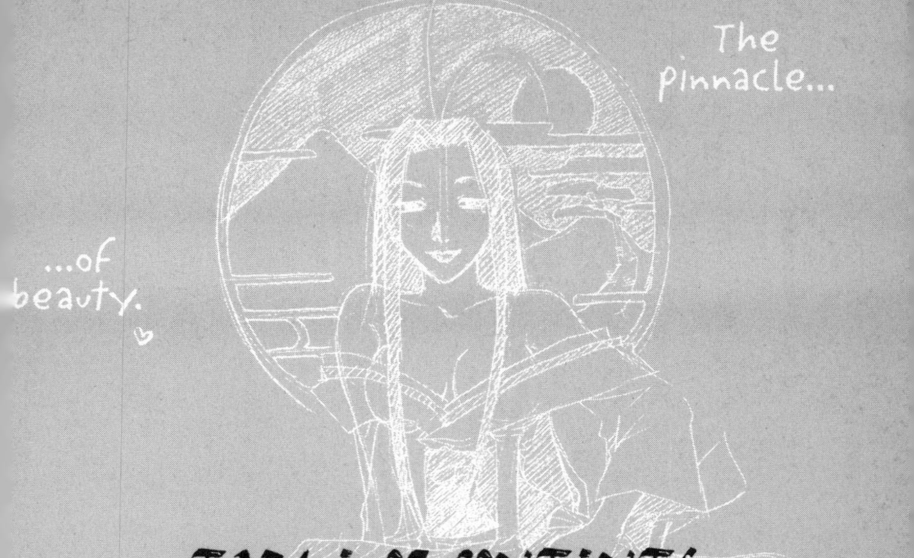
The pinnacle...
...of beauty.

TABLE OF CONTENTS

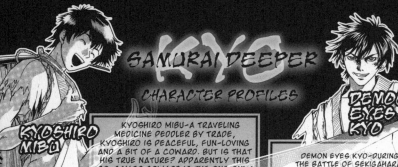

Samurai Deeper KYO

Character Profiles

Kyoshiro Mibu

KYOSHIRO MIBU–A TRAVELING MEDICINE PEDDLER BY TRADE, KYOSHIRO IS PEACEFUL, FUN-LOVING AND A BIT OF A COWARD. BUT IS THAT HIS TRUE NATURE? APPARENTLY THIS SO-CALLED COWARD IS THE ONE ONLY ONE TO EVER DEFEAT DEMON EYES KYO. WHAT REALLY HAPPENED AT SEKIGAHARA?

Demon Eyes Kyo

DEMON EYES KYO–DURING THE BATTLE OF SEKIGAHARA, ONIME NO KYO, OR "DEMON EYES KYO," WAS SAID TO HAVE KILLED 1000 MEN, AND FOR HIS CRIMES A ONE MILLION RYO BOUNTY HAS BEEN PLACED ON HIS HEAD. SOMEHOW, AFTER SEKIGAHARA, KYO'S SPIRIT BECAME TRAPPED INSIDE KYOSHIRO'S BODY. NOW KYOSHIRO'S SPIRIT IS TRAPPED AND KYO'S SPIRIT CONTROLS THE BODY.

Yuya Shiina

YUYA SHIINA–A BOUNTY HUNTRESS WHO SAYS SHE'S THE BEST ON KOKAIDO-CHU. SHE ONLY GOES AFTER THE MOST HIGH-PROFILE CRIMINALS WITH THE HIGHEST BOUNTIES. SHE IS ARMED WITH A THREE-BARRELED PISTOL AND SHE CAN THROW KNIVES WITH DEADLY ACCURACY, BUT PERHAPS HER GREATEST WEAPON IS HER FEMININE WILES. IN ADDITION TO HER BOUNTY HUNTING, SHE ALSO SEARCHES FOR A MAN WITH A SCAR WHO IS SOMEHOW CONNECTED TO HER PAST.

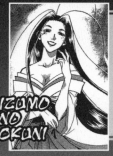

Izumo no Okuni

IZUMO NO OKUNI–A PAID INFORMANT, THIS BEAUTIFUL BACK-STABBER IS MORE THAN SHE LETS ON. SHE KNOWS DEMON EYES KYO AND SEEMS TO HAVE HAD SOME SORT OF RELATIONSHIP WITH HIM IN THE PAST.

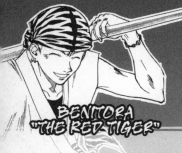

Yukimura Sanada

YUKIMURA SANADA–SON OF A WEALTHY AND POWERFUL FAMILY, SANADA WANTS THE HEAD OF IEYASU TOKUGAWA AND HOPES KYO WILL GET IT FOR HIM. HE IS FOND OF DRINK AND WOMEN, BUT WHEN THE OCCASION CALLS FOR IT, HE IS A MASTER WITH THE SWORD.

Benitora "The Red Tiger"

BENITORA, "THE RED TIGER"–DON'T LET HIS KITTEN-LIKE EXTERIOR FOOL YOU. THIS TIGER'S TRUE STRIPES ARE OF A MUCH MORE SAVAGE NATURE. BENITORA'S WEAPON OF CHOICE IS THE CROSS HAND SPEAR, A COLLAPSIBLE POLE WITH A THREE-BLADED CROSS AT THE END. HE SPEAKS IN KANSAI DIALECT AND IS A SHAMELESS FLIRT.

Mahiro "The Black Widow"

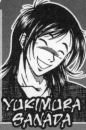

THIS DEADLY ASSASSIN KILLS WITH TRAINED SPIDERS AND POISONED WIRES. SHE SEEKS TO KILL DEMON EYES KYO TO AVENGE HER SISTER'S DEATH

KYO-SAN... DO WE HAVE A DEAL? YOU BRING ME THE SHOGUN IEYASU TOKUGAWA'S HEAD...

...D I'LL ...L YOU ...ERE ...SHIRO YOUR ...ODY.

SAMURAI DEEPER

Yukimura Sanada, enemy of the Tokugawa Shogunate, came to Demon Eyes Kyo with an interesting **proposition...**

I CANNOT ALLOW YOU TO LEAVE HERE ALIVE.

HEH-HEH-HEH.

WHAT?

A MILITIA! And samurai!

In order to reach Ieyasu, Kyo and his companions entered the **shogun's tournament** *at Edo. But after making it to the final round, they discover that the tournament was a trap.*

Tokugawa orders his men to kill Kyo...

...but Kyo defeats the milita.

NOW YOU'RE GOING TO TELL ME WHERE THE REAL IEYASU IS!

With no one left in his way, Kyo storms the shogun's palace to confront the so-called Ieyasu...

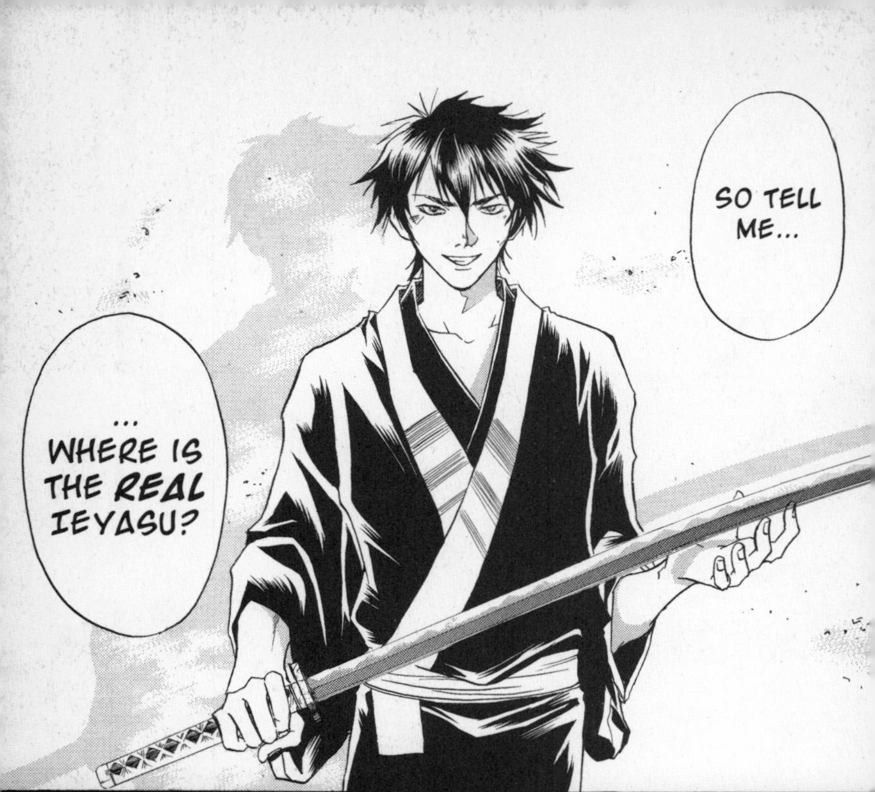
SO TELL ME...
... WHERE IS THE *REAL* IEYASU?

CHAPTER 33
DEATH WITHOUT HONOR

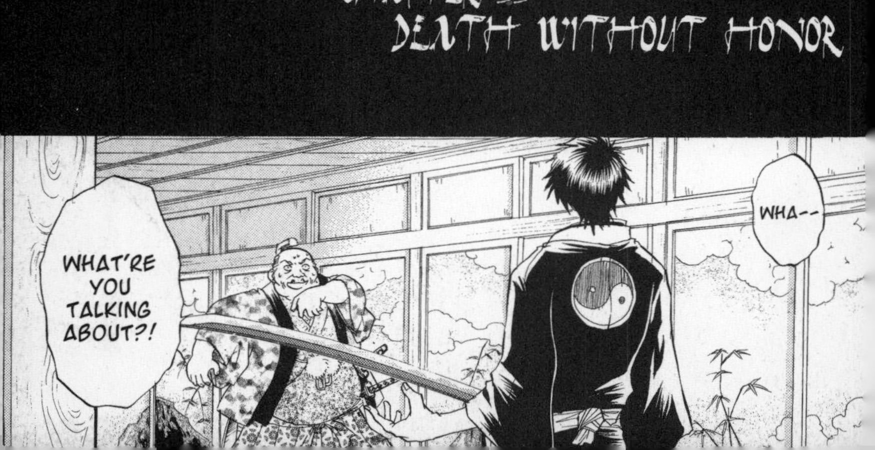
WHA--
WHAT'RE YOU TALKING ABOUT?!

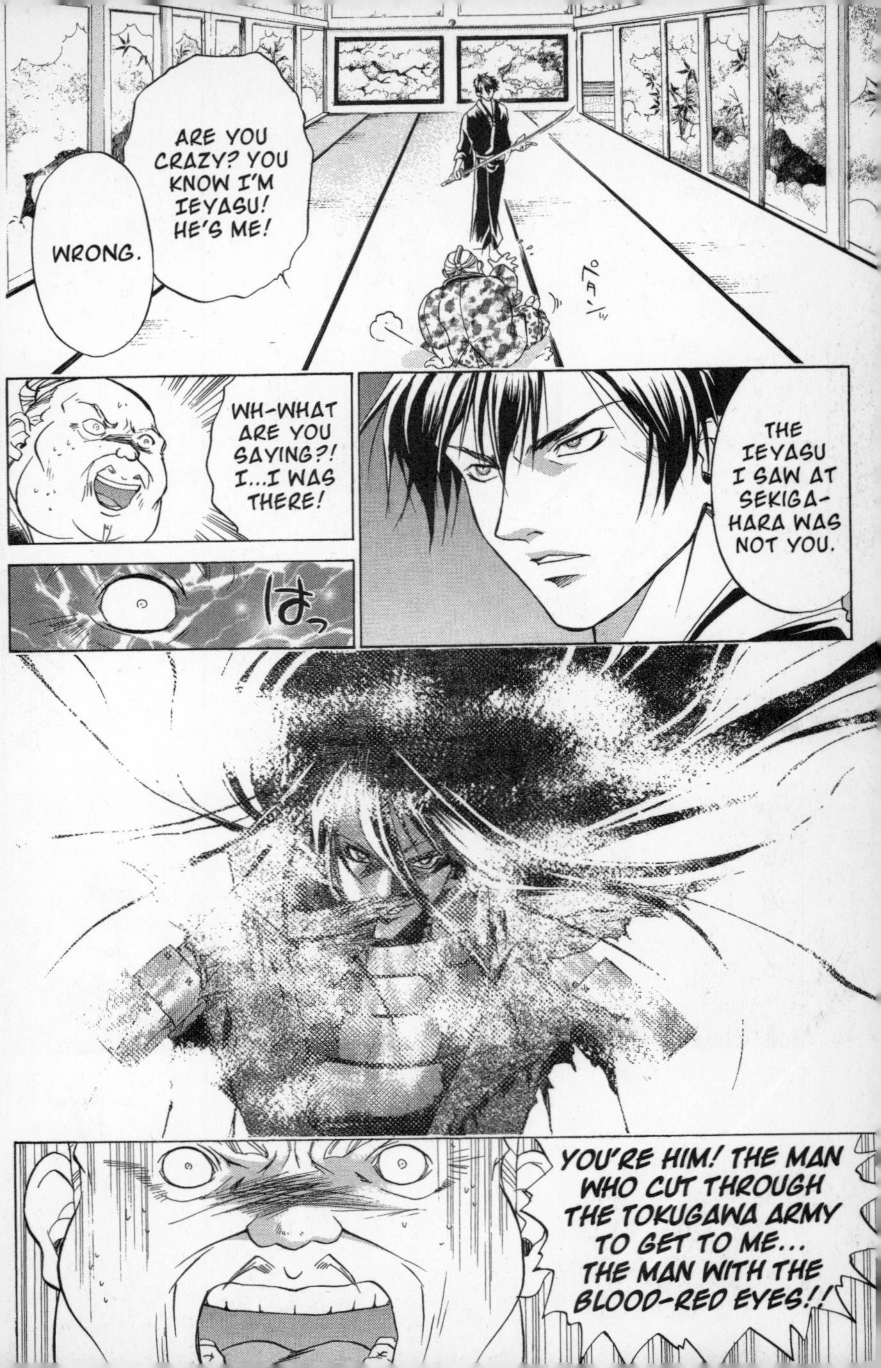
ARE YOU CRAZY? YOU KNOW I'M IEYASU! HE'S ME!
WRONG.
THE IEYASU I SAW AT SEKIGA-HARA WAS NOT YOU.
WH-WHAT ARE YOU SAYING?! I...I WAS THERE!
はっ
YOU'RE HIM! THE MAN WHO CUT THROUGH THE TOKUGAWA ARMY TO GET TO ME... THE MAN WITH THE BLOOD-RED EYES!!

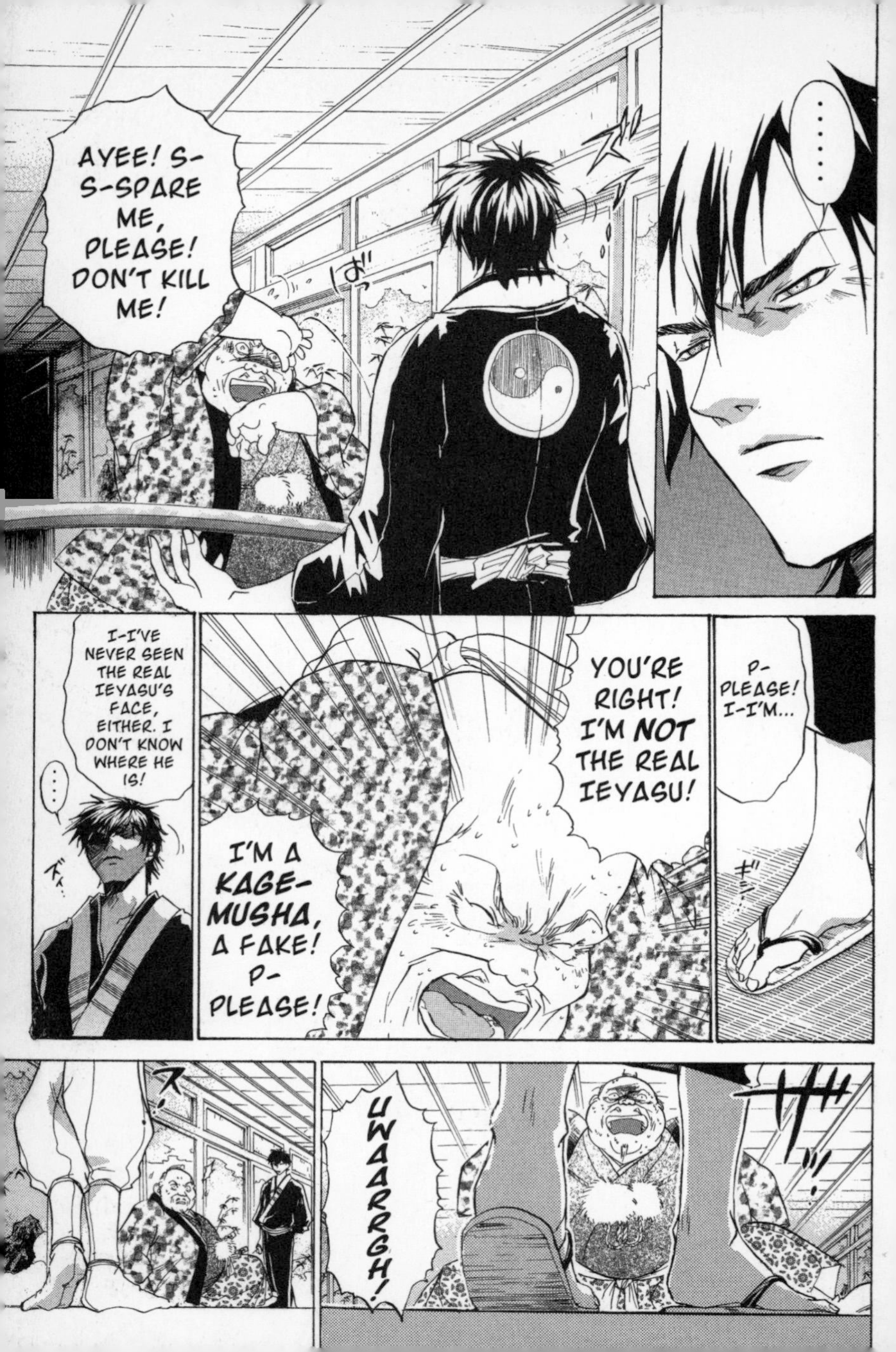
......
AYEE! S-S-SPARE ME, PLEASE! DON'T KILL ME!
P-PLEASE! I-I'M...
YOU'RE RIGHT! I'M NOT THE REAL IEYASU!
I'M A KAGE-MUSHA, A FAKE! P-PLEASE!
I-I'VE NEVER SEEN THE REAL IEYASU'S FACE, EITHER. I DON'T KNOW WHERE HE IS!
......
UWAARRGH!

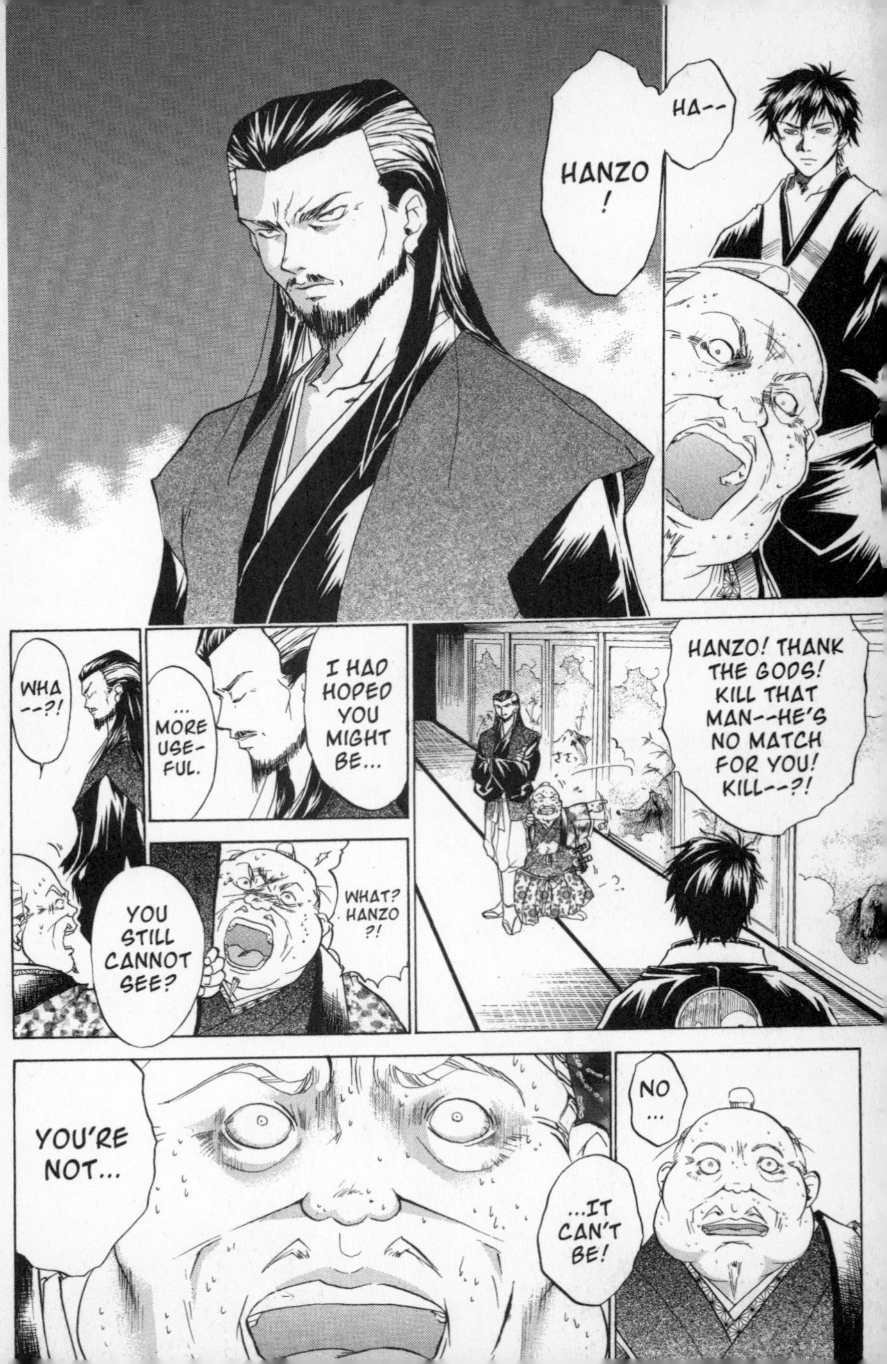
HA-- HANZO!
HANZO! THANK THE GODS! KILL THAT MAN--HE'S NO MATCH FOR YOU! KILL--?!
I HAD HOPED YOU MIGHT BE...
... MORE USE-FUL.
WHAT? HANZO?!
YOU STILL CANNOT SEE?
WHA--?!
NO...
...IT CAN'T BE!
YOU'RE NOT...

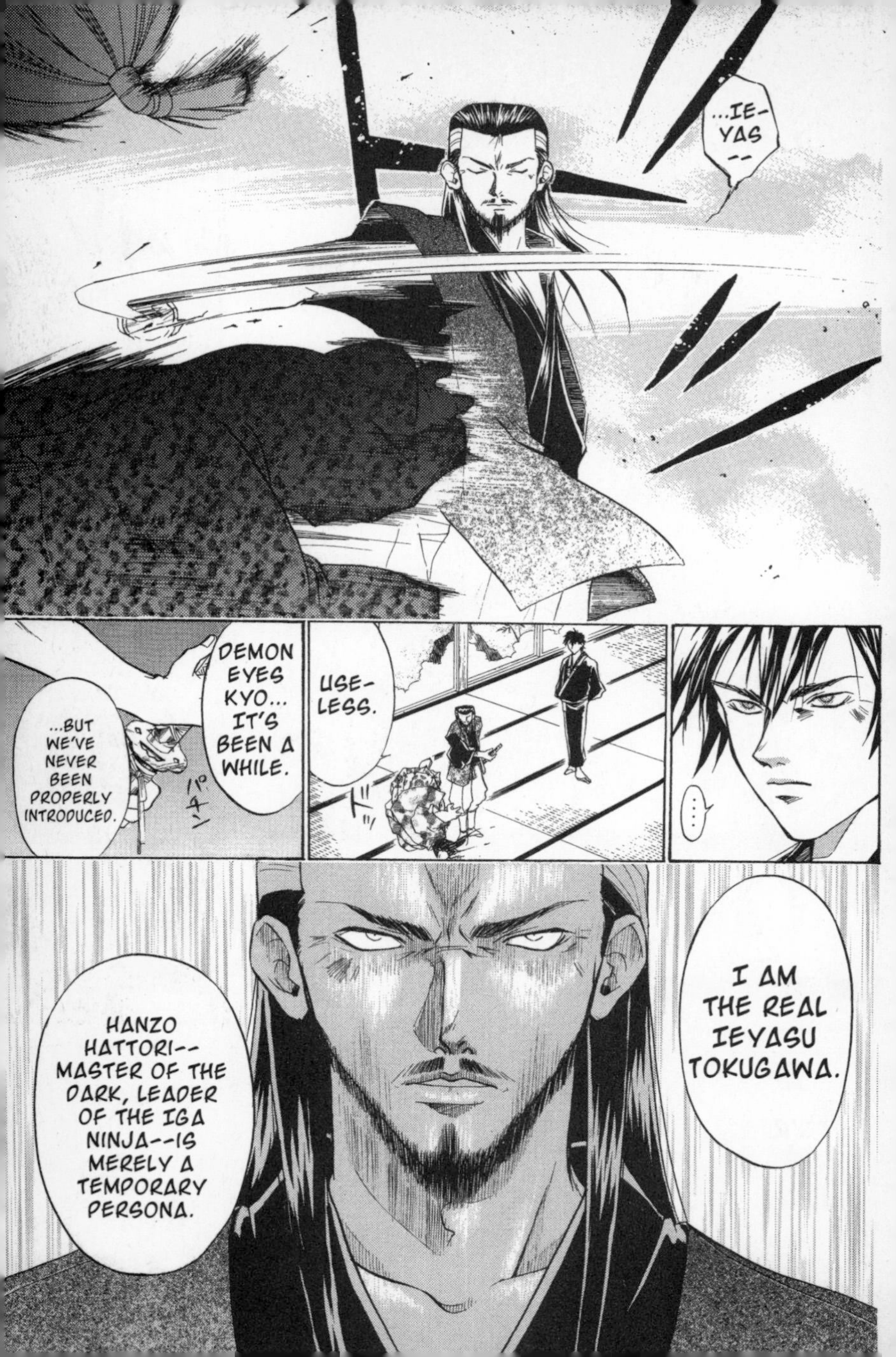

...IE-YAS--
...
USE-LESS.
DEMON EYES KYO... IT'S BEEN A WHILE.
...BUT WE'VE NEVER BEEN PROPERLY INTRODUCED.
I AM THE REAL IEYASU TOKUGAWA.
HANZO HATTORI--MASTER OF THE DARK, LEADER OF THE IGA NINJA--IS MERELY A TEMPORARY PERSONA.

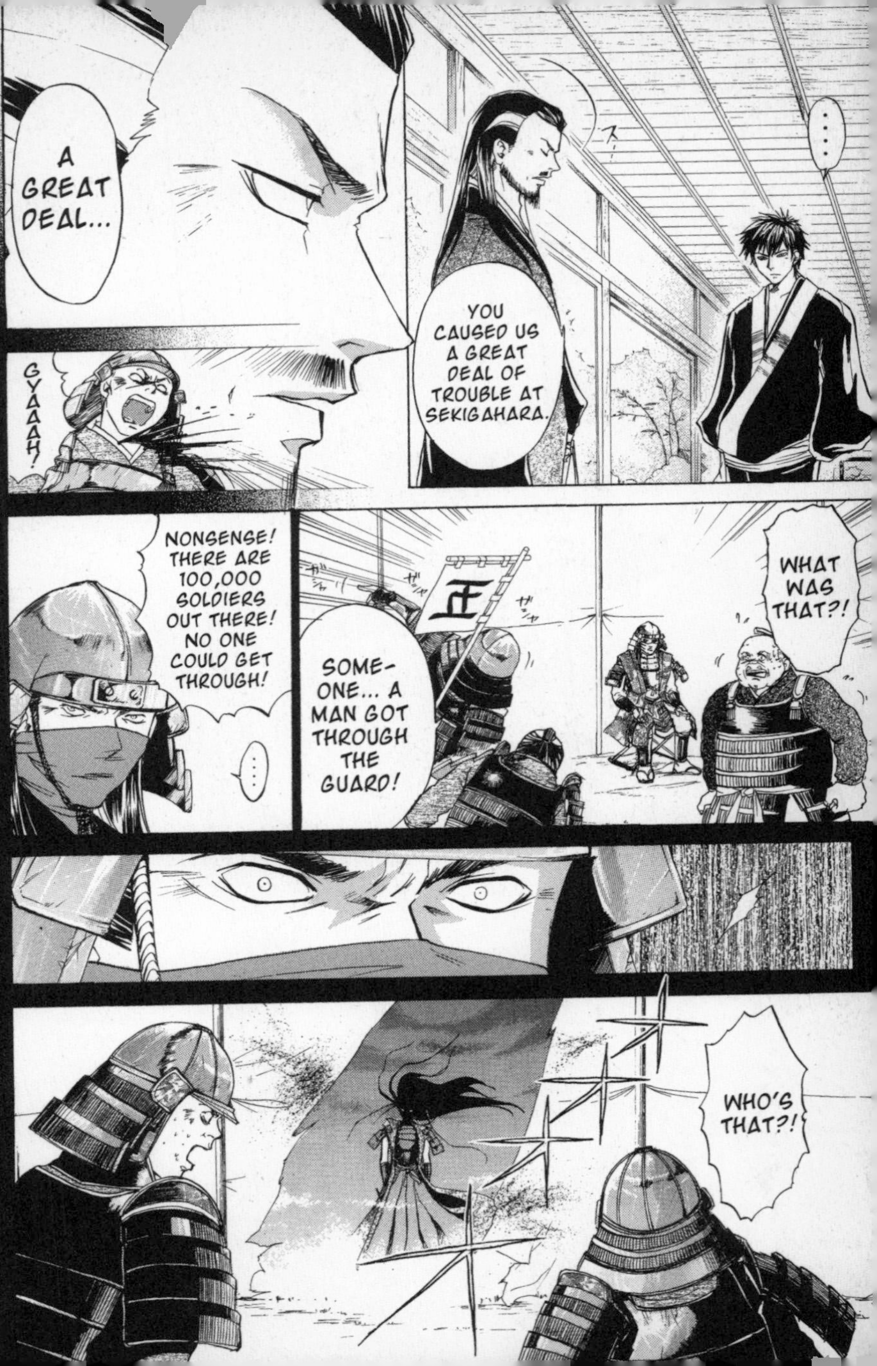

...
YOU CAUSED US A GREAT DEAL OF TROUBLE AT SEKIGAHARA.
A GREAT DEAL...
GYAAAH!
WHAT WAS THAT?!
SOME-ONE... A MAN GOT THROUGH THE GUARD!
NONSENSE! THERE ARE 100,000 SOLDIERS OUT THERE! NO ONE COULD GET THROUGH!
...
WHO'S THAT?!

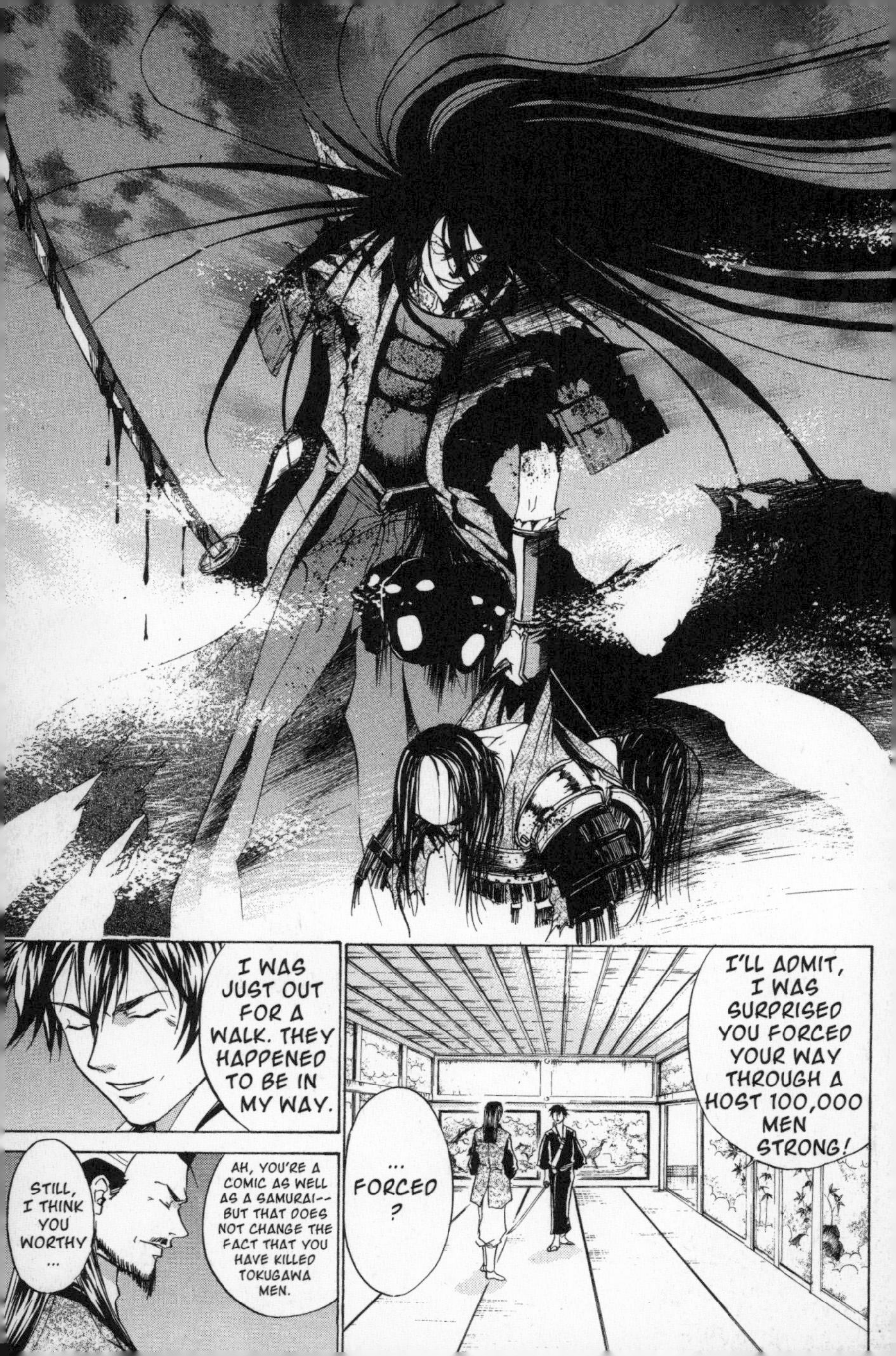
I'LL ADMIT, I WAS SURPRISED YOU FORCED YOUR WAY THROUGH A HOST 100,000 MEN STRONG!
... FORCED?
I WAS JUST OUT FOR A WALK. THEY HAPPENED TO BE IN MY WAY.
AH, YOU'RE A COMIC AS WELL AS A SAMURAI-- BUT THAT DOES NOT CHANGE THE FACT THAT YOU HAVE KILLED TOKUGAWA MEN.
STILL, I THINK YOU WORTHY ...

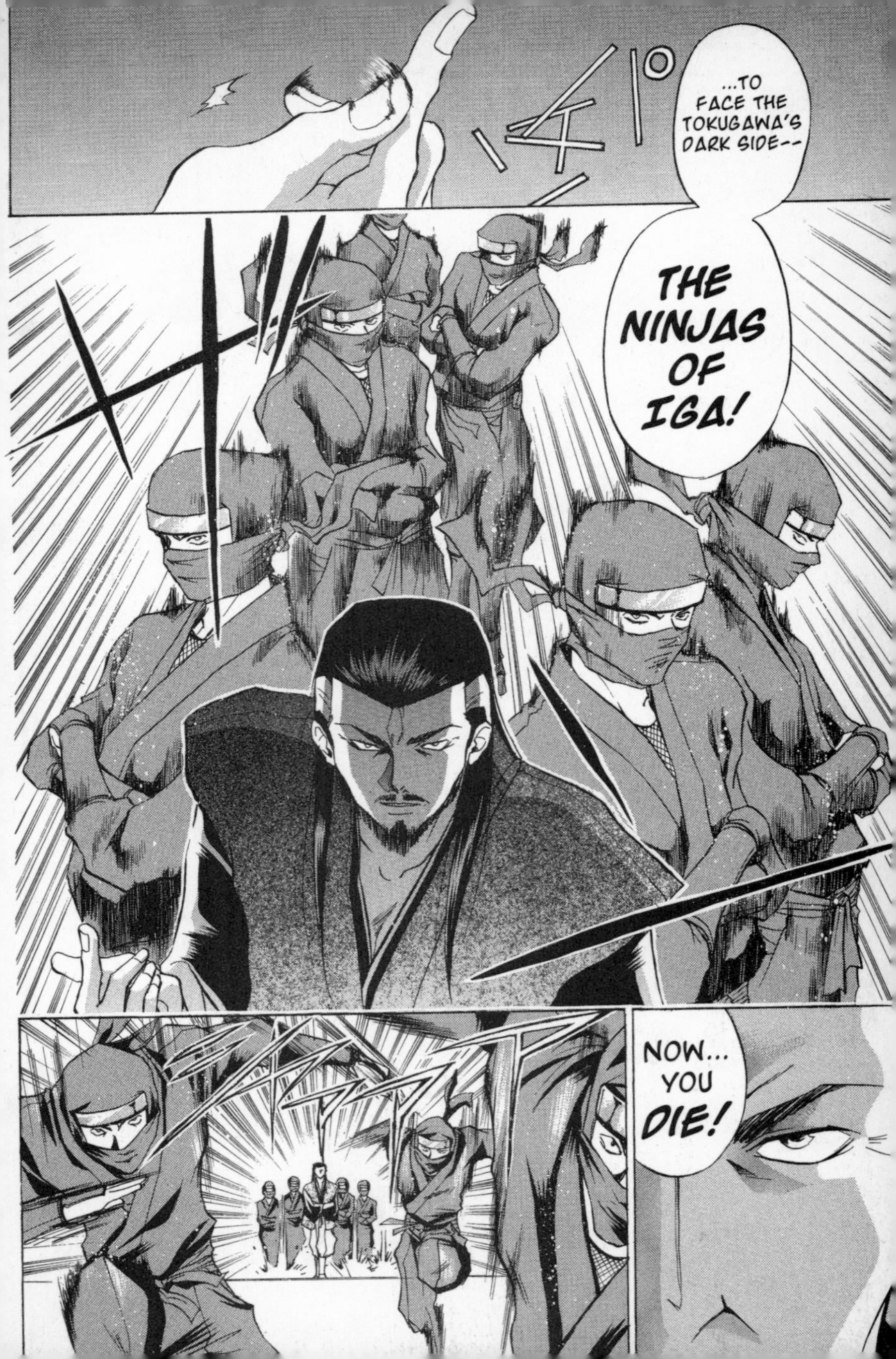
...TO FACE THE TOKUGAWA'S DARK SIDE--
THE NINJAS OF IGA!
NOW... YOU DIE!

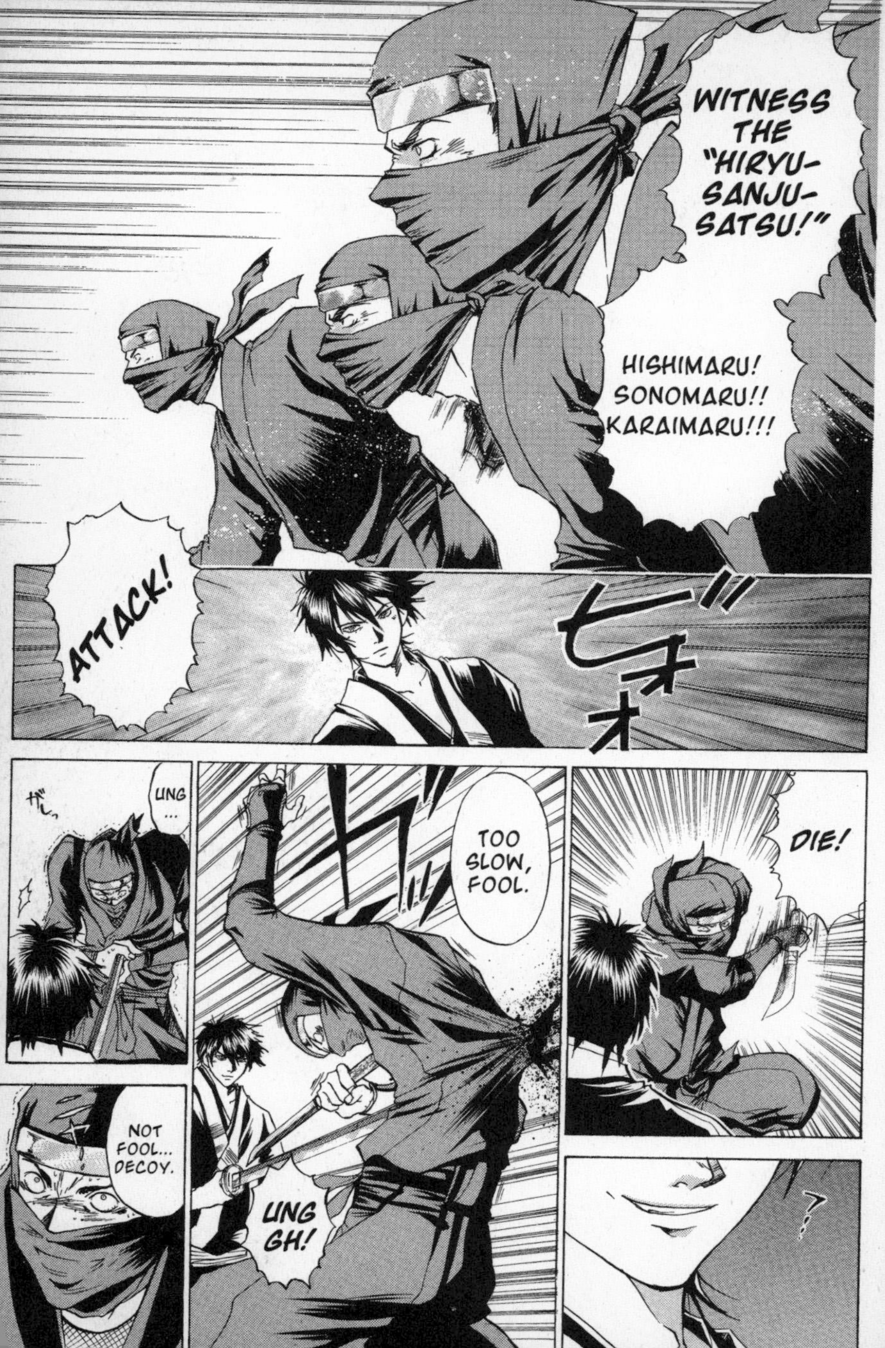
WITNESS THE "HIRYU-SANJU-SATSU!"
HISHIMARU! SONOMARU!! KARAIMARU!!!
ATTACK!
DIE!
?...
TOO SLOW, FOOL.
UNGGH!
UNG ...
NOT FOOL... DECOY.

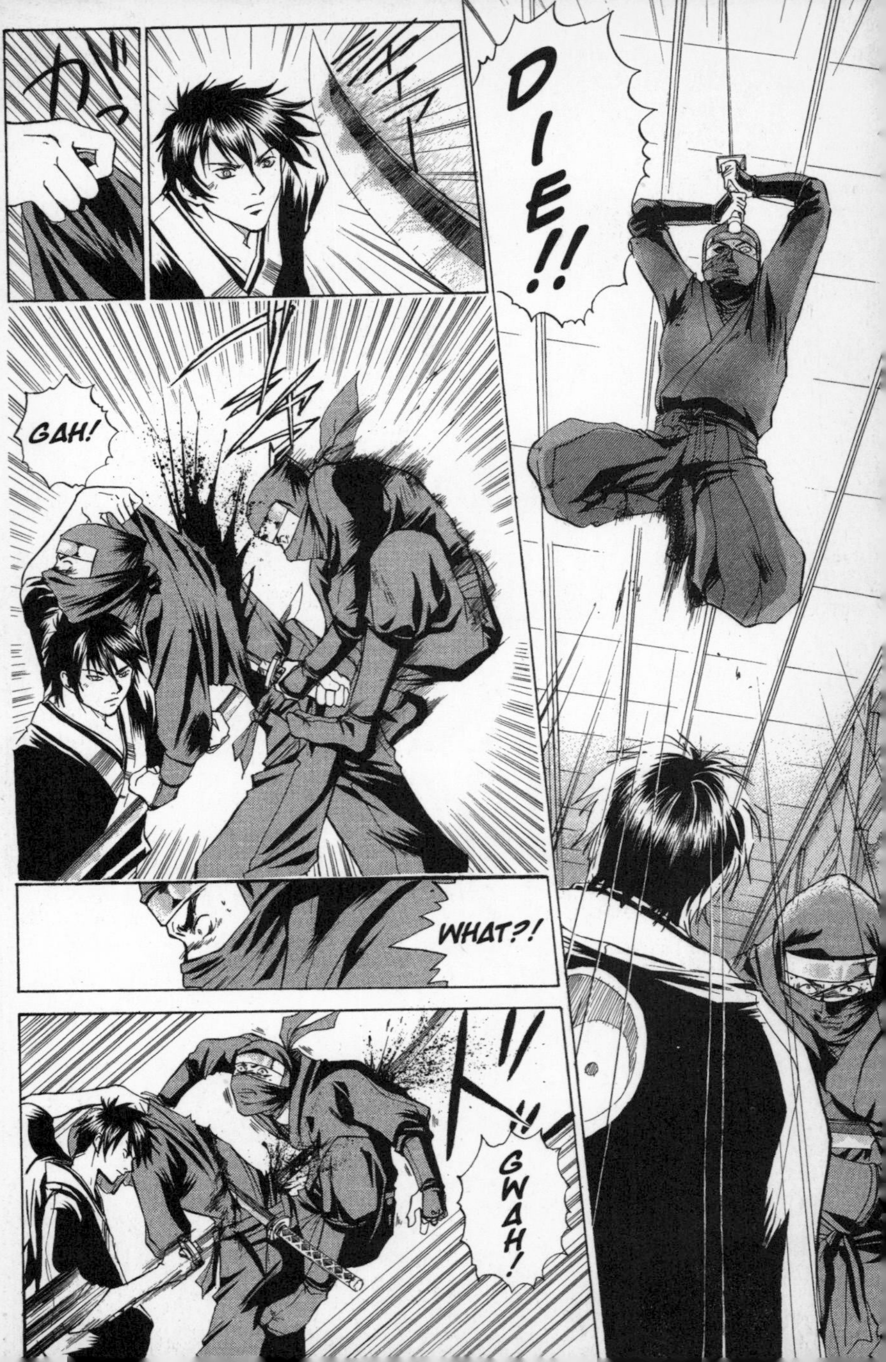
DIE!!
GAH!
WHAT?!
GWAH!

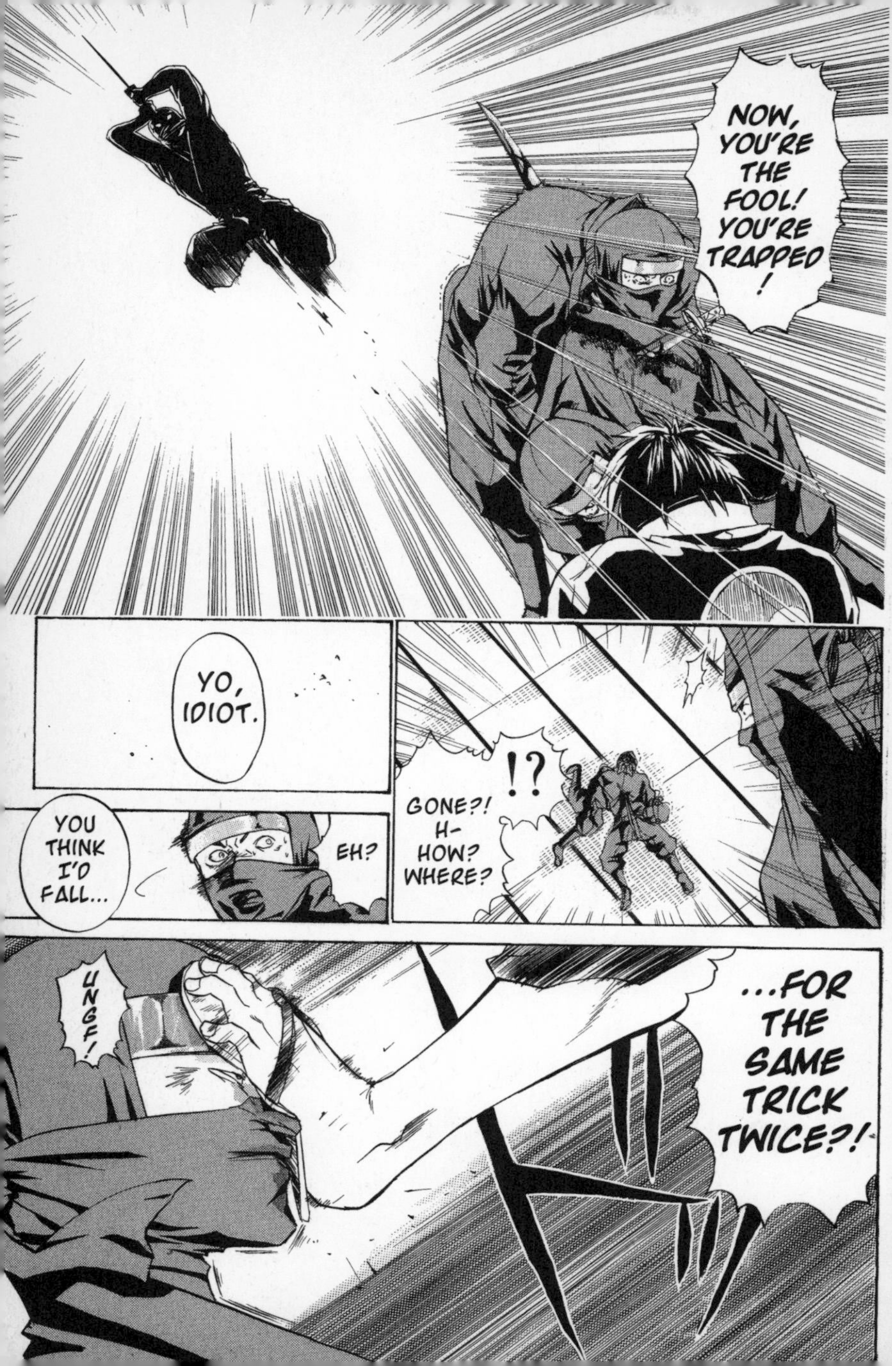
NOW, YOU'RE THE FOOL! YOU'RE TRAPPED!
!?
GONE?! H-HOW? WHERE?
YO, IDIOT.
EH?
YOU THINK I'D FALL...
...FOR THE SAME TRICK TWICE?!
UNGF!

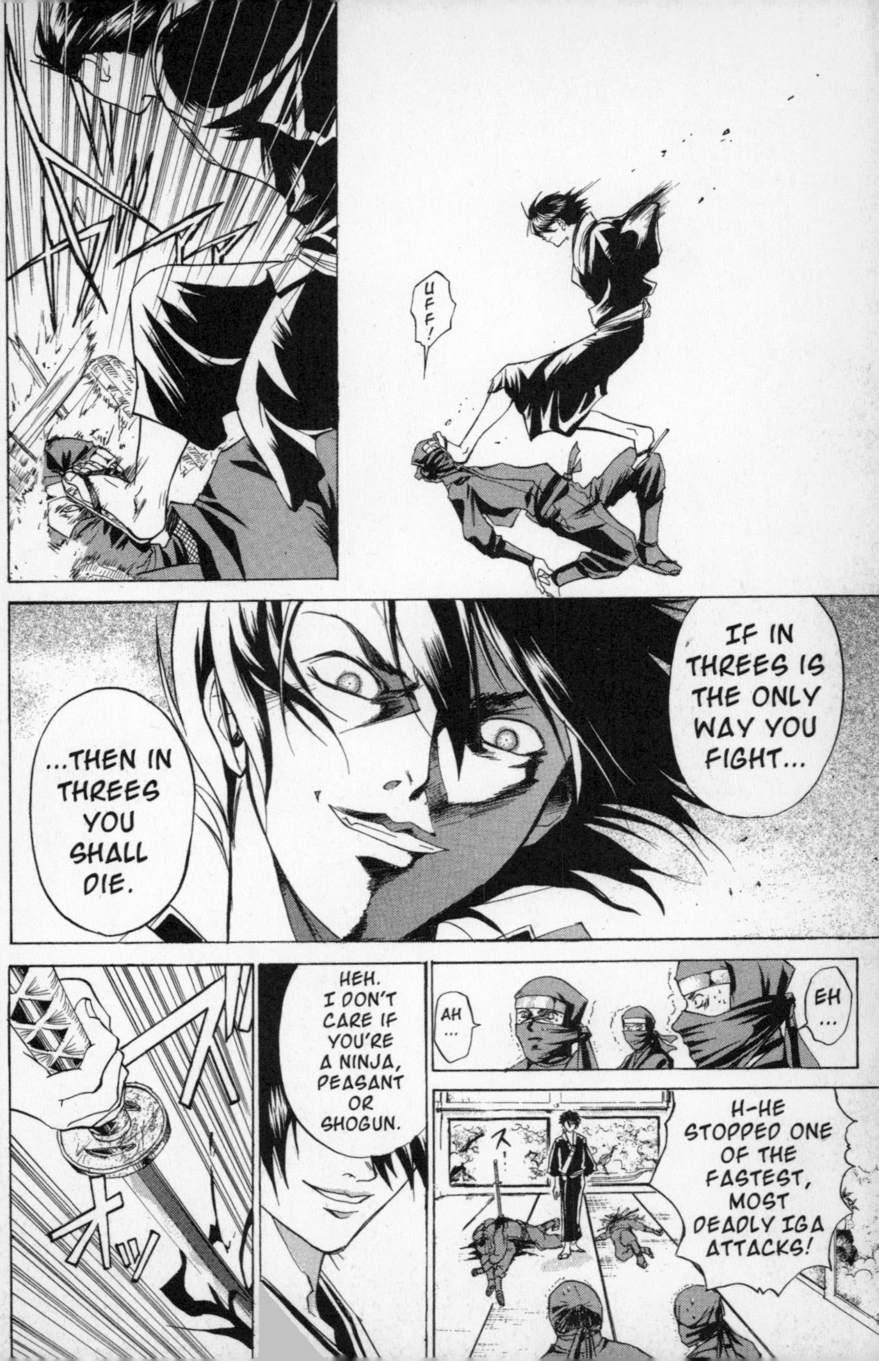
UFF!
IF IN THREES IS THE ONLY WAY YOU FIGHT...
...THEN IN THREES YOU SHALL DIE.
EH ...
AH ...
H-HE STOPPED ONE OF THE FASTEST, MOST DEADLY IGA ATTACKS!
HEH. I DON'T CARE IF YOU'RE A NINJA, PEASANT OR SHOGUN.

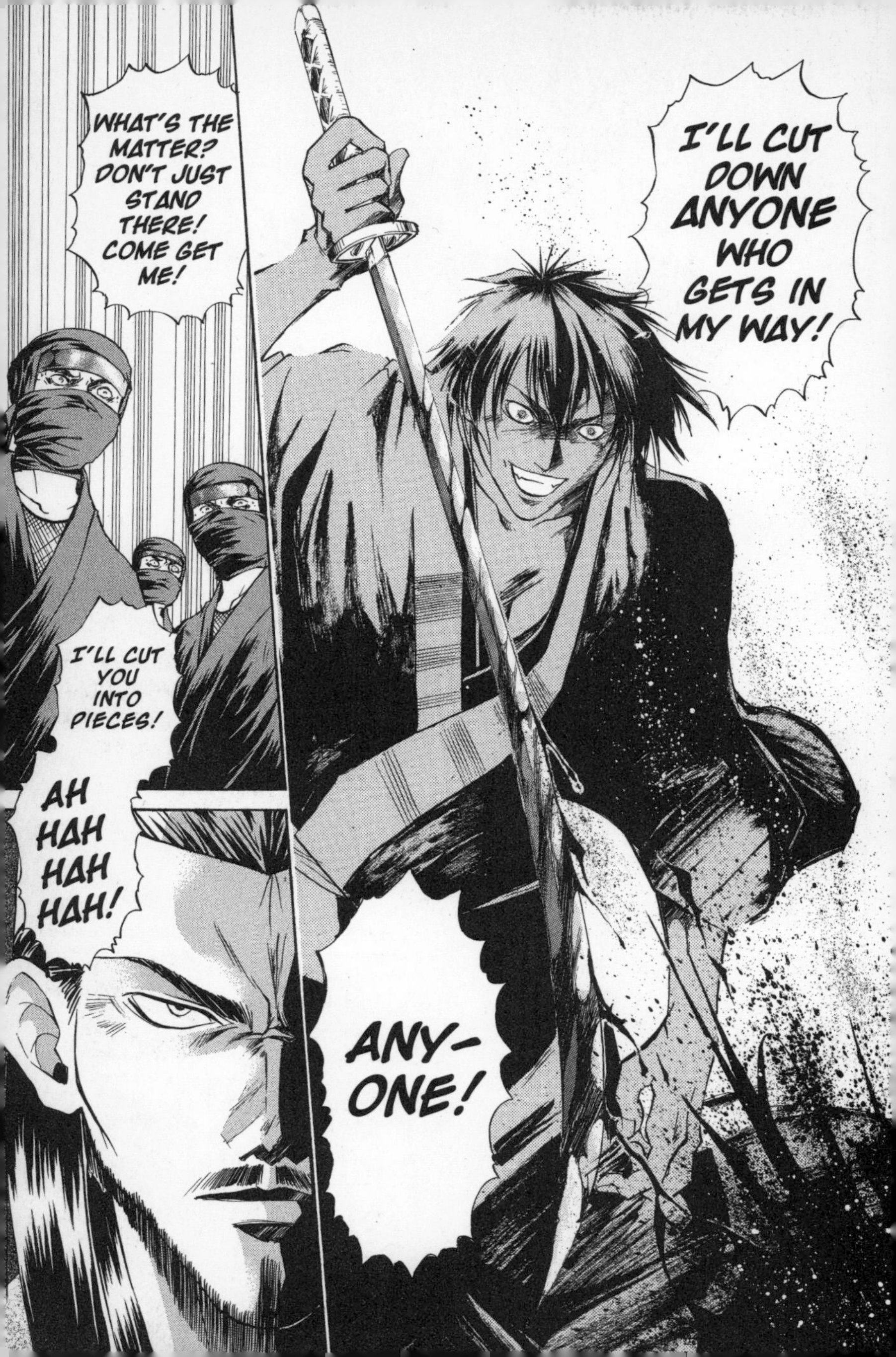
I'LL CUT DOWN ANYONE WHO GETS IN MY WAY!
ANY-ONE!
WHAT'S THE MATTER? DON'T JUST STAND THERE! COME GET ME!
I'LL CUT YOU INTO PIECES!
AH HAH HAH HAH!

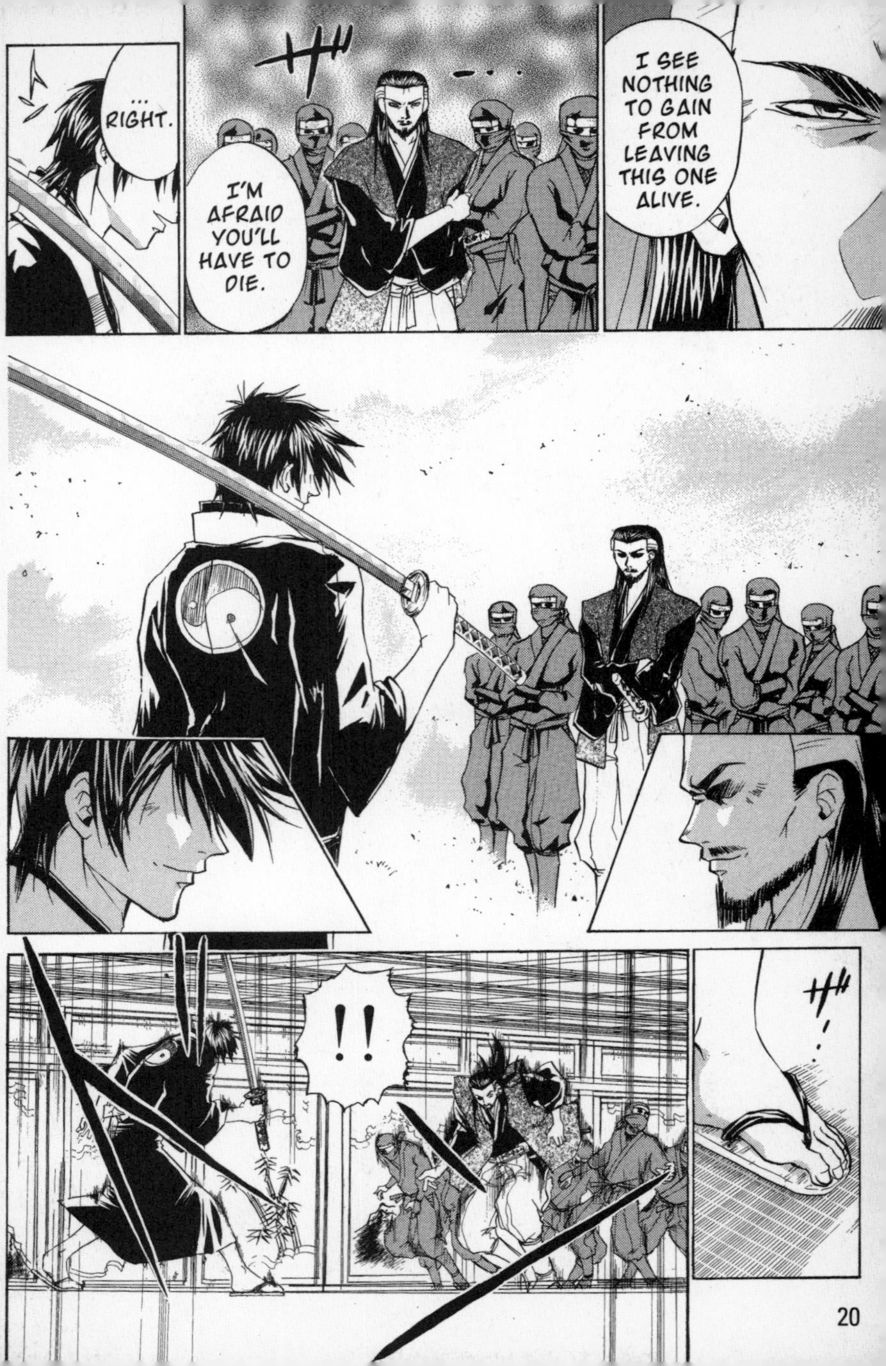
I SEE NOTHING TO GAIN FROM LEAVING THIS ONE ALIVE.
I'M AFRAID YOU'LL HAVE TO DIE.
... RIGHT.
!!

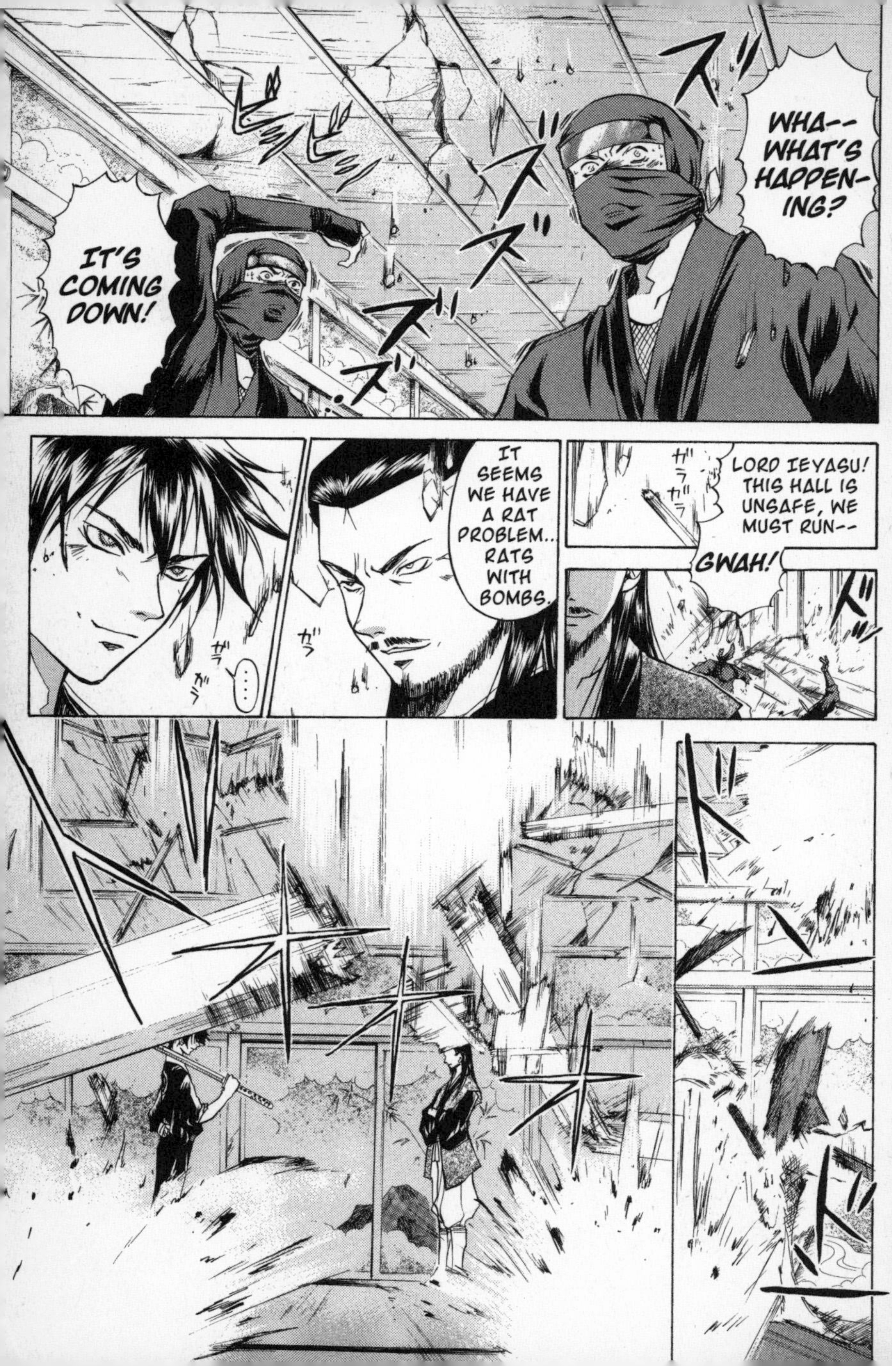
WHA-- WHAT'S HAPPENING?
IT'S COMING DOWN!
LORD IEYASU! THIS HALL IS UNSAFE, WE MUST RUN--
GWAH!
IT SEEMS WE HAVE A RAT PROBLEM... RATS WITH BOMBS.
...

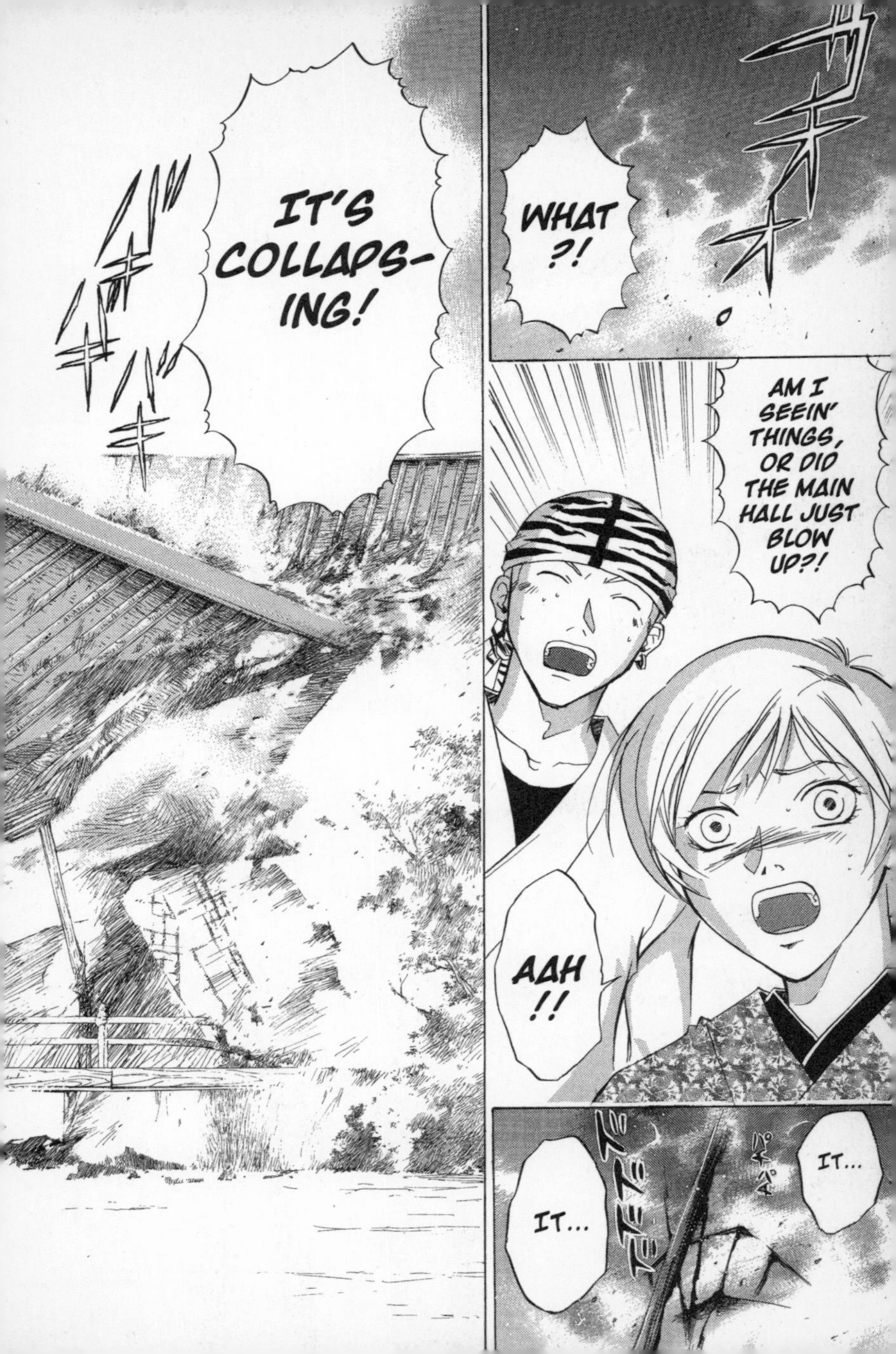
WHAT?!
AM I SEEIN' THINGS, OR DID THE MAIN HALL JUST BLOW UP?!
AAH!!
IT...
IT...
IT'S COLLAPSING!

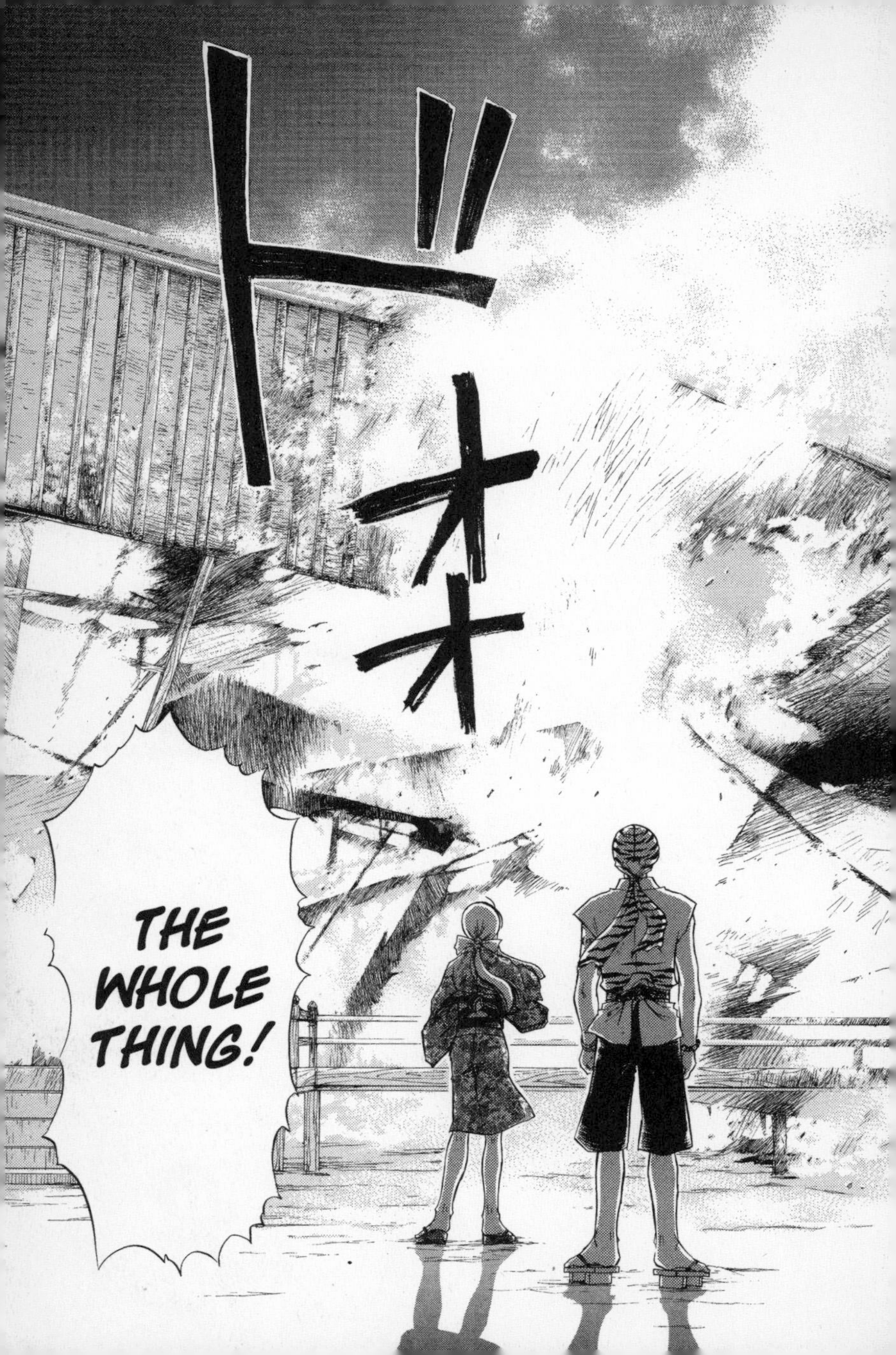
ドオオ
THE WHOLE THING!

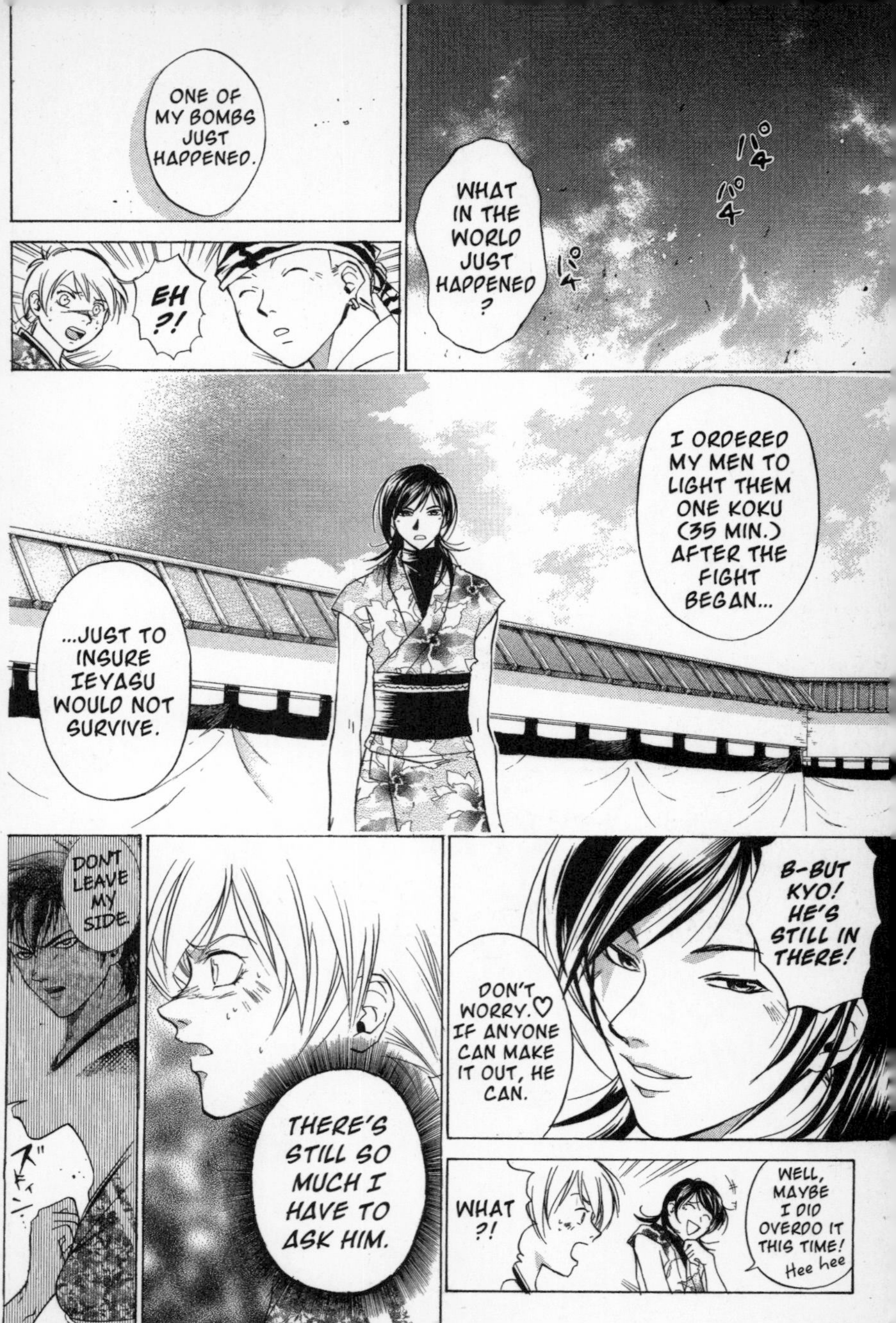
WHAT IN THE WORLD JUST HAPPENED?
ONE OF MY BOMBS JUST HAPPENED.
EH?!
I ORDERED MY MEN TO LIGHT THEM ONE KOKU (35 MIN.) AFTER THE FIGHT BEGAN...
...JUST TO INSURE IEYASU WOULD NOT SURVIVE.
B-BUT KYO! HE'S STILL IN THERE!
DON'T WORRY.♡ IF ANYONE CAN MAKE IT OUT, HE CAN.
WELL, MAYBE I DID OVERDO IT THIS TIME! Hee hee
WHAT?!
THERE'S STILL SO MUCH I HAVE TO ASK HIM.
DON'T LEAVE MY SIDE.

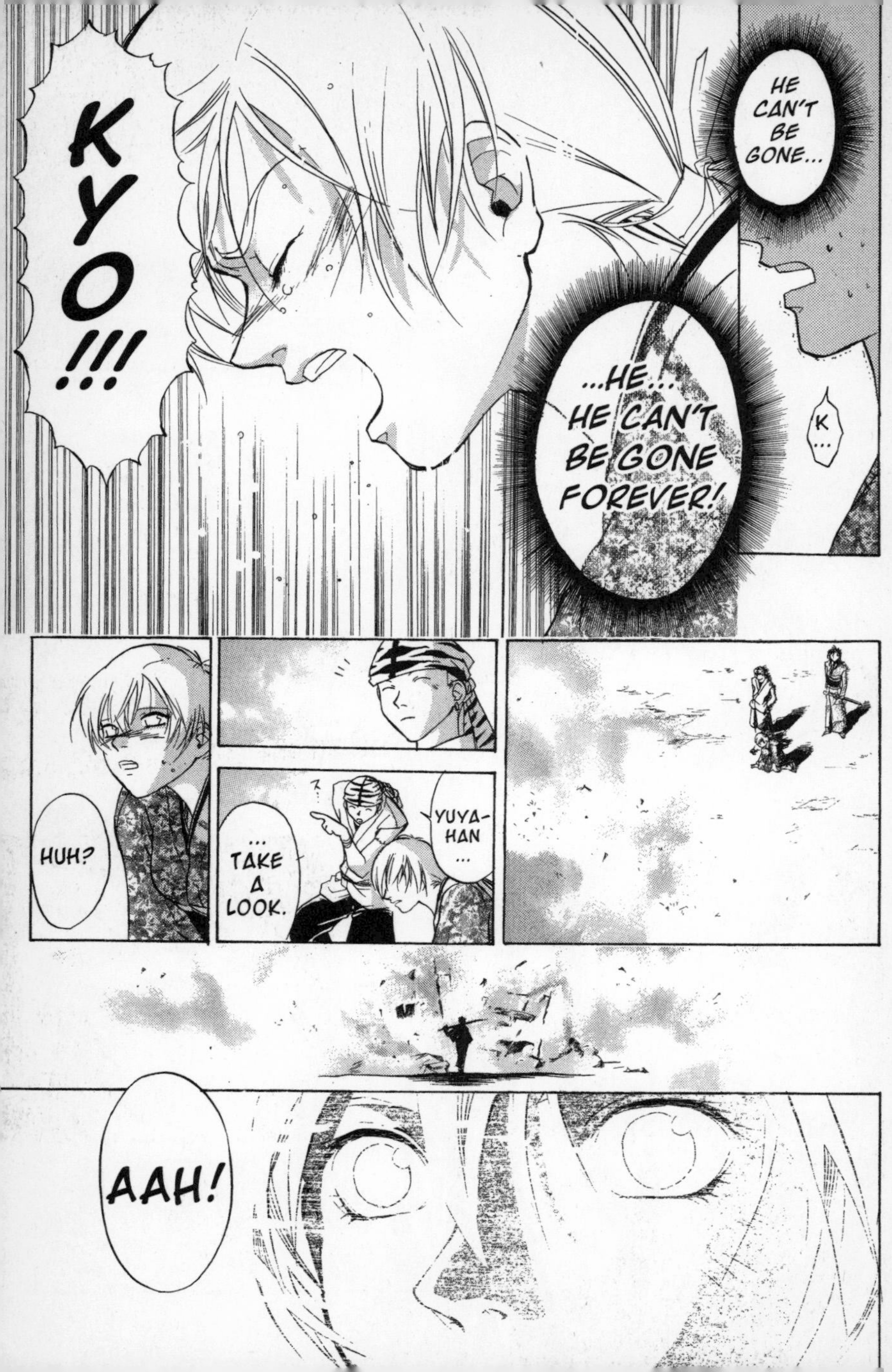

HE CAN'T BE GONE...
K ...
...HE... HE CAN'T BE GONE FOREVER!
KYO!!!
YUYA-HAN ...
... TAKE A LOOK.
HUH?
AAH!

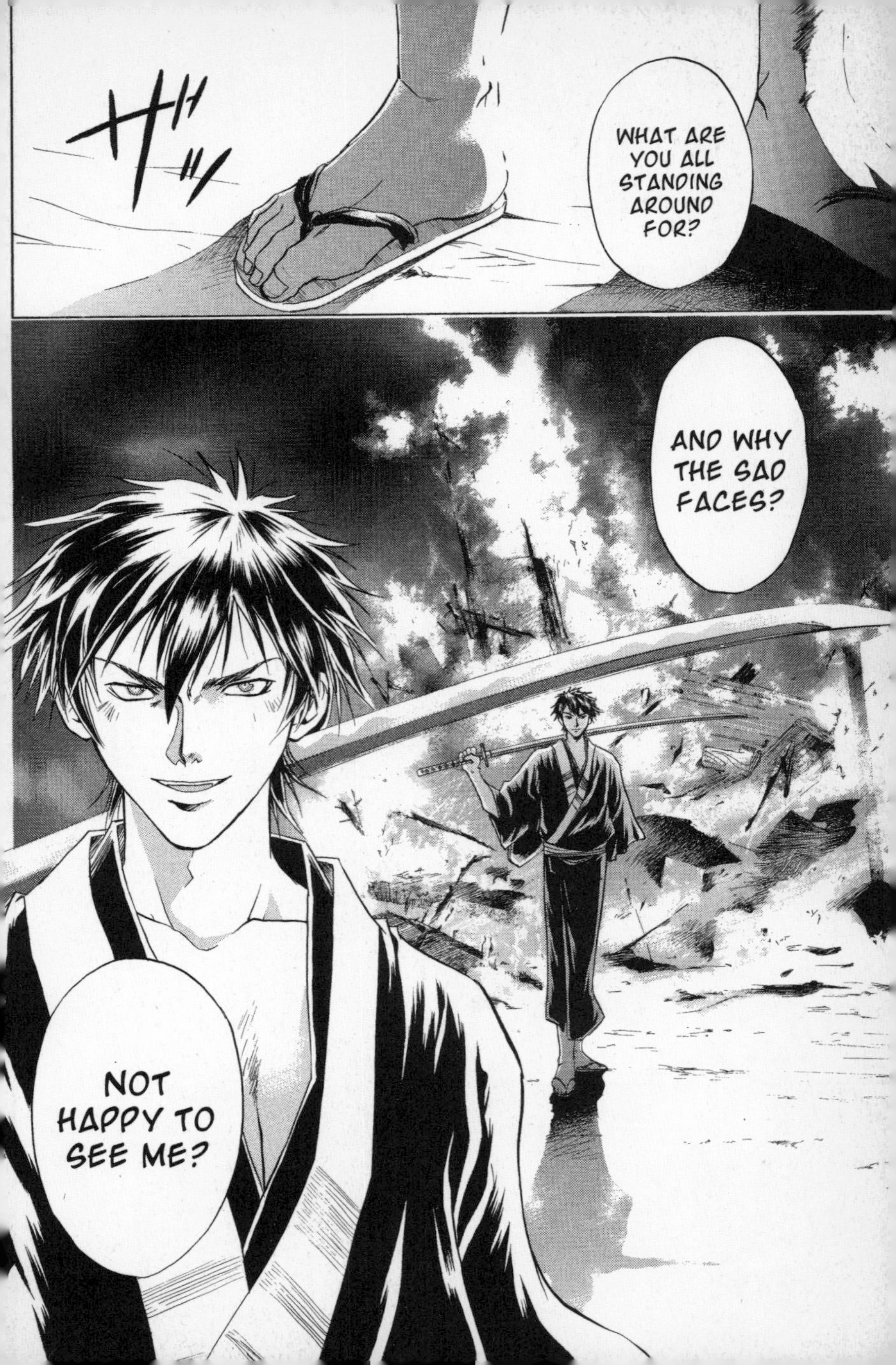
WHAT ARE YOU ALL STANDING AROUND FOR?
AND WHY THE SAD FACES?
NOT HAPPY TO SEE ME?

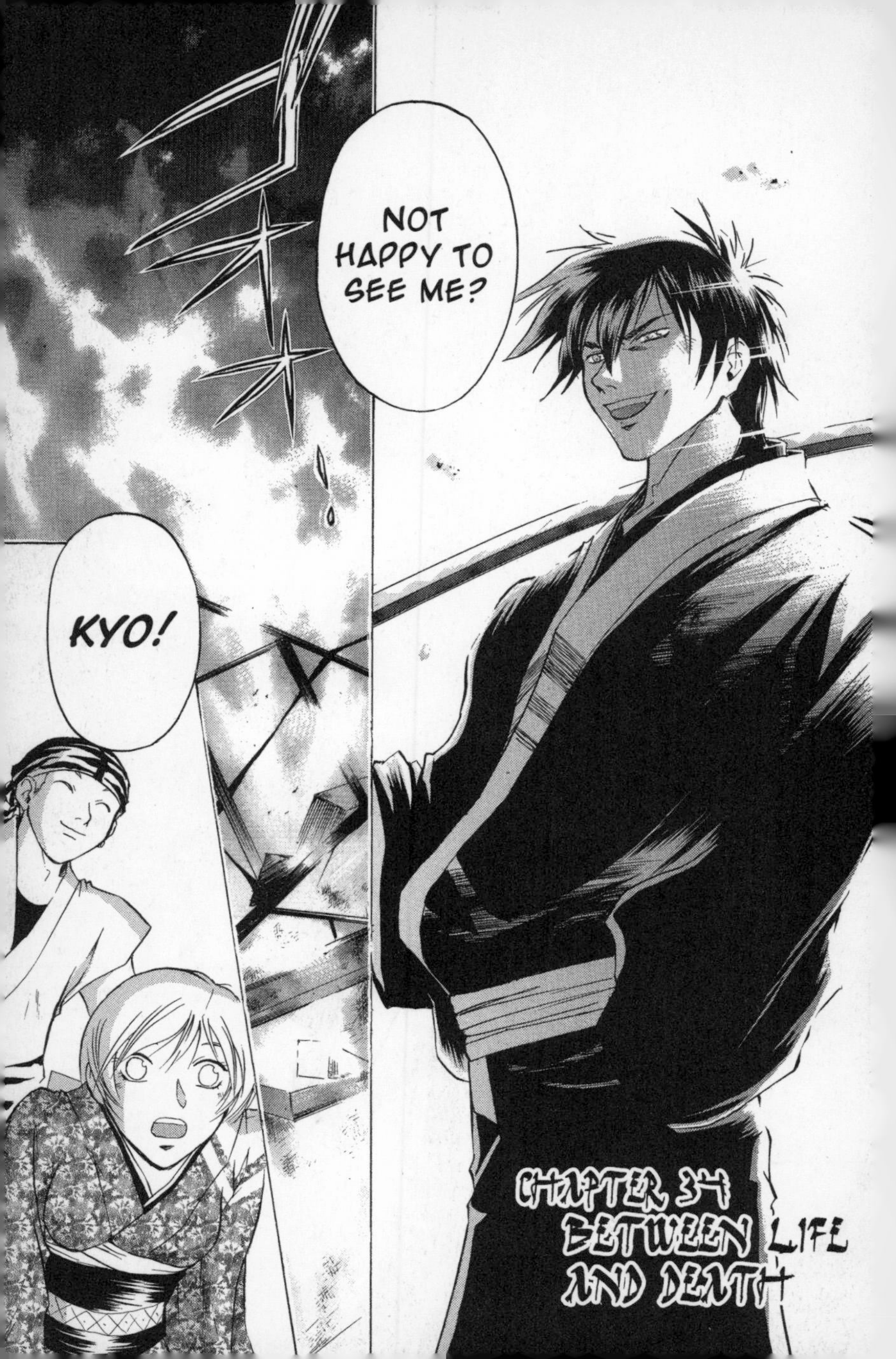
NOT HAPPY TO SEE ME?
CHAPTER 34
BETWEEN LIFE AND DEATH
KYO!

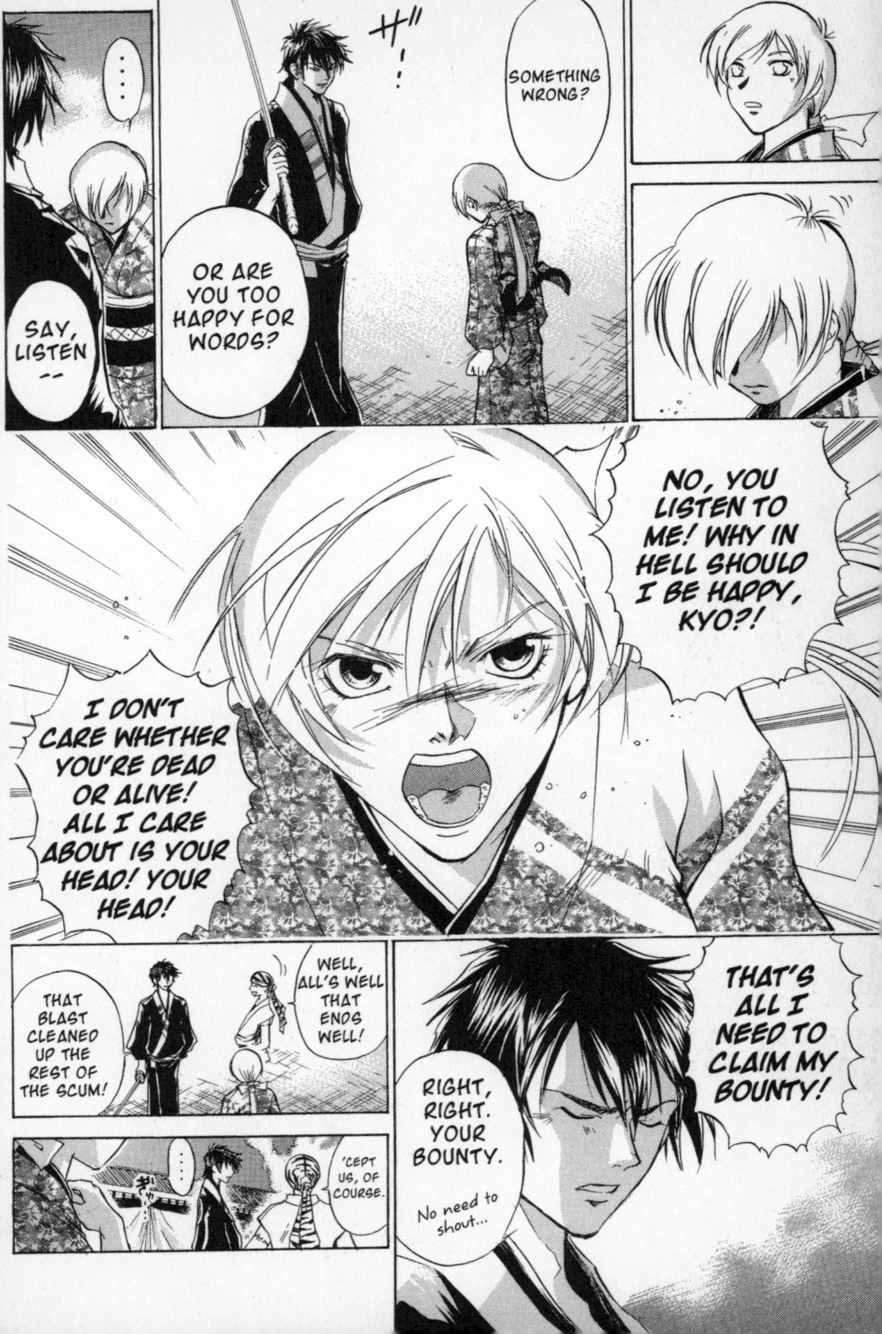
SOMETHING WRONG?
OR ARE YOU TOO HAPPY FOR WORDS?
. . . .
SAY, LISTEN --
NO, YOU LISTEN TO ME! WHY IN HELL SHOULD I BE HAPPY, KYO?!
I DON'T CARE WHETHER YOU'RE DEAD OR ALIVE! ALL I CARE ABOUT IS YOUR HEAD! YOUR HEAD!
THAT'S ALL I NEED TO CLAIM MY BOUNTY!
RIGHT, RIGHT. YOUR BOUNTY.
No need to shout...
WELL, ALL'S WELL THAT ENDS WELL!
THAT BLAST CLEANED UP THE REST OF THE SCUM!
'CEPT US, OF COURSE.
. . .

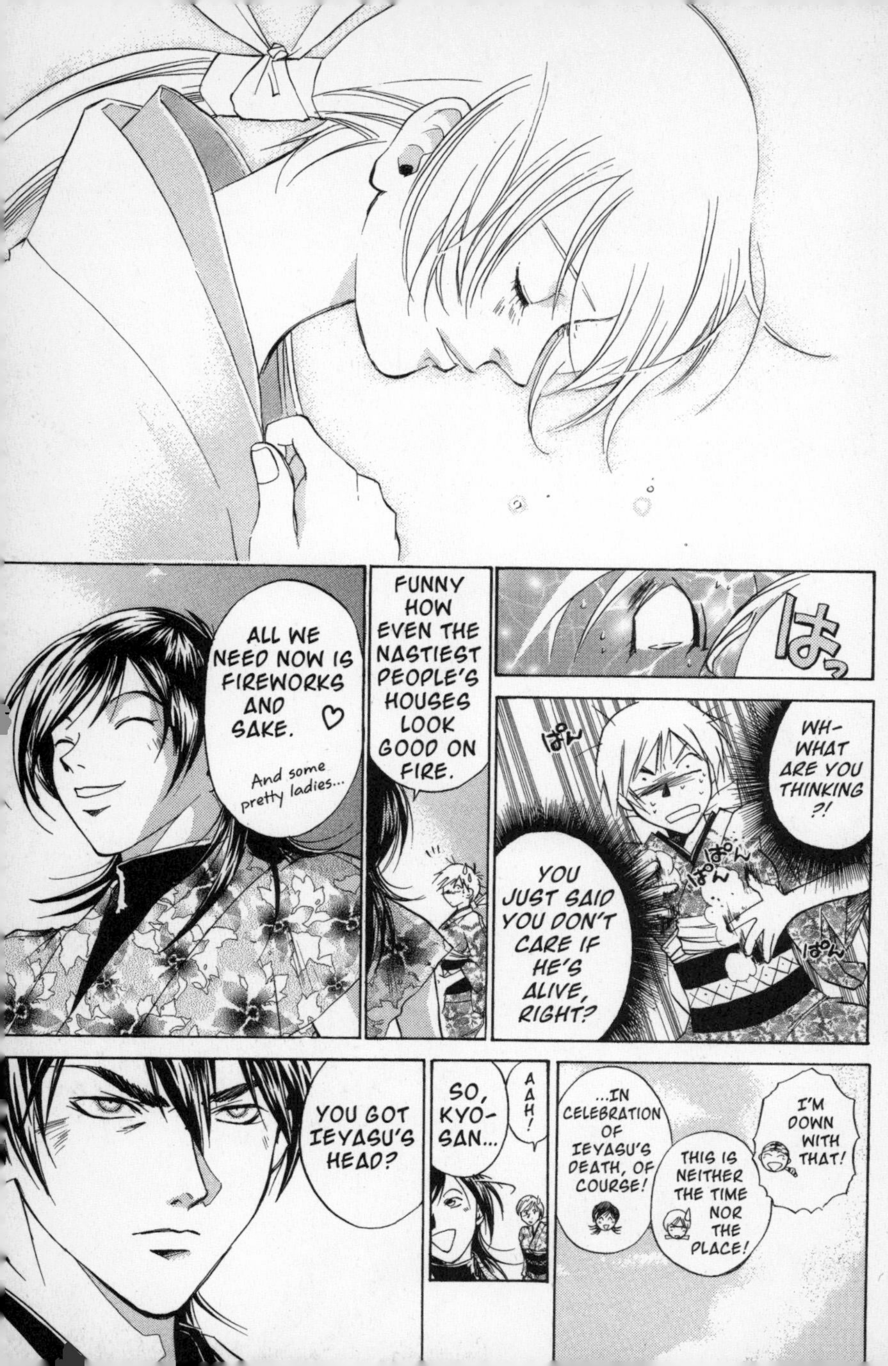
はっ
WH-WHAT ARE YOU THINKING?!
ぱん
YOU JUST SAID YOU DON'T CARE IF HE'S ALIVE, RIGHT?
ぱん ぱん ぱん
FUNNY HOW EVEN THE NASTIEST PEOPLE'S HOUSES LOOK GOOD ON FIRE.
ALL WE NEED NOW IS FIREWORKS AND SAKE. ♡
And some pretty ladies...
...IN CELEBRATION OF IEYASU'S DEATH, OF COURSE!
I'M DOWN WITH THAT!
THIS IS NEITHER THE TIME NOR THE PLACE!
AAAH!
SO, KYO-SAN...
YOU GOT IEYASU'S HEAD?

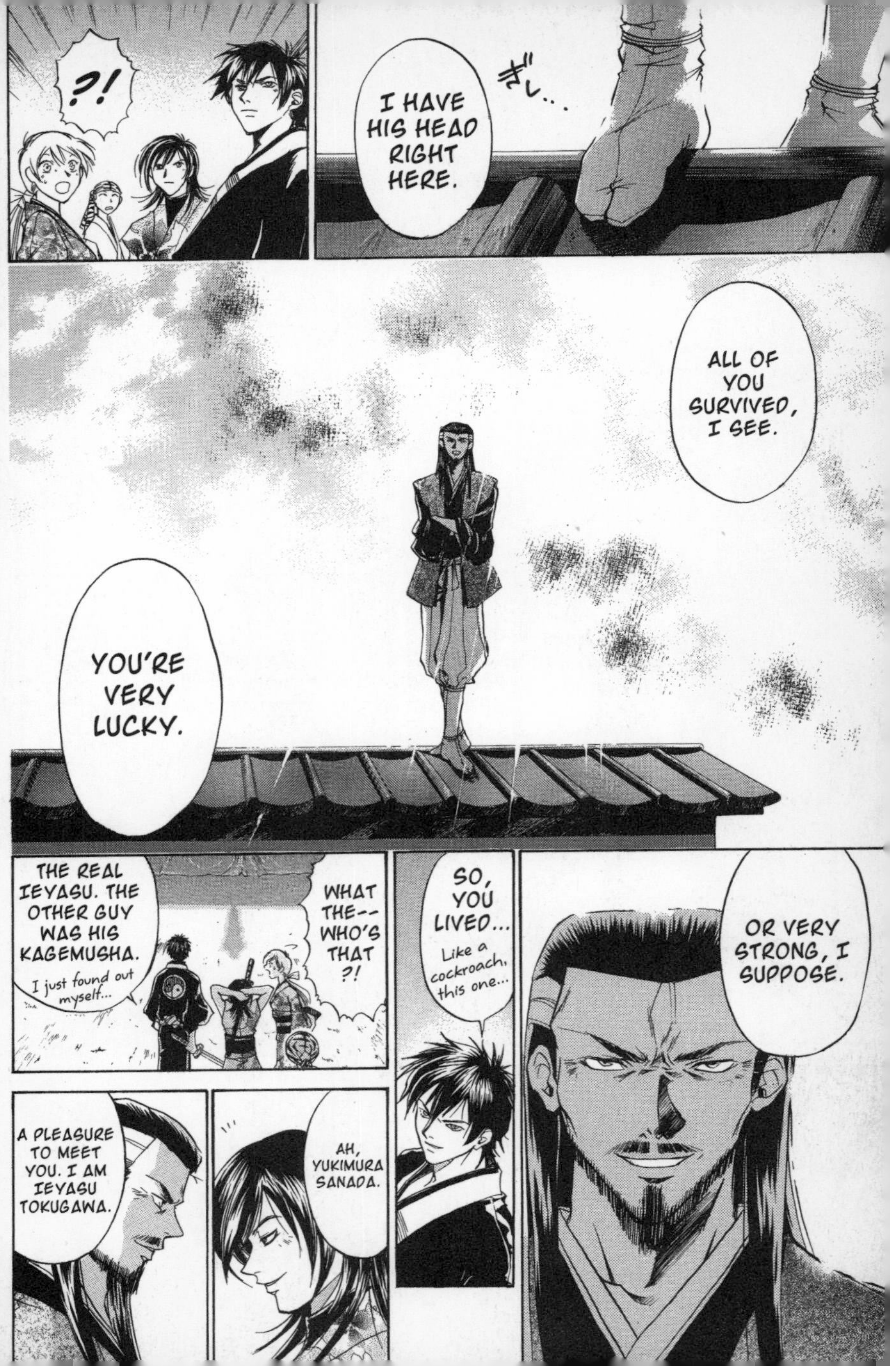

ぎし…
I HAVE HIS HEAD RIGHT HERE.
?!
ALL OF YOU SURVIVED, I SEE.
YOU'RE VERY LUCKY.
OR VERY STRONG, I SUPPOSE.
SO, YOU LIVED...
Like a cockroach, this one...
WHAT THE-- WHO'S THAT ?!
THE REAL IEYASU. THE OTHER GUY WAS HIS KAGEMUSHA.
I just found out myself...
AH, YUKIMURA SANADA.
A PLEASURE TO MEET YOU. I AM IEYASU TOKUGAWA.

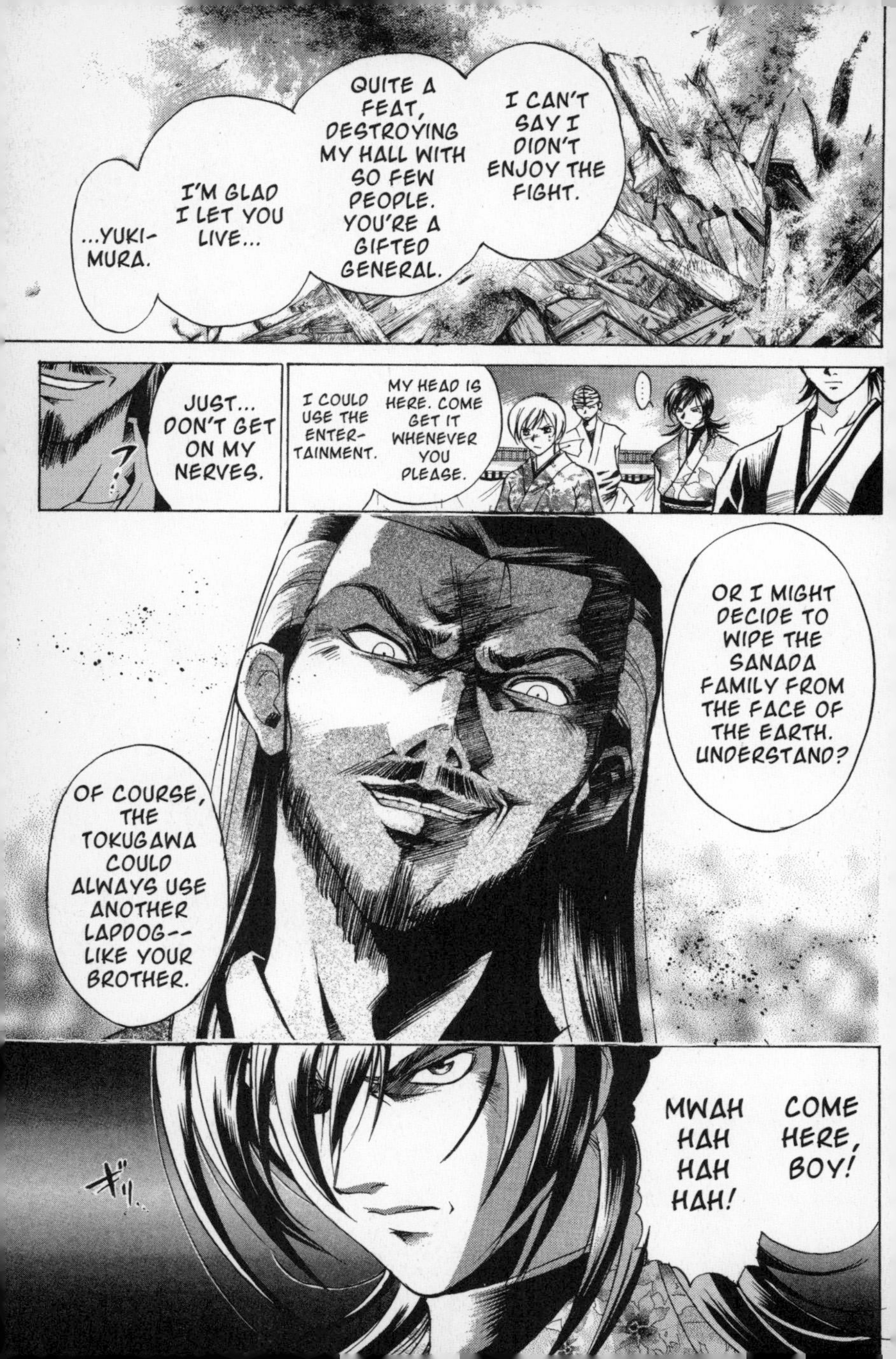
I CAN'T SAY I DIDN'T ENJOY THE FIGHT.
QUITE A FEAT, DESTROYING MY HALL WITH SO FEW PEOPLE. YOU'RE A GIFTED GENERAL.
I'M GLAD I LET YOU LIVE...
...YUKI-MURA.
...
MY HEAD IS HERE. COME GET IT WHENEVER YOU PLEASE.
I COULD USE THE ENTER-TAINMENT.
JUST... DON'T GET ON MY NERVES.
OR I MIGHT DECIDE TO WIPE THE SANADA FAMILY FROM THE FACE OF THE EARTH. UNDERSTAND?
OF COURSE, THE TOKUGAWA COULD ALWAYS USE ANOTHER LAPDOG--LIKE YOUR BROTHER.
COME HERE, BOY!
MWAH HAH HAH HAH!
ギリ..

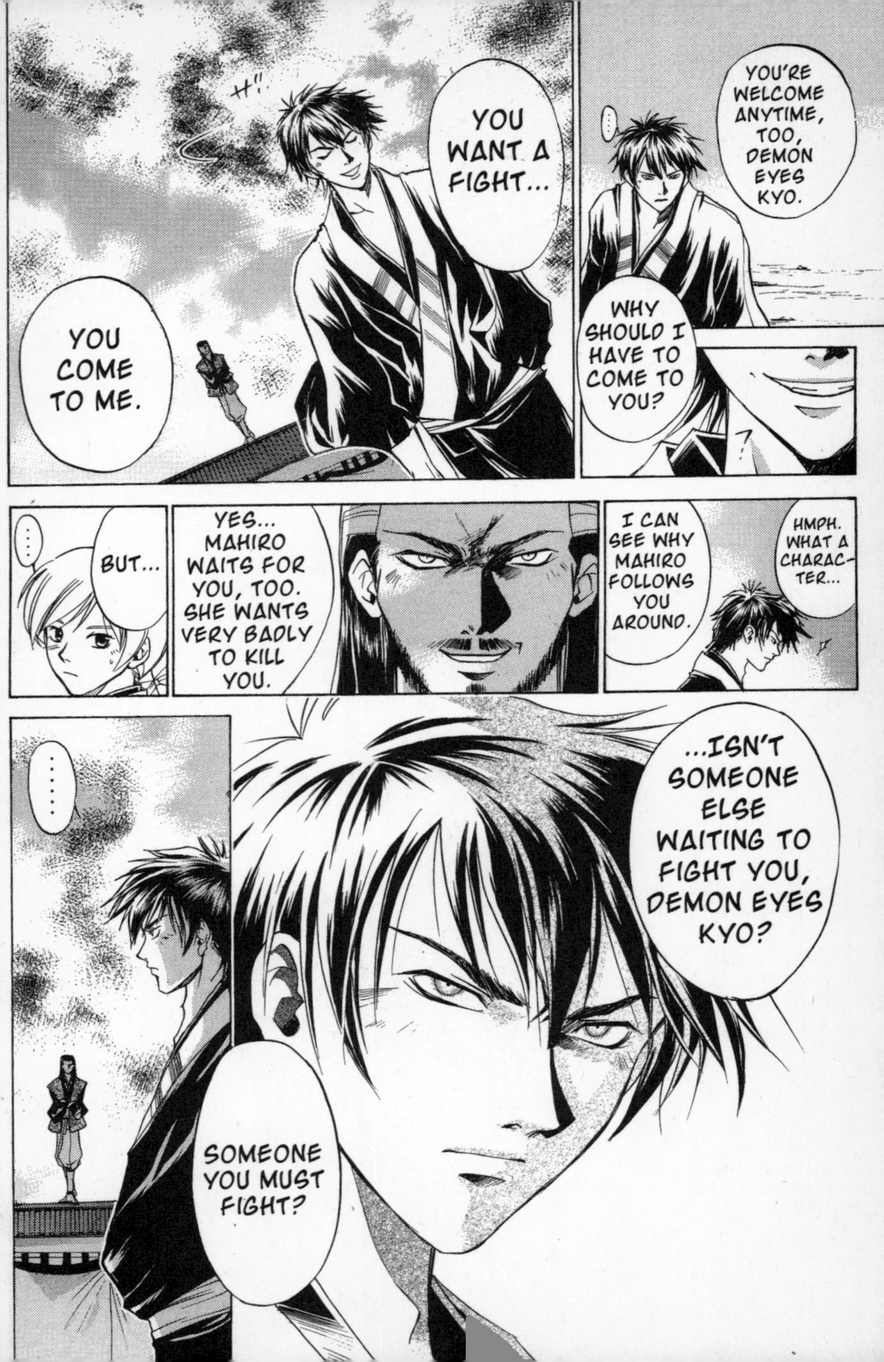

...
YOU'RE WELCOME ANYTIME, TOO, DEMON EYES KYO.
WHY SHOULD I HAVE TO COME TO YOU?
YOU WANT A FIGHT...
YOU COME TO ME.
HMPH. WHAT A CHARAC-TER...
I CAN SEE WHY MAHIRO FOLLOWS YOU AROUND.
YES... MAHIRO WAITS FOR YOU, TOO. SHE WANTS VERY BADLY TO KILL YOU.
BUT...
....
...ISN'T SOMEONE ELSE WAITING TO FIGHT YOU, DEMON EYES KYO?
SOMEONE YOU MUST FIGHT?
......

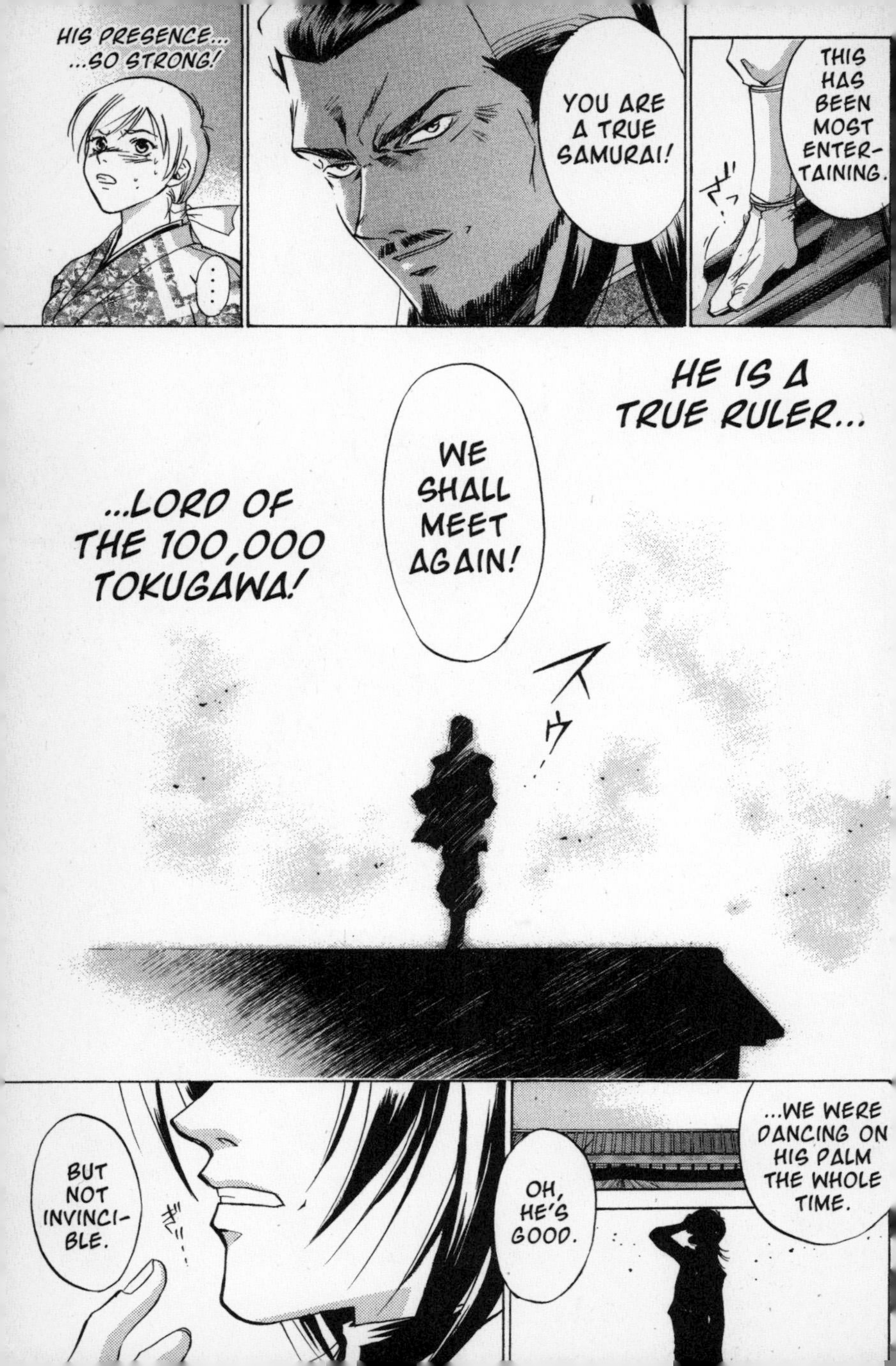
THIS HAS BEEN MOST ENTERTAINING.
YOU ARE A TRUE SAMURAI!
HIS PRESENCE... ...SO STRONG!
....
HE IS A TRUE RULER...
WE SHALL MEET AGAIN!
...LORD OF THE 100,000 TOKUGAWA!
スゥ
...WE WERE DANCING ON HIS PALM THE WHOLE TIME.
OH, HE'S GOOD.
BUT NOT INVINCIBLE.

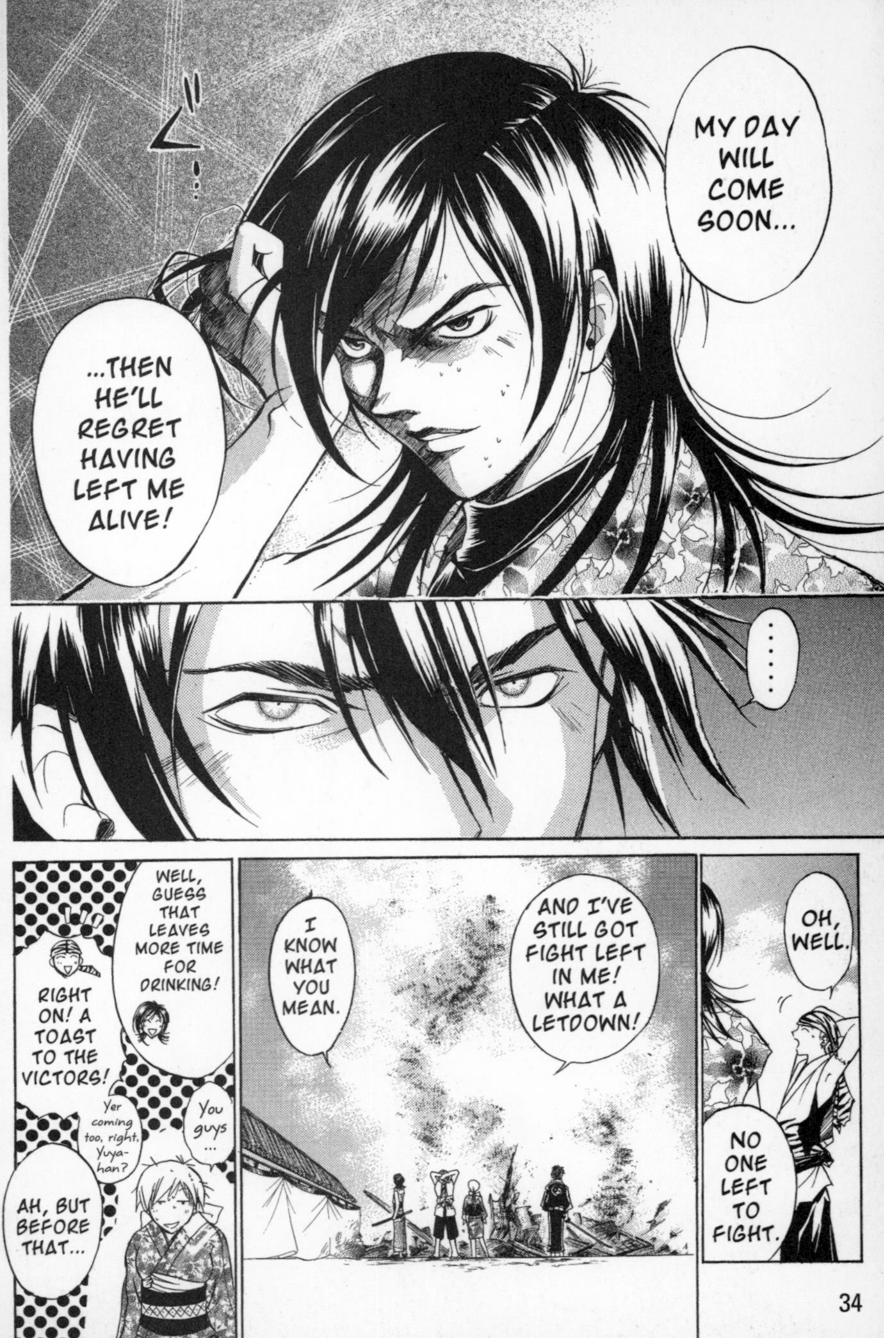
MY DAY WILL COME SOON...
...THEN HE'LL REGRET HAVING LEFT ME ALIVE!
......
OH, WELL.
NO ONE LEFT TO FIGHT.
AND I'VE STILL GOT FIGHT LEFT IN ME! WHAT A LETDOWN!
I KNOW WHAT YOU MEAN.
WELL, GUESS THAT LEAVES MORE TIME FOR DRINKING!
RIGHT ON! A TOAST TO THE VICTORS!
You guys ...
Yer coming too, right, Yuya-han?
AH, BUT BEFORE THAT...

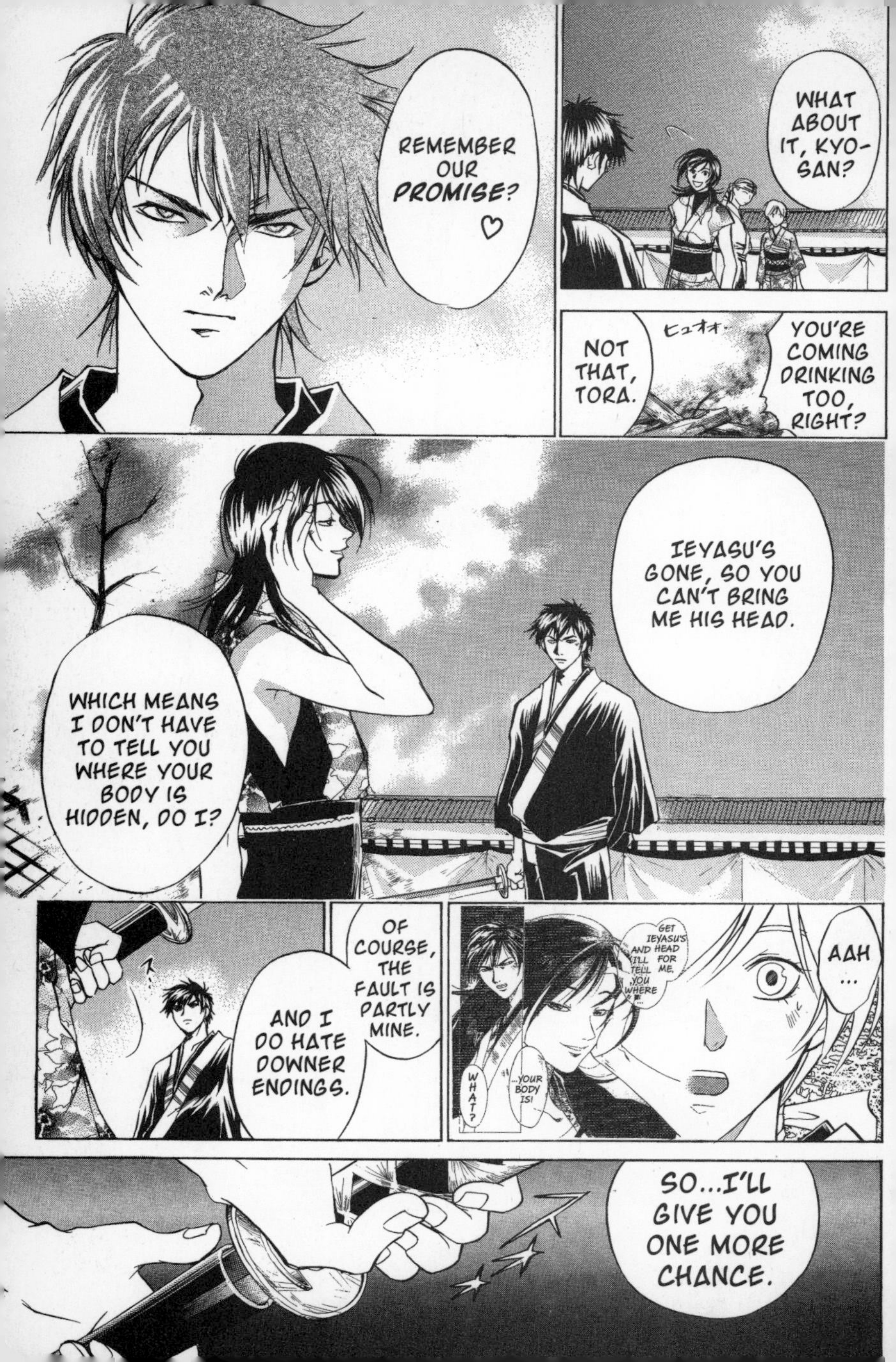
WHAT ABOUT IT, KYO-SAN?
YOU'RE COMING DRINKING TOO, RIGHT?
ヒュオオ
NOT THAT, TORA.
REMEMBER OUR PROMISE? ♡
IEYASU'S GONE, SO YOU CAN'T BRING ME HIS HEAD.
WHICH MEANS I DON'T HAVE TO TELL YOU WHERE YOUR BODY IS HIDDEN, DO I?
AAH ...
GET IEYASU'S HEAD FOR ME, AND I'LL TELL YOU WHERE ...
...YOUR BODY IS!
WHAT?
OF COURSE, THE FAULT IS PARTLY MINE.
AND I DO HATE DOWNER ENDINGS.
SO...I'LL GIVE YOU ONE MORE CHANCE.

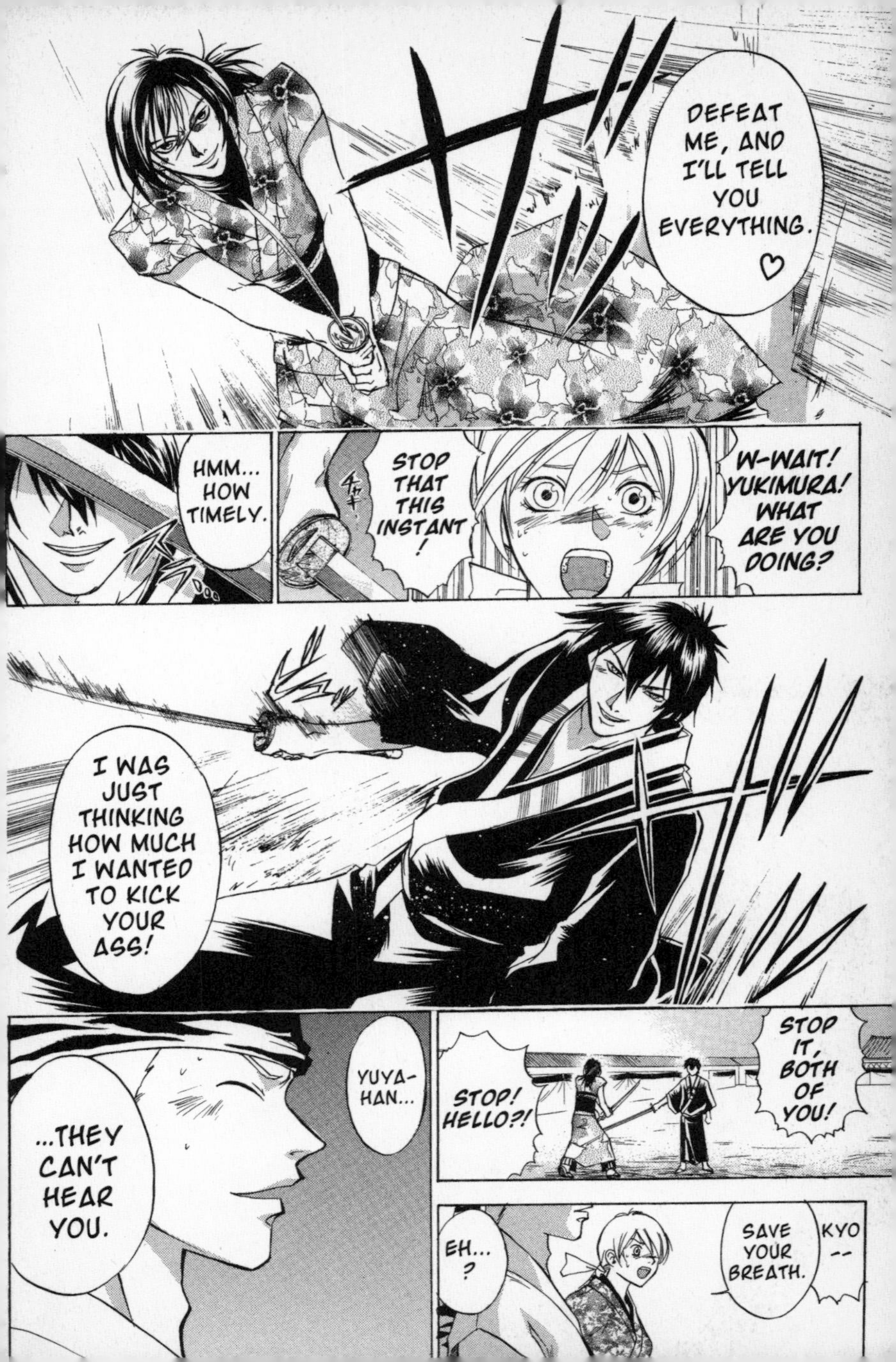
DEFEAT ME, AND I'LL TELL YOU EVERYTHING. ♡
W-WAIT! YUKIMURA! WHAT ARE YOU DOING?
STOP THAT THIS INSTANT!
HMM... HOW TIMELY.
I WAS JUST THINKING HOW MUCH I WANTED TO KICK YOUR ASS!
STOP IT, BOTH OF YOU!
STOP! HELLO?!
KYO--
SAVE YOUR BREATH.
EH...?
YUYA-HAN...
...THEY CAN'T HEAR YOU.

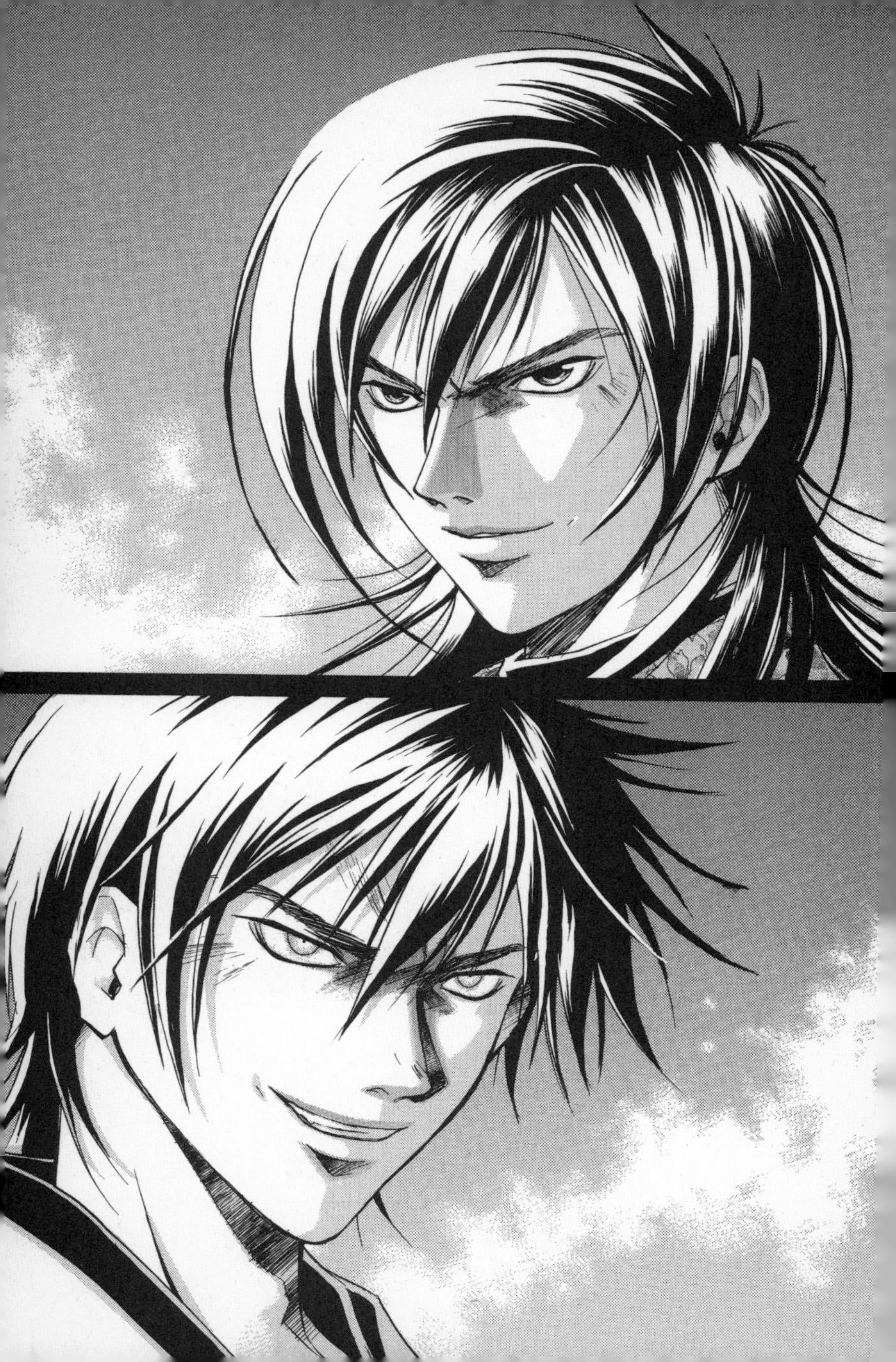

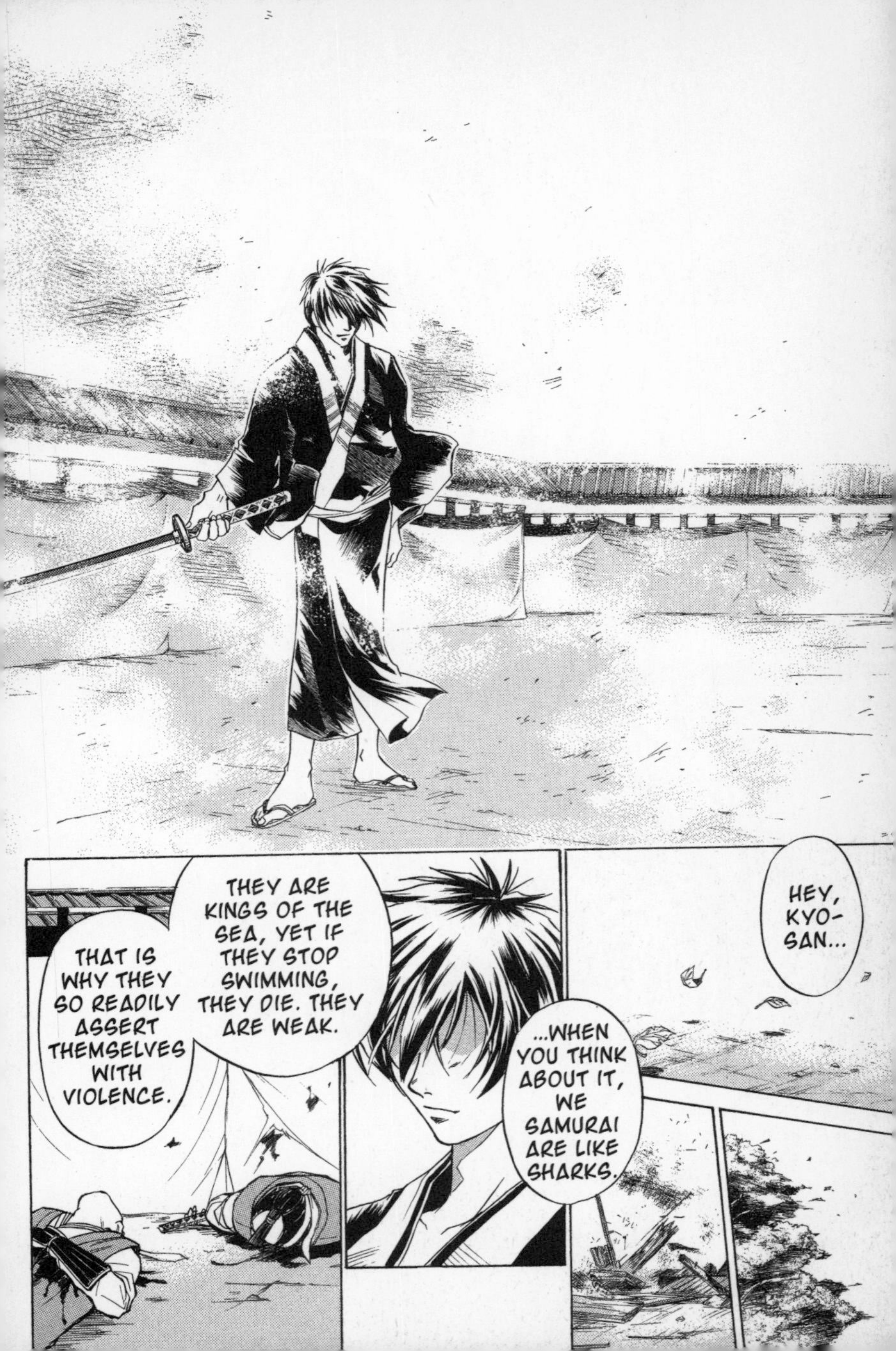
HEY, KYO-SAN...
...WHEN YOU THINK ABOUT IT, WE SAMURAI ARE LIKE SHARKS.
THEY ARE KINGS OF THE SEA, YET IF THEY STOP SWIMMING, THEY DIE. THEY ARE WEAK.
THAT IS WHY THEY SO READILY ASSERT THEMSELVES WITH VIOLENCE.

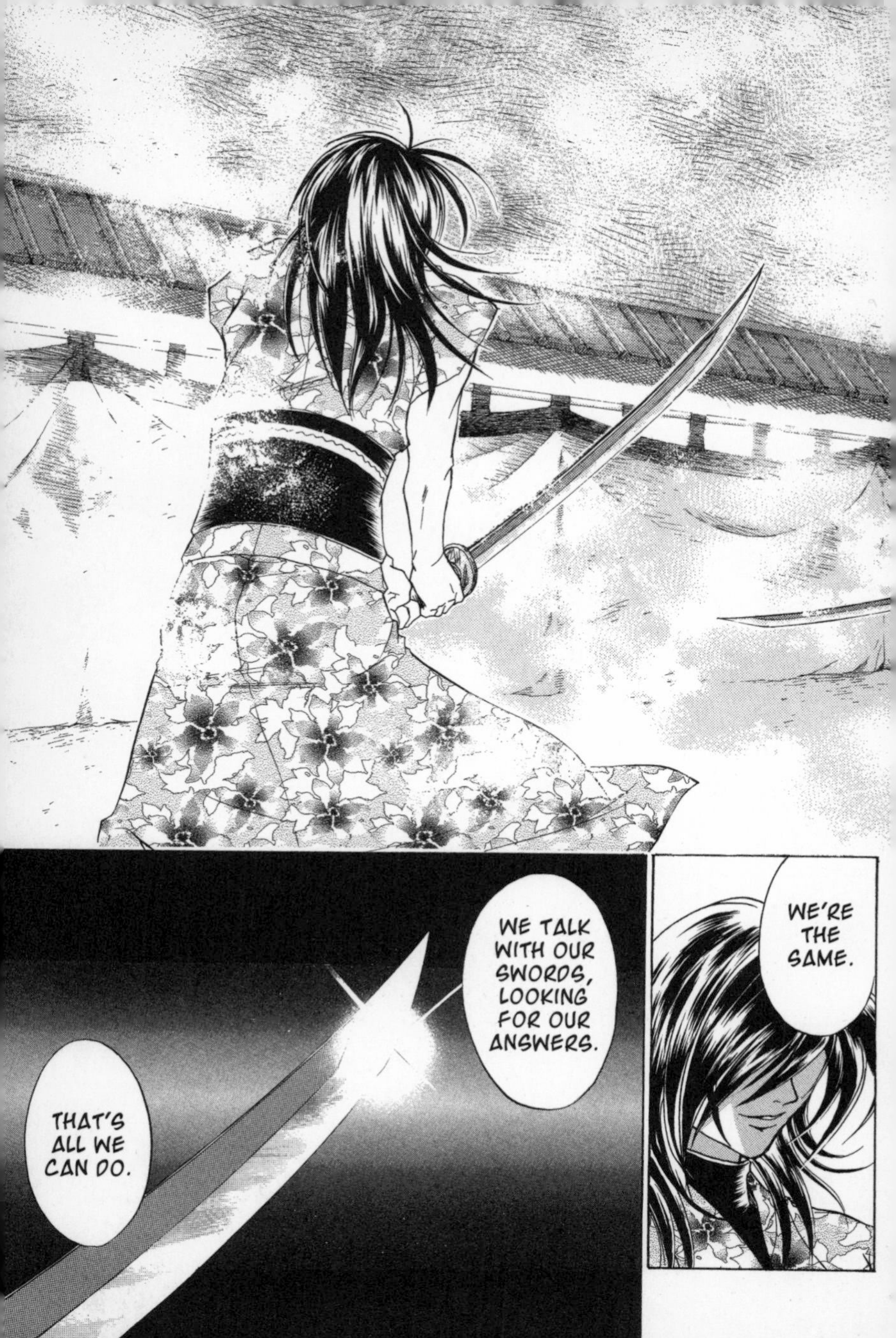
WE'RE THE SAME.
WE TALK WITH OUR SWORDS, LOOKING FOR OUR ANSWERS.
THAT'S ALL WE CAN DO.

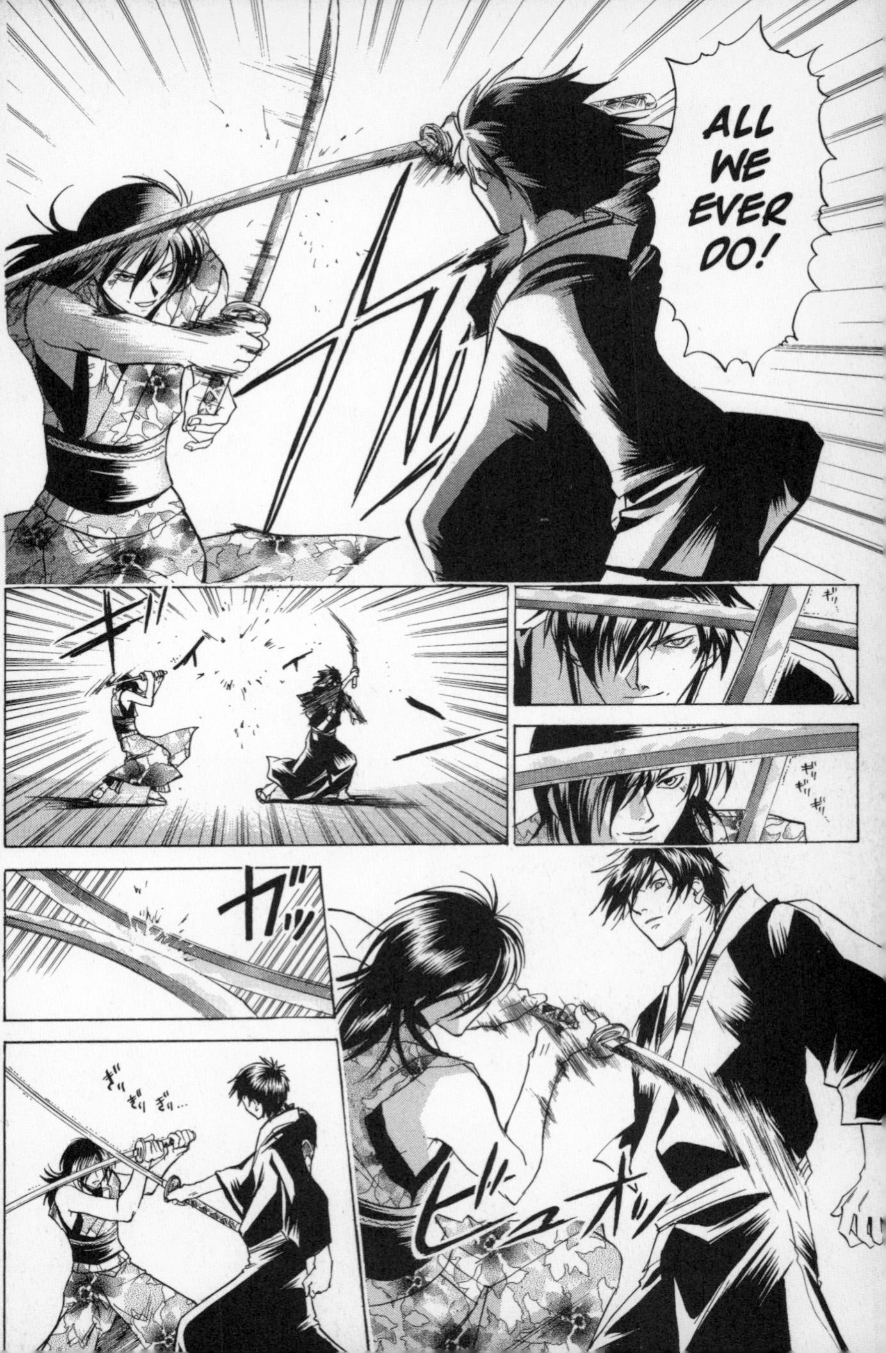
ALL WE EVER DO!
ビュオッ
ガッ
ぎりぎりぎり…

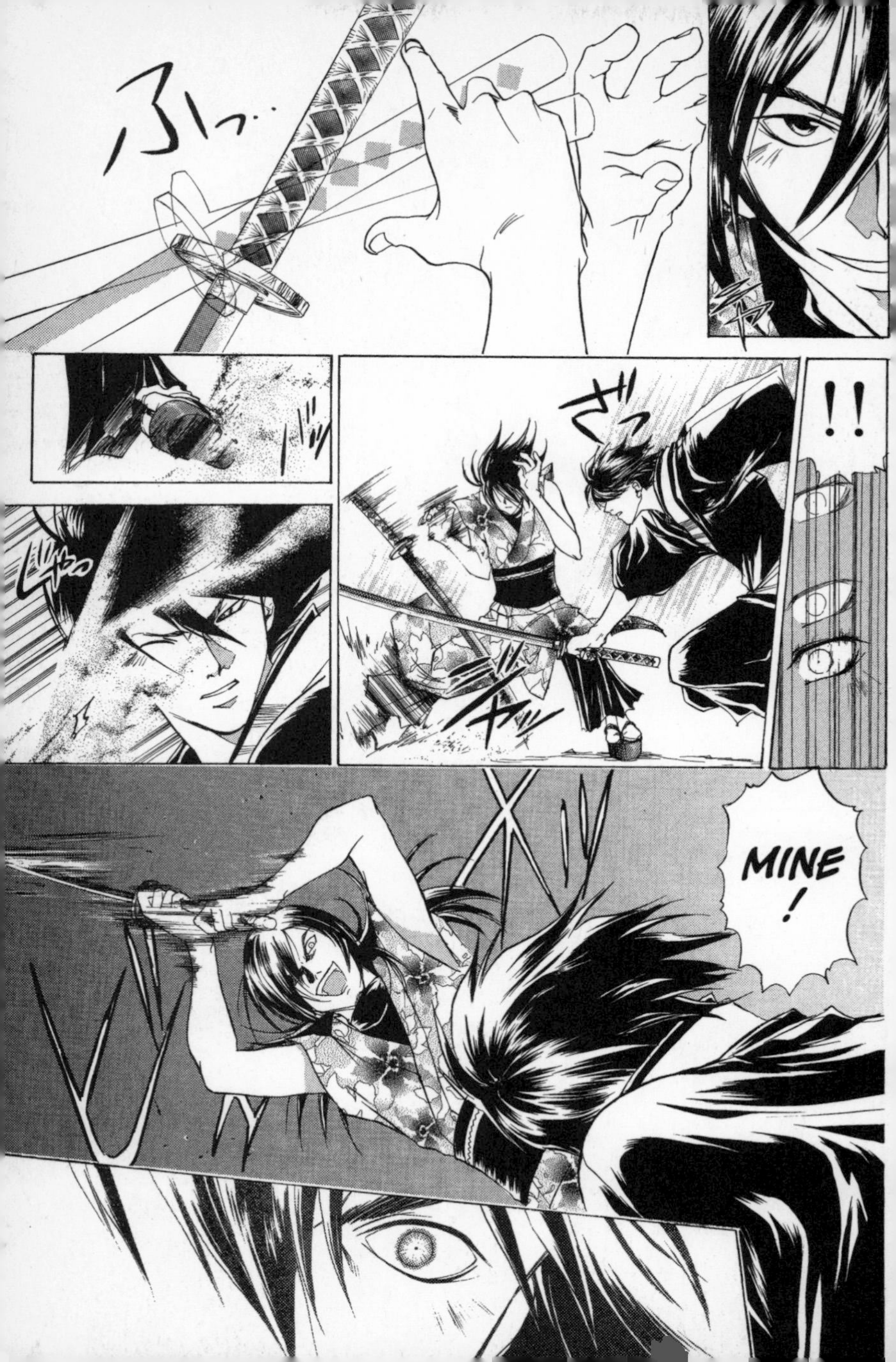
ふっ…
!!
ざっ
MINE!

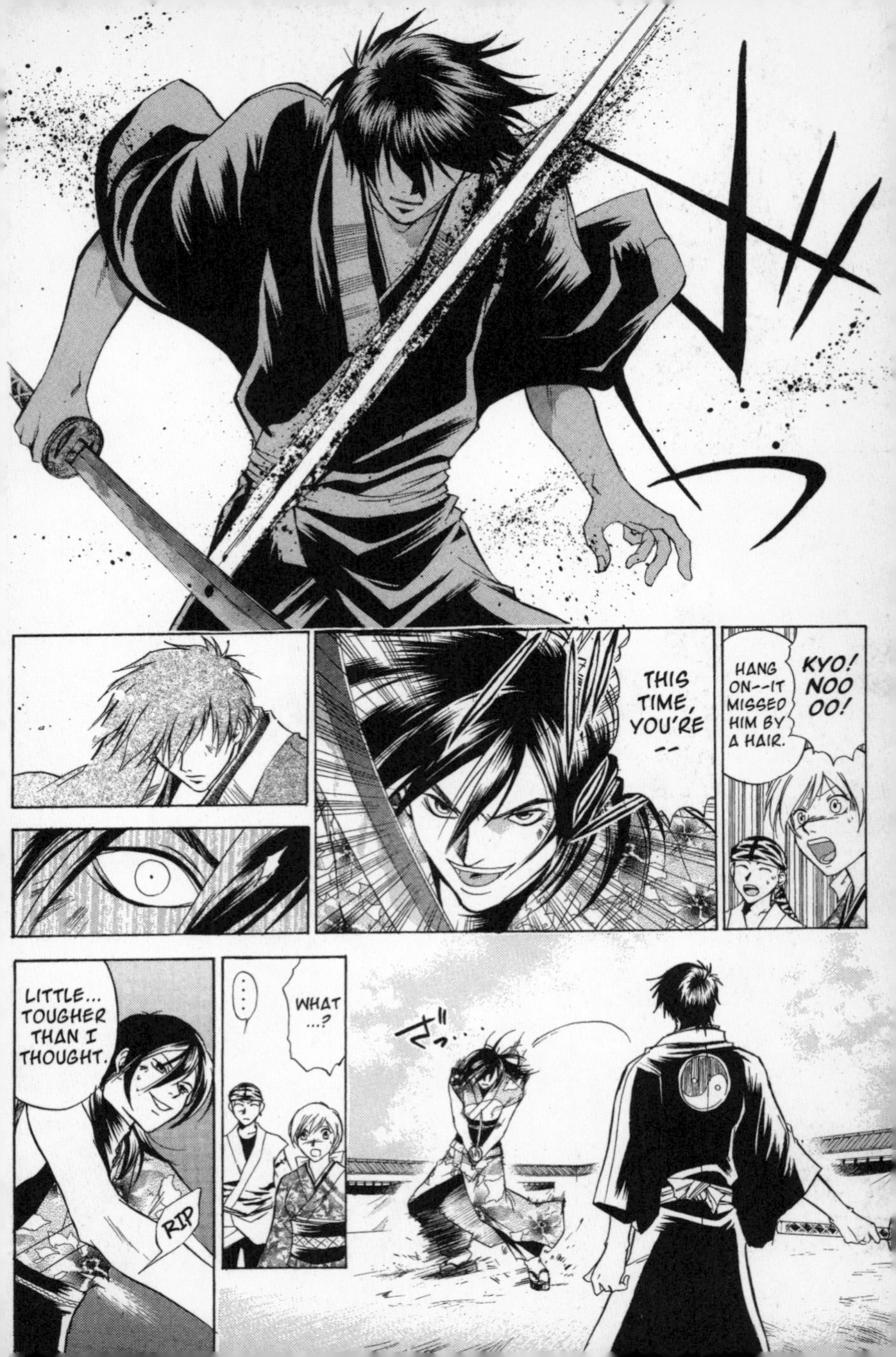

KYO! NOOOO!
HANG ON--IT MISSED HIM BY A HAIR.
THIS TIME, YOU'RE --
ざっ...
WHAT ...?
....
LITTLE... TOUGHER THAN I THOUGHT.
RIP

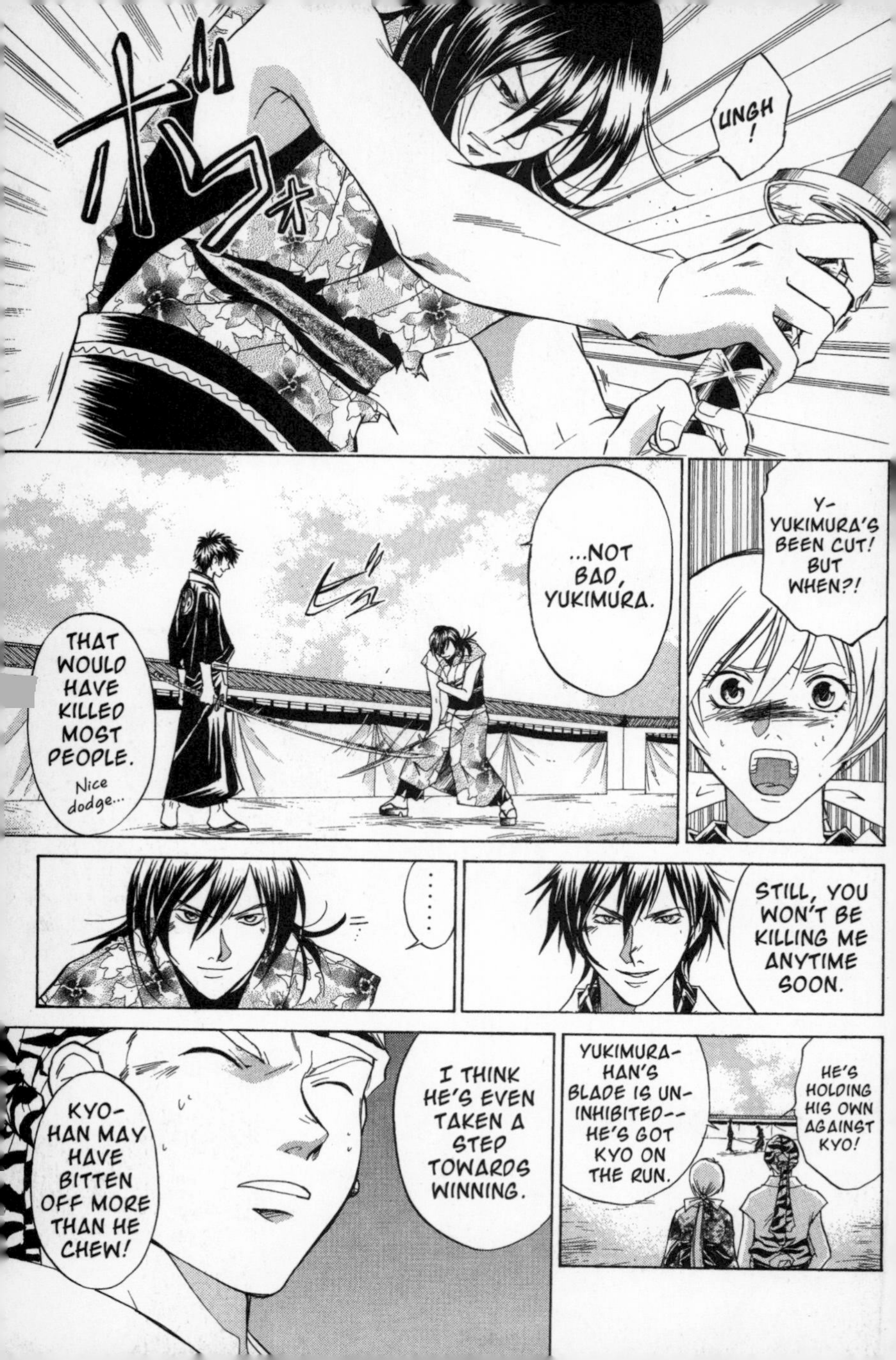
UNGH!
Y-YUKIMURA'S BEEN CUT! BUT WHEN?!
...NOT BAD, YUKIMURA.
THAT WOULD HAVE KILLED MOST PEOPLE.
Nice dodge...
STILL, YOU WON'T BE KILLING ME ANYTIME SOON.
......
HE'S HOLDING HIS OWN AGAINST KYO!
YUKIMURA-HAN'S BLADE IS UN-INHIBITED--HE'S GOT KYO ON THE RUN.
I THINK HE'S EVEN TAKEN A STEP TOWARDS WINNING.
KYO-HAN MAY HAVE BITTEN OFF MORE THAN HE CHEW!

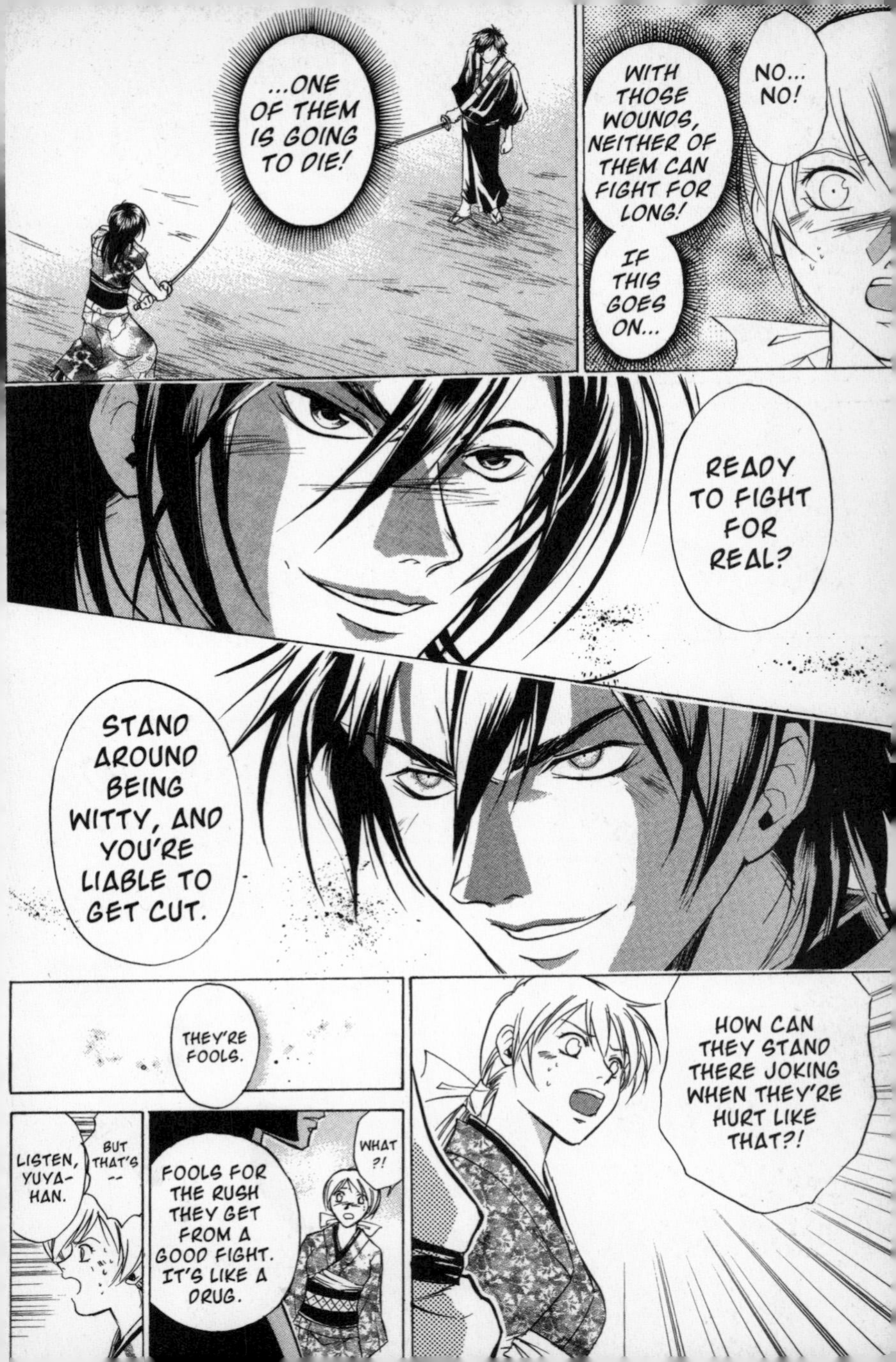
NO... NO!
WITH THOSE WOUNDS, NEITHER OF THEM CAN FIGHT FOR LONG!
IF THIS GOES ON...
...ONE OF THEM IS GOING TO DIE!
READY TO FIGHT FOR REAL?
STAND AROUND BEING WITTY, AND YOU'RE LIABLE TO GET CUT.
HOW CAN THEY STAND THERE JOKING WHEN THEY'RE HURT LIKE THAT?!
THEY'RE FOOLS.
WHAT ?!
FOOLS FOR THE RUSH THEY GET FROM A GOOD FIGHT. IT'S LIKE A DRUG.
BUT THAT'S --
LISTEN, YUYA-HAN.

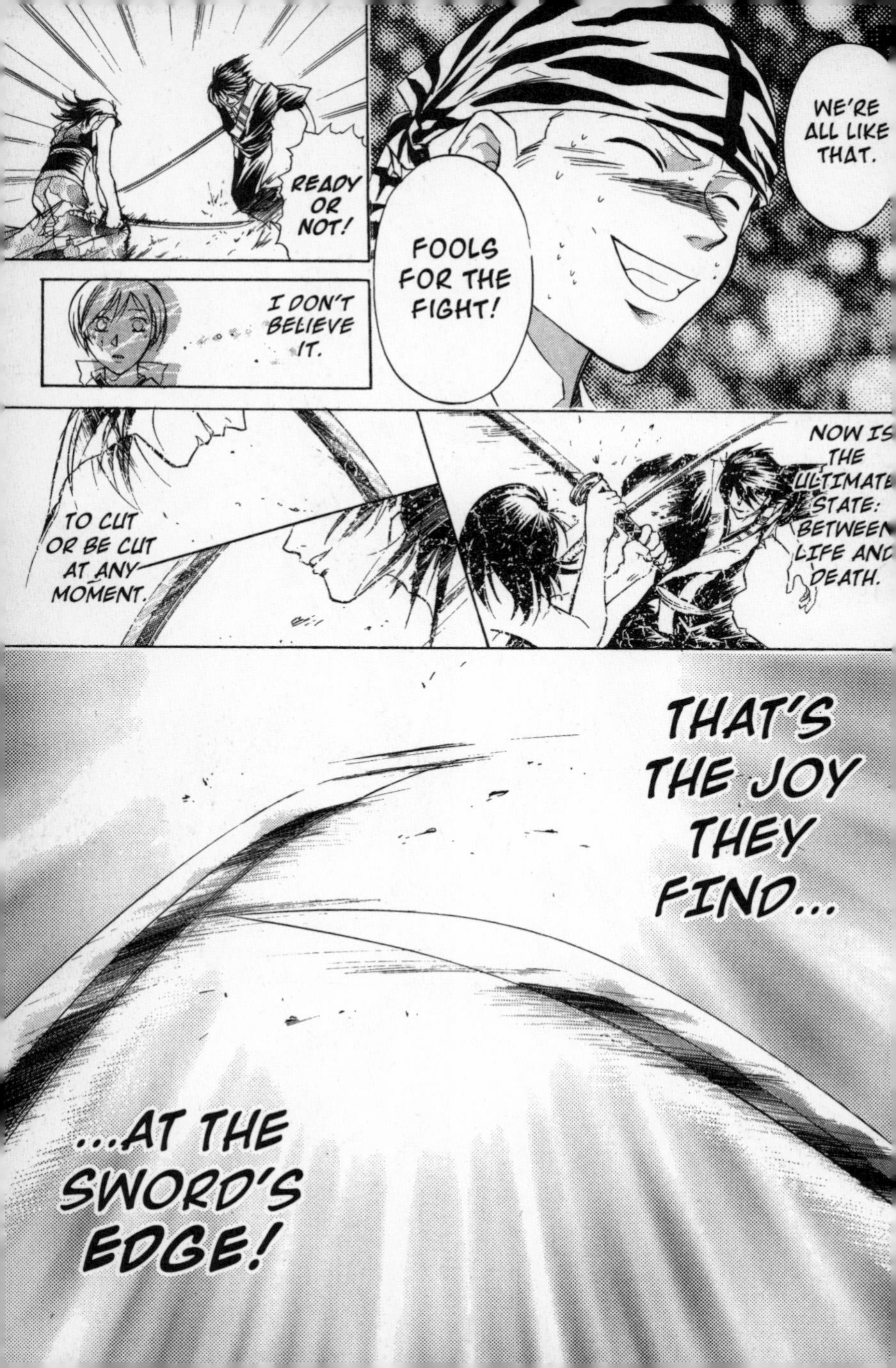
WE'RE ALL LIKE THAT.
FOOLS FOR THE FIGHT!
READY OR NOT!
I DON'T BELIEVE IT.
NOW IS THE ULTIMATE STATE: BETWEEN LIFE AND DEATH.
TO CUT OR BE CUT AT ANY MOMENT.
THAT'S THE JOY THEY FIND...
...AT THE SWORD'S EDGE!

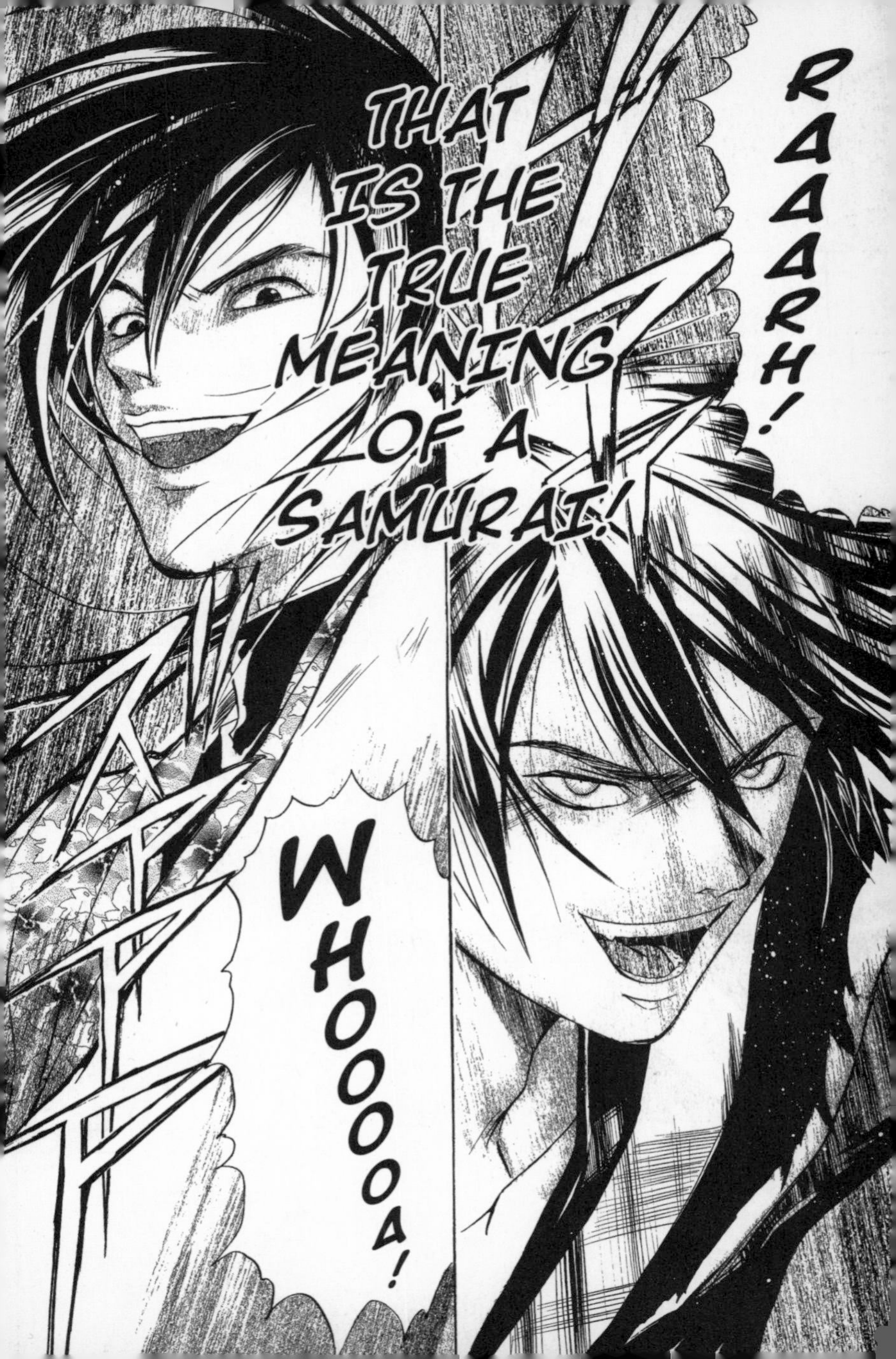
RAAARH!
THAT IS THE TRUE MEANING OF A SAMURAI!
WHOOOOA!

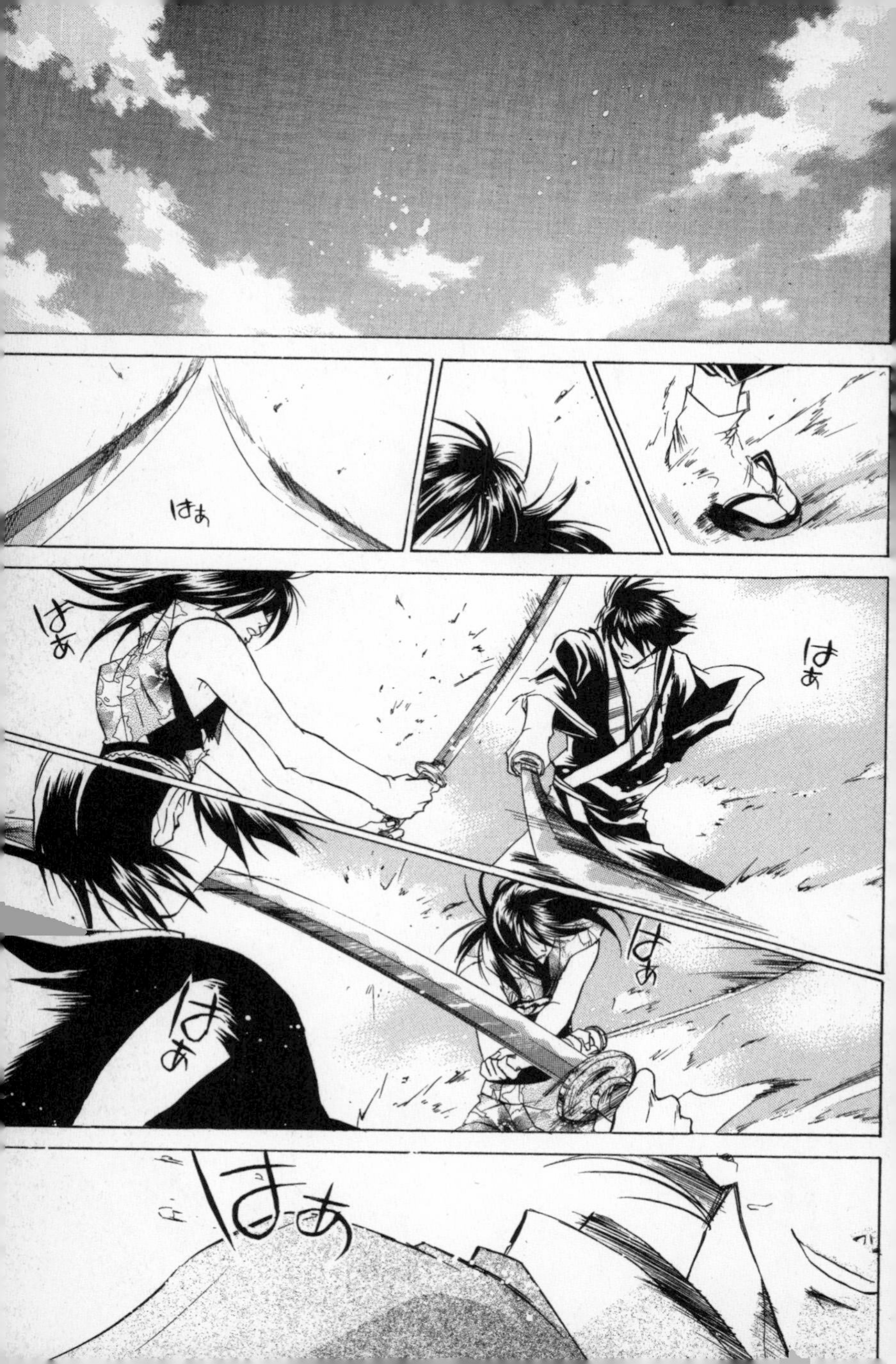
はぁ
はぁ
はぁ
はぁ
はぁ
はぁ

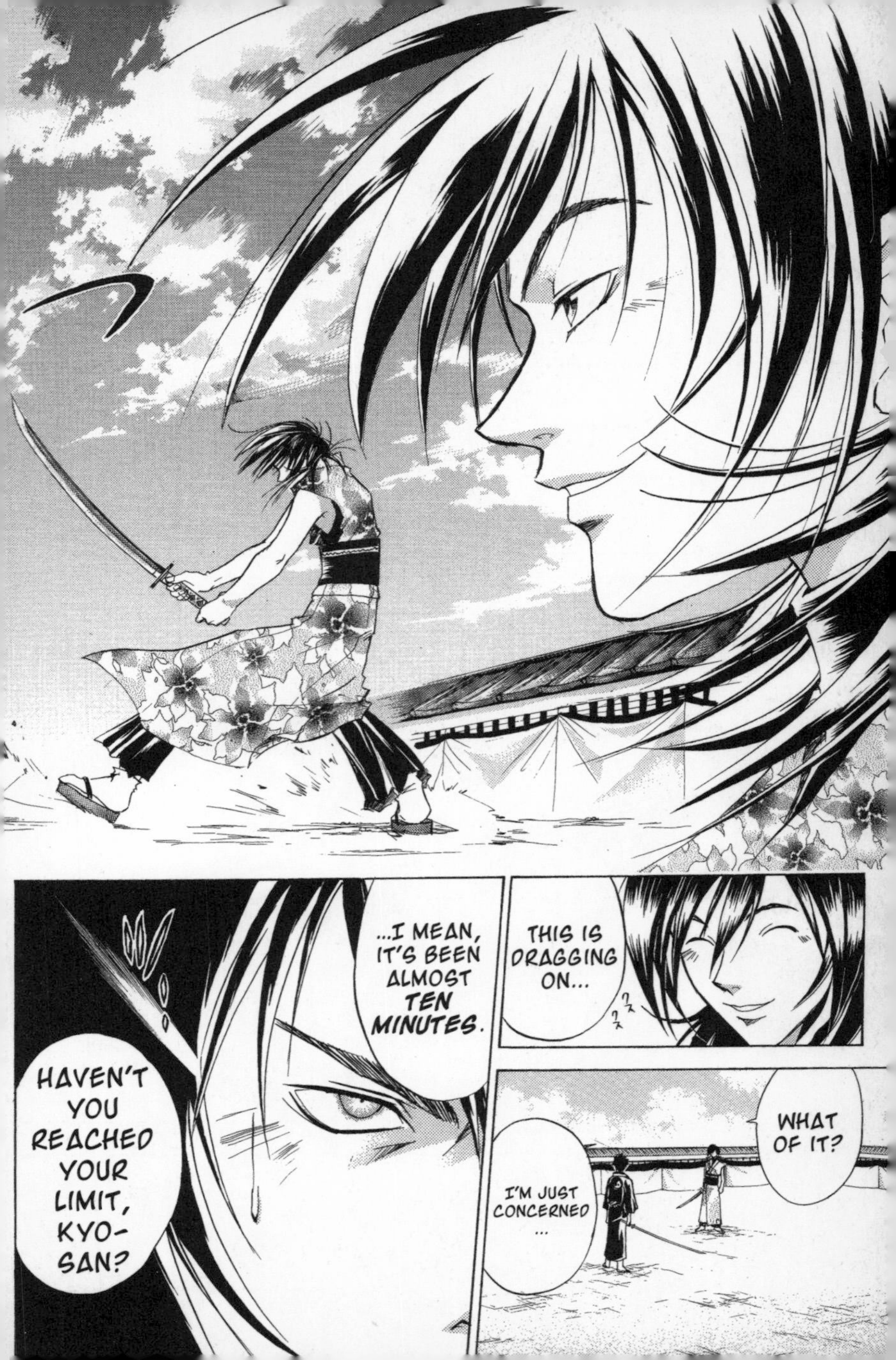
THIS IS DRAGGING ON...
WHAT OF IT?
I'M JUST CONCERNED...
...I MEAN, IT'S BEEN ALMOST TEN MINUTES.
HAVEN'T YOU REACHED YOUR LIMIT, KYO-SAN?

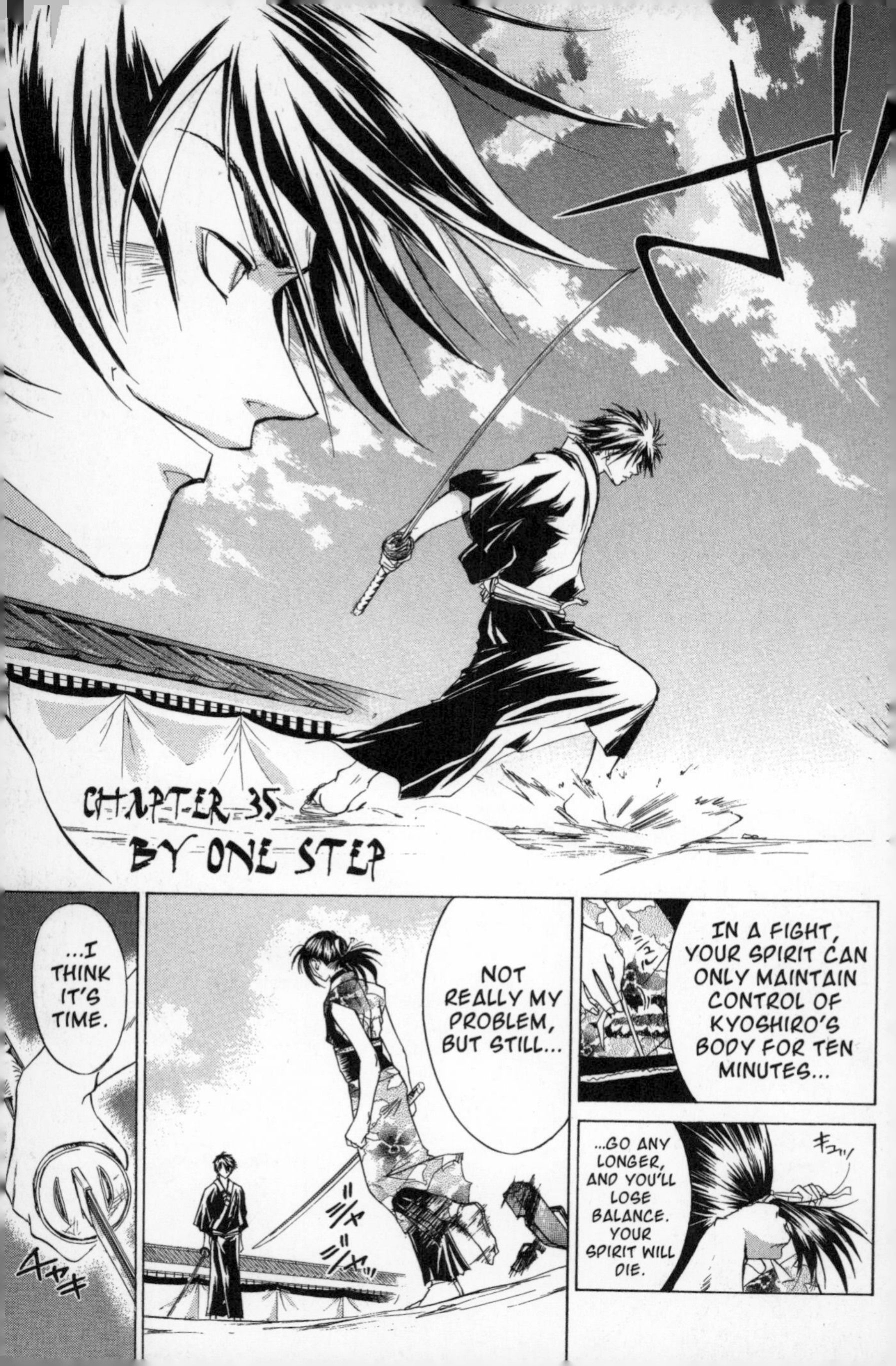
CHAPTER 35
BY ONE STEP
IN A FIGHT, YOUR SPIRIT CAN ONLY MAINTAIN CONTROL OF KYOSHIRO'S BODY FOR TEN MINUTES...
...GO ANY LONGER, AND YOU'LL LOSE BALANCE. YOUR SPIRIT WILL DIE.
NOT REALLY MY PROBLEM, BUT STILL...
...I THINK IT'S TIME.

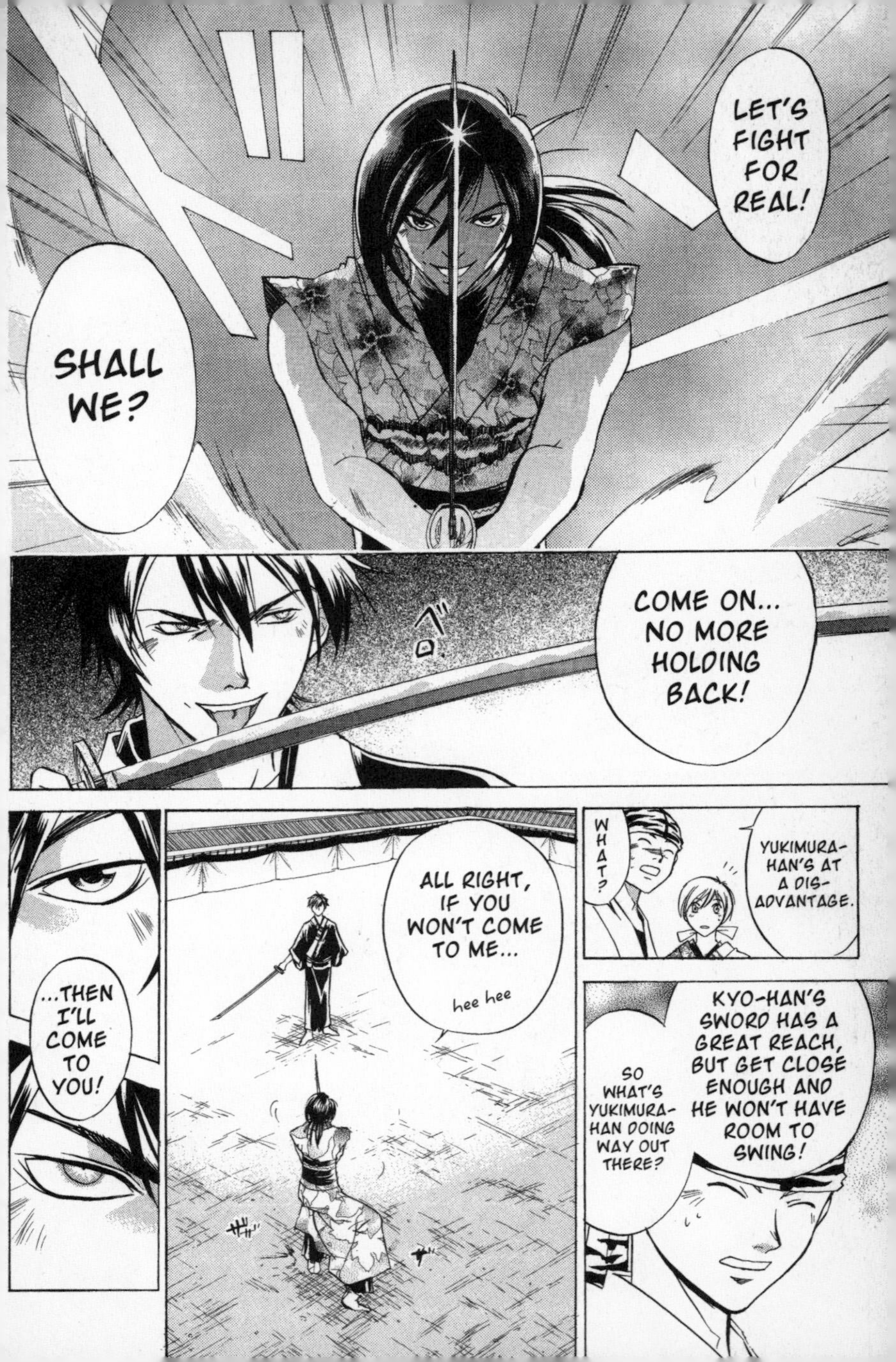
LET'S FIGHT FOR REAL!
SHALL WE?
COME ON... NO MORE HOLDING BACK!
YUKIMURA-HAN'S AT A DIS-ADVANTAGE.
WHAT?
KYO-HAN'S SWORD HAS A GREAT REACH, BUT GET CLOSE ENOUGH AND HE WON'T HAVE ROOM TO SWING!
SO WHAT'S YUKIMURA-HAN DOING WAY OUT THERE?
ALL RIGHT, IF YOU WON'T COME TO ME...
hee hee
...THEN I'LL COME TO YOU!

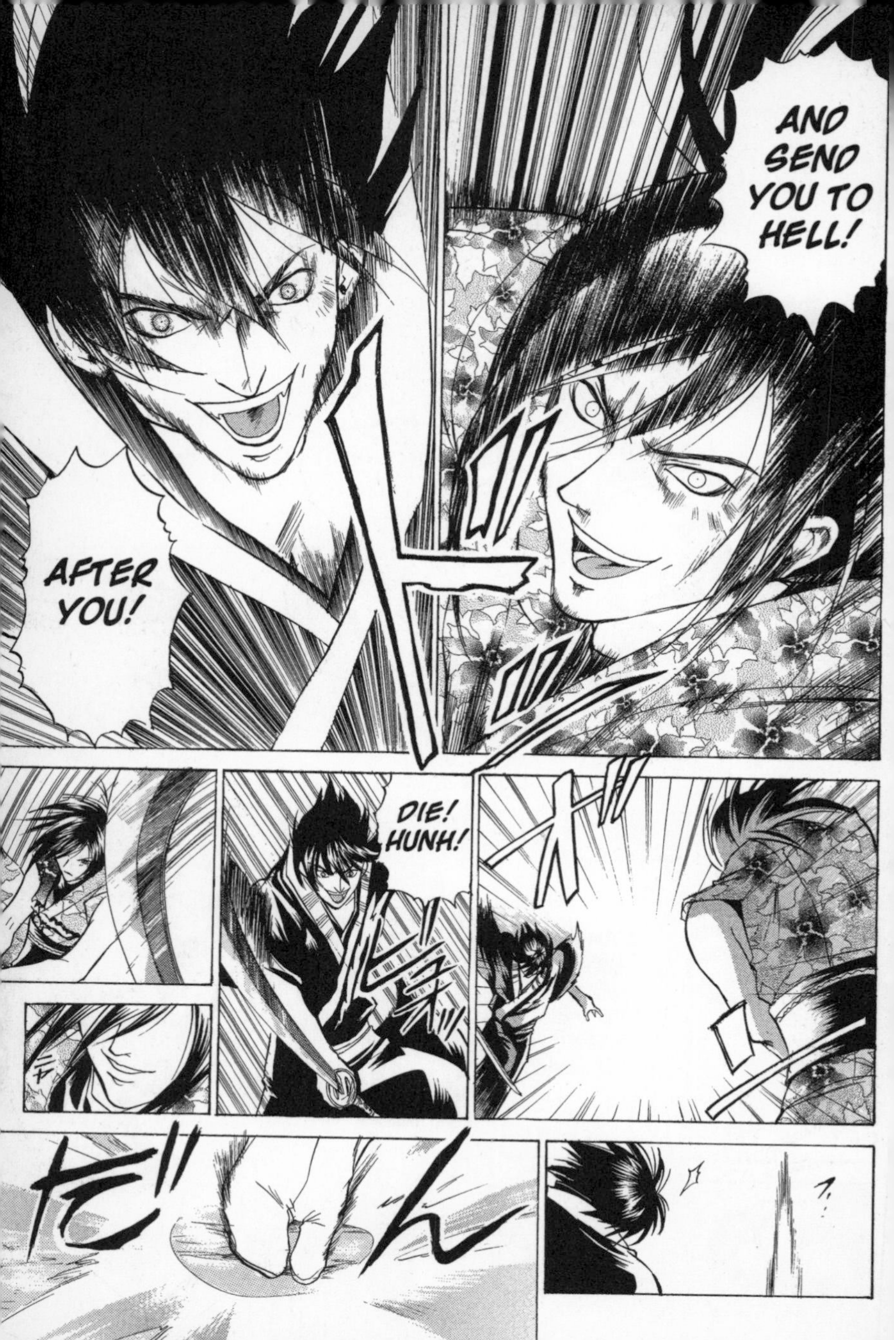
AND SEND YOU TO HELL!
AFTER YOU!
DIE! HUNH!
だん

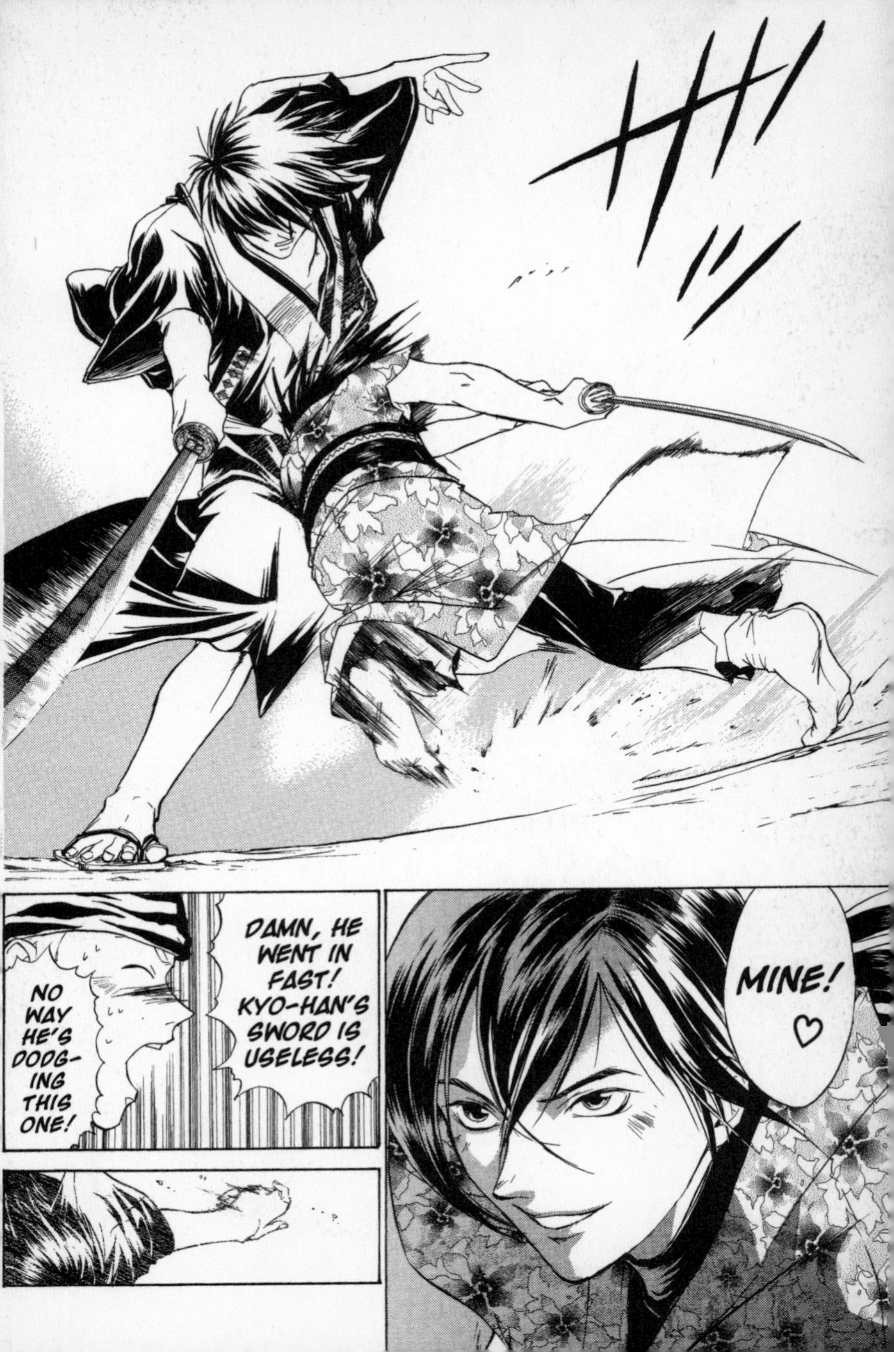
MINE! ♥
DAMN, HE WENT IN FAST! KYO-HAN'S SWORD IS USELESS!
NO WAY HE'S DODGING THIS ONE!

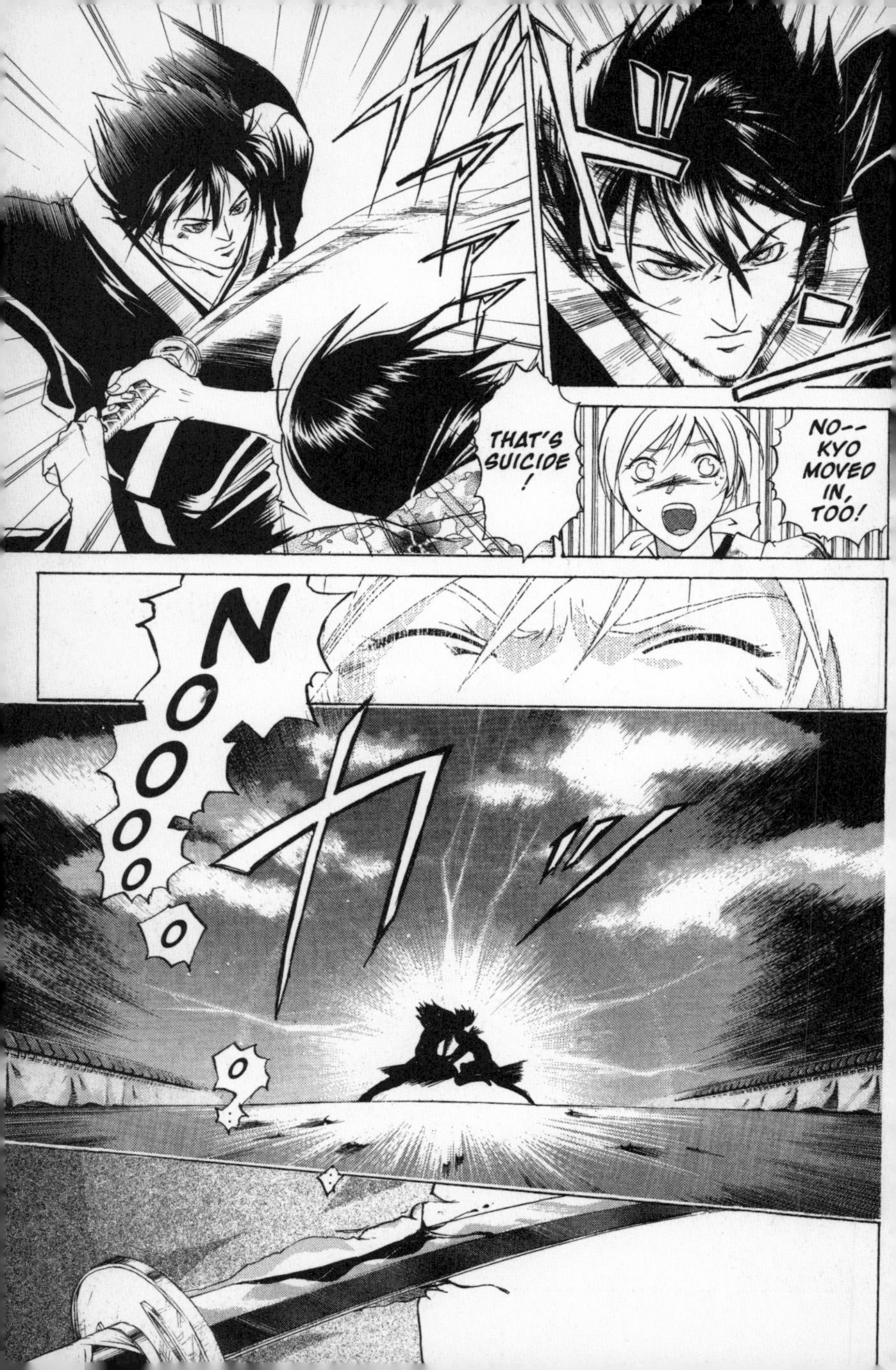
NO-- KYO MOVED IN, TOO!
THAT'S SUICIDE!
NOOOOOOOO

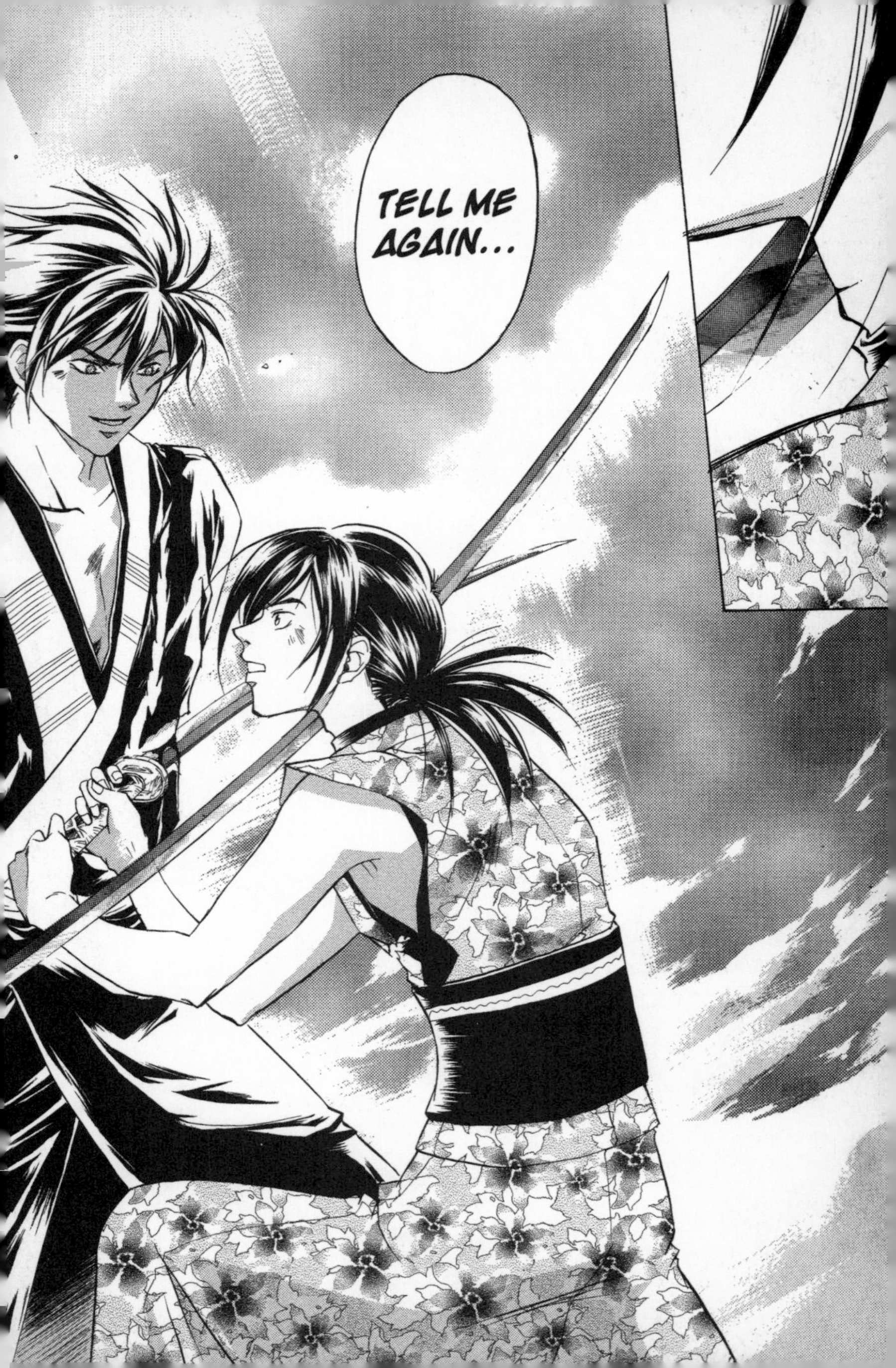
TELL ME AGAIN...

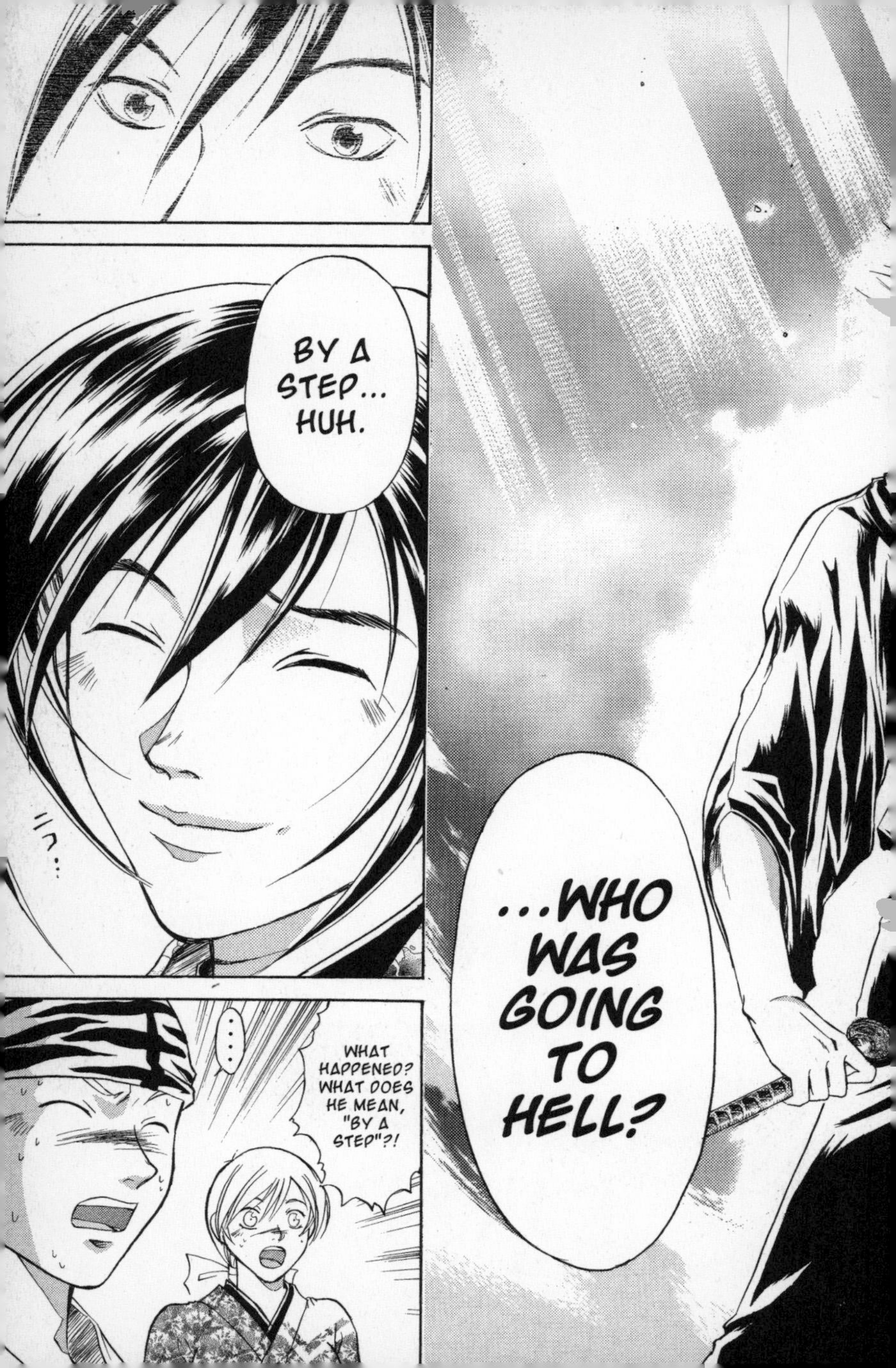

...WHO WAS GOING TO HELL?
BY A STEP... HUH.
ニコ…
WHAT HAPPENED? WHAT DOES HE MEAN, "BY A STEP"?!
....

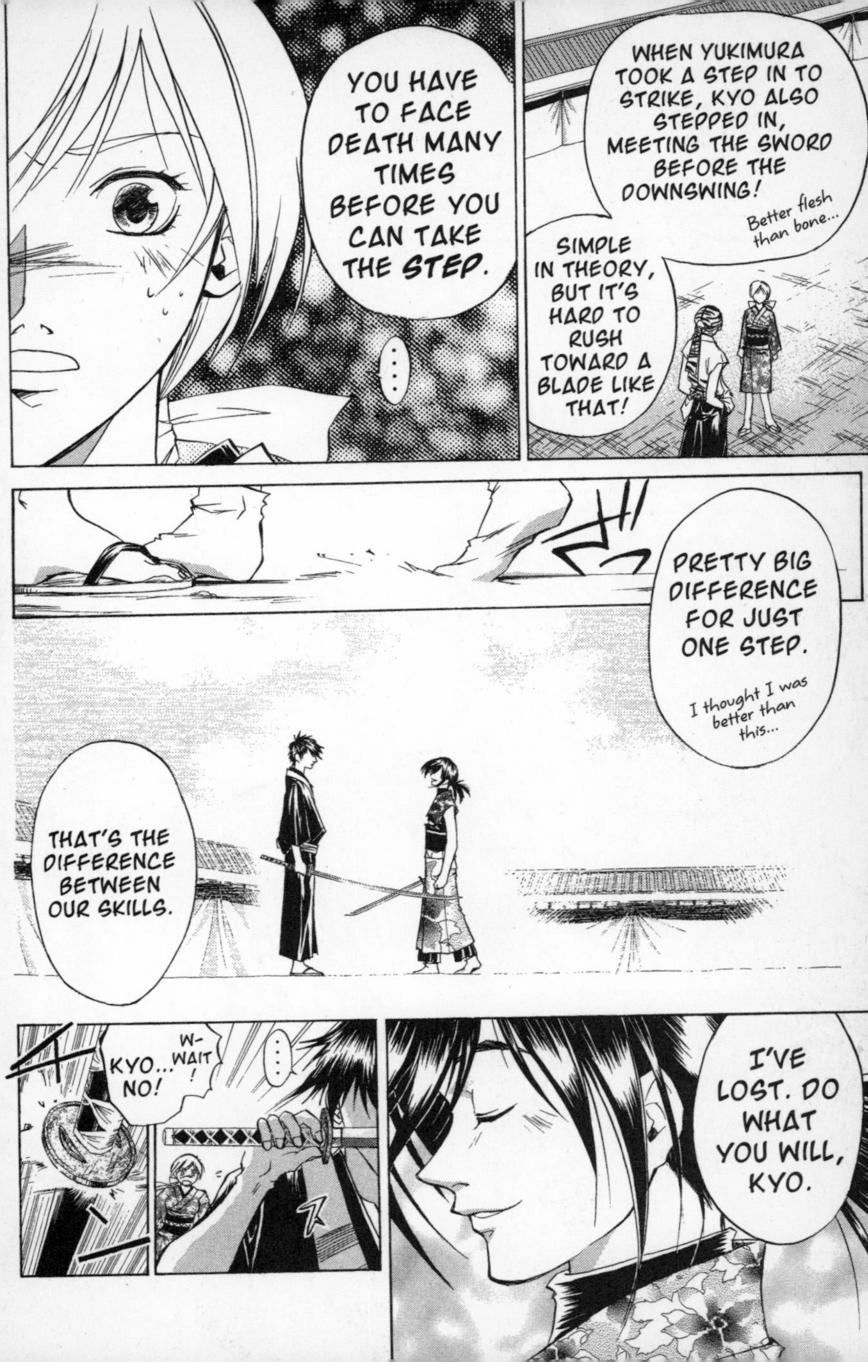
WHEN YUKIMURA TOOK A STEP IN TO STRIKE, KYO ALSO STEPPED IN, MEETING THE SWORD BEFORE THE DOWNSWING!
Better flesh than bone...
SIMPLE IN THEORY, BUT IT'S HARD TO RUSH TOWARD A BLADE LIKE THAT!
YOU HAVE TO FACE DEATH MANY TIMES BEFORE YOU CAN TAKE THE STEP.
...
PRETTY BIG DIFFERENCE FOR JUST ONE STEP.
I thought I was better than this...
THAT'S THE DIFFERENCE BETWEEN OUR SKILLS.
I'VE LOST. DO WHAT YOU WILL, KYO.
...
W-WAIT!
KYO... NO!

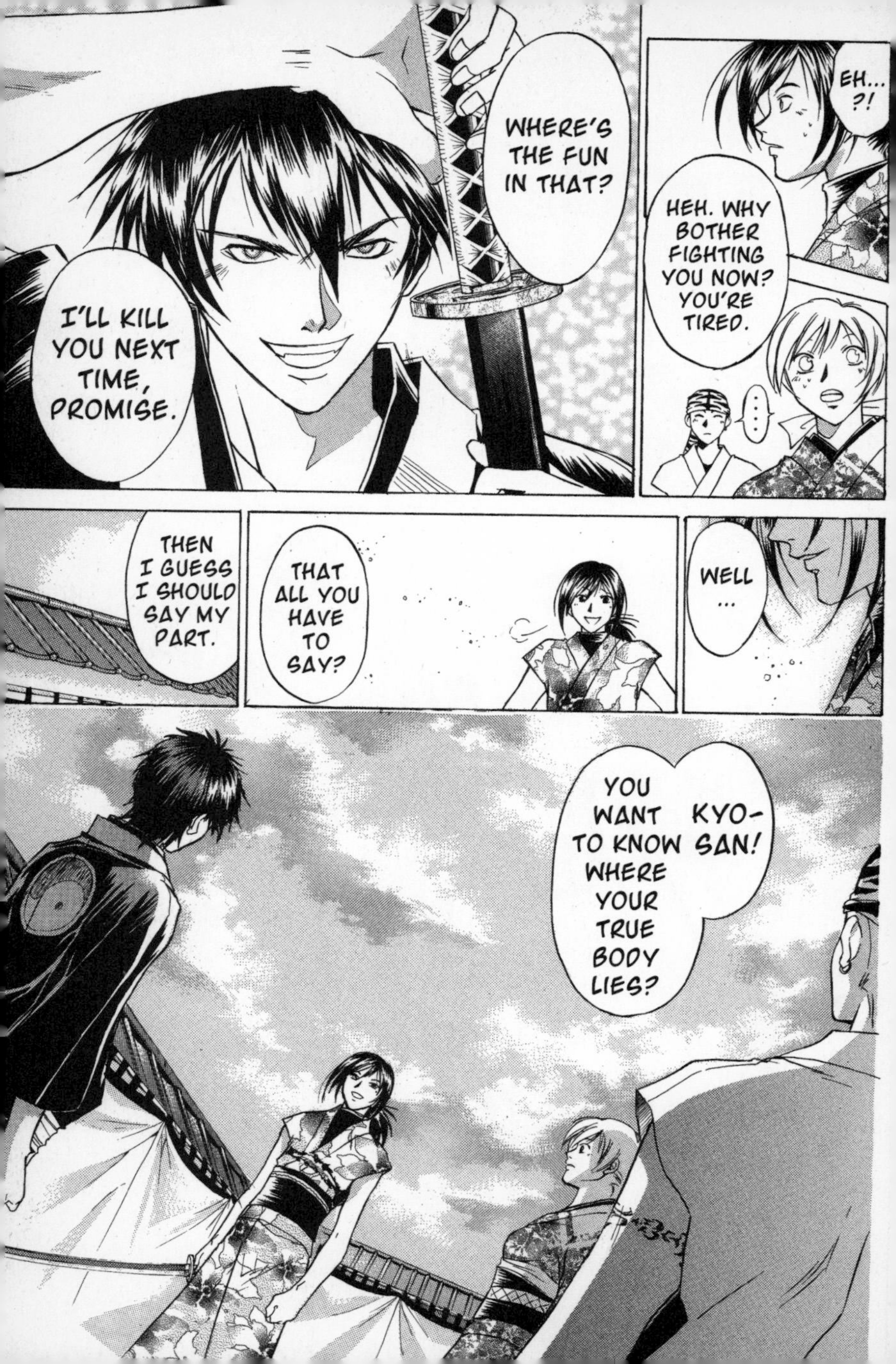
EH... ?!
HEH. WHY BOTHER FIGHTING YOU NOW? YOU'RE TIRED.
....
WHERE'S THE FUN IN THAT?
I'LL KILL YOU NEXT TIME, PROMISE.
WELL ...
THAT ALL YOU HAVE TO SAY?
THEN I GUESS I SHOULD SAY MY PART.
KYO-SAN! YOU WANT TO KNOW WHERE YOUR TRUE BODY LIES?

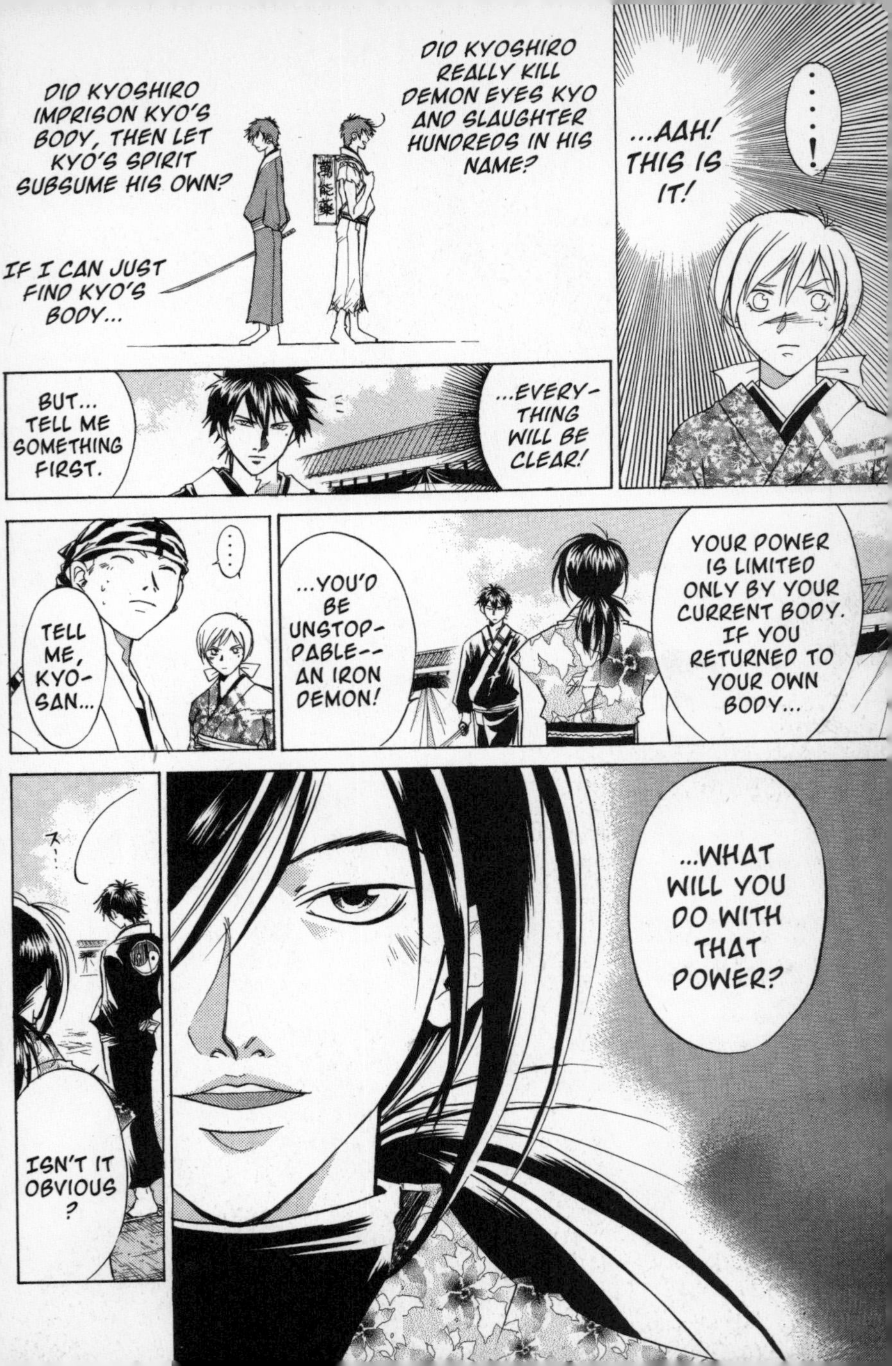
....!
...AAH! THIS IS IT!
DID KYOSHIRO REALLY KILL DEMON EYES KYO AND SLAUGHTER HUNDREDS IN HIS NAME?
DID KYOSHIRO IMPRISON KYO'S BODY, THEN LET KYO'S SPIRIT SUBSUME HIS OWN?
IF I CAN JUST FIND KYO'S BODY...
...EVERY-THING WILL BE CLEAR!
BUT... TELL ME SOMETHING FIRST.
YOUR POWER IS LIMITED ONLY BY YOUR CURRENT BODY. IF YOU RETURNED TO YOUR OWN BODY...
...YOU'D BE UNSTOP-PABLE-- AN IRON DEMON!
....
TELL ME, KYO-SAN...
...WHAT WILL YOU DO WITH THAT POWER?
ISN'T IT OBVIOUS?

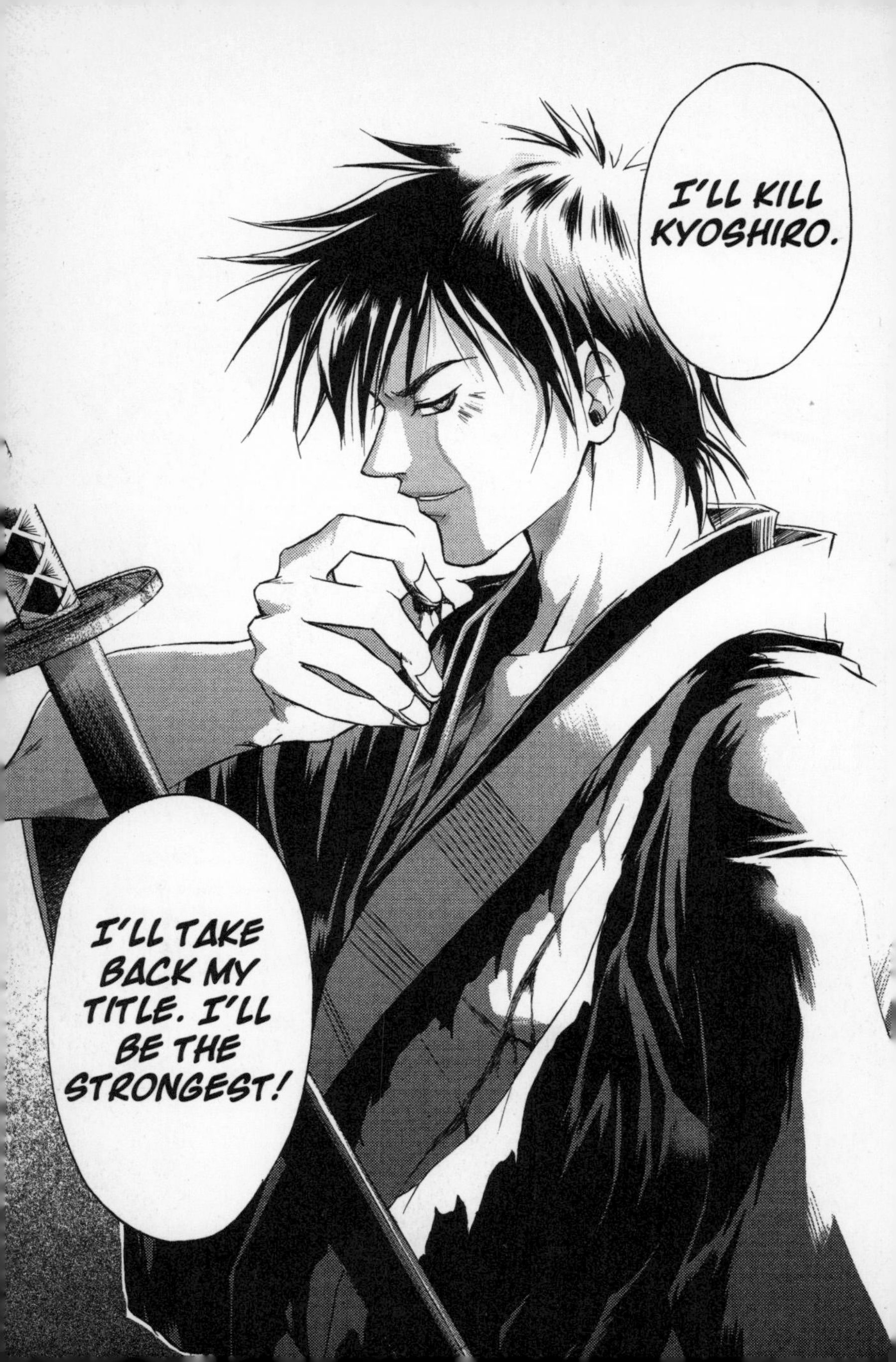
I'LL KILL KYOSHIRO.
I'LL TAKE BACK MY TITLE. I'LL BE THE STRONGEST!

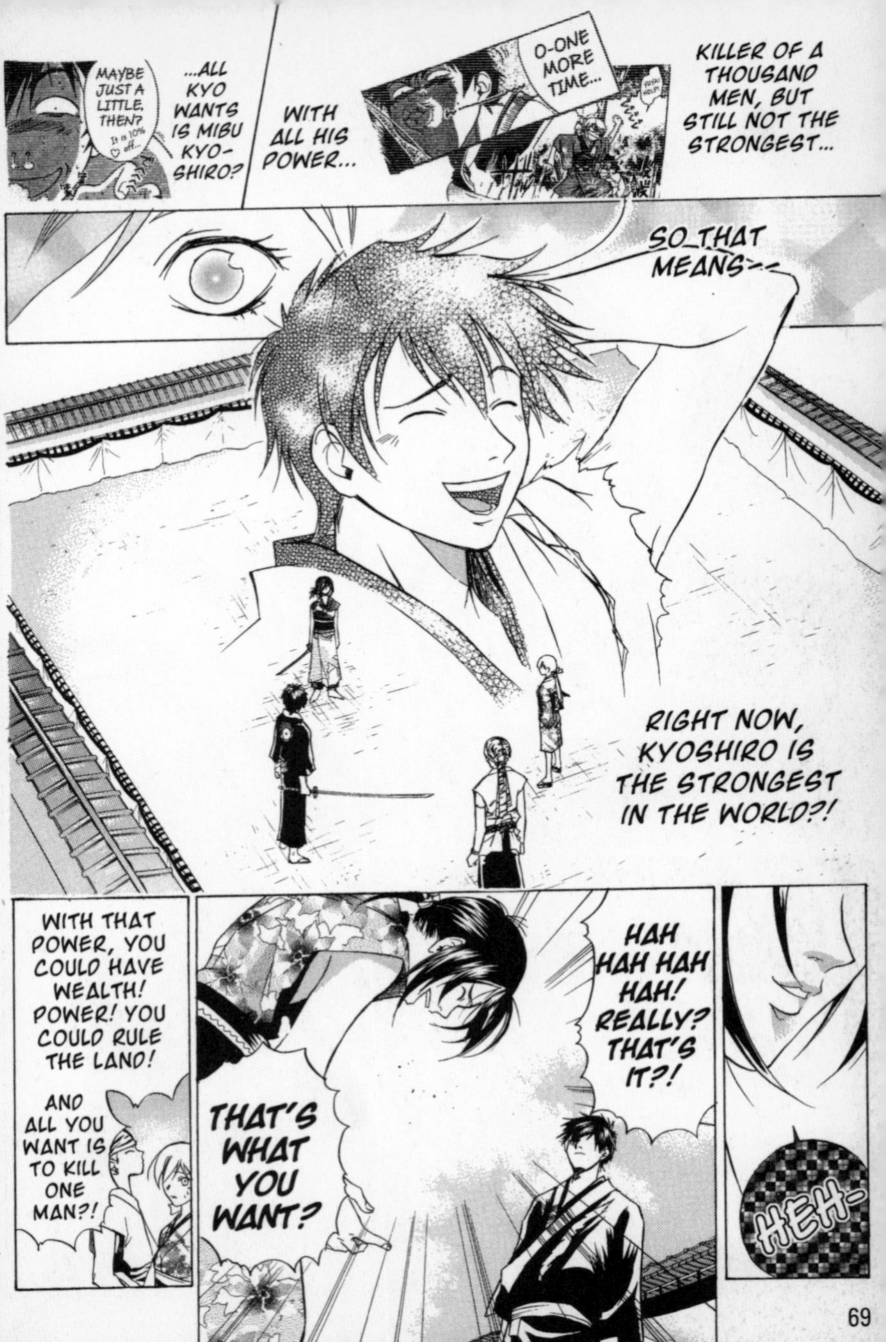
KILLER OF A THOUSAND MEN, BUT STILL NOT THE STRONGEST...
O-ONE MORE TIME...
YUYA! HELP!
WITH ALL HIS POWER...
...ALL KYO WANTS IS MIBU KYO-SHIRO?
MAYBE JUST A LITTLE, THEN?
It is 10% off...
SO THAT MEANS...
RIGHT NOW, KYOSHIRO IS THE STRONGEST IN THE WORLD?!
HEH-
HAH HAH HAH HAH! REALLY? THAT'S IT?!
THAT'S WHAT YOU WANT?
WITH THAT POWER, YOU COULD HAVE WEALTH! POWER! YOU COULD RULE THE LAND!
AND ALL YOU WANT IS TO KILL ONE MAN?!

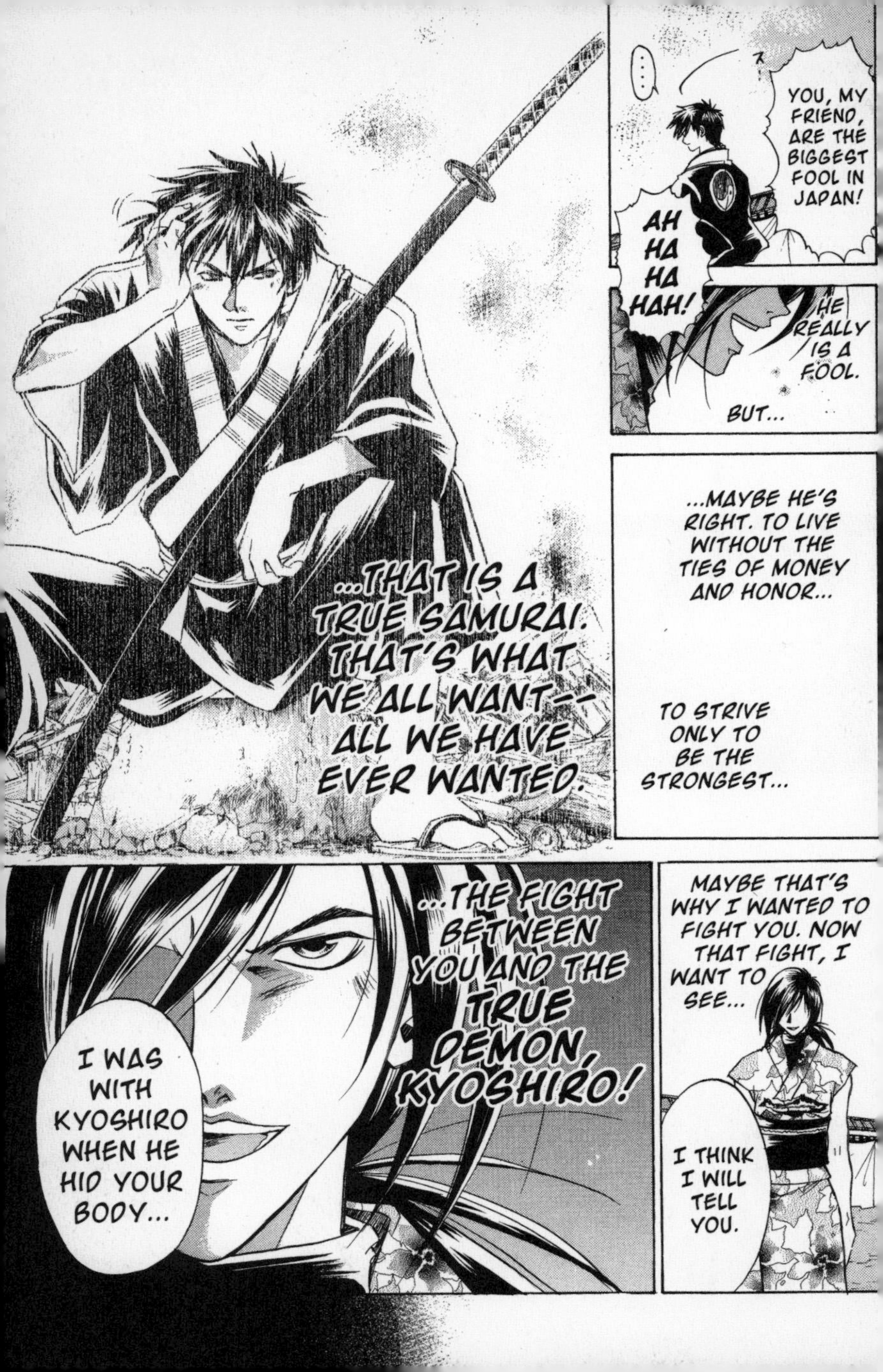
YOU, MY FRIEND, ARE THE BIGGEST FOOL IN JAPAN!
AH HA HA HAH!
....
HE REALLY IS A FOOL.
BUT...
...MAYBE HE'S RIGHT. TO LIVE WITHOUT THE TIES OF MONEY AND HONOR...
TO STRIVE ONLY TO BE THE STRONGEST...
...THAT IS A TRUE SAMURAI. THAT'S WHAT WE ALL WANT-- ALL WE HAVE EVER WANTED.
MAYBE THAT'S WHY I WANTED TO FIGHT YOU. NOW THAT FIGHT, I WANT TO SEE...
I THINK I WILL TELL YOU.
...THE FIGHT BETWEEN YOU AND THE TRUE DEMON, KYOSHIRO!
I WAS WITH KYOSHIRO WHEN HE HID YOUR BODY...

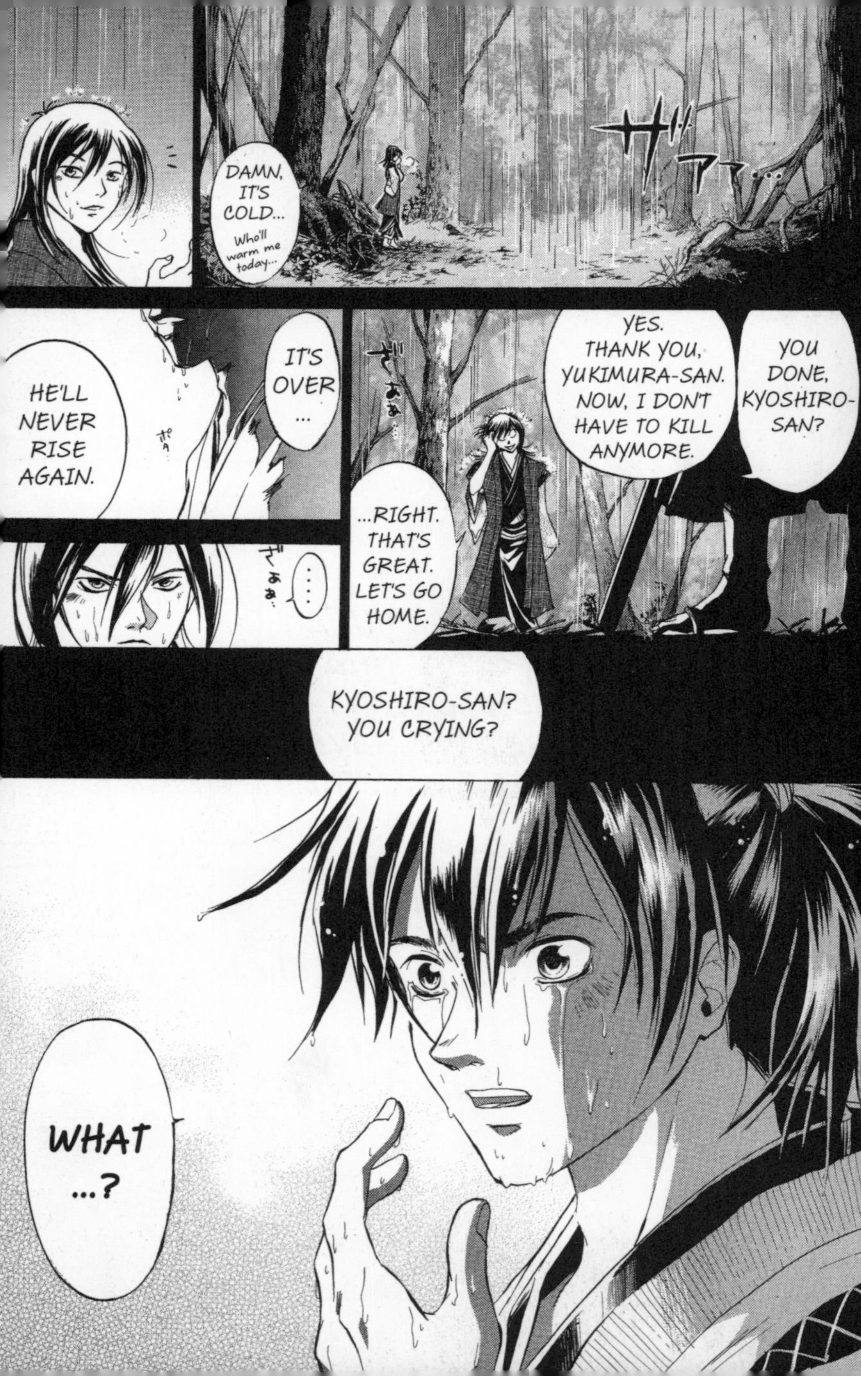
DAMN, IT'S COLD... Who'll warm me today...
YOU DONE, KYOSHIRO-SAN?
YES. THANK YOU, YUKIMURA-SAN. NOW, I DON'T HAVE TO KILL ANYMORE.
...RIGHT. THAT'S GREAT. LET'S GO HOME.
IT'S OVER...
HE'LL NEVER RISE AGAIN.
....
KYOSHIRO-SAN? YOU CRYING?
WHAT...?

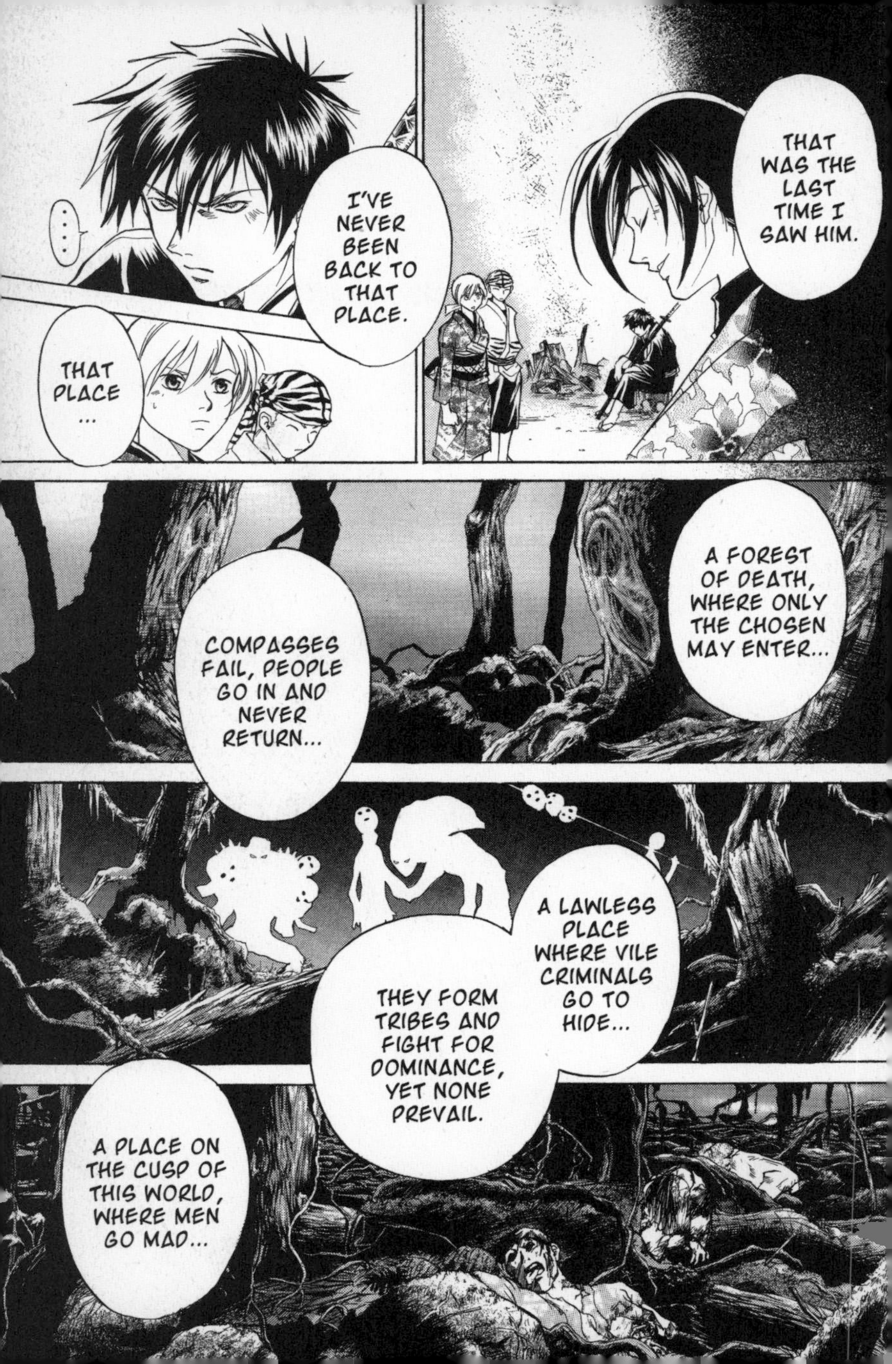
THAT WAS THE LAST TIME I SAW HIM.
I'VE NEVER BEEN BACK TO THAT PLACE.
...
THAT PLACE ...
A FOREST OF DEATH, WHERE ONLY THE CHOSEN MAY ENTER...
COMPASSES FAIL, PEOPLE GO IN AND NEVER RETURN...
A LAWLESS PLACE WHERE VILE CRIMINALS GO TO HIDE...
THEY FORM TRIBES AND FIGHT FOR DOMINANCE, YET NONE PREVAIL.
A PLACE ON THE CUSP OF THIS WORLD, WHERE MEN GO MAD...

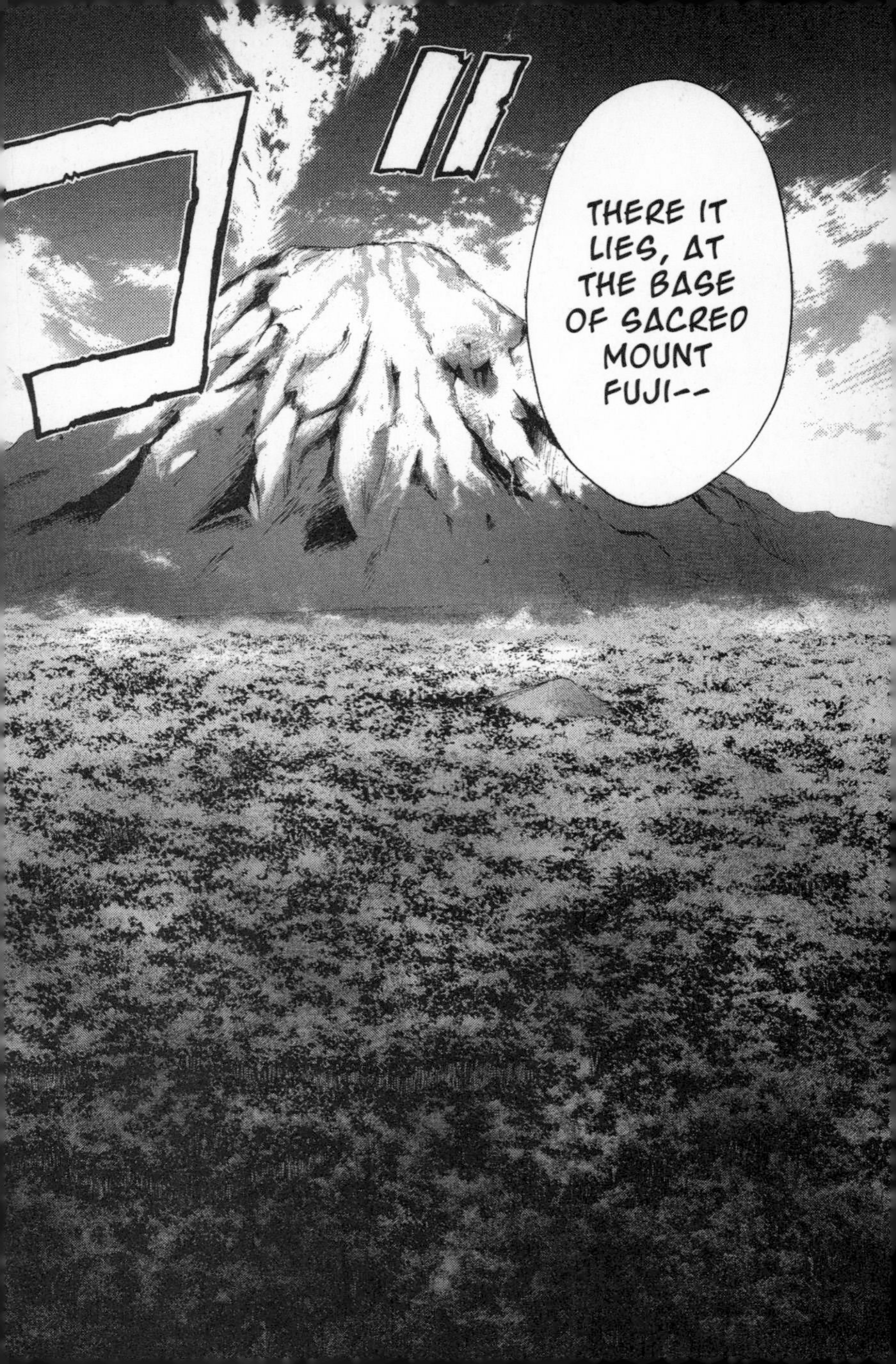
THERE IT LIES, AT THE BASE OF SACRED MOUNT FUJI--

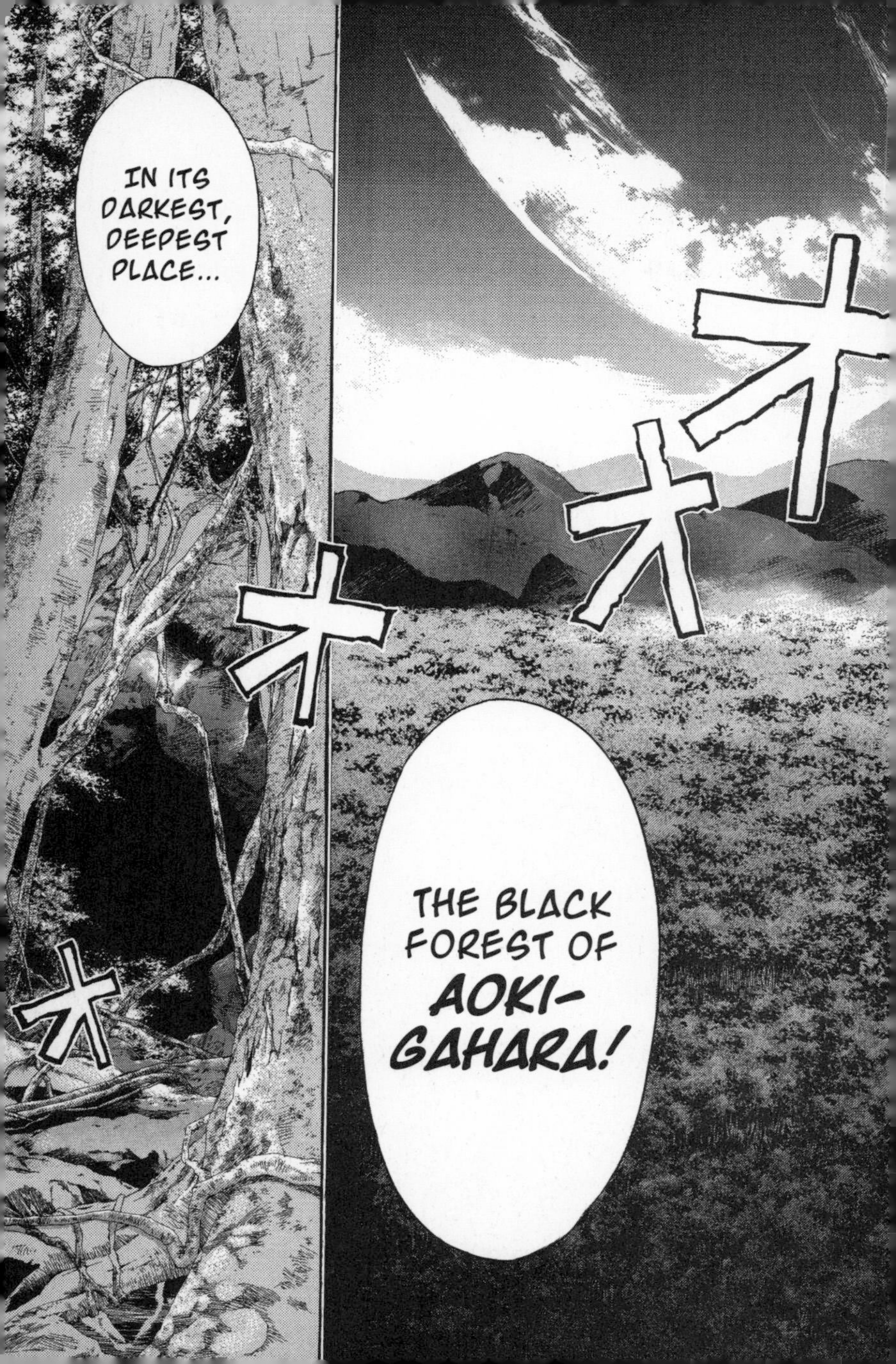
オオオオ
THE BLACK FOREST OF AOKI-GAHARA!
IN ITS DARKEST, DEEPEST PLACE...

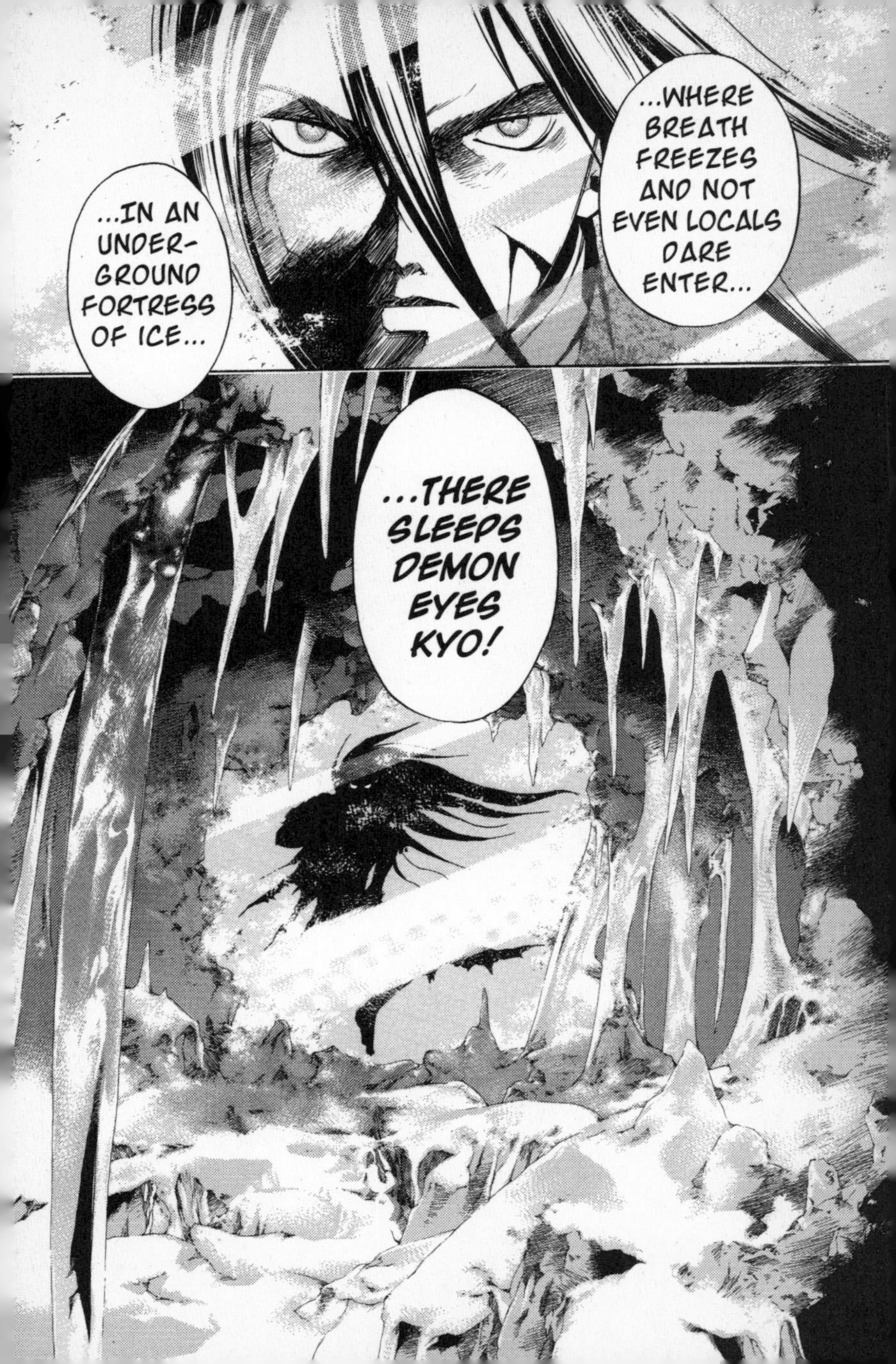
...WHERE BREATH FREEZES AND NOT EVEN LOCALS DARE ENTER...
...IN AN UNDER-GROUND FORTRESS OF ICE...
...THERE SLEEPS DEMON EYES KYO!

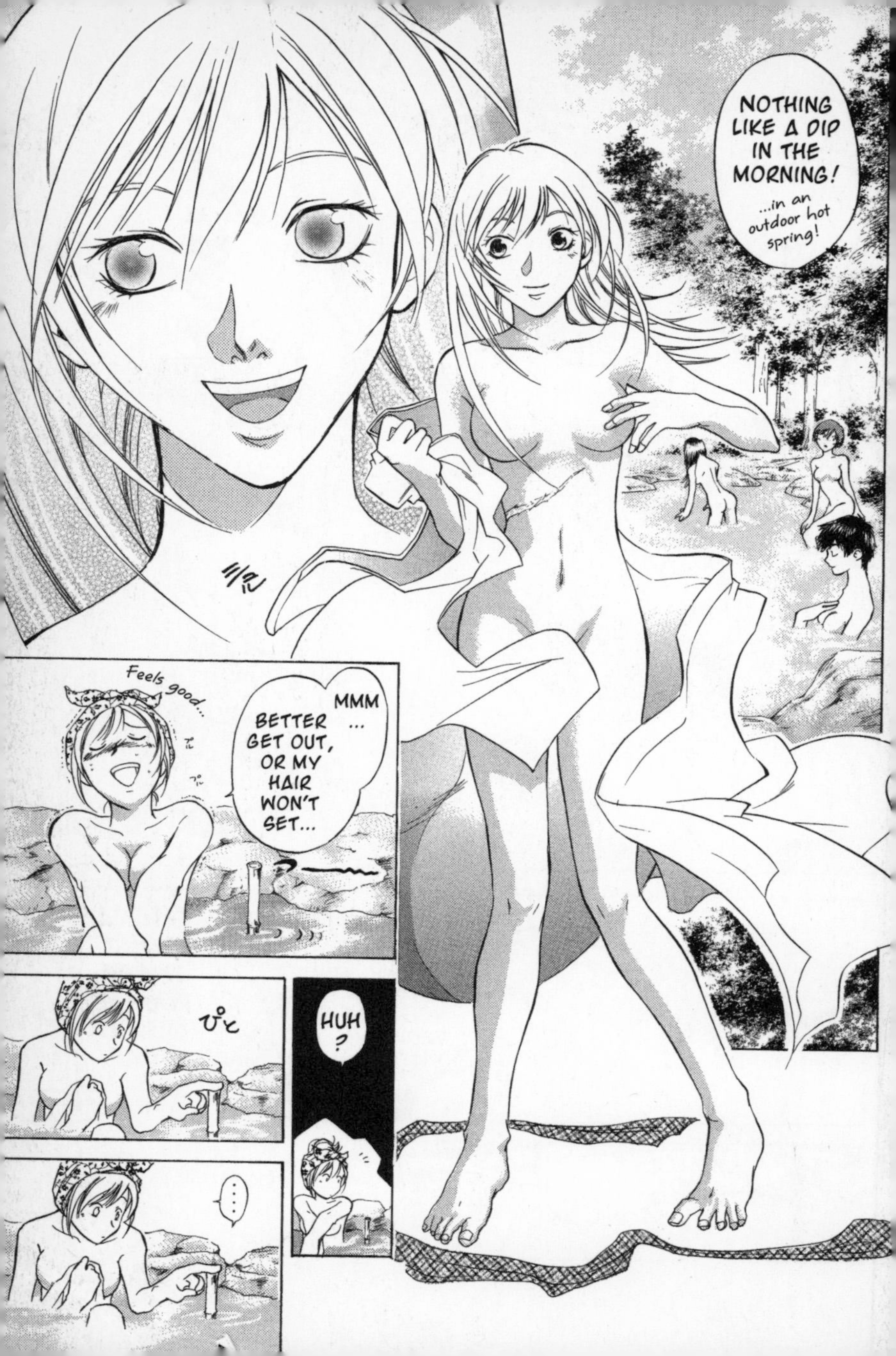
NOTHING LIKE A DIP IN THE MORNING!
...in an outdoor hot spring!
Feels good...
MMM... BETTER GET OUT, OR MY HAIR WON'T SET...
HUH?
ぴと
...

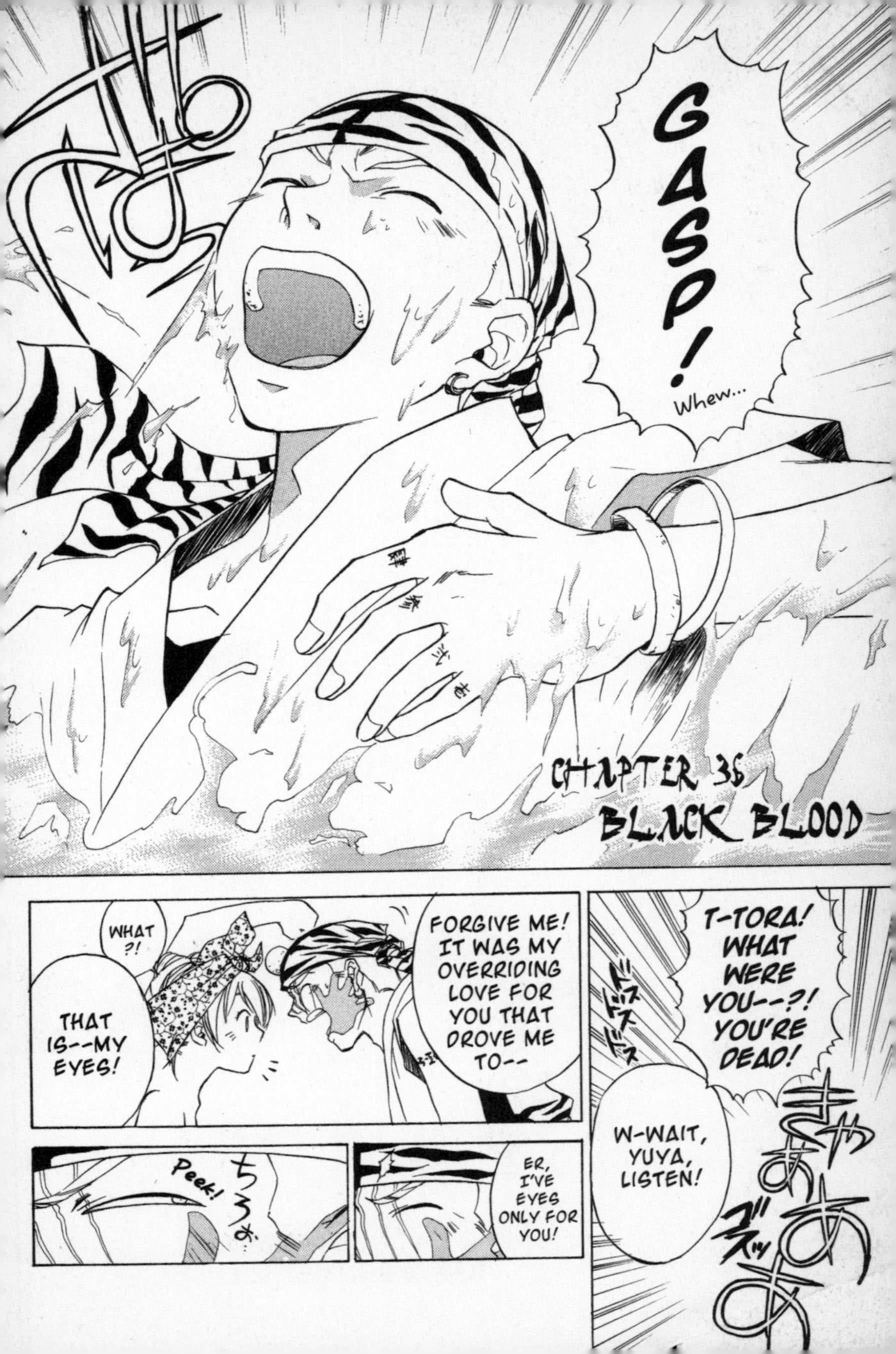
GASP!
Whew...
CHAPTER 36
BLACK BLOOD
T-TORA! WHAT WERE YOU--?! YOU'RE DEAD!
W-WAIT, YUYA, LISTEN!
FORGIVE ME! IT WAS MY OVERRIDING LOVE FOR YOU THAT DROVE ME TO--
WHAT ?!
THAT IS--MY EYES!
ER, I'VE EYES ONLY FOR YOU!
Peek!

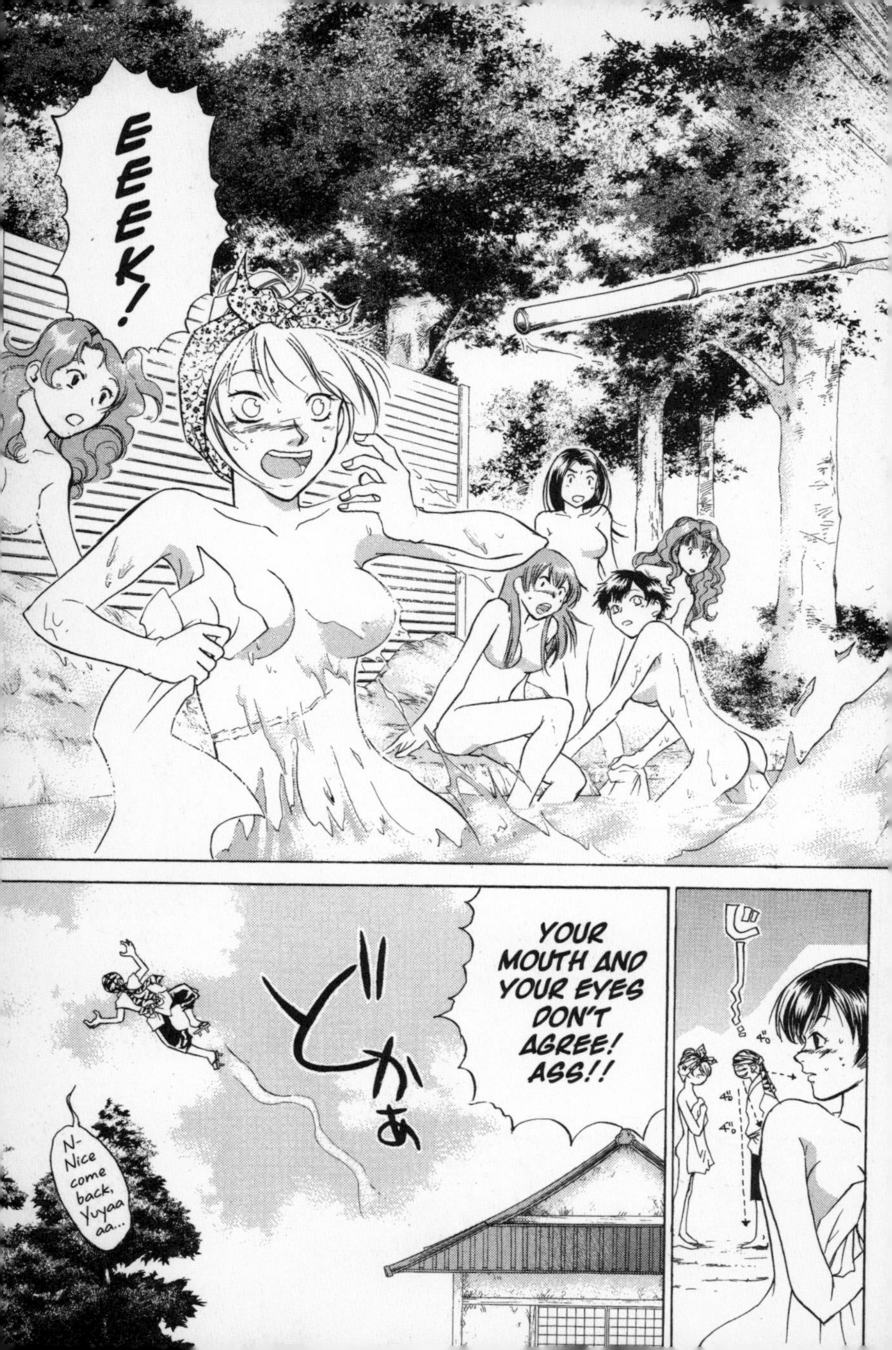
EEEEK!
じー
YOUR MOUTH AND YOUR EYES DON'T AGREE! ASS!!
どかぁ
N-Nice come back, Yuyaa aa...

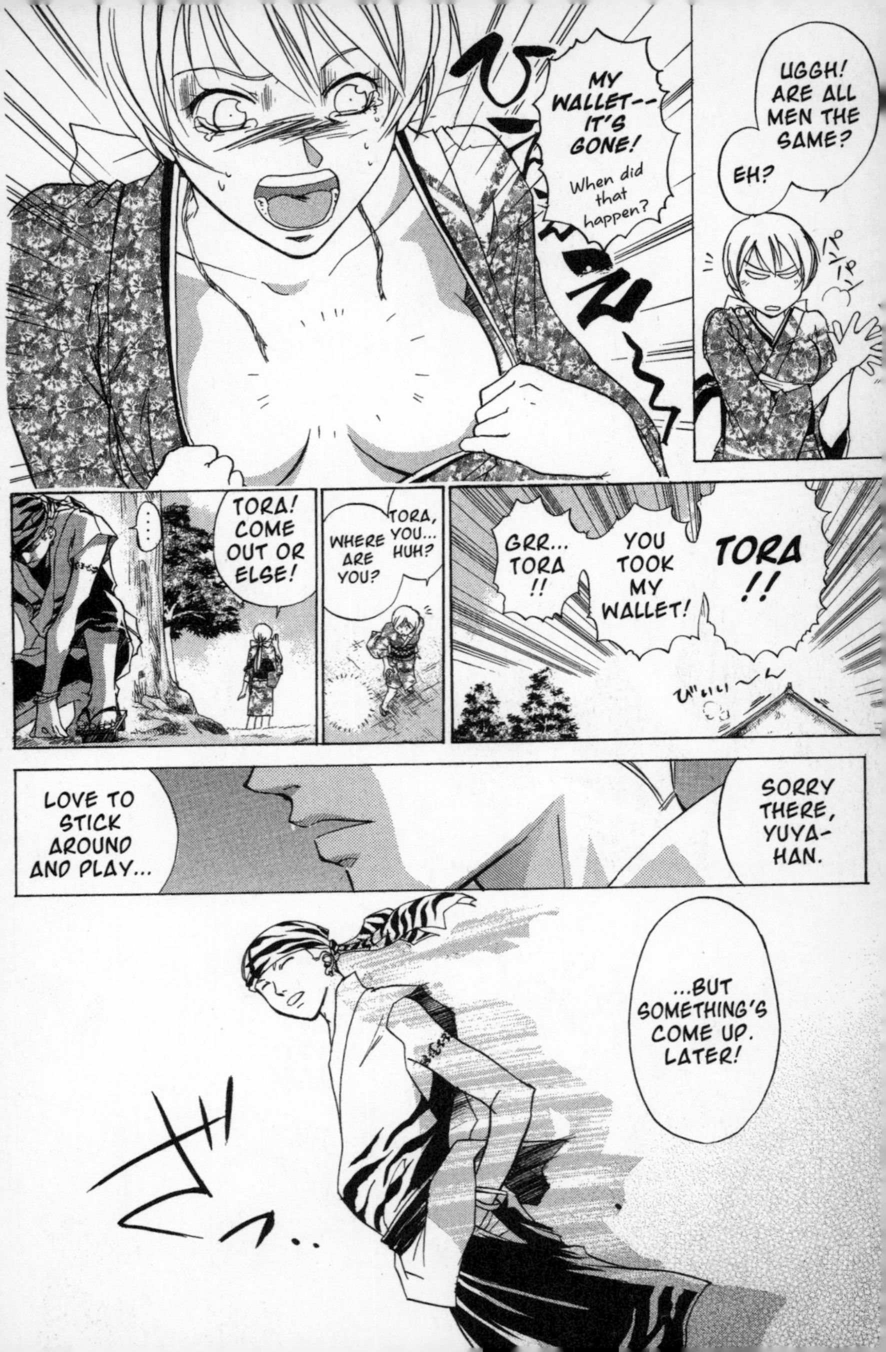
UGGH! ARE ALL MEN THE SAME?
EH?
MY WALLET--IT'S GONE!
When did that happen?
TORA!!
YOU TOOK MY WALLET!
GRR... TORA!!
TORA, YOU... HUH?
WHERE ARE YOU?
TORA! COME OUT OR ELSE!
...
SORRY THERE, YUYA-HAN.
LOVE TO STICK AROUND AND PLAY...
...BUT SOMETHING'S COME UP. LATER!

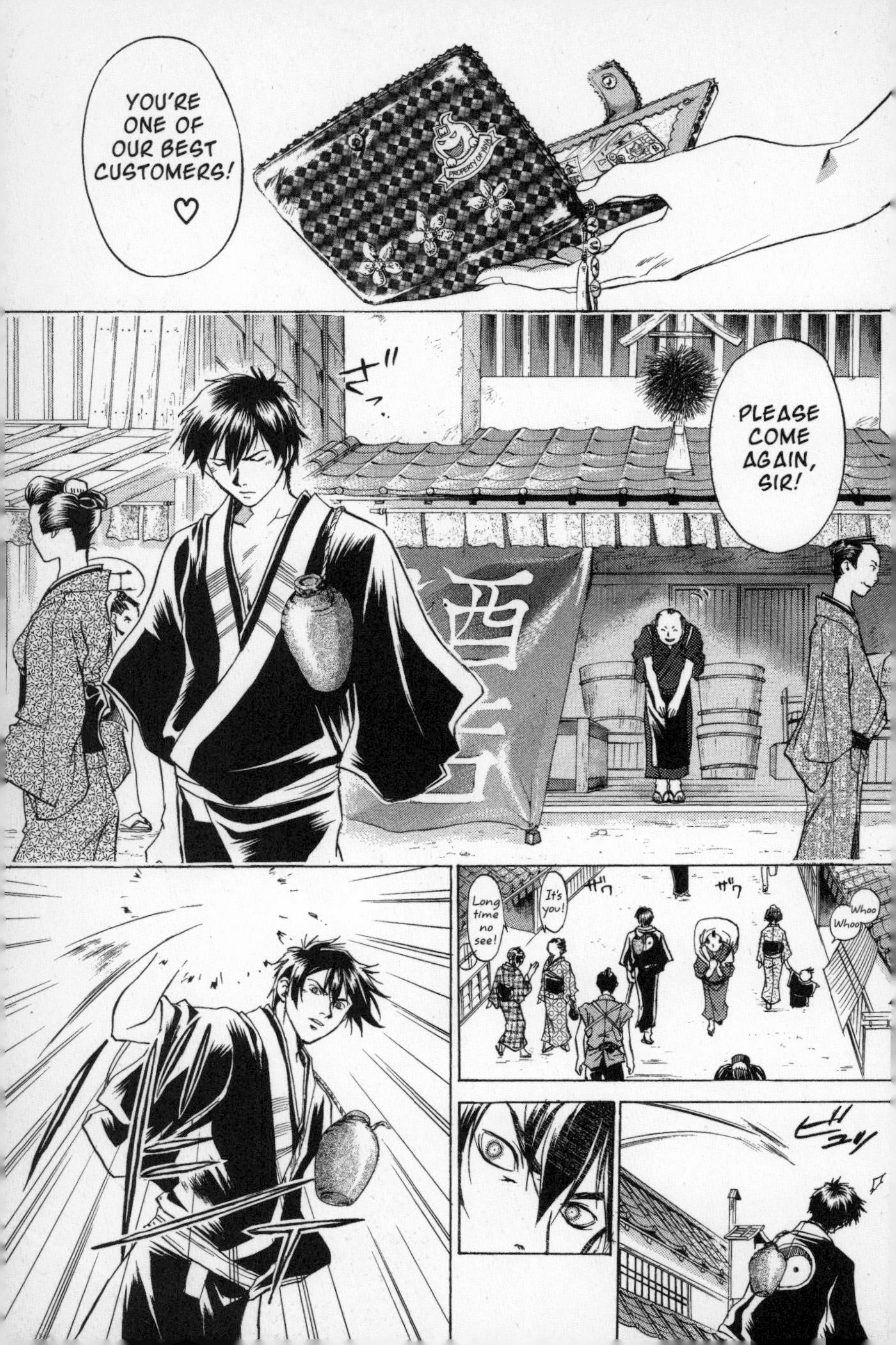
YOU'RE ONE OF OUR BEST CUSTOMERS! ♡
PLEASE COME AGAIN, SIR!
Whoo Whoo
It's you!
Long time no see!

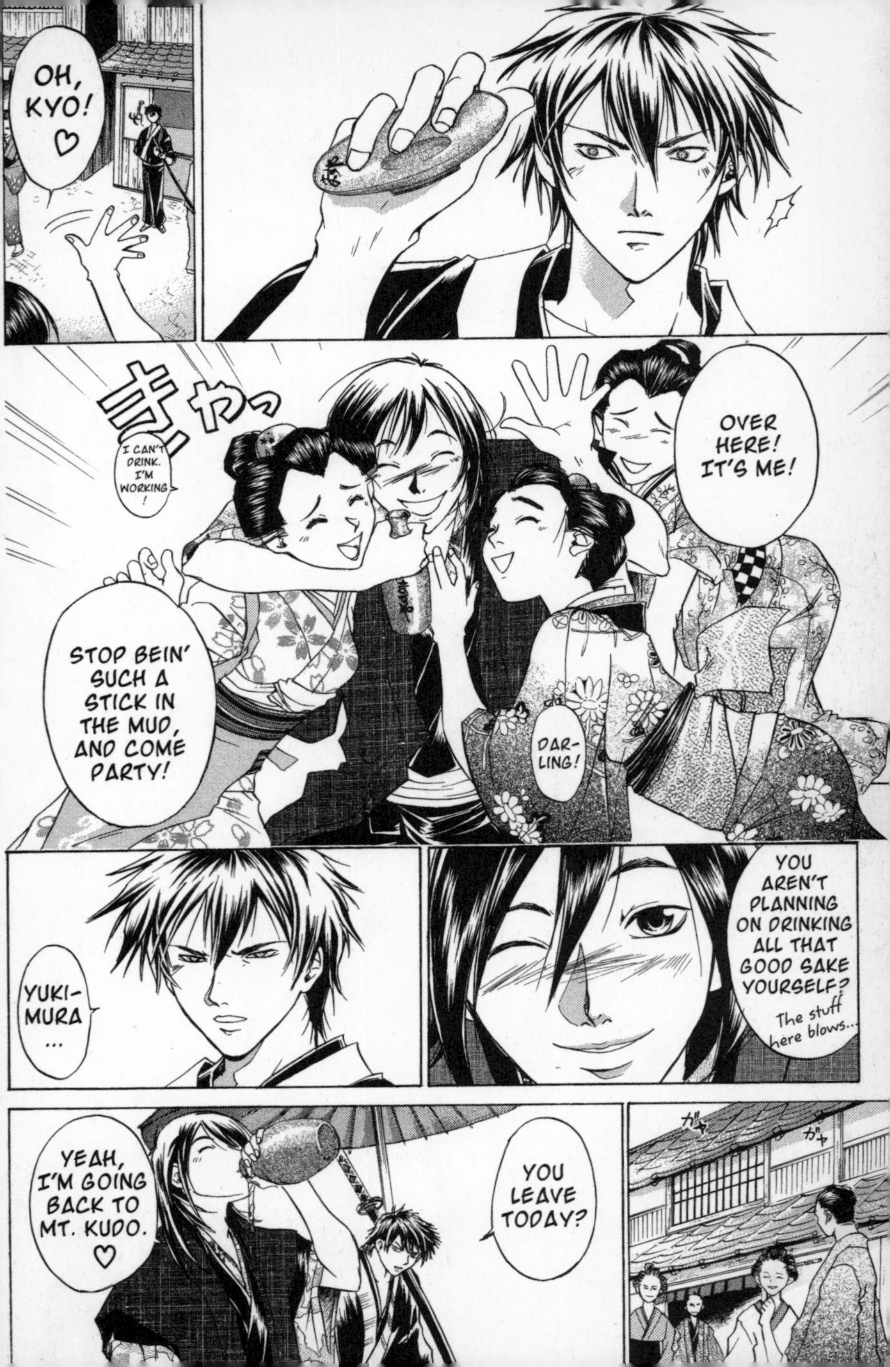
OH, KYO! ♡
OVER HERE! IT'S ME!
きゃっ
I CAN'T DRINK. I'M WORKING!
DARLING!
STOP BEIN' SUCH A STICK IN THE MUD, AND COME PARTY!
YOU AREN'T PLANNING ON DRINKING ALL THAT GOOD SAKE YOURSELF?
The stuff here blows...
YUKIMURA...
ガヤ
ガヤ
YOU LEAVE TODAY?
YEAH, I'M GOING BACK TO MT. KUDO. ♡

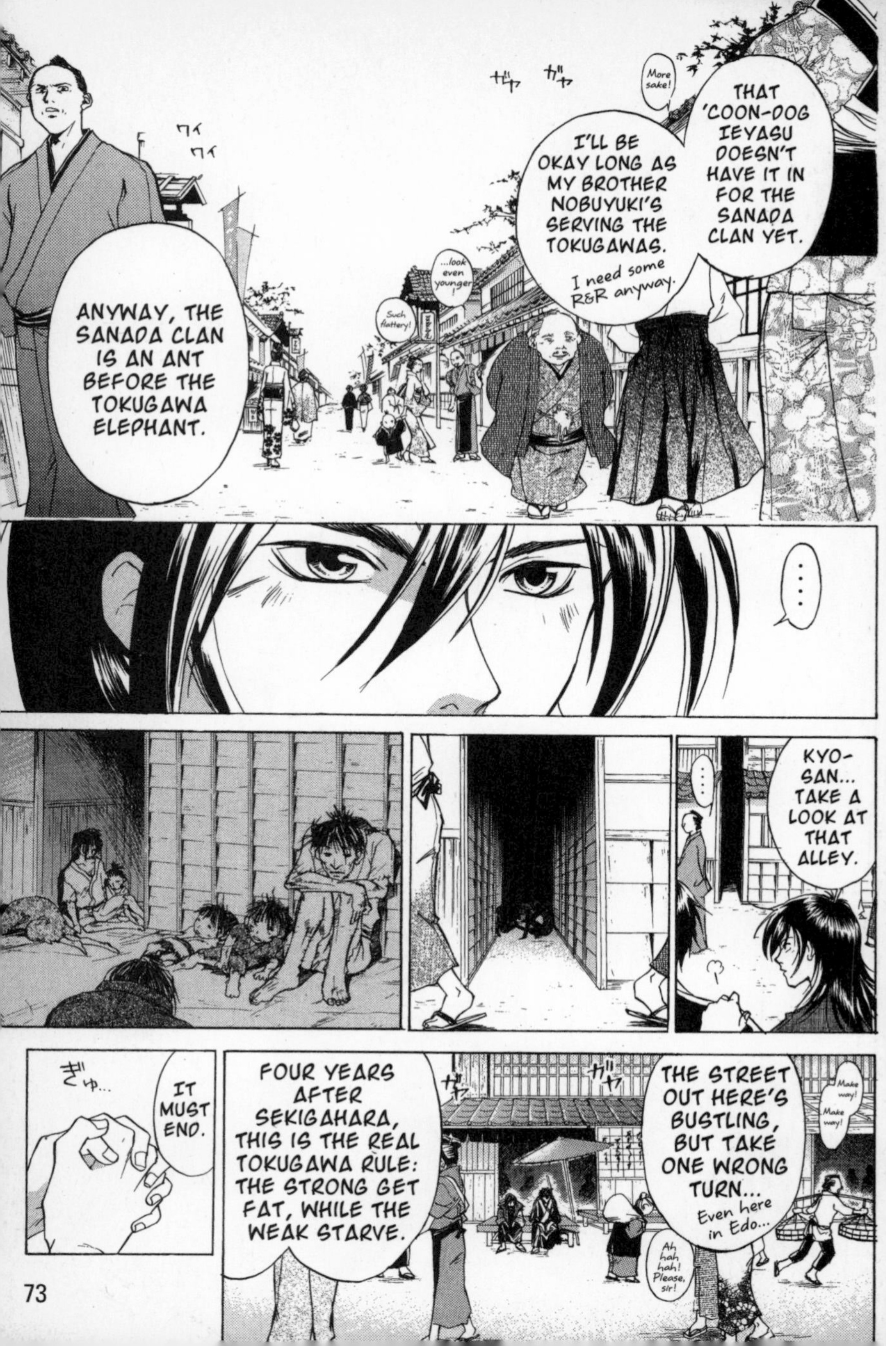
ガヤ ガヤ
More sake!
THAT 'COON-DOG IEYASU DOESN'T HAVE IT IN FOR THE SANADA CLAN YET.
I'LL BE OKAY LONG AS MY BROTHER NOBUYUKI'S SERVING THE TOKUGAWAS.
I need some R&R anyway.
...look even younger!
Such flattery!
ワイ ワイ
ANYWAY, THE SANADA CLAN IS AN ANT BEFORE THE TOKUGAWA ELEPHANT.
....
KYO-SAN... TAKE A LOOK AT THAT ALLEY.
....
Make way!
Make way!
THE STREET OUT HERE'S BUSTLING, BUT TAKE ONE WRONG TURN...
Even here in Edo...
Ah hah hah! Please, sir!
ガヤ ガヤ
FOUR YEARS AFTER SEKIGAHARA, THIS IS THE REAL TOKUGAWA RULE: THE STRONG GET FAT, WHILE THE WEAK STARVE.
ぎゅ...
IT MUST END.

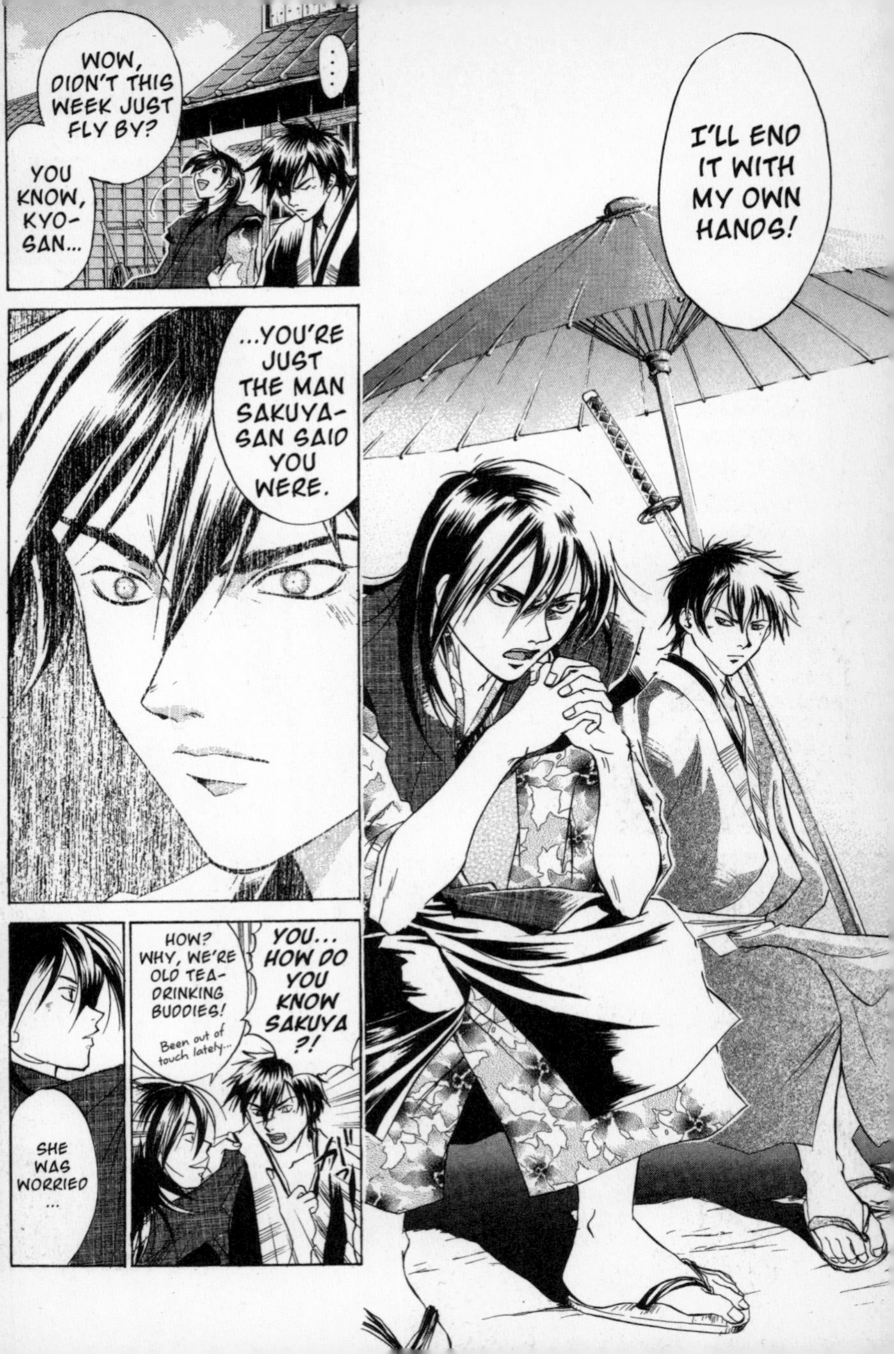
I'LL END IT WITH MY OWN HANDS!
...
WOW, DIDN'T THIS WEEK JUST FLY BY?
YOU KNOW, KYO-SAN...
...YOU'RE JUST THE MAN SAKUYA-SAN SAID YOU WERE.
YOU... HOW DO YOU KNOW SAKUYA?!
HOW? WHY, WE'RE OLD TEA-DRINKING BUDDIES!
Been out of touch lately...
SHE WAS WORRIED...

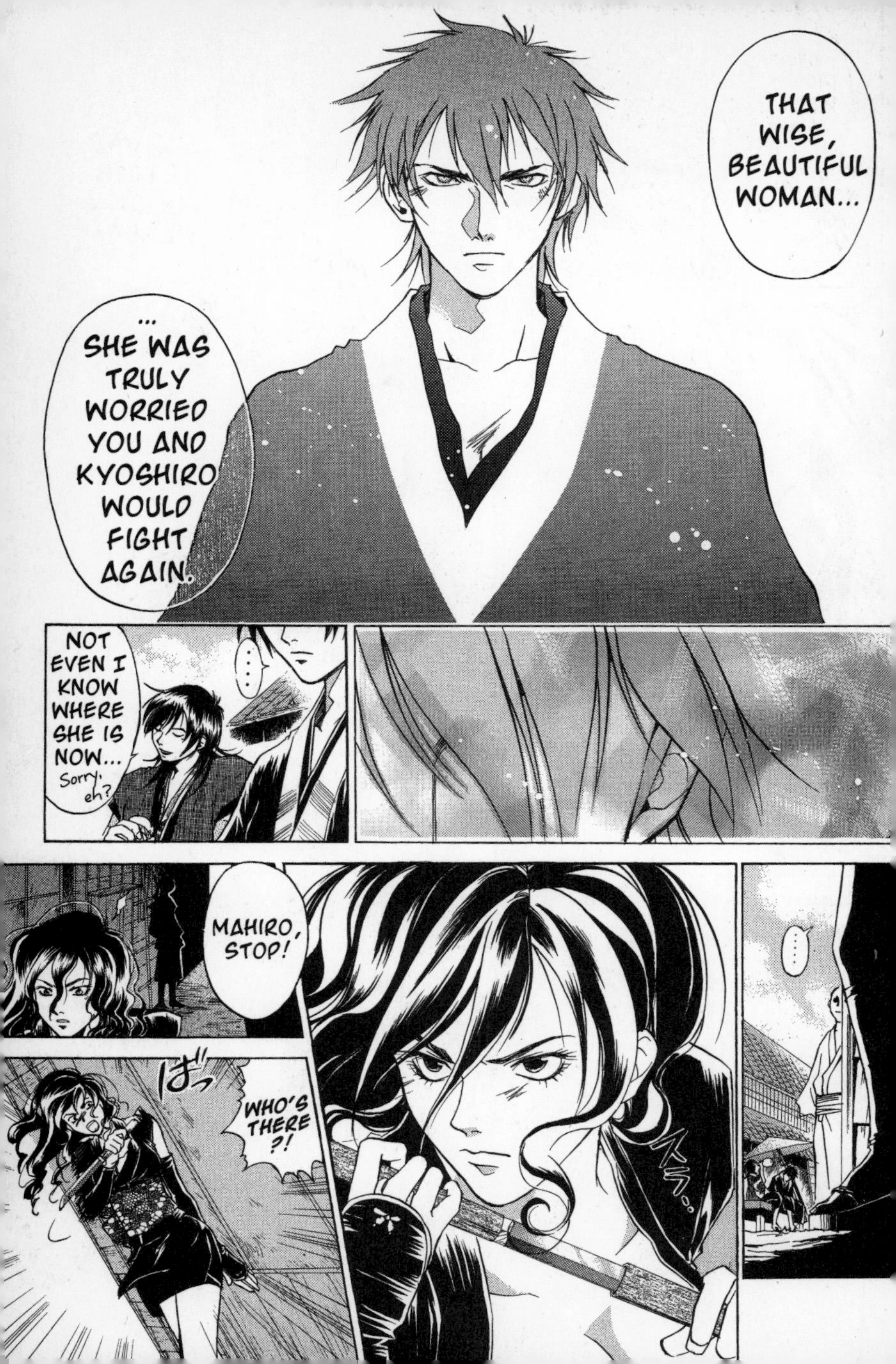
THAT WISE, BEAUTIFUL WOMAN...
...SHE WAS TRULY WORRIED YOU AND KYOSHIRO WOULD FIGHT AGAIN.
...
NOT EVEN I KNOW WHERE SHE IS NOW...
Sorry, eh?
...
MAHIRO, STOP!
ぱっ
WHO'S THERE?!

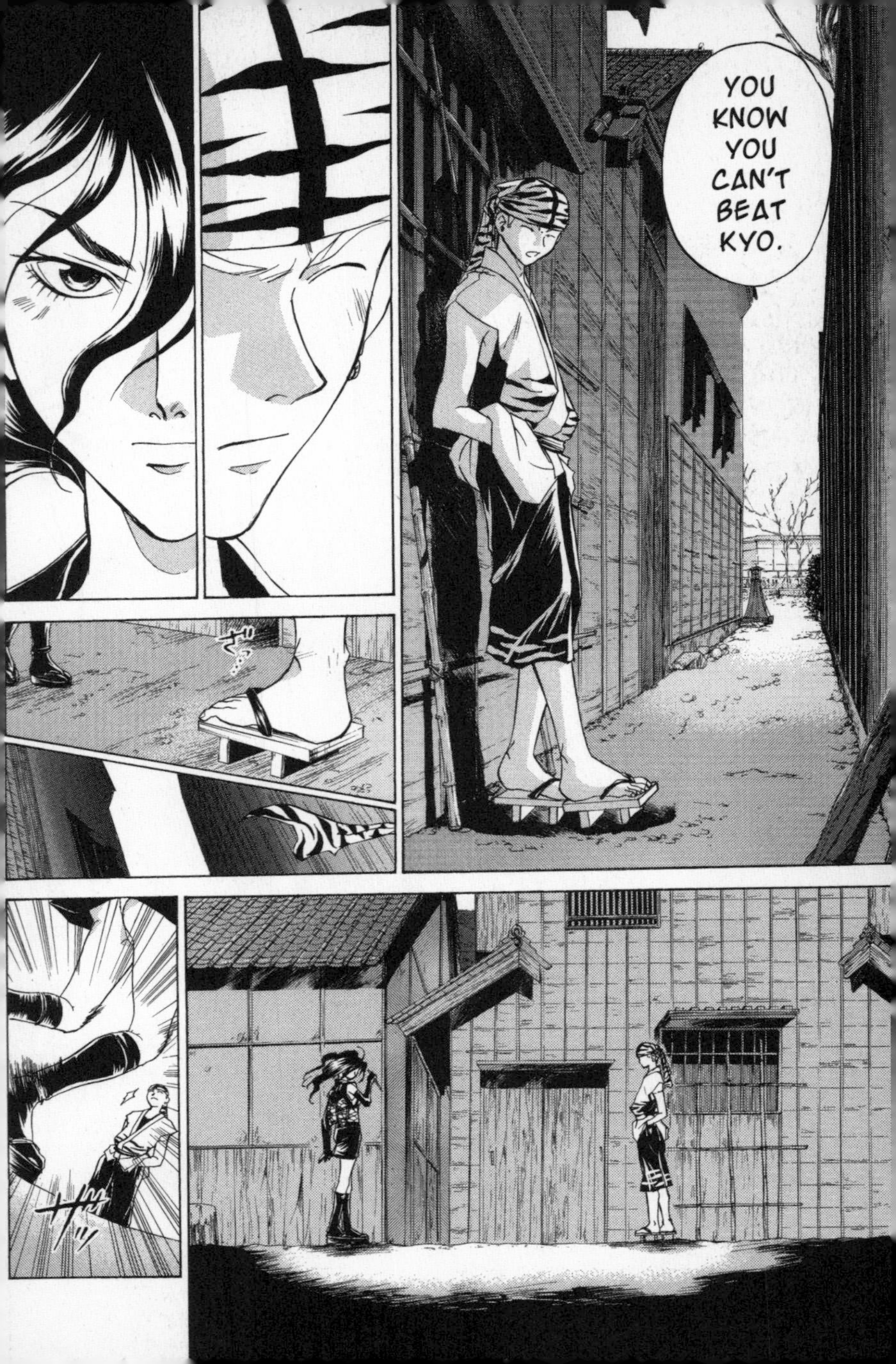
YOU KNOW YOU CAN'T BEAT KYO.

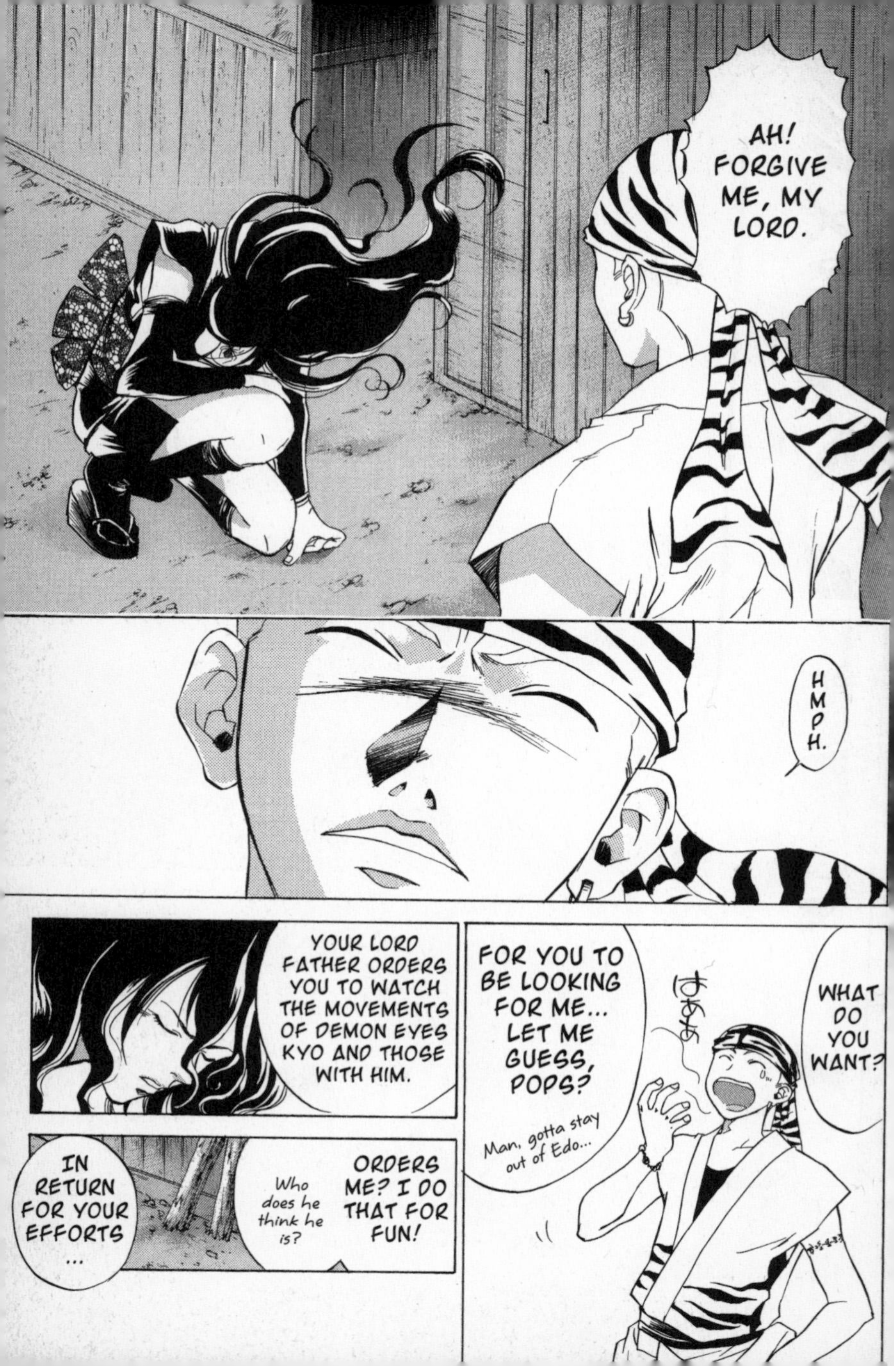
AH! FORGIVE ME, MY LORD.
HMPH.
WHAT DO YOU WANT?
FOR YOU TO BE LOOKING FOR ME... LET ME GUESS, POPS?
はああ
Man, gotta stay out of Edo...
YOUR LORD FATHER ORDERS YOU TO WATCH THE MOVEMENTS OF DEMON EYES KYO AND THOSE WITH HIM.
ORDERS ME? I DO THAT FOR FUN!
Who does he think he is?
IN RETURN FOR YOUR EFFORTS ...

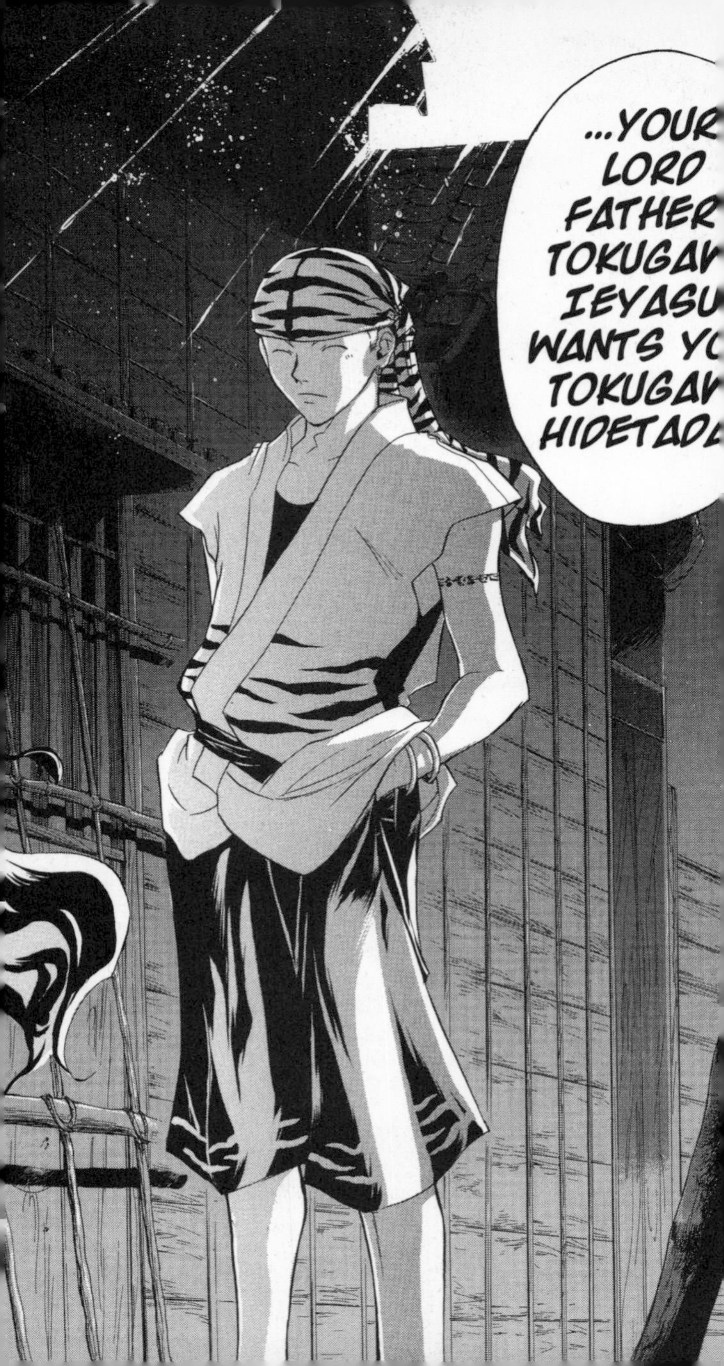
...YOUR LORD FATHER TOKUGAW IEYASU WANTS YO TOKUGAW HIDETADA

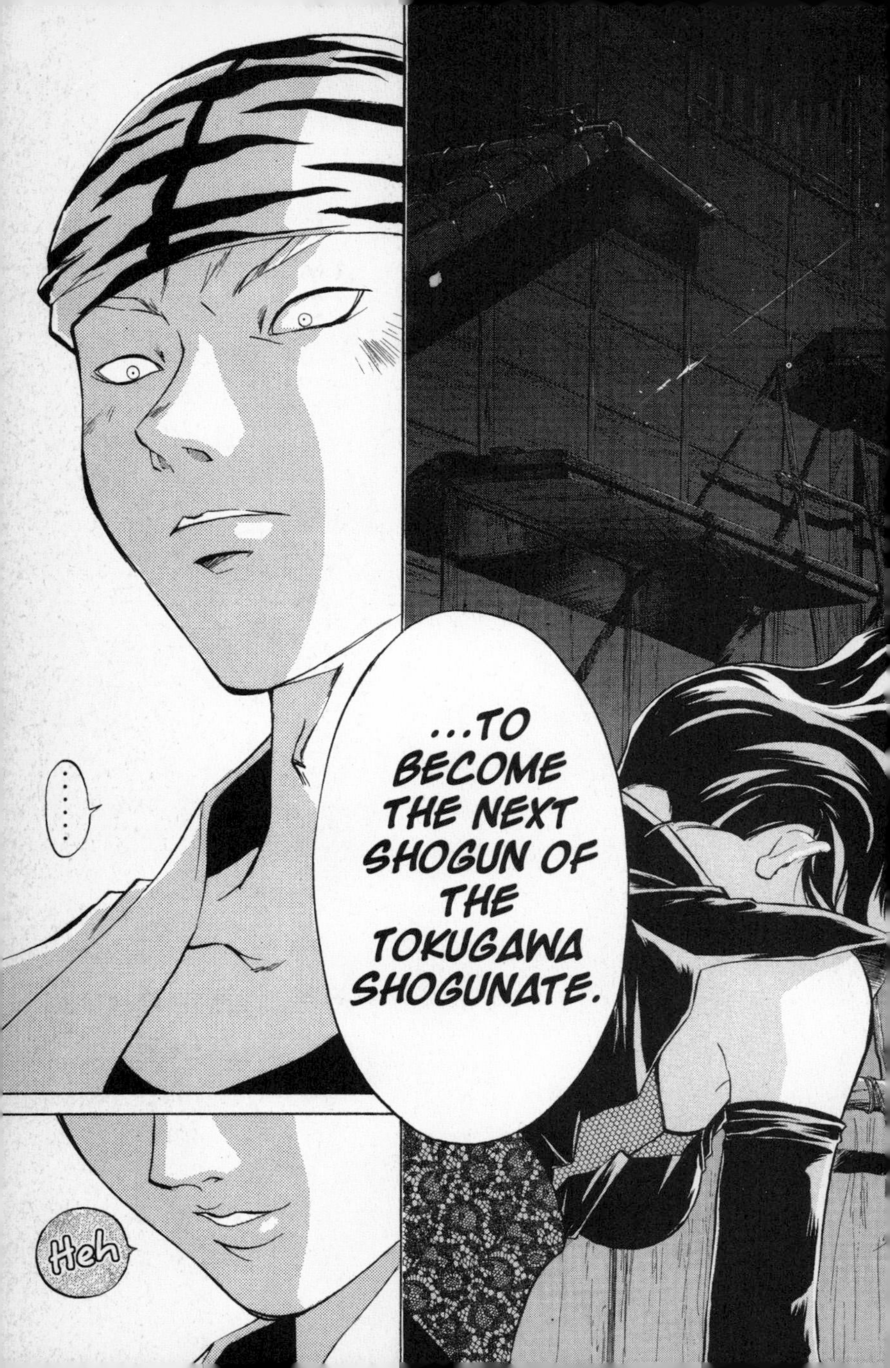
...TO BECOME THE NEXT SHOGUN OF THE TOKUGAWA SHOGUNATE.
......
Heh

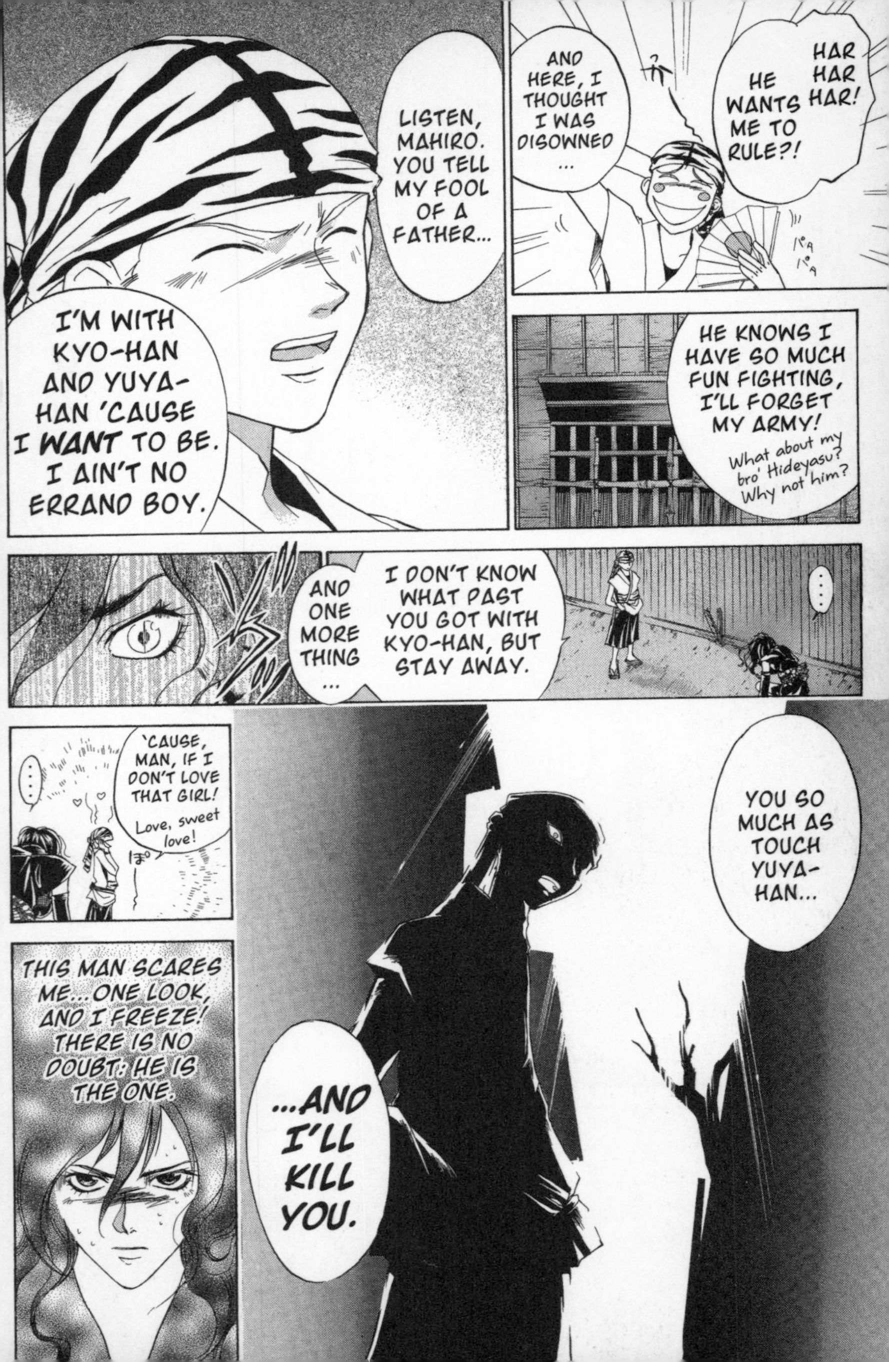
HE WANTS ME TO RULE?! HAR HAR HAR!
AND HERE, I THOUGHT I WAS DISOWNED...
HE KNOWS I HAVE SO MUCH FUN FIGHTING, I'LL FORGET MY ARMY!
What about my bro' Hideyasu? Why not him?
LISTEN, MAHIRO. YOU TELL MY FOOL OF A FATHER...
I'M WITH KYO-HAN AND YUYA-HAN 'CAUSE I **WANT** TO BE. I AIN'T NO ERRAND BOY.
...
I DON'T KNOW WHAT PAST YOU GOT WITH KYO-HAN, BUT STAY AWAY.
AND ONE MORE THING...
YOU SO MUCH AS TOUCH YUYA-HAN...
...AND I'LL KILL YOU.
'CAUSE, MAN, IF I DON'T LOVE THAT GIRL!
Love, sweet love!
...
THIS MAN SCARES ME...ONE LOOK, AND I FREEZE! THERE IS NO DOUBT: HE IS THE ONE.

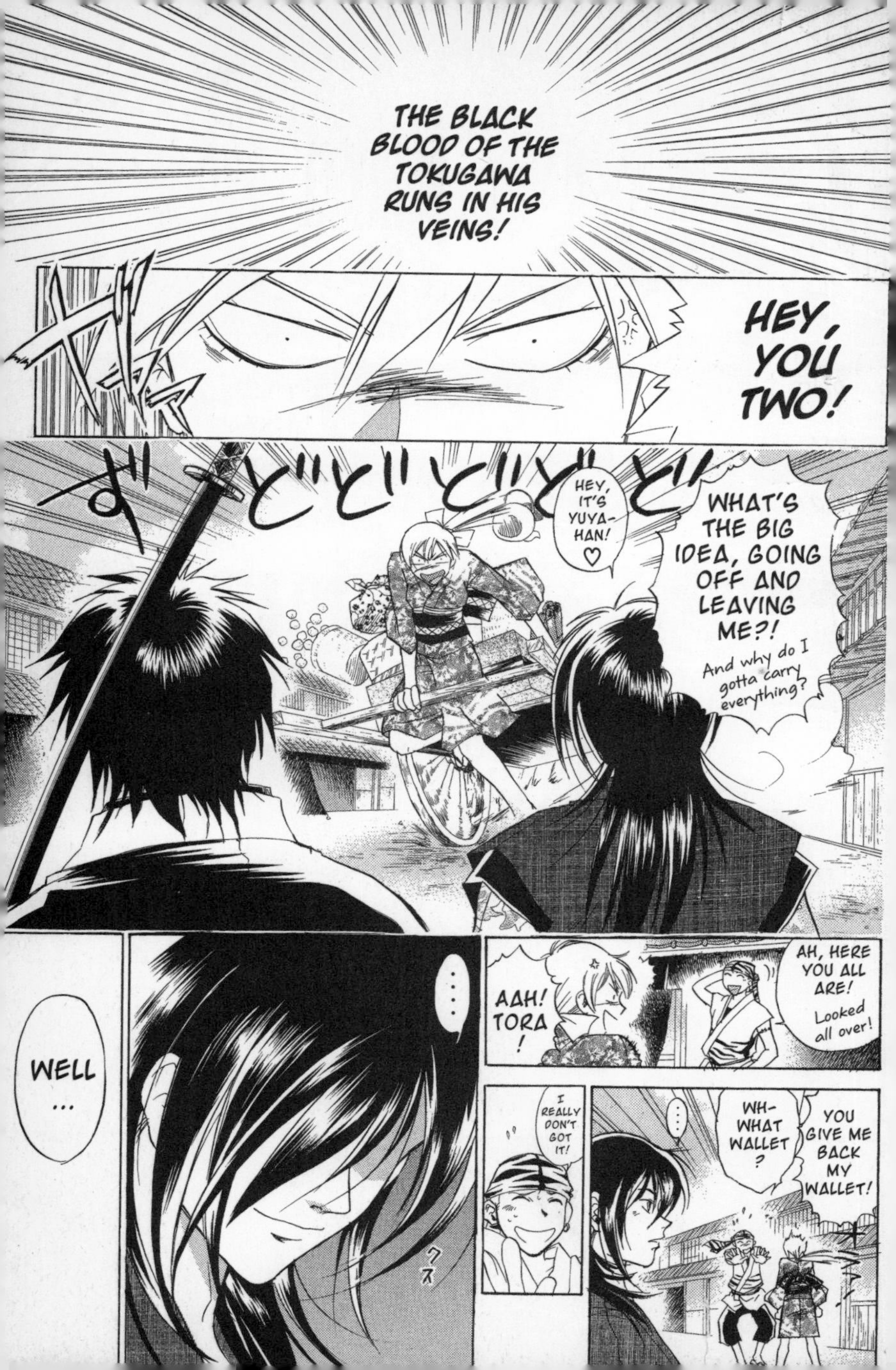
THE BLACK BLOOD OF THE TOKUGAWA RUNS IN HIS VEINS!
HEY, YOU TWO!
WHAT'S THE BIG IDEA, GOING OFF AND LEAVING ME?!
And why do I gotta carry everything?
HEY, IT'S YUYA-HAN! ♡
AH, HERE YOU ALL ARE!
Looked all over!
AAH! TORA!
YOU GIVE ME BACK MY WALLET!
WH-WHAT WALLET?
....
I REALLY DON'T GOT IT!
....
WELL ...

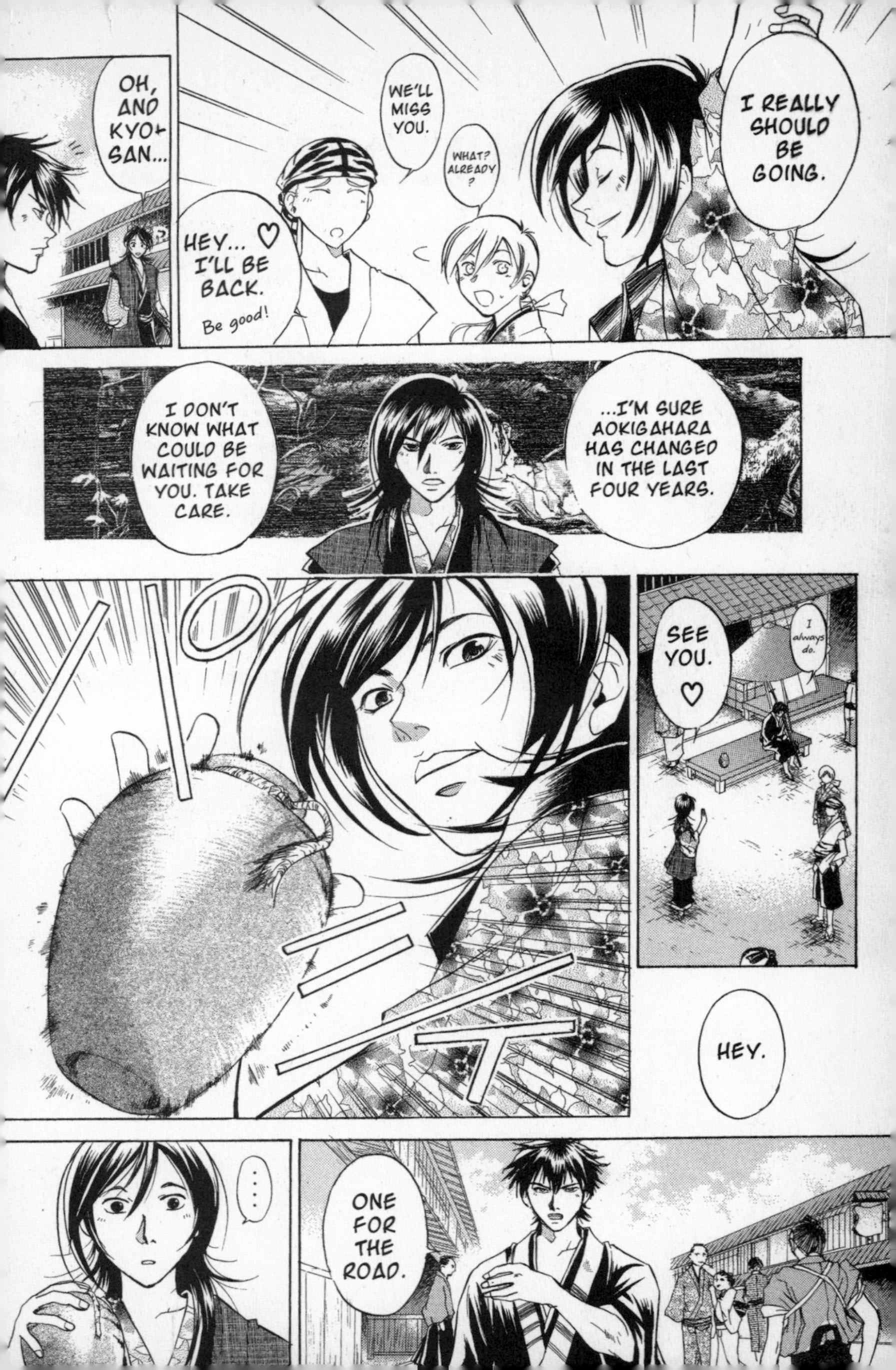
I REALLY SHOULD BE GOING.
WHAT? ALREADY?
WE'LL MISS YOU.
HEY... ♡ I'LL BE BACK.
Be good!
OH, AND KYO-SAN...
...I'M SURE AOKIGAHARA HAS CHANGED IN THE LAST FOUR YEARS.
I DON'T KNOW WHAT COULD BE WAITING FOR YOU. TAKE CARE.
SEE YOU. ♡
I always do.
HEY.
ONE FOR THE ROAD.
...

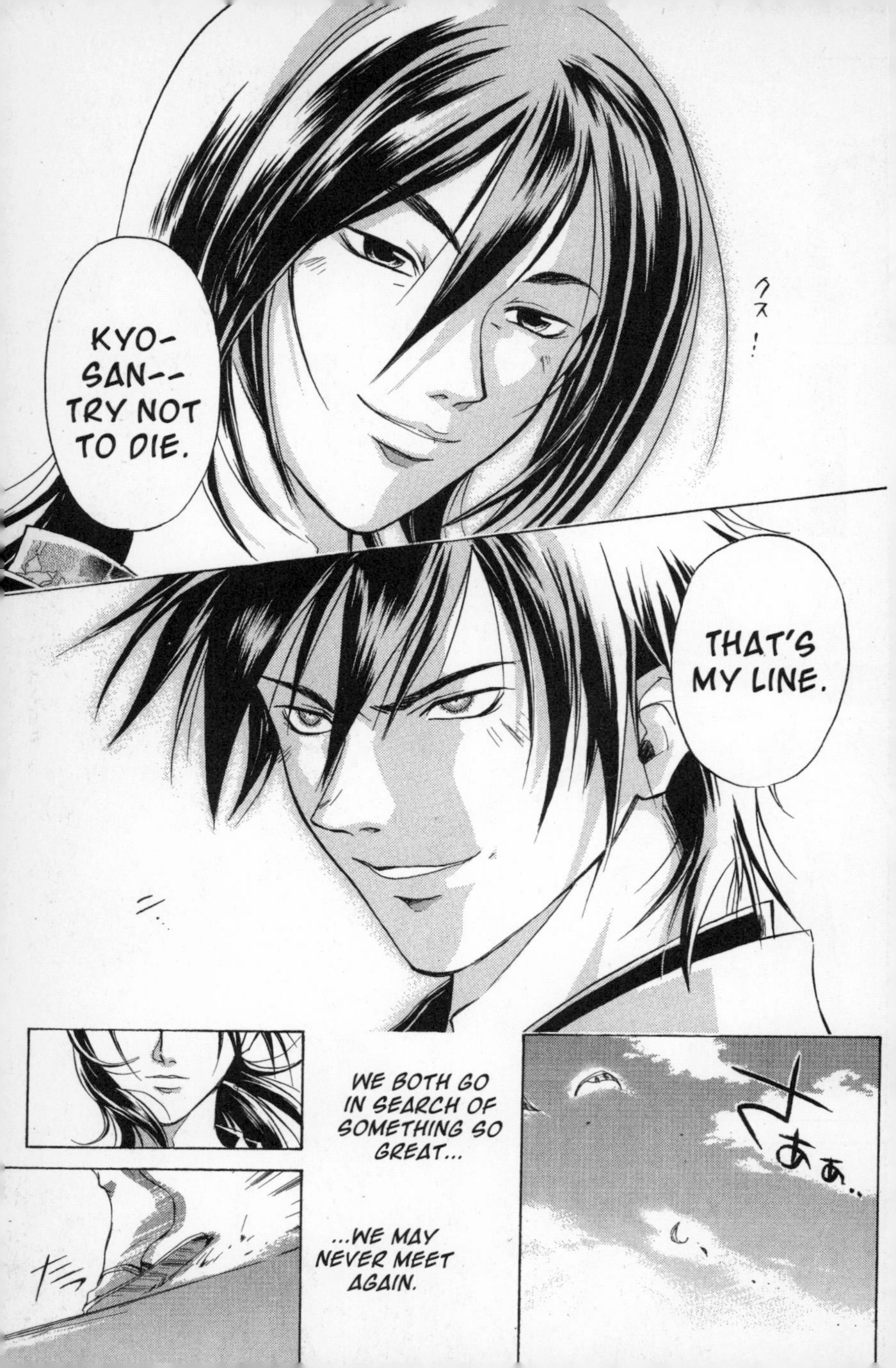
KYO-SAN--TRY NOT TO DIE.
クス！
THAT'S MY LINE.
さぁぁ..
WE BOTH GO IN SEARCH OF SOMETHING SO GREAT...
...WE MAY NEVER MEET AGAIN.

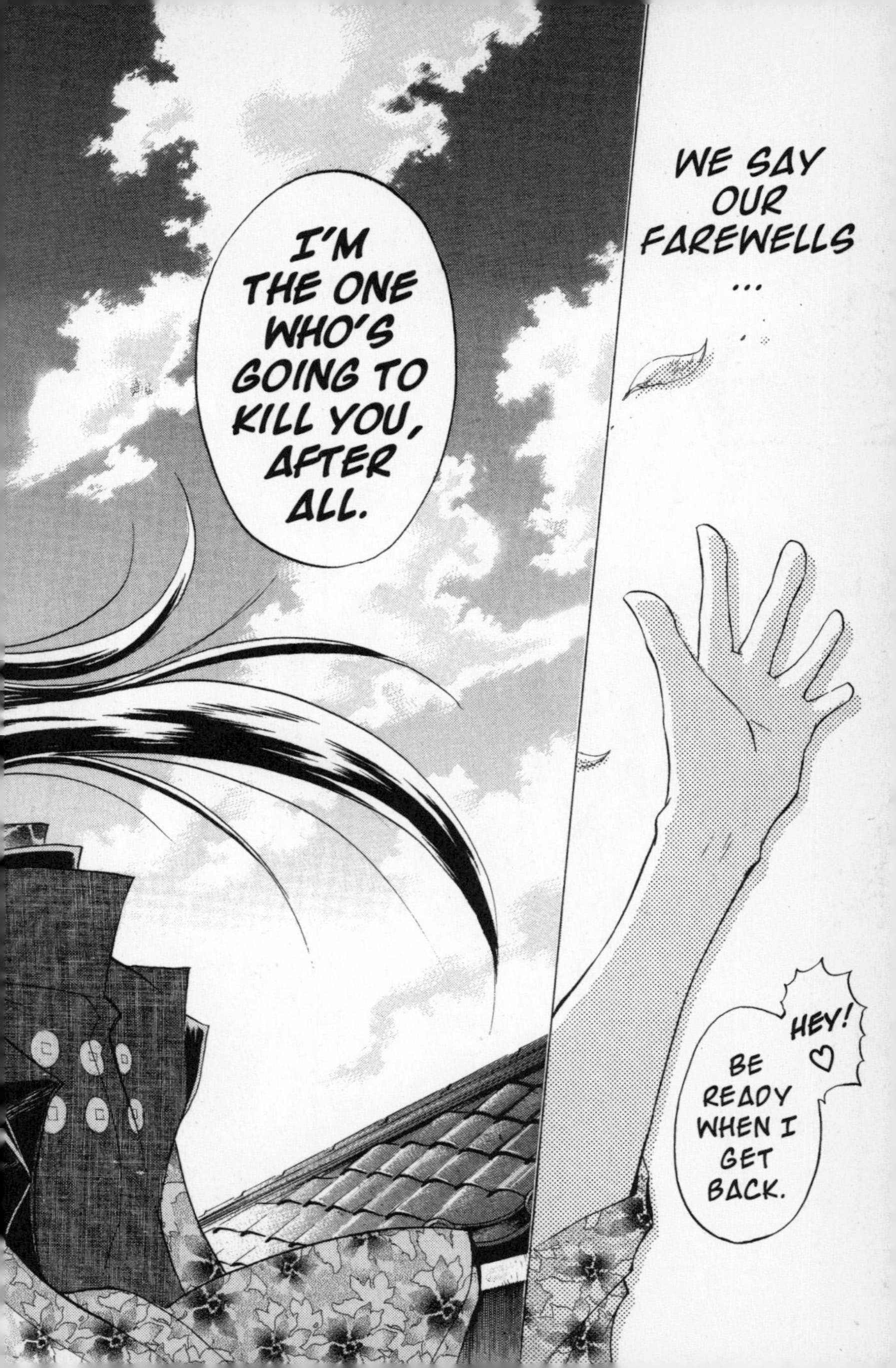
WE SAY OUR FAREWELLS ...
HEY! ♡ BE READY WHEN I GET BACK.
I'M THE ONE WHO'S GOING TO KILL YOU, AFTER ALL.

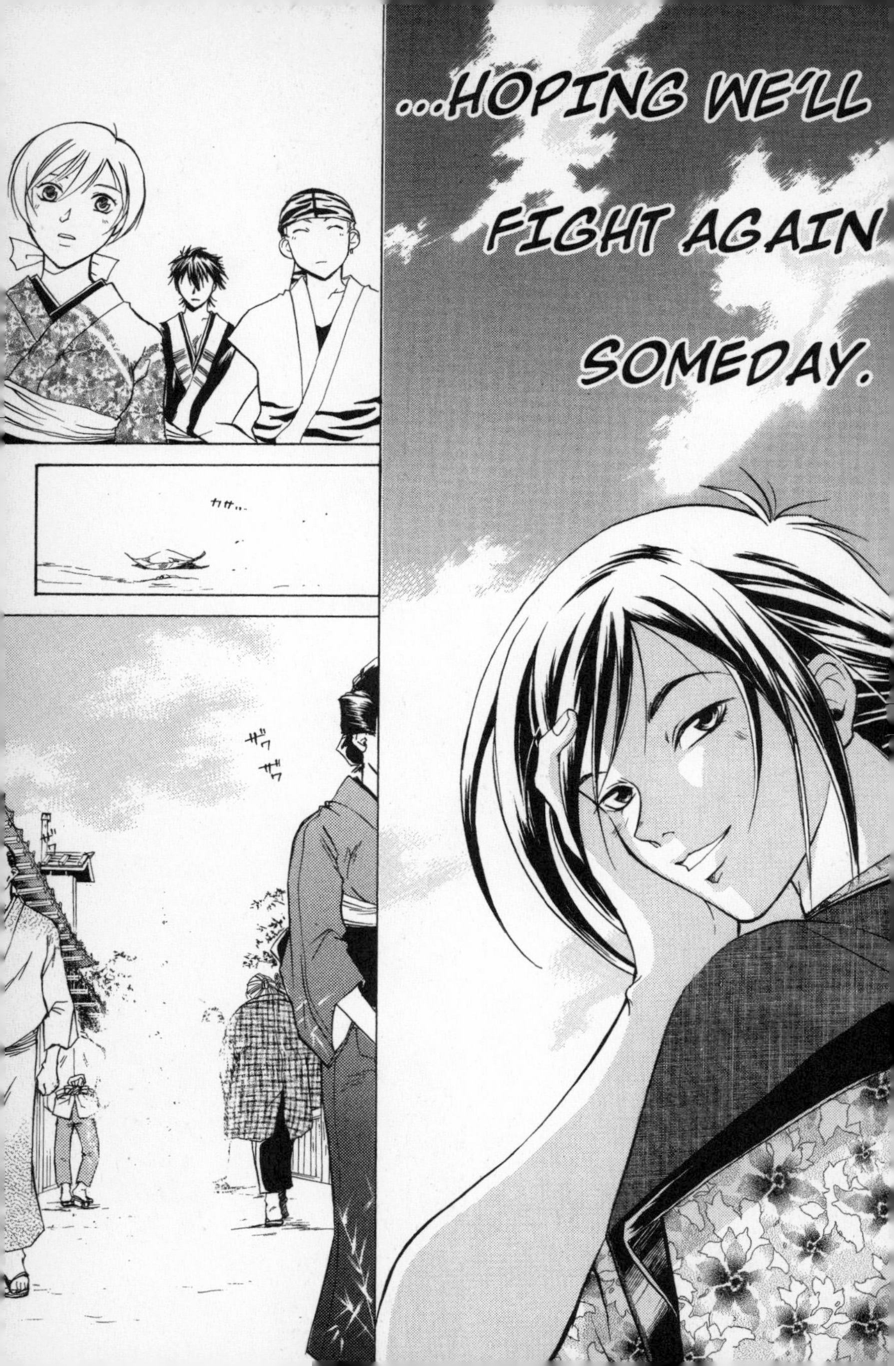
...HOPING WE'LL FIGHT AGAIN SOMEDAY.
カサ…
ザワ ザワ

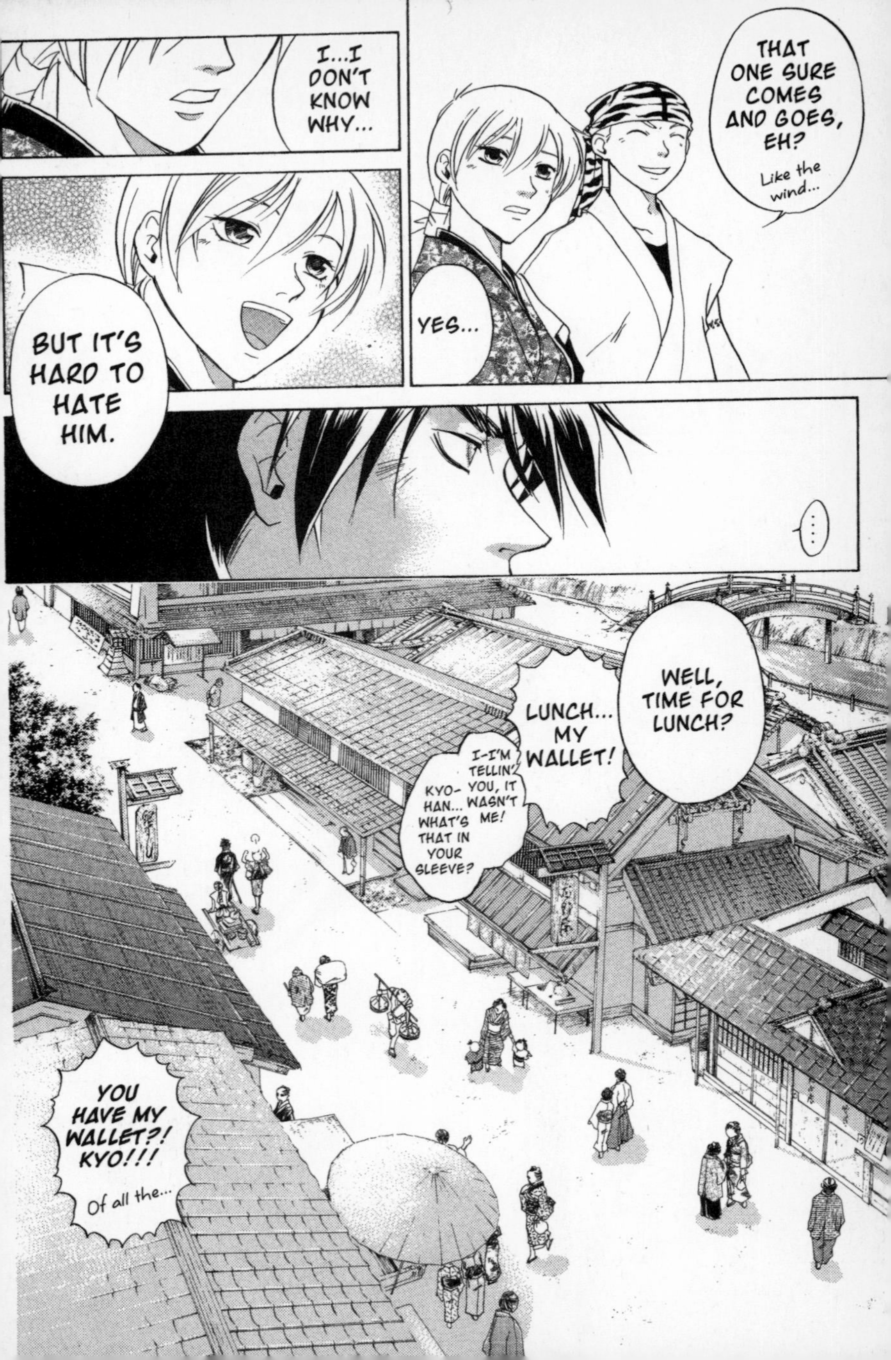
THAT ONE SURE COMES AND GOES, EH?
Like the wind...
YES...
I...I DON'T KNOW WHY...
BUT IT'S HARD TO HATE HIM.
...
WELL, TIME FOR LUNCH?
LUNCH... MY WALLET!
I-I'M TELLIN' YOU, IT WASN'T ME!
KYO-HAN... WHAT'S THAT IN YOUR SLEEVE?
YOU HAVE MY WALLET?! KYO!!!
Of all the...

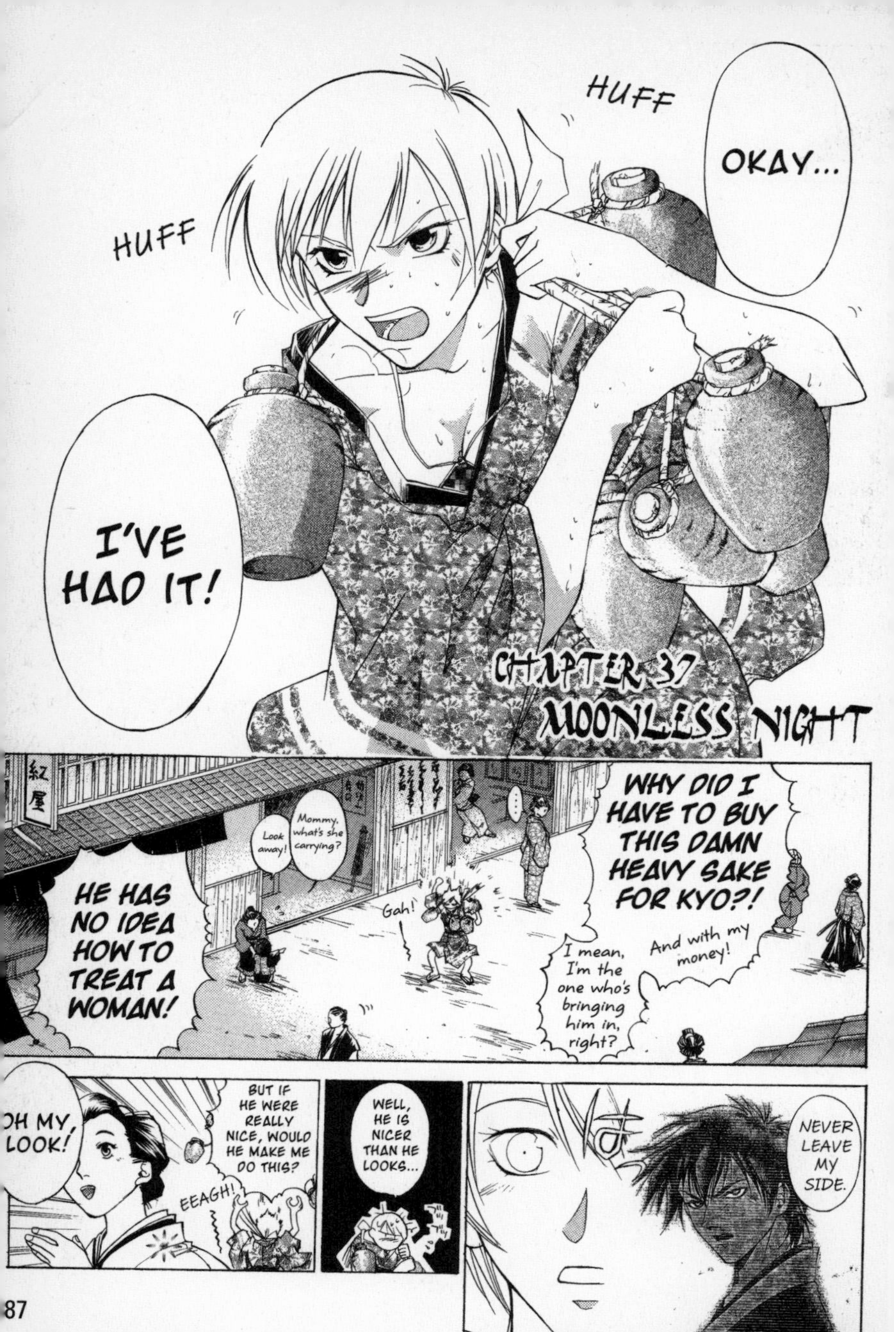

OKAY...
HUFF
HUFF
I'VE HAD IT!
CHAPTER 37
MOONLESS NIGHT
WHY DID I HAVE TO BUY THIS DAMN HEAVY SAKE FOR KYO?!
And with my money!
I mean, I'm the one who's bringing him in, right?
Gah!
Mommy, what's she carrying?
Look away!
HE HAS NO IDEA HOW TO TREAT A WOMAN!
NEVER LEAVE MY SIDE.
WELL, HE IS NICER THAN HE LOOKS...
BUT IF HE WERE REALLY NICE, WOULD HE MAKE ME DO THIS?
EEAGH!
OH MY, LOOK!

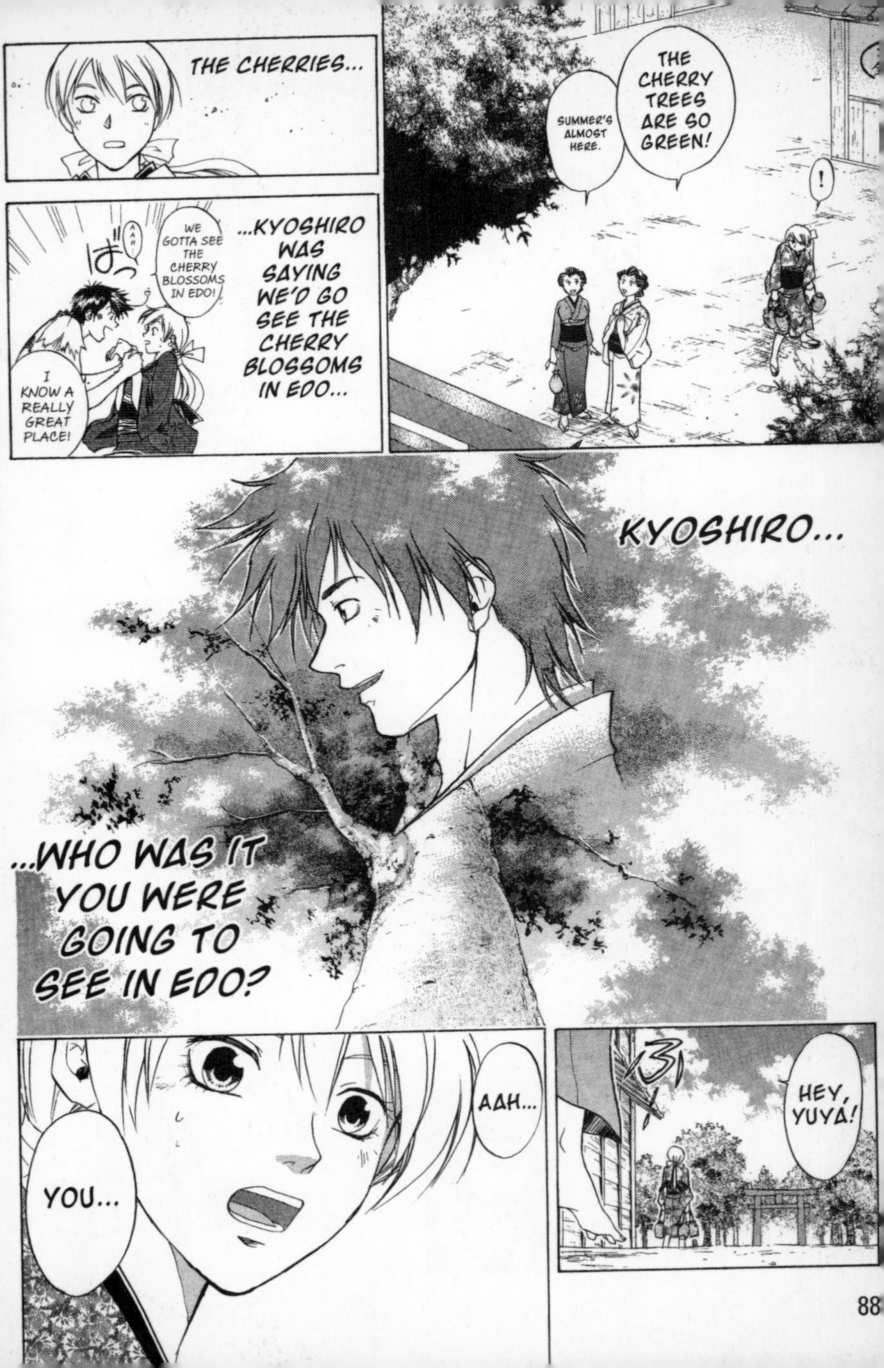
THE CHERRY TREES ARE SO GREEN!
SUMMER'S ALMOST HERE.
!
THE CHERRIES...
...KYOSHIRO WAS SAYING WE'D GO SEE THE CHERRY BLOSSOMS IN EDO...
WE GOTTA SEE THE CHERRY BLOSSOMS IN EDO!
AAH...
ばっ
I KNOW A REALLY GREAT PLACE!
KYOSHIRO...
...WHO WAS IT YOU WERE GOING TO SEE IN EDO?
HEY, YUYA!
AAH...
YOU...

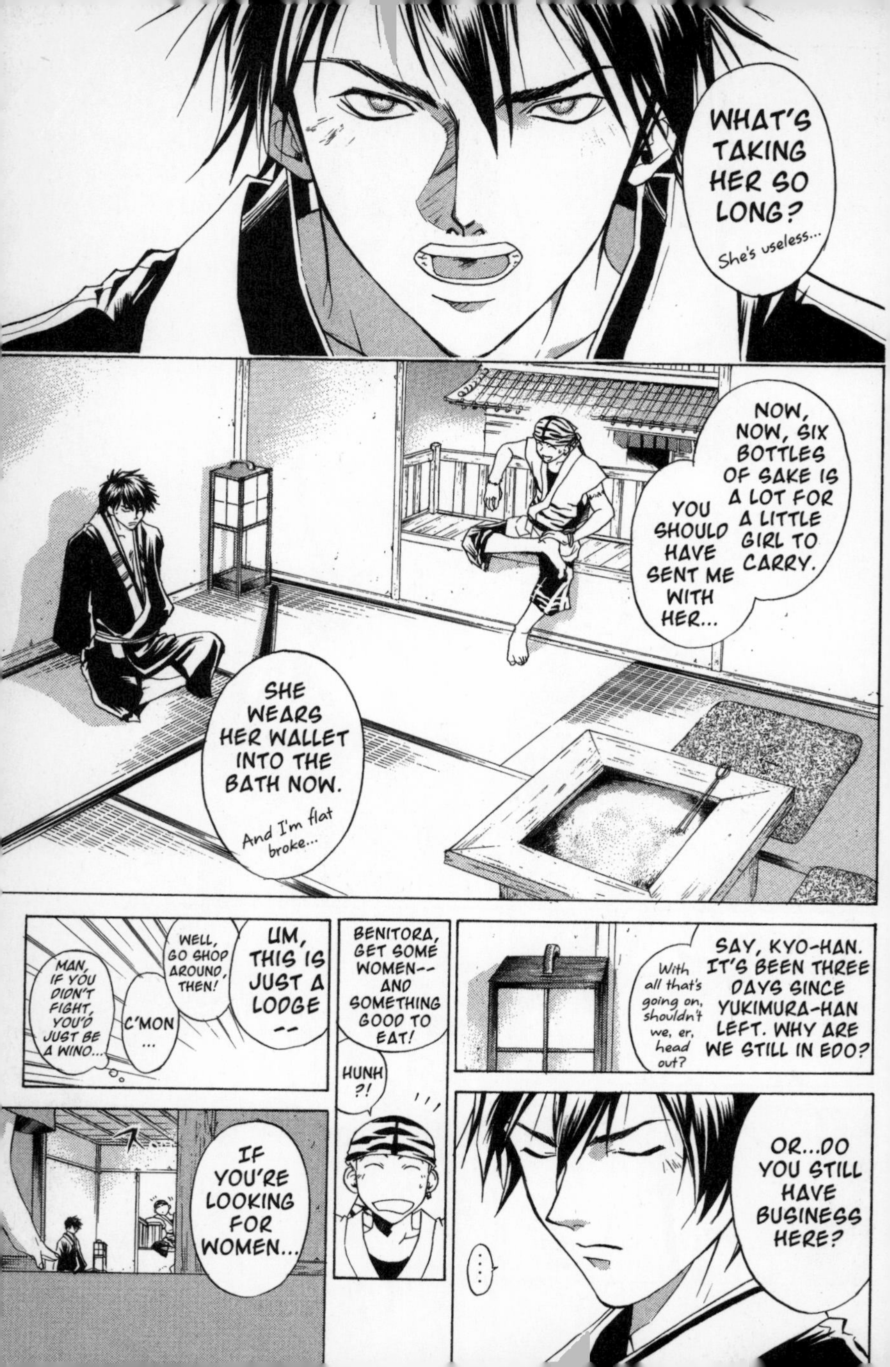
WHAT'S TAKING HER SO LONG?
She's useless...
NOW, NOW, SIX BOTTLES OF SAKE IS A LOT FOR A LITTLE GIRL TO CARRY.
YOU SHOULD HAVE SENT ME WITH HER...
SHE WEARS HER WALLET INTO THE BATH NOW.
And I'm flat broke...
SAY, KYO-HAN. IT'S BEEN THREE DAYS SINCE YUKIMURA-HAN LEFT. WHY ARE WE STILL IN EDO?
With all that's going on, shouldn't we, er, head out?
OR...DO YOU STILL HAVE BUSINESS HERE?
....
BENITORA, GET SOME WOMEN--AND SOMETHING GOOD TO EAT!
HUNH?!
UM, THIS IS JUST A LODGE--
WELL, GO SHOP AROUND, THEN!
C'MON...
MAN, IF YOU DIDN'T FIGHT, YOU'D JUST BE A WINO...
IF YOU'RE LOOKING FOR WOMEN...

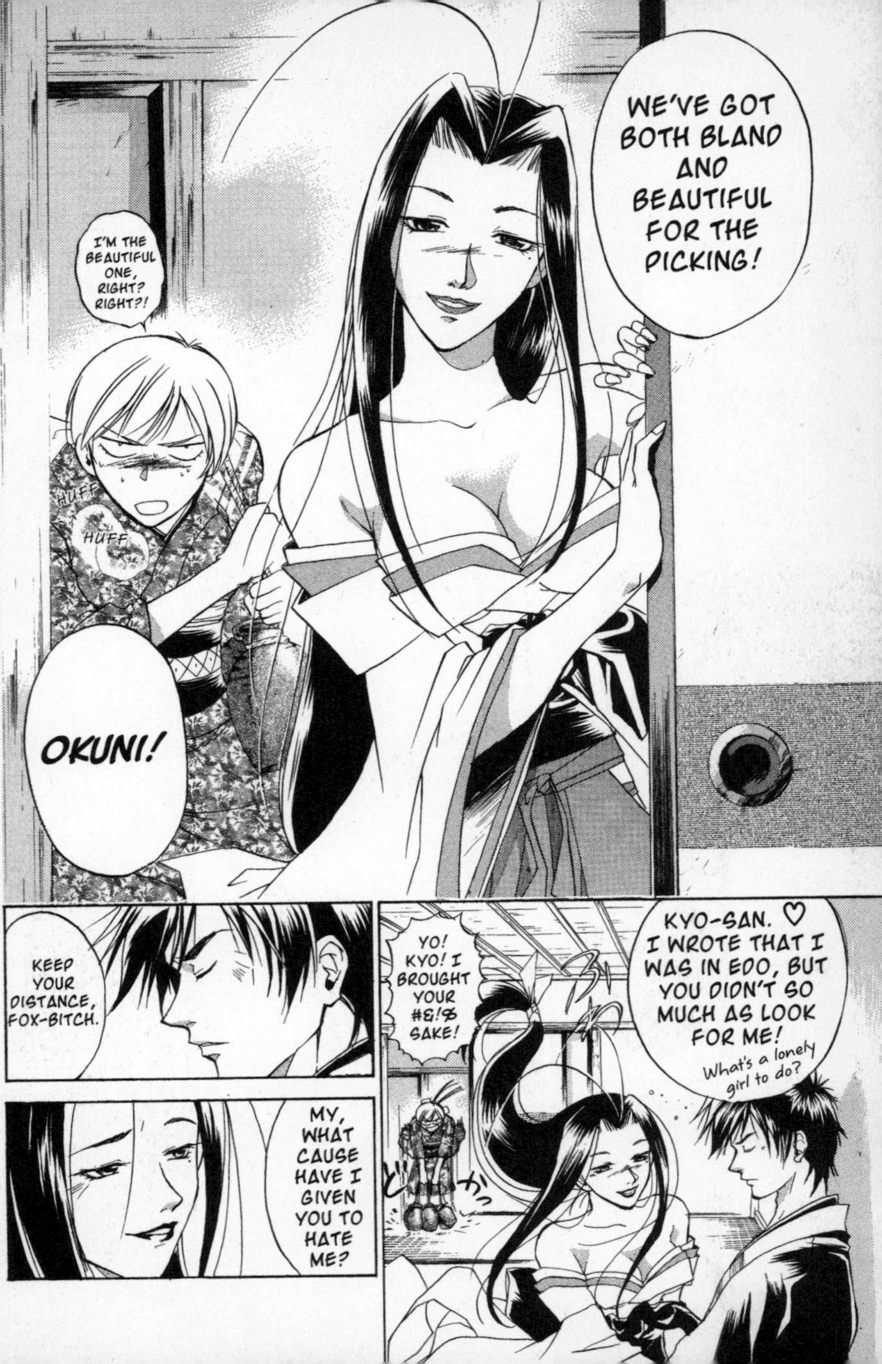
WE'VE GOT BOTH BLAND AND BEAUTIFUL FOR THE PICKING!
I'M THE BEAUTIFUL ONE, RIGHT? RIGHT?!
HUFF
HUFF
OKUNI!
KYO-SAN. ♡ I WROTE THAT I WAS IN EDO, BUT YOU DIDN'T SO MUCH AS LOOK FOR ME!
What's a lonely girl to do?
YO! KYO! I BROUGHT YOUR #&!% SAKE!
KEEP YOUR DISTANCE, FOX-BITCH.
MY, WHAT CAUSE HAVE I GIVEN YOU TO HATE ME?

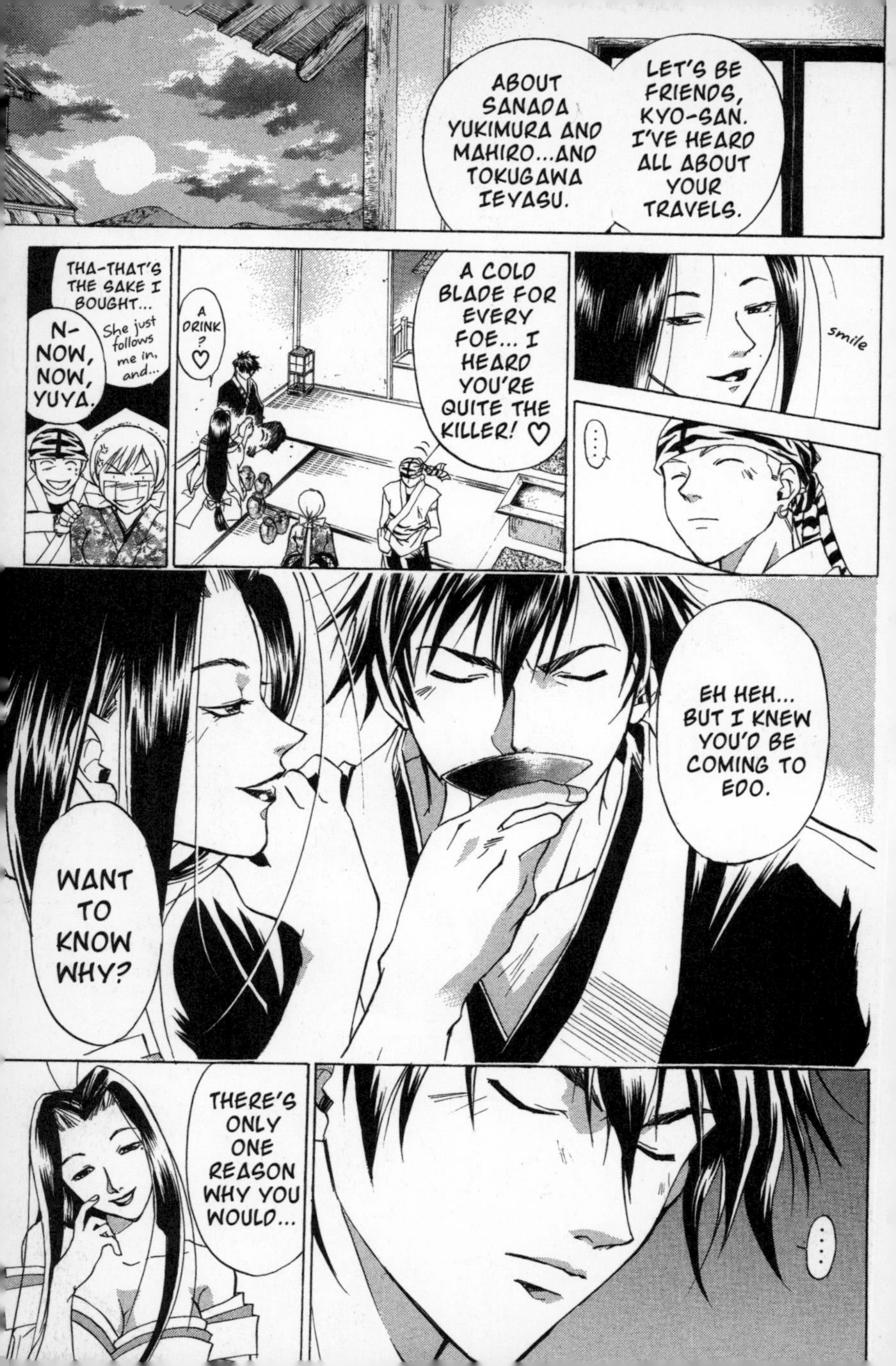
LET'S BE FRIENDS, KYO-SAN. I'VE HEARD ALL ABOUT YOUR TRAVELS.
ABOUT SANADA YUKIMURA AND MAHIRO...AND TOKUGAWA IEYASU.
smile
....
A COLD BLADE FOR EVERY FOE... I HEARD YOU'RE QUITE THE KILLER! ♥
A DRINK? ♥
THA-THAT'S THE SAKE I BOUGHT...
She just follows me in, and...
N-NOW, NOW, YUYA.
EH HEH... BUT I KNEW YOU'D BE COMING TO EDO.
WANT TO KNOW WHY?
....
THERE'S ONLY ONE REASON WHY YOU WOULD...

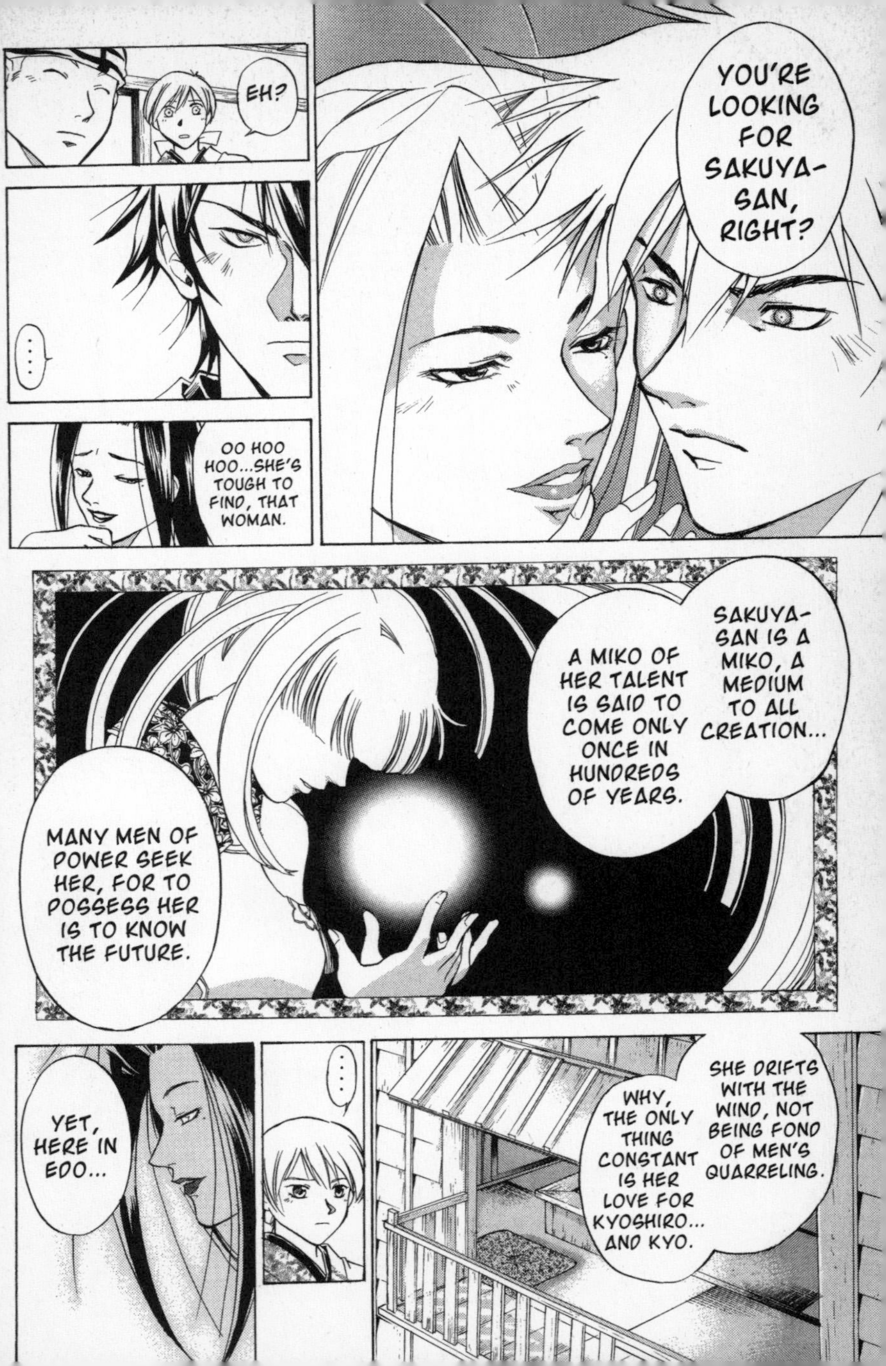
YOU'RE LOOKING FOR SAKUYA-SAN, RIGHT?
EH?
....
OO HOO HOO...SHE'S TOUGH TO FIND, THAT WOMAN.
SAKUYA-SAN IS A MIKO, A MEDIUM TO ALL CREATION...
A MIKO OF HER TALENT IS SAID TO COME ONLY ONCE IN HUNDREDS OF YEARS.
MANY MEN OF POWER SEEK HER, FOR TO POSSESS HER IS TO KNOW THE FUTURE.
SHE DRIFTS WITH THE WIND, NOT BEING FOND OF MEN'S QUARRELING.
WHY, THE ONLY THING CONSTANT IS HER LOVE FOR KYOSHIRO... AND KYO.
....
YET, HERE IN EDO...

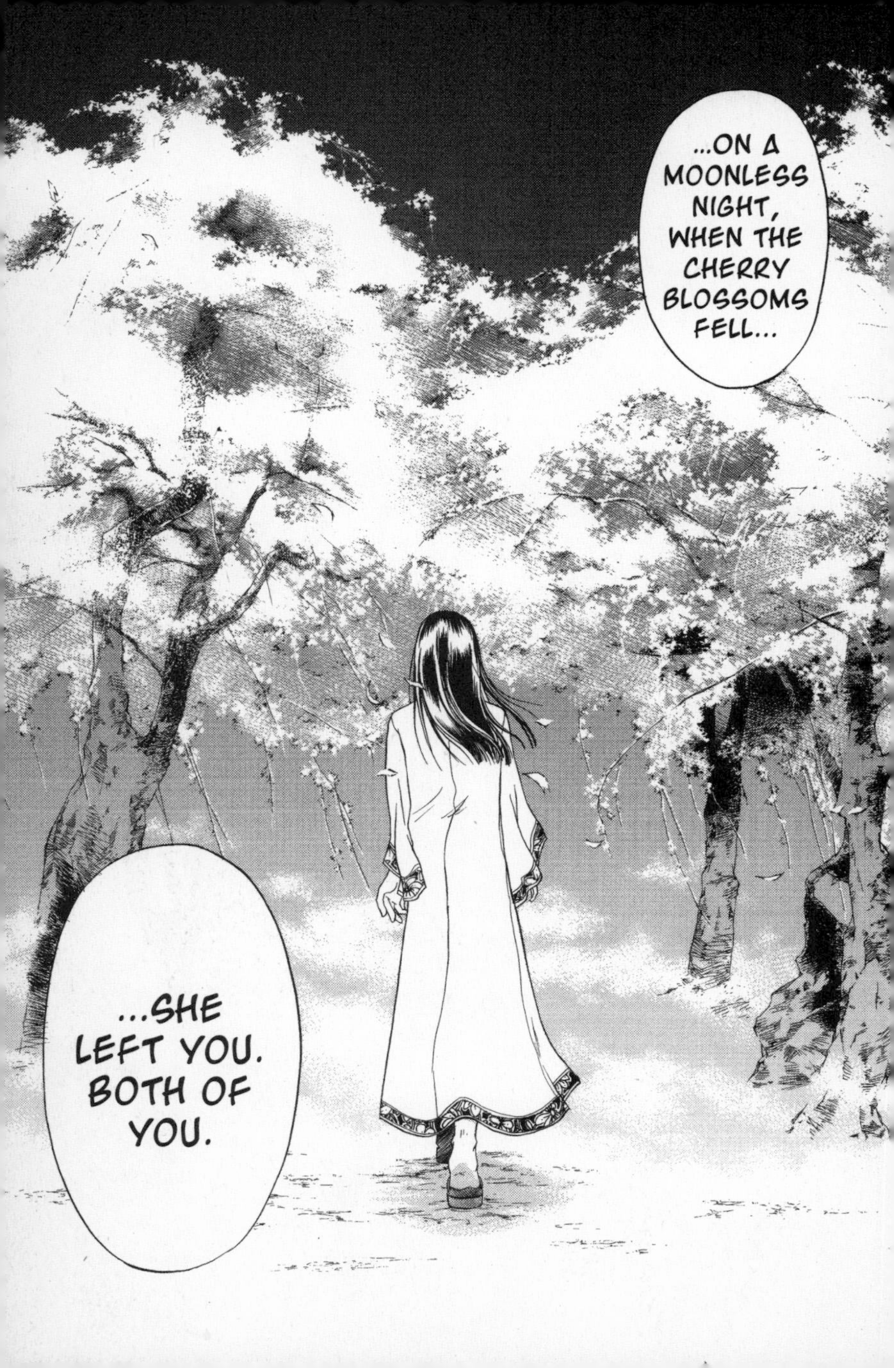
...ON A MOONLESS NIGHT, WHEN THE CHERRY BLOSSOMS FELL...
...SHE LEFT YOU. BOTH OF YOU.

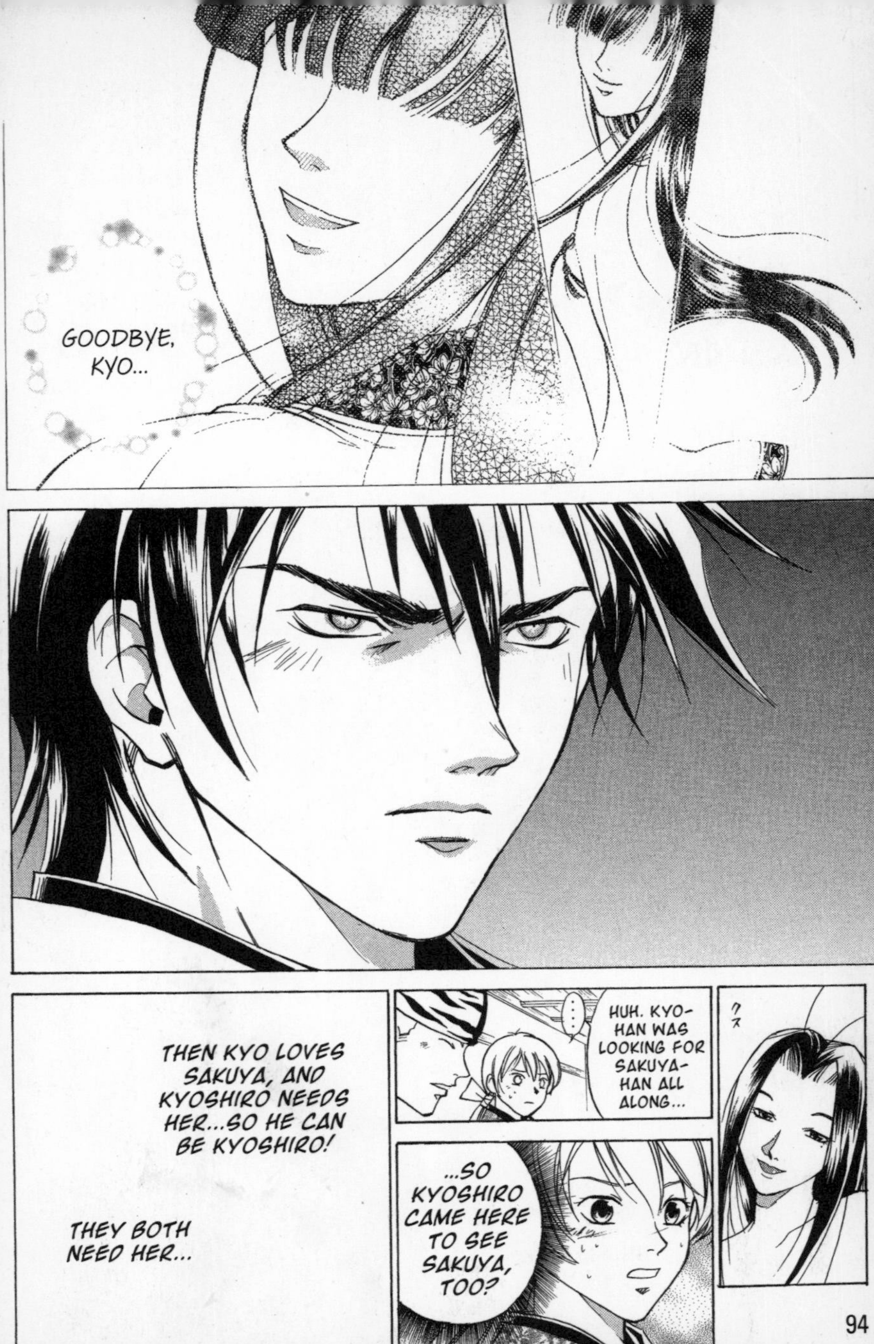
GOODBYE, KYO...
クス
...
HUH. KYO-HAN WAS LOOKING FOR SAKUYA-HAN ALL ALONG...
...SO KYOSHIRO CAME HERE TO SEE SAKUYA, TOO?
THEN KYO LOVES SAKUYA, AND KYOSHIRO NEEDS HER...SO HE CAN BE KYOSHIRO!
THEY BOTH NEED HER...

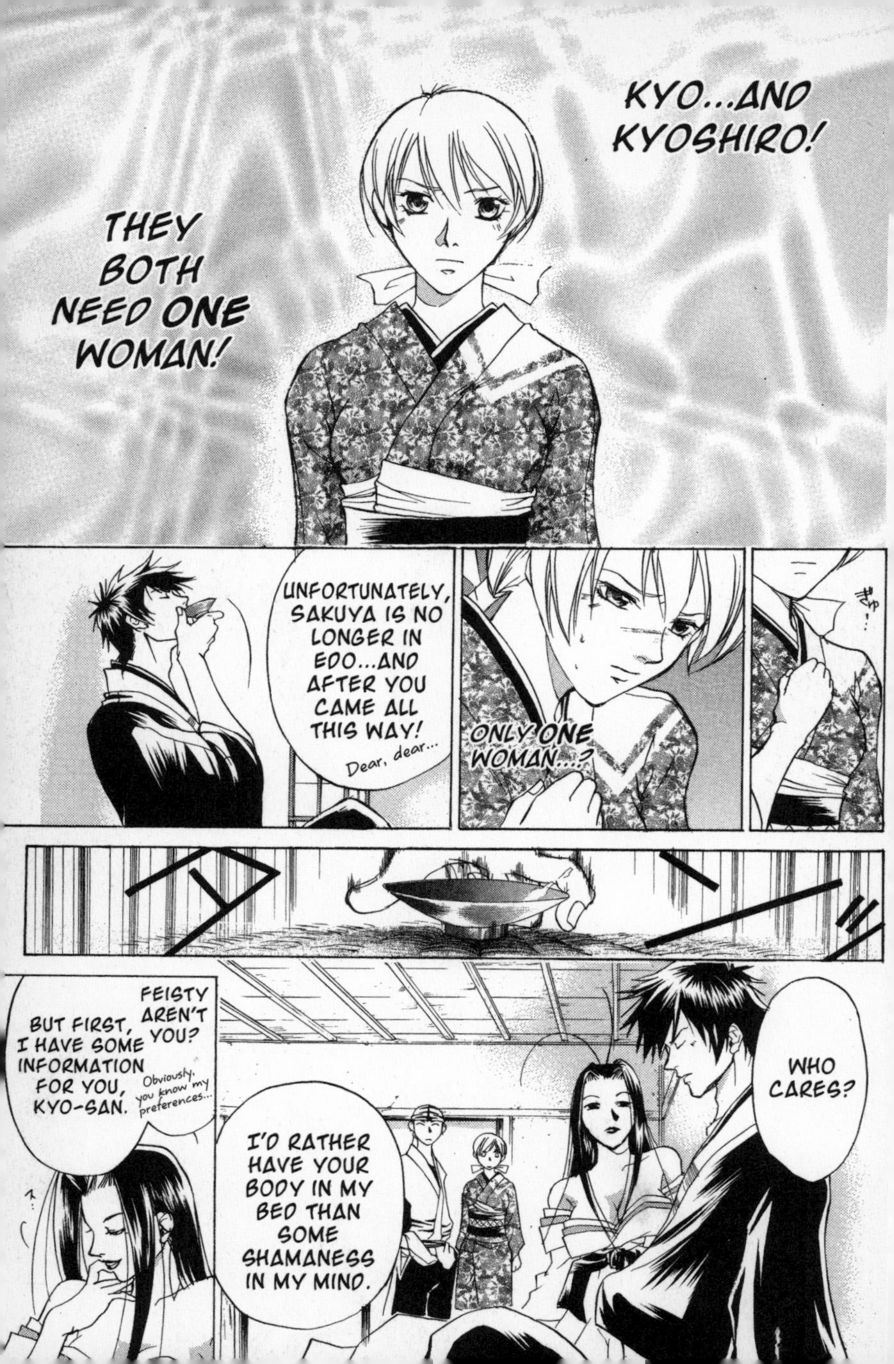
KYO...AND KYOSHIRO!
THEY BOTH NEED ONE WOMAN!
ONLY ONE WOMAN...?
UNFORTUNATELY, SAKUYA IS NO LONGER IN EDO...AND AFTER YOU CAME ALL THIS WAY!
Dear, dear...
WHO CARES?
I'D RATHER HAVE YOUR BODY IN MY BED THAN SOME SHAMANESS IN MY MIND.
FEISTY AREN'T YOU?
BUT FIRST, I HAVE SOME INFORMATION FOR YOU, KYO-SAN.
Obviously, you know my preferences...

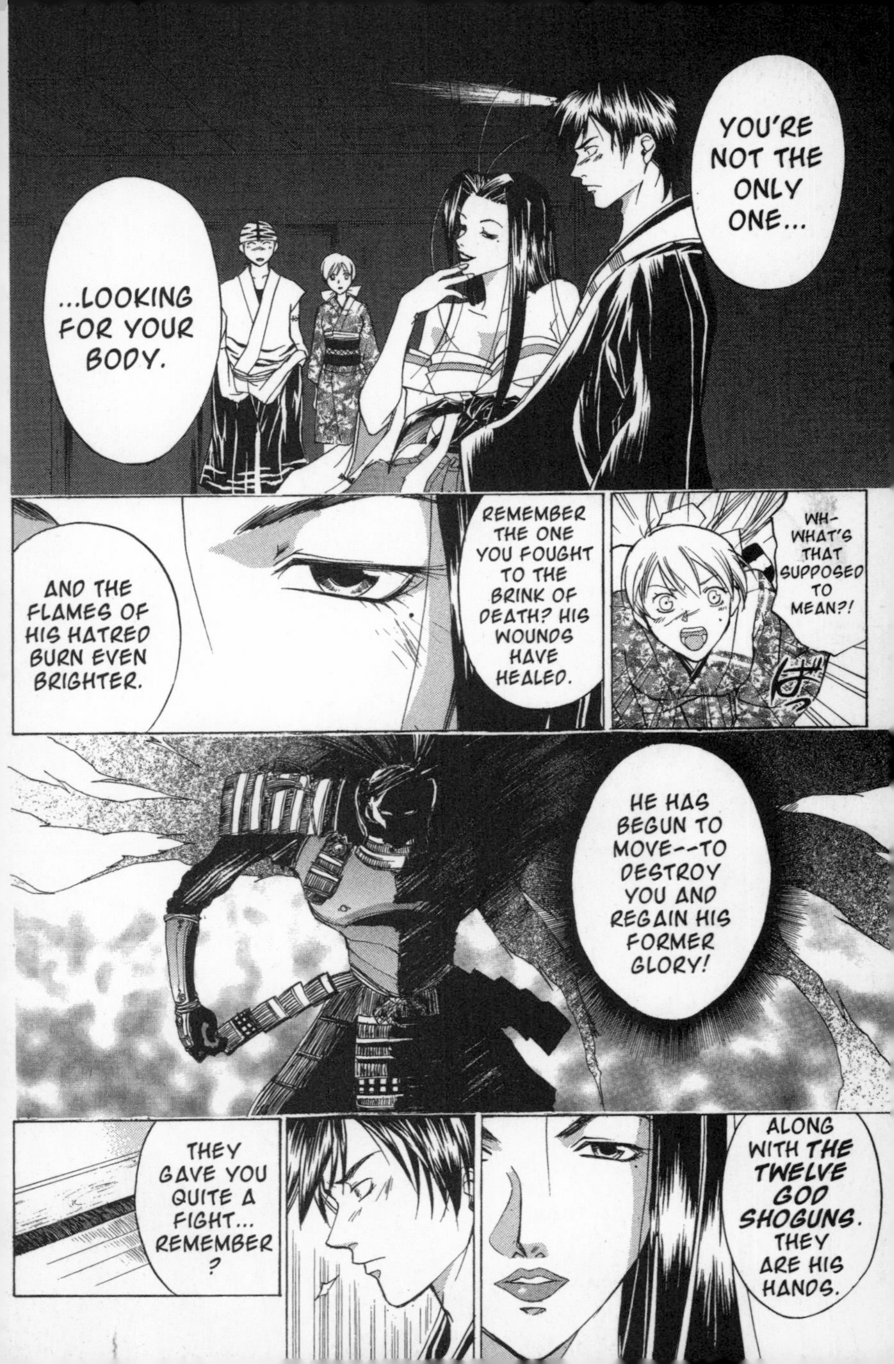
YOU'RE NOT THE ONLY ONE...
...LOOKING FOR YOUR BODY.
WH-WHAT'S THAT SUPPOSED TO MEAN?!
ばっ
REMEMBER THE ONE YOU FOUGHT TO THE BRINK OF DEATH? HIS WOUNDS HAVE HEALED.
AND THE FLAMES OF HIS HATRED BURN EVEN BRIGHTER.
HE HAS BEGUN TO MOVE--TO DESTROY YOU AND REGAIN HIS FORMER GLORY!
ALONG WITH **THE TWELVE GOD SHOGUNS**. THEY ARE HIS HANDS.
THEY GAVE YOU QUITE A FIGHT... REMEMBER?

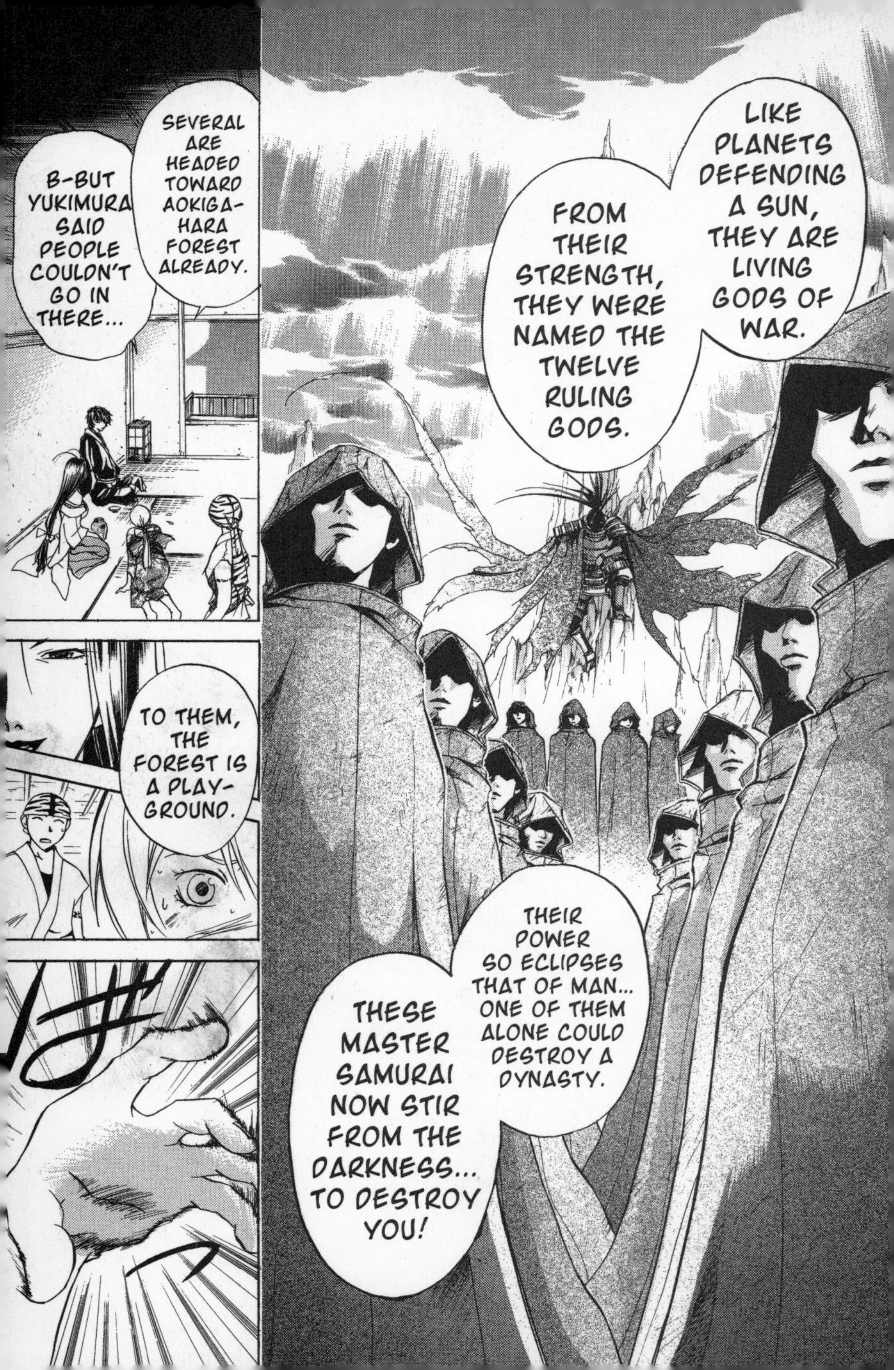

LIKE PLANETS DEFENDING A SUN, THEY ARE LIVING GODS OF WAR.
FROM THEIR STRENGTH, THEY WERE NAMED THE TWELVE RULING GODS.
THEIR POWER SO ECLIPSES THAT OF MAN... ONE OF THEM ALONE COULD DESTROY A DYNASTY.
THESE MASTER SAMURAI NOW STIR FROM THE DARKNESS... TO DESTROY YOU!
SEVERAL ARE HEADED TOWARD AOKIGA-HARA FOREST ALREADY.
B-BUT YUKIMURA SAID PEOPLE COULDN'T GO IN THERE...
TO THEM, THE FOREST IS A PLAY-GROUND.

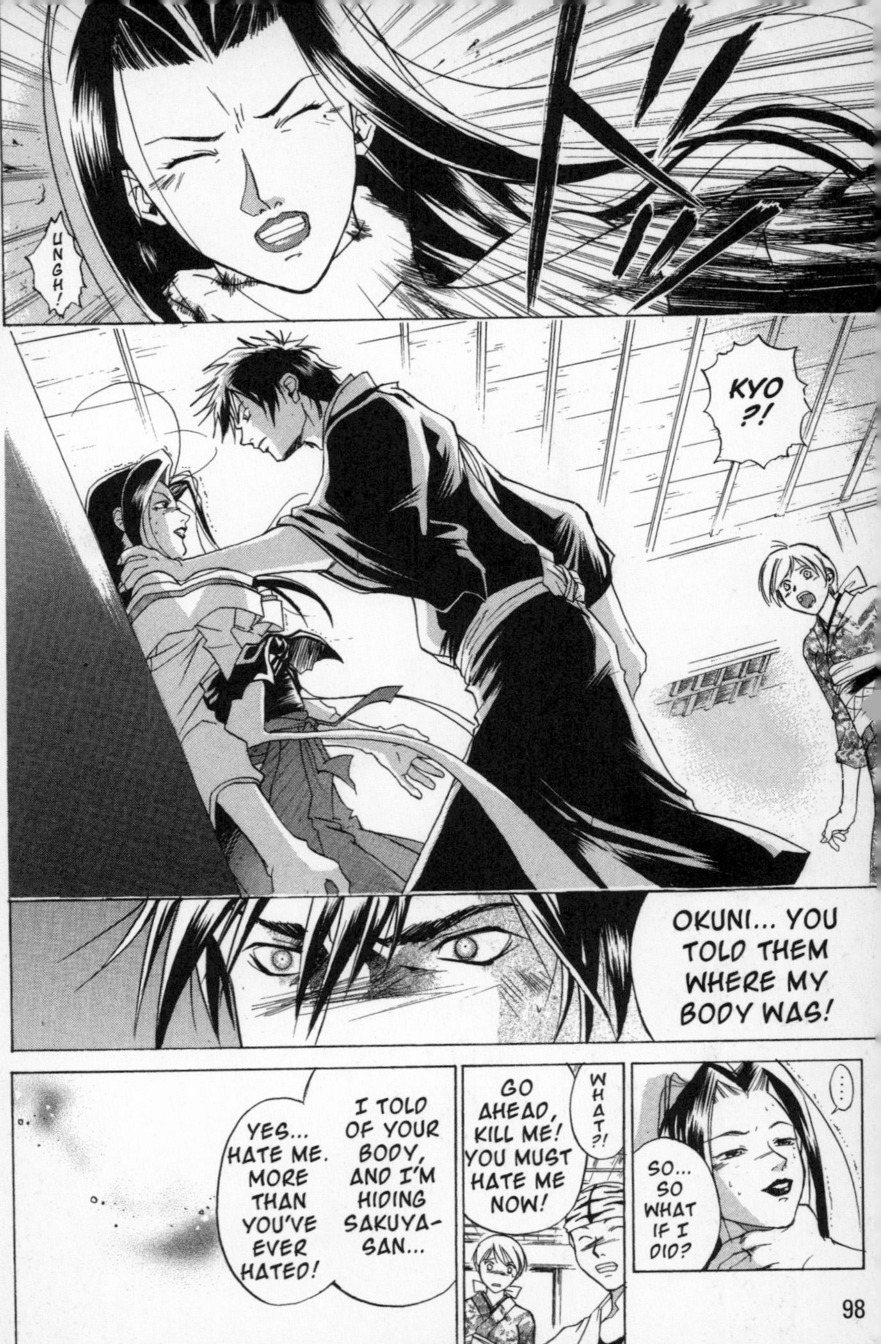
UNGH!
KYO ?!
OKUNI... YOU TOLD THEM WHERE MY BODY WAS!
....
SO... SO WHAT IF I DID?
WHAT?!
GO AHEAD, KILL ME! YOU MUST HATE ME NOW!
I TOLD OF YOUR BODY, AND I'M HIDING SAKUYA-SAN...
YES... HATE ME. MORE THAN YOU'VE EVER HATED!

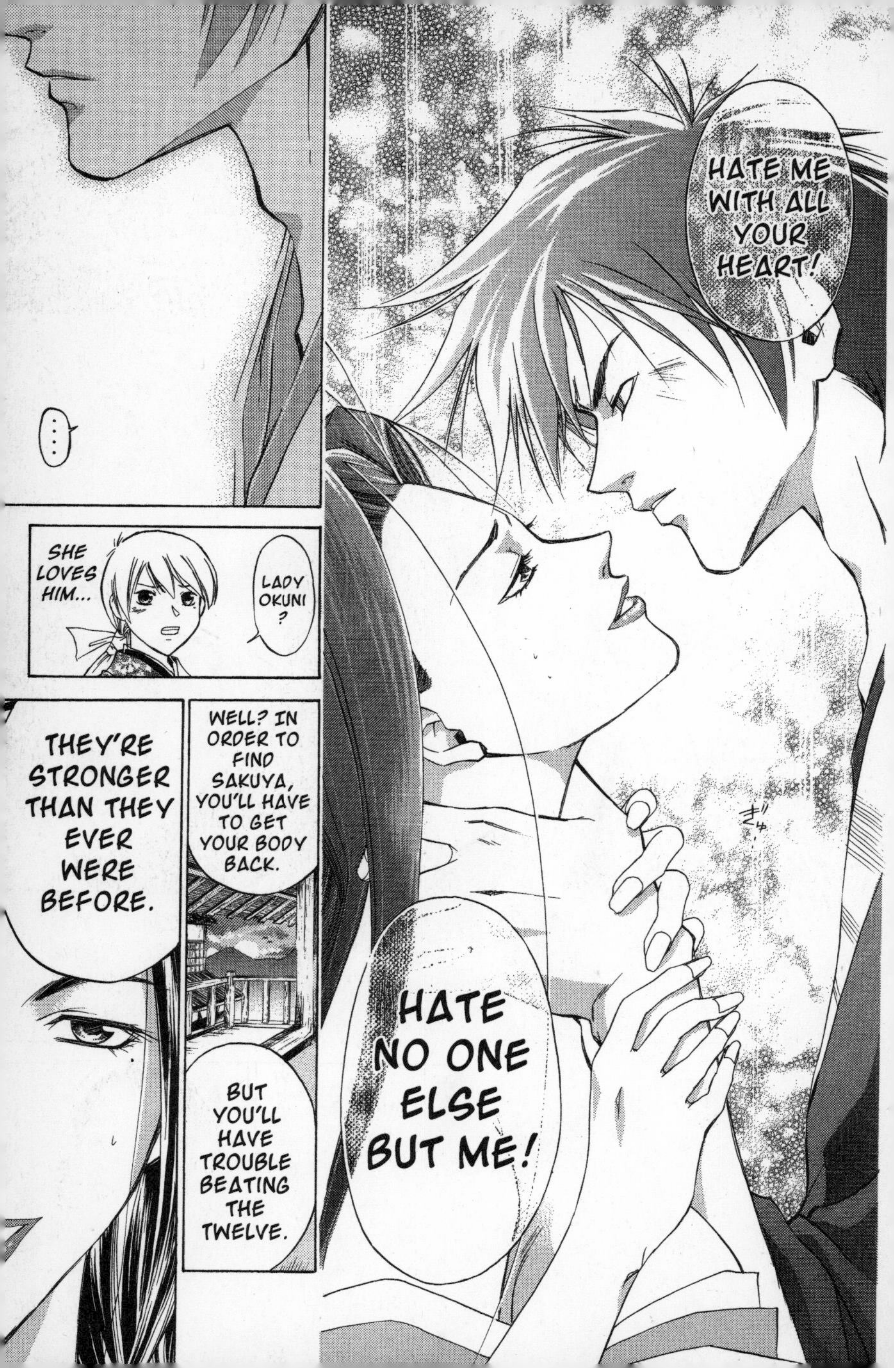
HATE ME WITH ALL YOUR HEART!
ぎゅ
HATE NO ONE ELSE BUT ME!
...
LADY OKUNI?
SHE LOVES HIM...
WELL? IN ORDER TO FIND SAKUYA, YOU'LL HAVE TO GET YOUR BODY BACK.
BUT YOU'LL HAVE TROUBLE BEATING THE TWELVE.
THEY'RE STRONGER THAN THEY EVER WERE BEFORE.

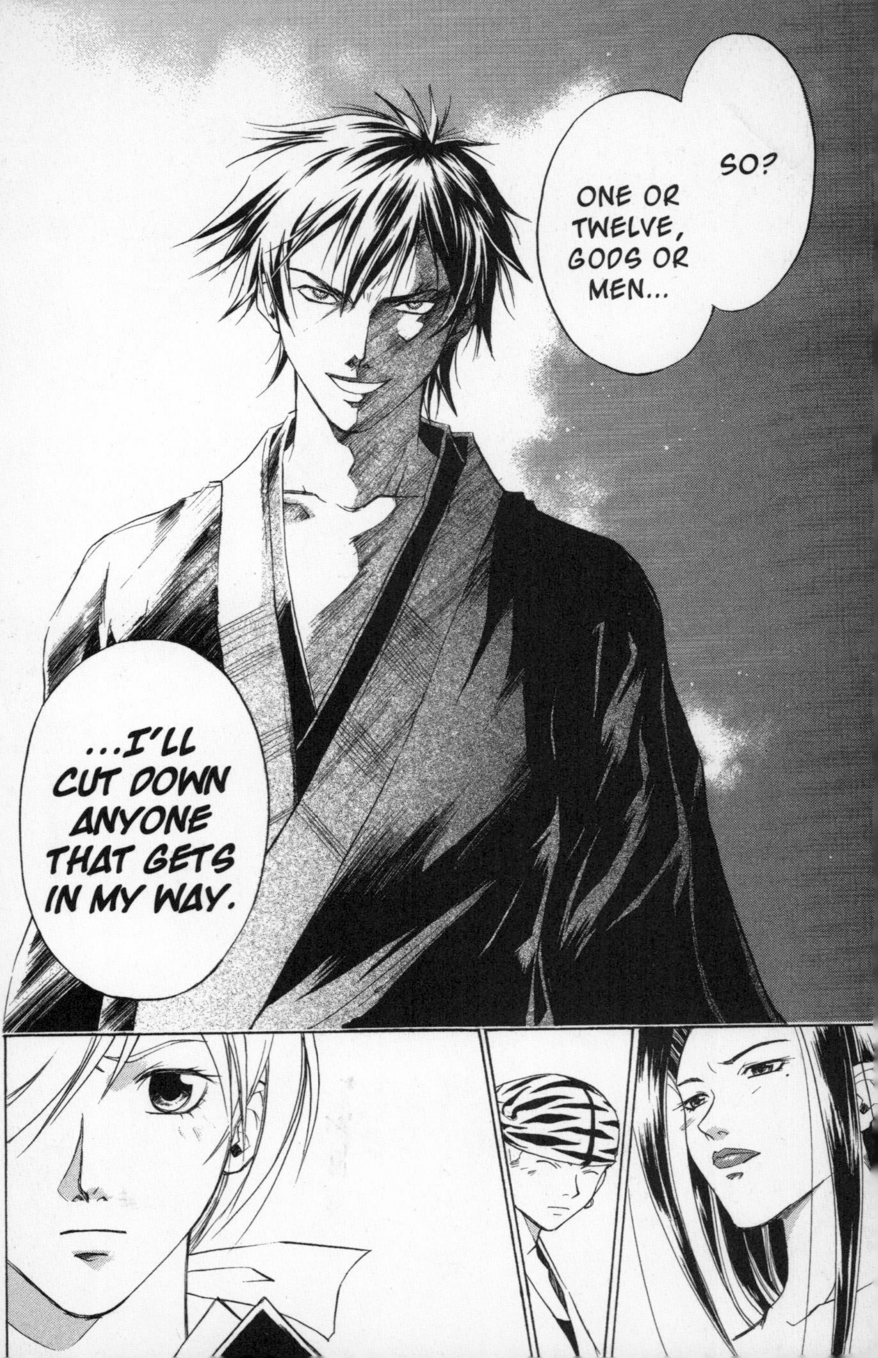
SO?
ONE OR TWELVE, GODS OR MEN...
...I'LL CUT DOWN ANYONE THAT GETS IN MY WAY.

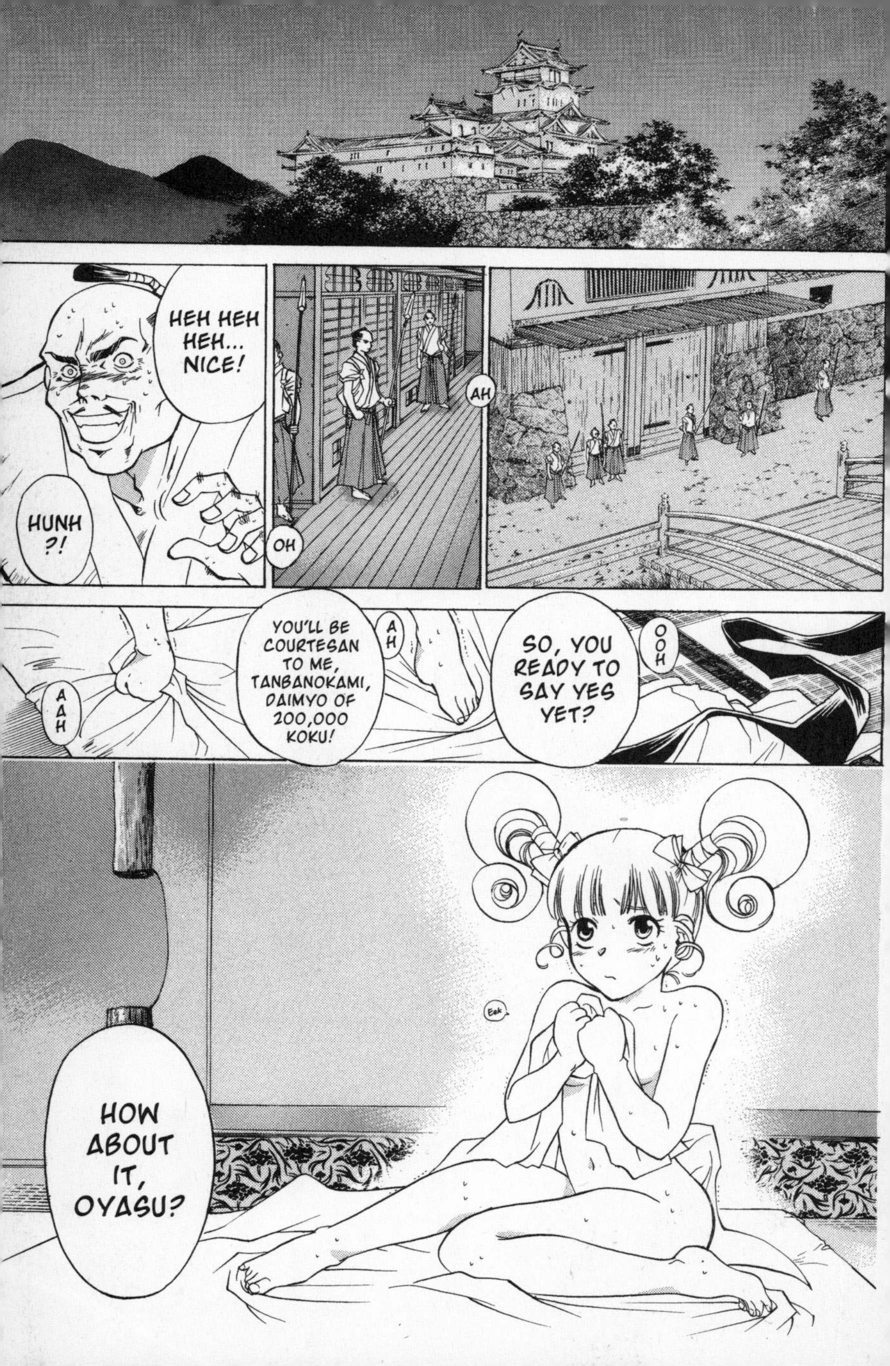
AH
OH
HEH HEH HEH... NICE!
HUNH ?!
OOH
SO, YOU READY TO SAY YES YET?
AH
YOU'LL BE COURTESAN TO ME, TANBANOKAMI, DAIMYO OF 200,000 KOKU!
AAH
Eek
HOW ABOUT IT, OYASU?

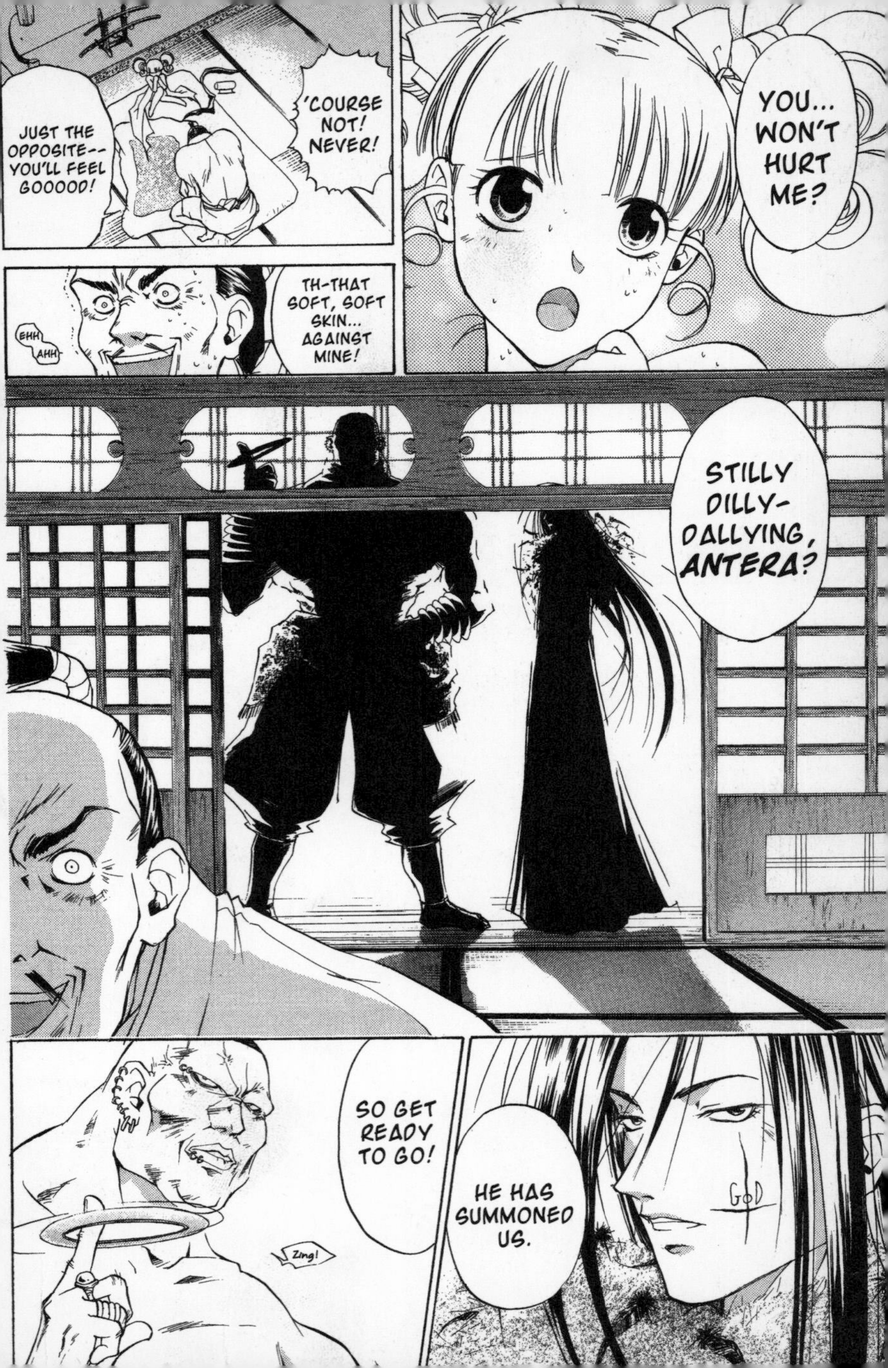
YOU... WON'T HURT ME?
'COURSE NOT! NEVER!
JUST THE OPPOSITE-- YOU'LL FEEL GOOOOD!
TH-THAT SOFT, SOFT SKIN... AGAINST MINE!
EHH AHH
STILLY DILLY-DALLYING, ANTERA?
HE HAS SUMMONED US.
GOD
SO GET READY TO GO!
Zing!

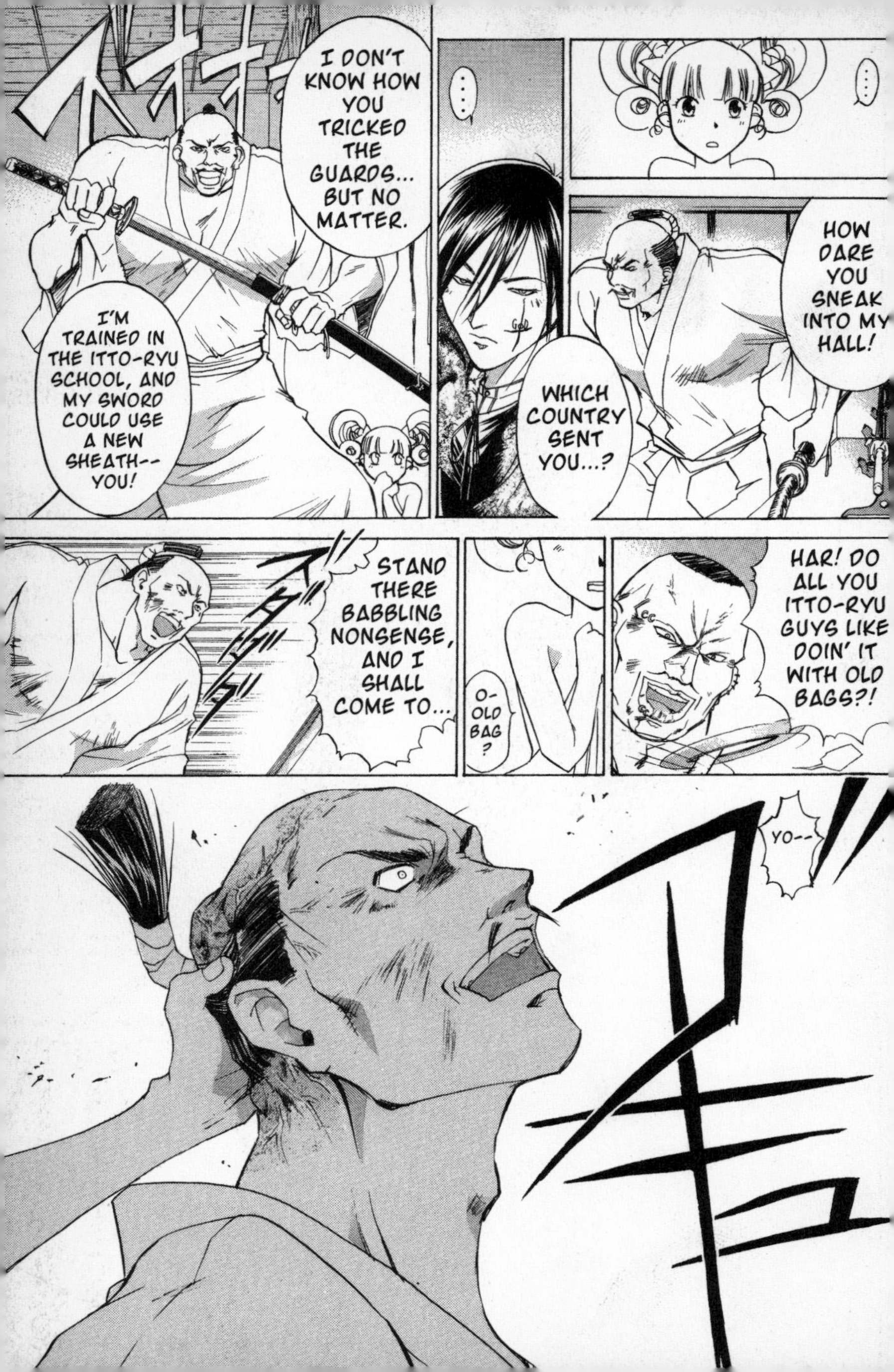
...
HOW DARE YOU SNEAK INTO MY HALL!
WHICH COUNTRY SENT YOU...?
...
I DON'T KNOW HOW YOU TRICKED THE GUARDS... BUT NO MATTER.
I'M TRAINED IN THE ITTO-RYU SCHOOL, AND MY SWORD COULD USE A NEW SHEATH--YOU!
HAR! DO ALL YOU ITTO-RYU GUYS LIKE DOIN' IT WITH OLD BAGS?!
O-OLD BAG?
STAND THERE BABBLING NONSENSE, AND I SHALL COME TO...
YO--

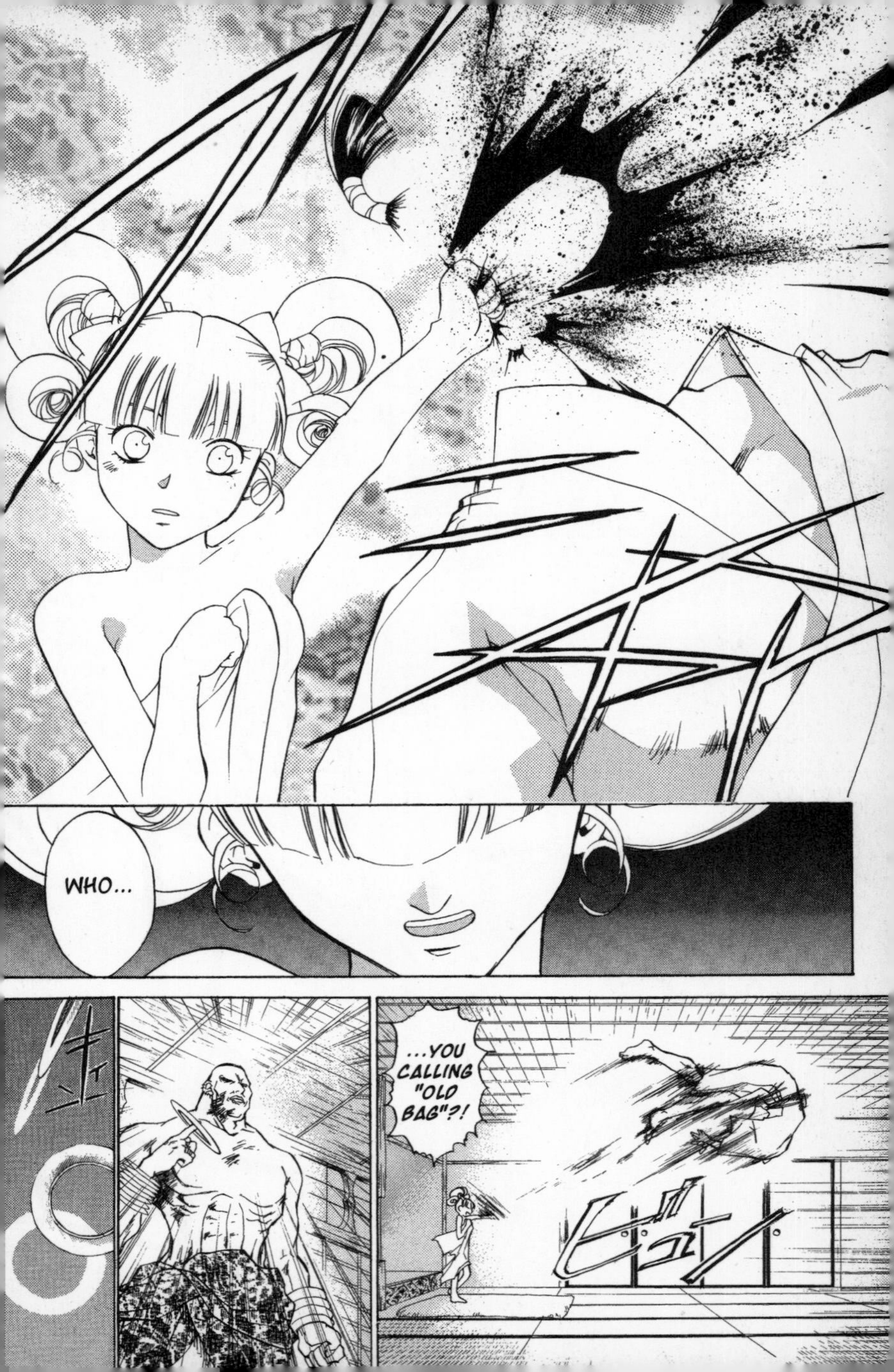
WHO...
...YOU CALLING "OLD BAG"?!

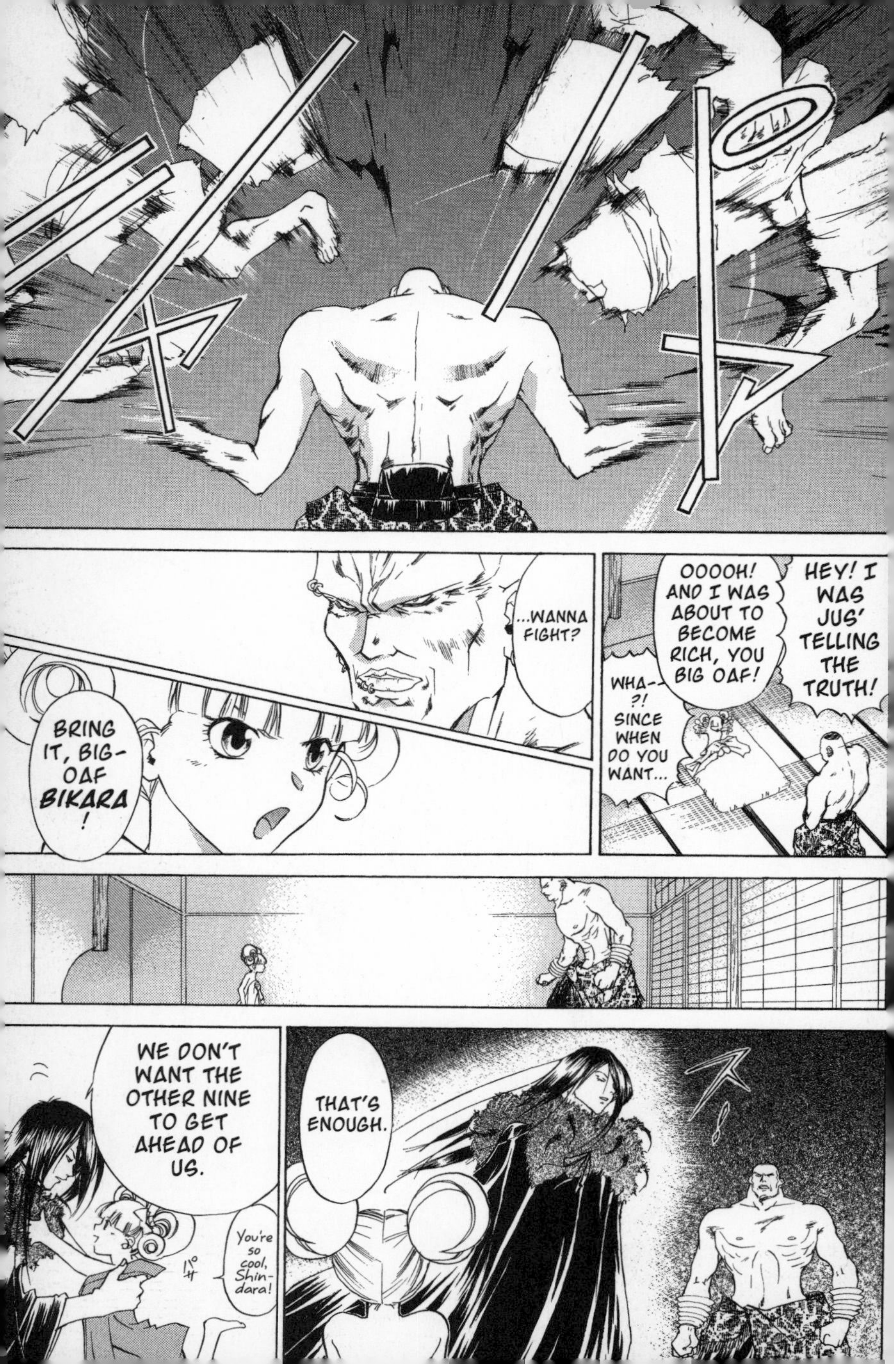
HEY! I WAS JUS' TELLING THE TRUTH!
OOOOH! AND I WAS ABOUT TO BECOME RICH, YOU BIG OAF!
WHA--?! SINCE WHEN DO YOU WANT...
...WANNA FIGHT?
BRING IT, BIG-OAF BIKARA!
THAT'S ENOUGH.
WE DON'T WANT THE OTHER NINE TO GET AHEAD OF US.
You're so cool, Shindara!

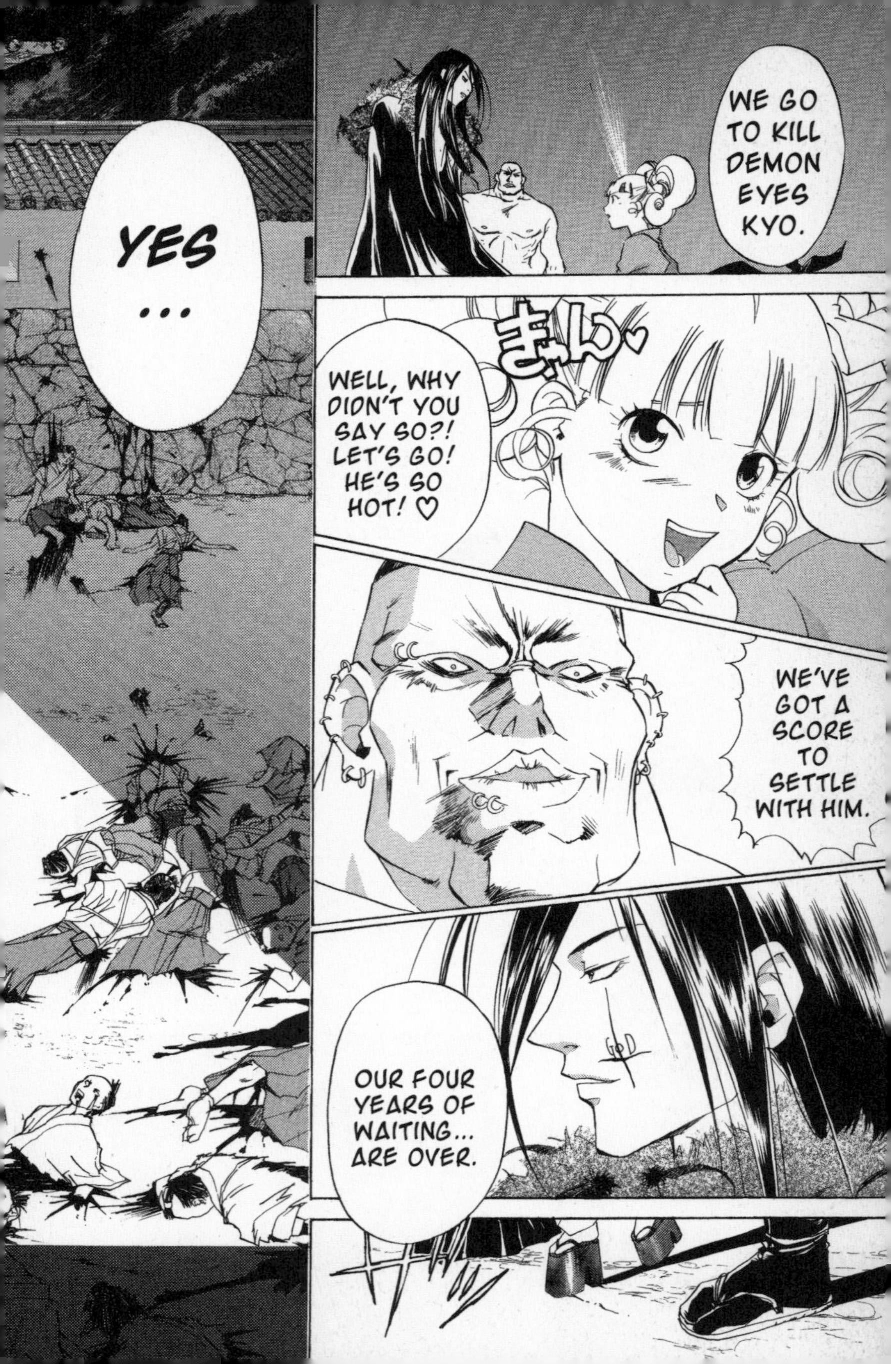
WE GO TO KILL DEMON EYES KYO.
きゅん♡
WELL, WHY DIDN'T YOU SAY SO?! LET'S GO! HE'S SO HOT! ♡
WE'VE GOT A SCORE TO SETTLE WITH HIM.
OUR FOUR YEARS OF WAITING... ARE OVER.
YES ...

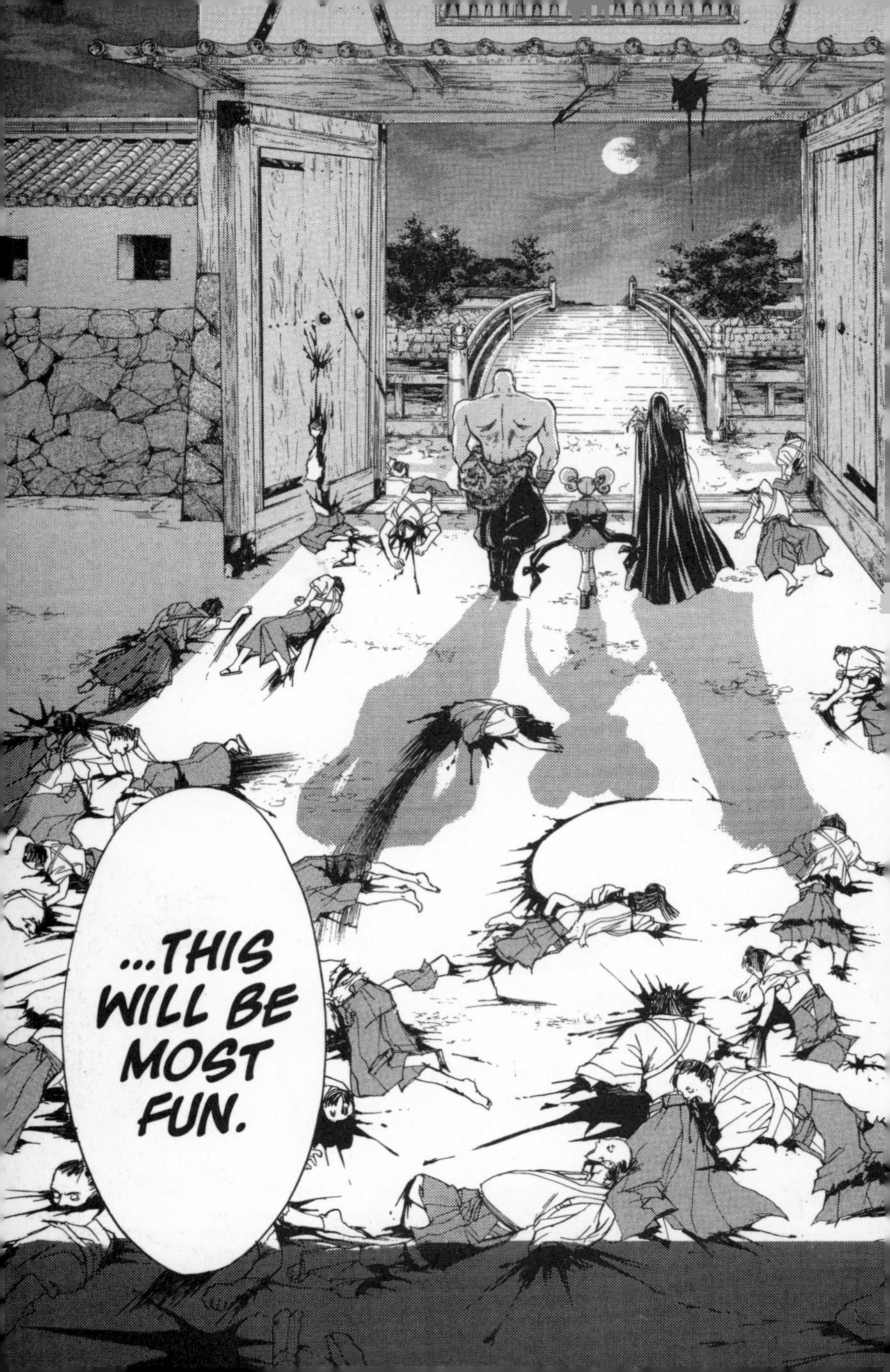
...THIS WILL BE MOST FUN.

Kamijyo Circumstances

The Best Meal Ever

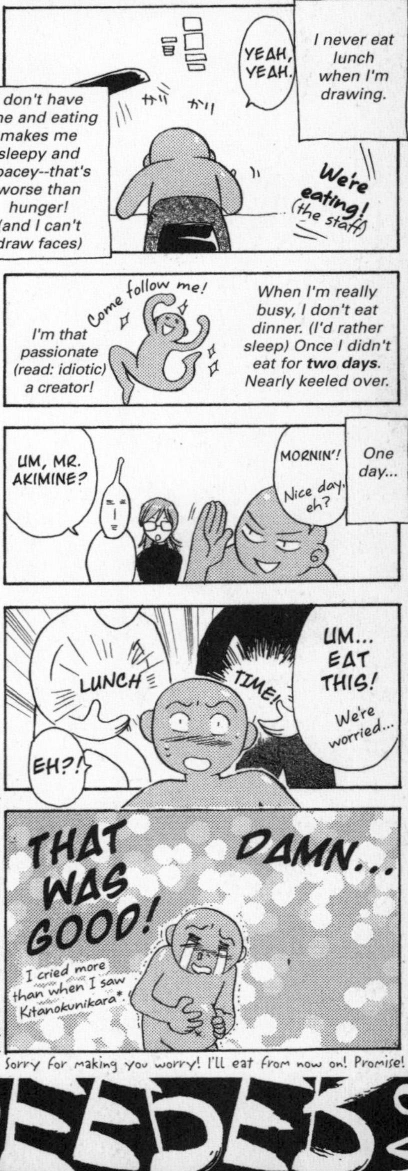
I never eat lunch when I'm drawing.
YEAH, YEAH.
I don't have time and eating makes me sleepy and spacey--that's worse than hunger! (and I can't draw faces)
We're eating! (the staff)
When I'm really busy, I don't eat dinner. (I'd rather sleep) Once I didn't eat for **two days**. Nearly keeled over.
Come follow me!
I'm that passionate (read: idiotic) a creator!
One day...
MORNIN'!
Nice day, eh?
UM, MR. AKIMINE?
UM... EAT THIS!
We're worried...
LUNCH
TIME!
EH?!
DAMN...
THAT WAS GOOD!
I cried more than when I saw Kitanokunikara*.
Sorry for making you worry! I'll eat from now on! Promise!

Tora Likes Yuya!

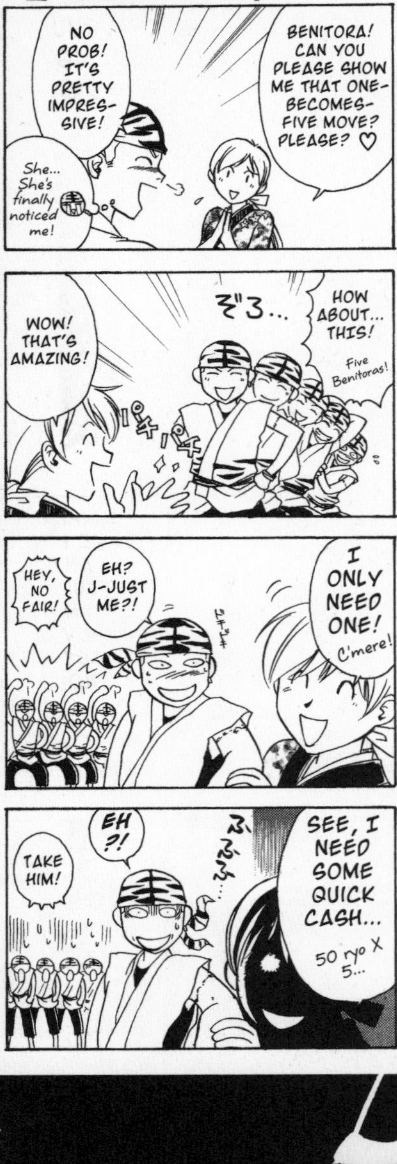
BENITORA! CAN YOU PLEASE SHOW ME THAT ONE-BECOMES-FIVE MOVE? PLEASE? ♡
NO PROB! IT'S PRETTY IMPRESSIVE!
She... She's finally noticed me!
HOW ABOUT... THIS!
Five Benitoras!
ぞろ...
WOW! THAT'S AMAZING!
I ONLY NEED ONE!
C'mere!
EH? J-JUST ME?!
HEY, NO FAIR!
SEE, I NEED SOME QUICK CASH...
50 ryo X 5...
EH?!
TAKE HIM!

*Kitanokunikara ("From the Northlands") was a popular miniseries in the 80s. A real tear-jerker.

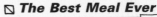

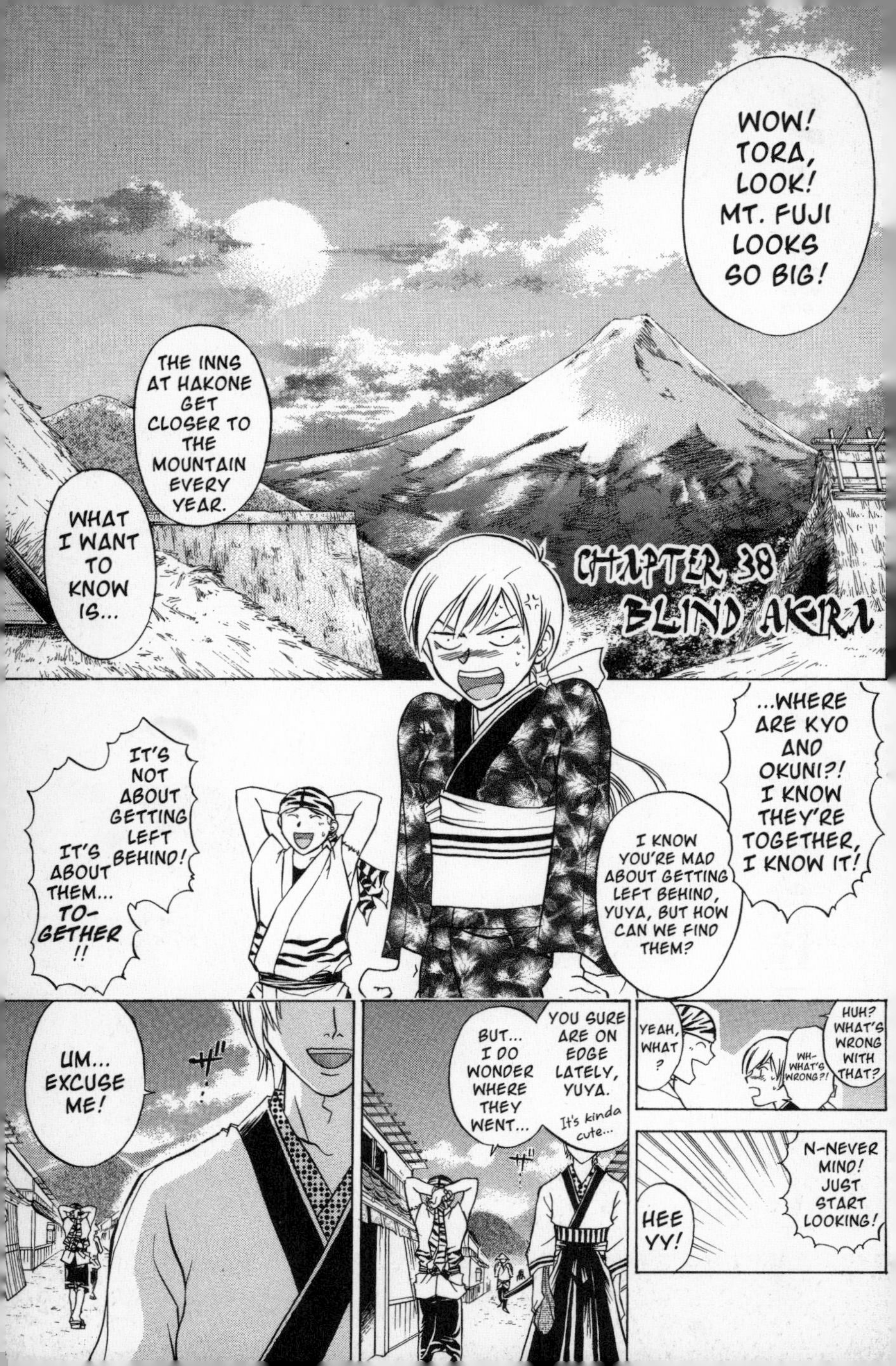
WOW! TORA, LOOK! MT. FUJI LOOKS SO BIG!
THE INNS AT HAKONE GET CLOSER TO THE MOUNTAIN EVERY YEAR.
WHAT I WANT TO KNOW IS...
CHAPTER 38
BLIND AKIRA
...WHERE ARE KYO AND OKUNI?! I KNOW THEY'RE TOGETHER, I KNOW IT!
I KNOW YOU'RE MAD ABOUT GETTING LEFT BEHIND, YUYA, BUT HOW CAN WE FIND THEM?
IT'S NOT ABOUT GETTING LEFT BEHIND!
IT'S ABOUT THEM... TO-GETHER!!
HUH? WHAT'S WRONG WITH THAT?
WH-WHAT'S WRONG?!
YEAH, WHAT?
N-NEVER MIND! JUST START LOOKING!
HEE YY!
YOU SURE ARE ON EDGE LATELY, YUYA.
It's kinda cute...
BUT... I DO WONDER WHERE THEY WENT...
UM... EXCUSE ME!

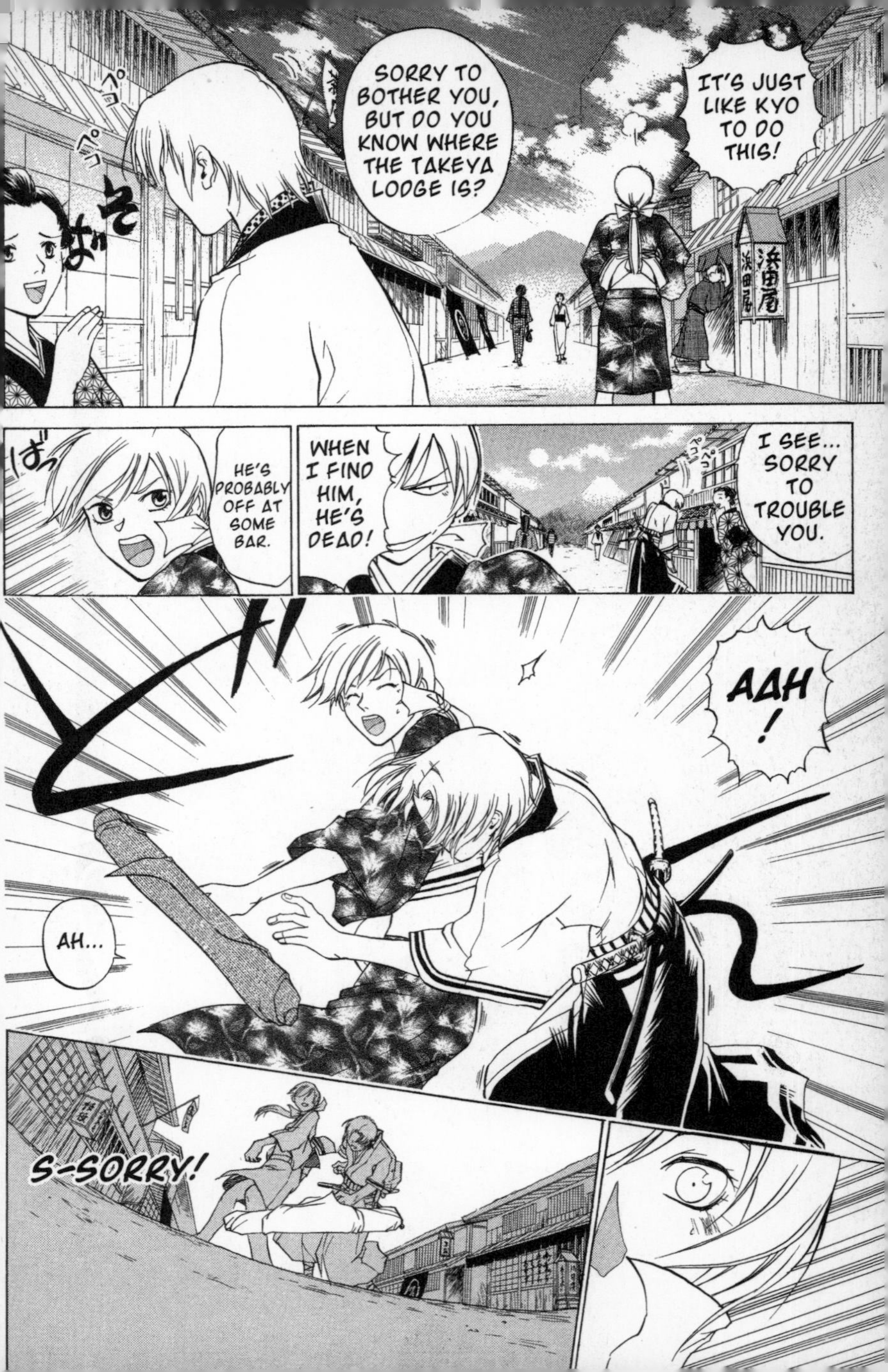

IT'S JUST LIKE KYO TO DO THIS!
SORRY TO BOTHER YOU, BUT DO YOU KNOW WHERE THE TAKEYA LODGE IS?
I SEE... SORRY TO TROUBLE YOU.
WHEN I FIND HIM, HE'S DEAD!
HE'S PROBABLY OFF AT SOME BAR.
AAH!
AH...
S-SORRY!

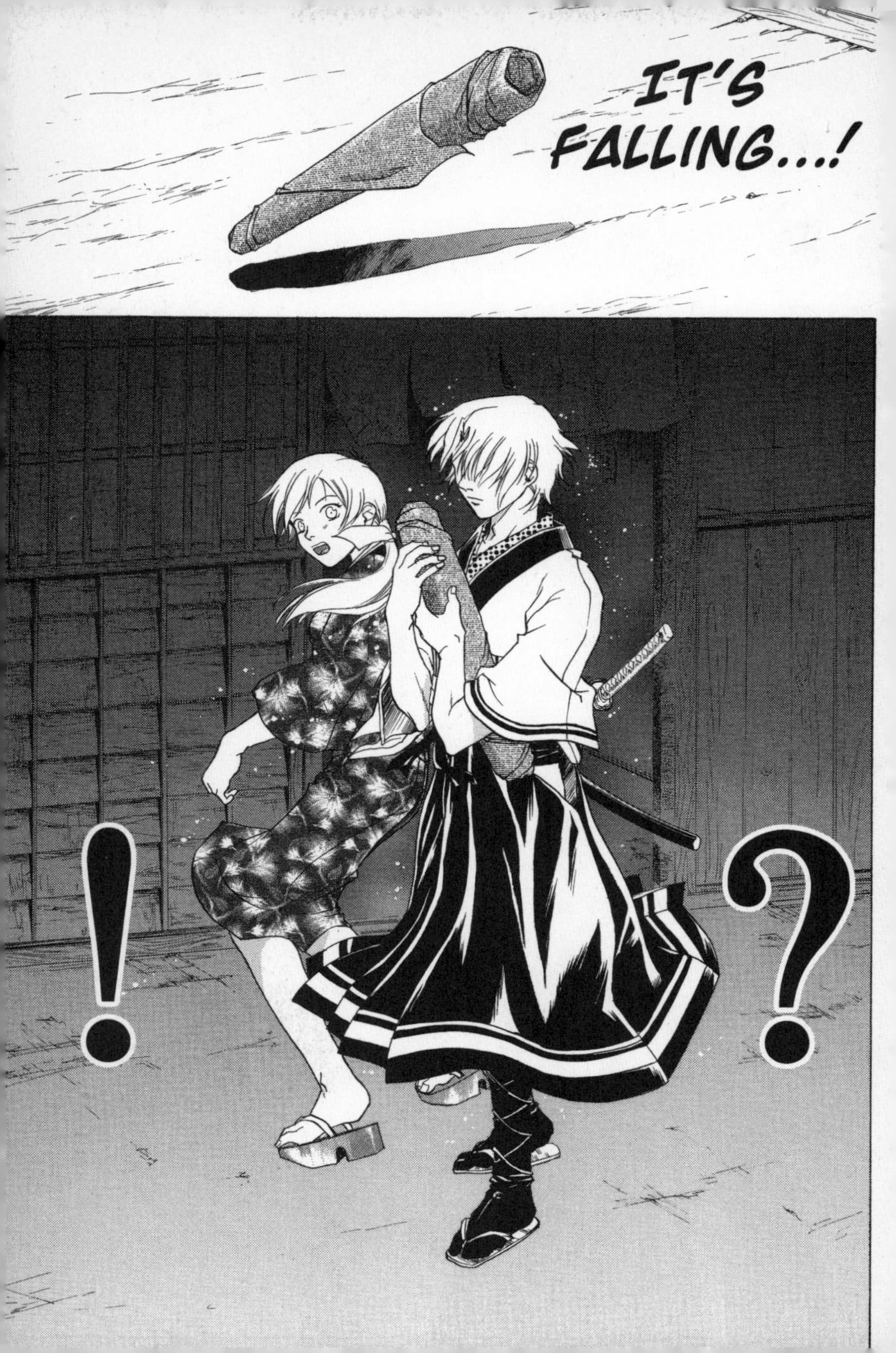
IT'S FALLING...!
!
?

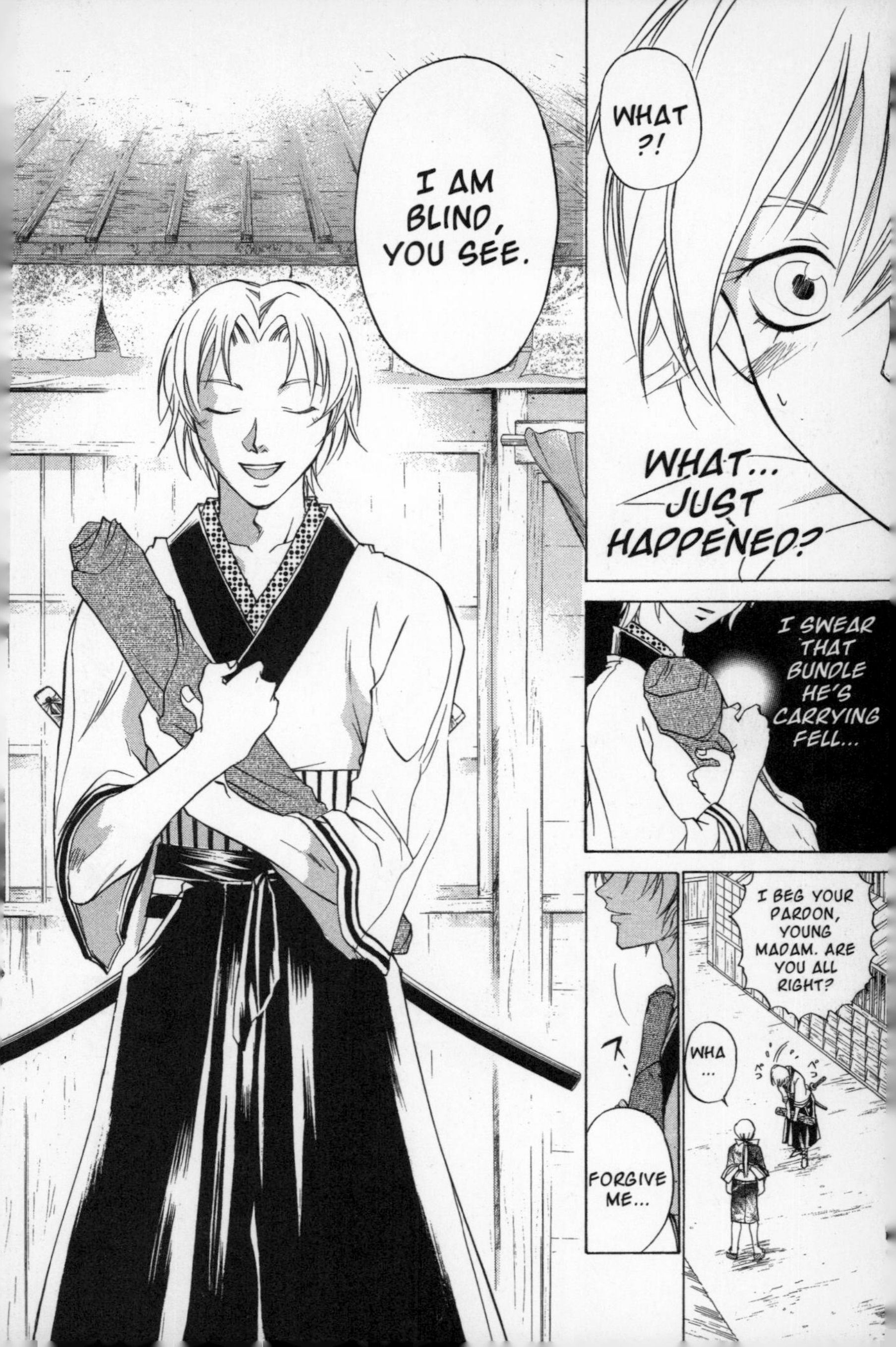
WHAT ?!
WHAT... JUST HAPPENED?
I SWEAR THAT BUNDLE HE'S CARRYING FELL...
I BEG YOUR PARDON, YOUNG MADAM. ARE YOU ALL RIGHT?
WHA ...
FORGIVE ME...
I AM BLIND, YOU SEE.

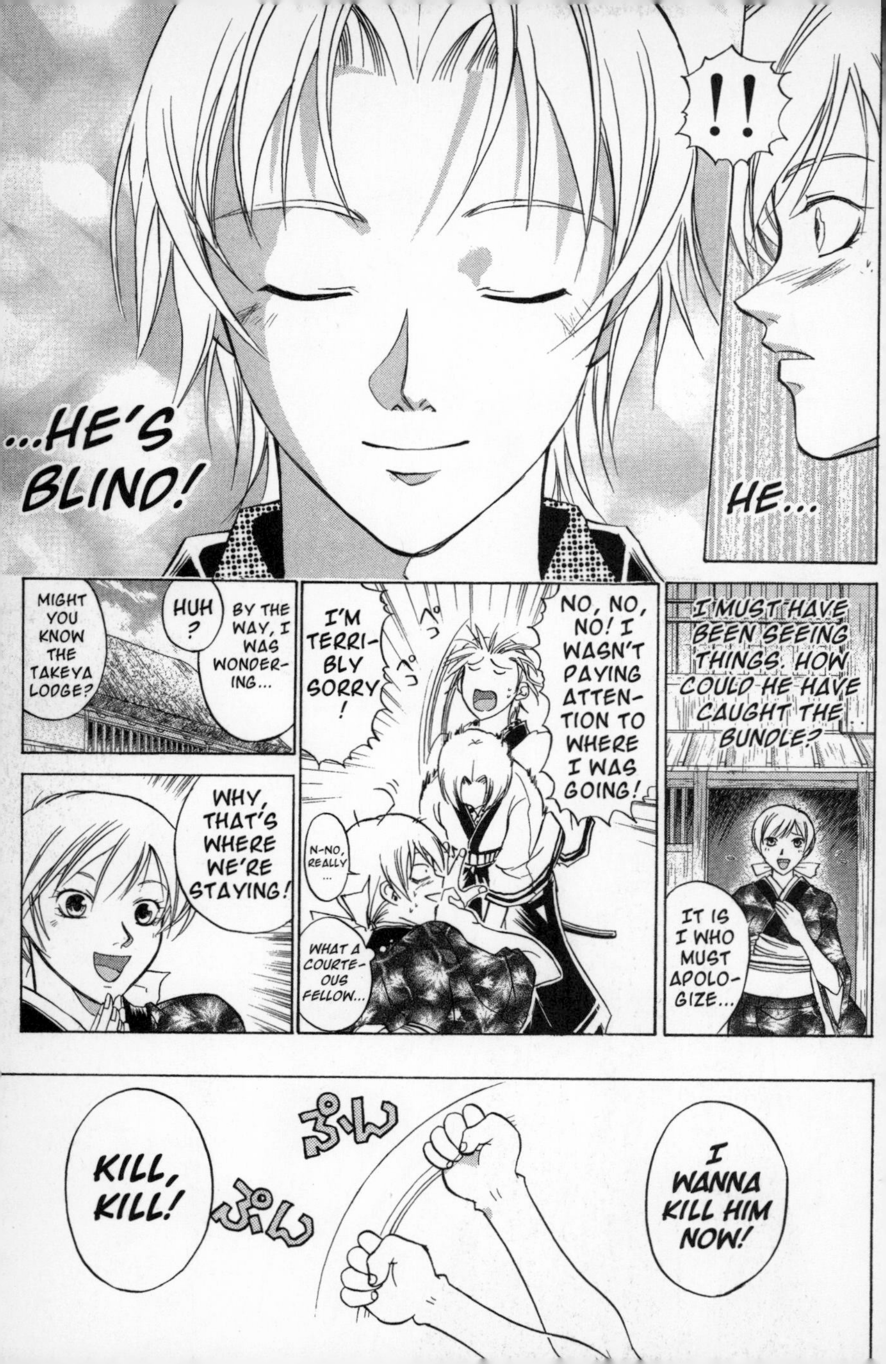
!!
HE...
...HE'S BLIND!
I MUST HAVE BEEN SEEING THINGS. HOW COULD HE HAVE CAUGHT THE BUNDLE?
IT IS I WHO MUST APOLOGIZE...
NO, NO, NO! I WASN'T PAYING ATTENTION TO WHERE I WAS GOING!
I'M TERRIBLY SORRY!
N-NO, REALLY...
WHAT A COURTEOUS FELLOW...
BY THE WAY, I WAS WONDERING...
HUH?
MIGHT YOU KNOW THE TAKEYA LODGE?
WHY, THAT'S WHERE WE'RE STAYING!
I WANNA KILL HIM NOW!
ぷん
ぷん
KILL, KILL!

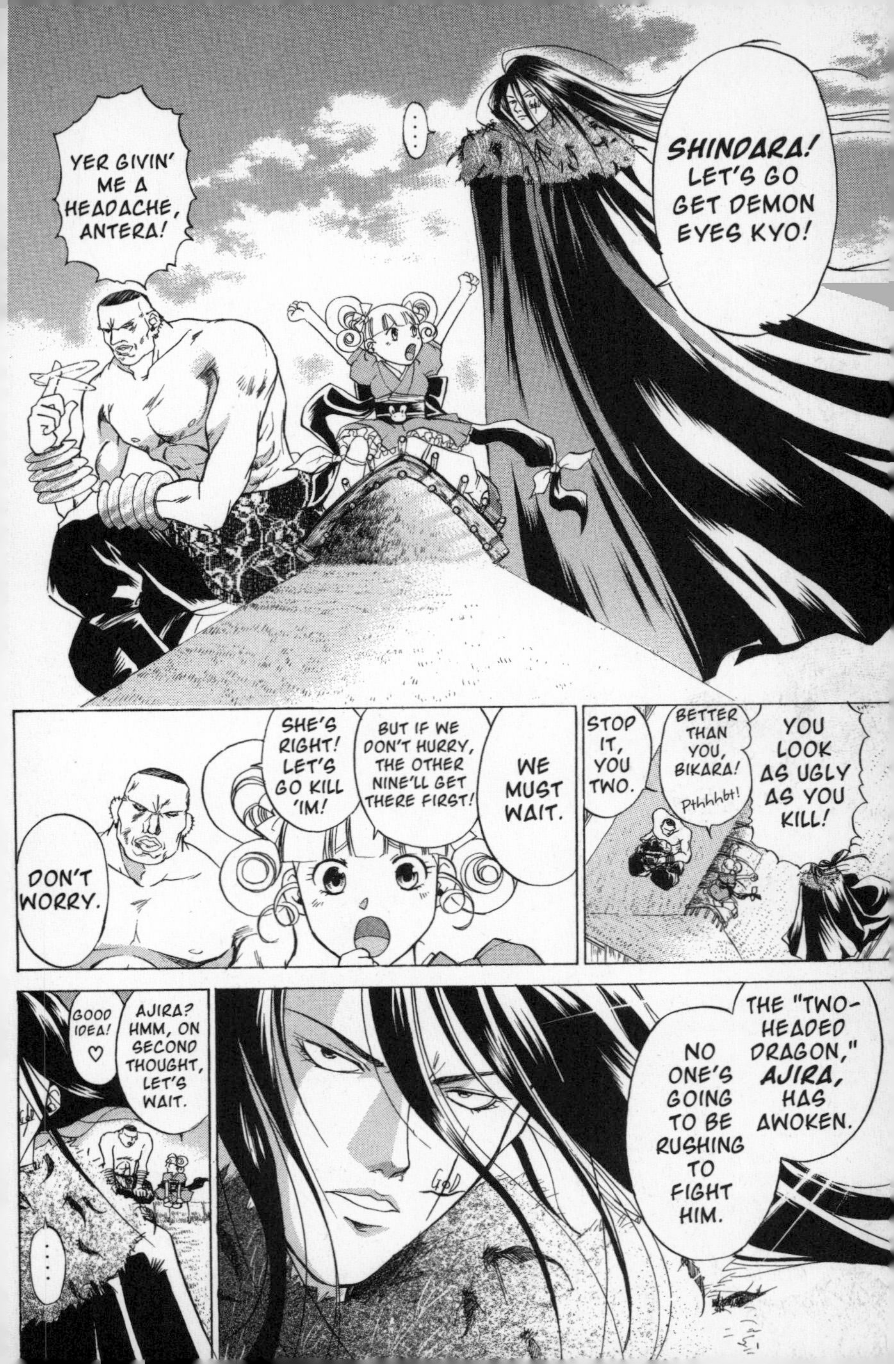
SHINDARA! LET'S GO GET DEMON EYES KYO!
...
YER GIVIN' ME A HEADACHE, ANTERA!
YOU LOOK AS UGLY AS YOU KILL!
BETTER THAN YOU, BIKARA!
Pthhhbt!
STOP IT, YOU TWO.
WE MUST WAIT.
BUT IF WE DON'T HURRY, THE OTHER NINE'LL GET THERE FIRST!
SHE'S RIGHT! LET'S GO KILL 'IM!
DON'T WORRY.
THE "TWO-HEADED DRAGON," AJIRA, HAS AWOKEN.
NO ONE'S GOING TO BE RUSHING TO FIGHT HIM.
AJIRA? HMM, ON SECOND THOUGHT, LET'S WAIT.
GOOD IDEA! ♡
...

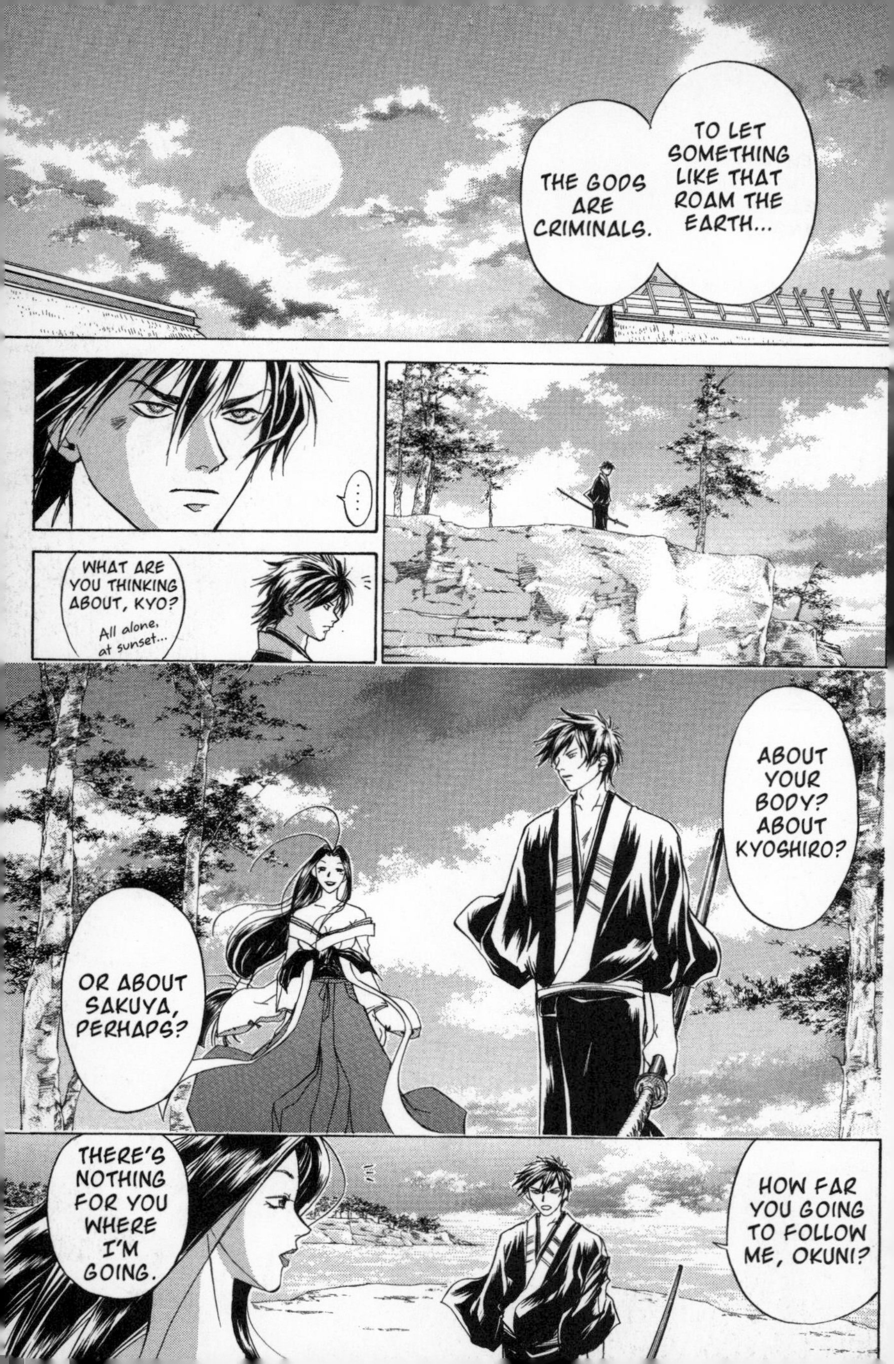
TO LET SOMETHING LIKE THAT ROAM THE EARTH...
THE GODS ARE CRIMINALS.
...
WHAT ARE YOU THINKING ABOUT, KYO?
All alone, at sunset...
ABOUT YOUR BODY? ABOUT KYOSHIRO?
OR ABOUT SAKUYA, PERHAPS?
HOW FAR YOU GOING TO FOLLOW ME, OKUNI?
THERE'S NOTHING FOR YOU WHERE I'M GOING.

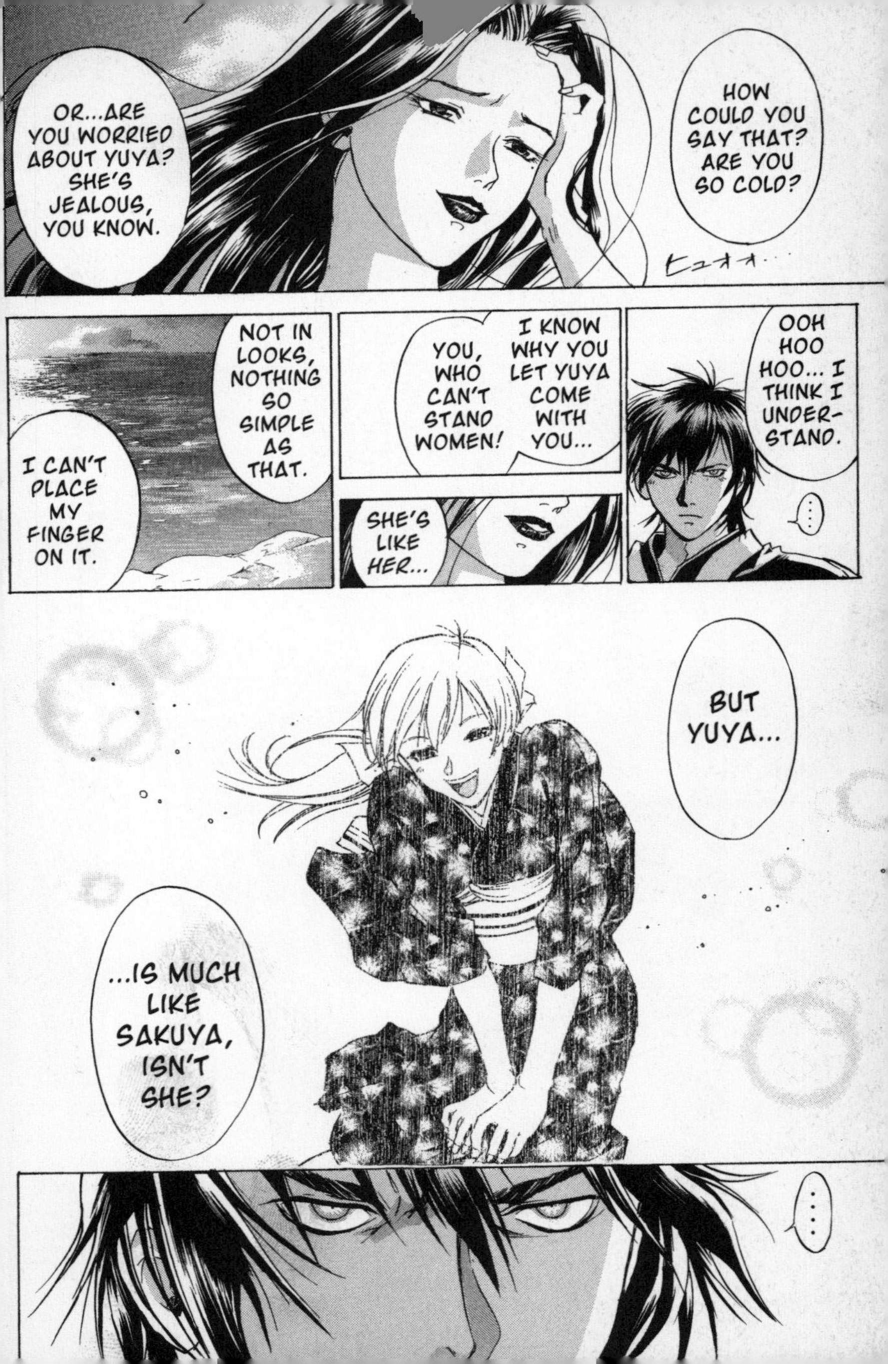
HOW COULD YOU SAY THAT? ARE YOU SO COLD?
OR...ARE YOU WORRIED ABOUT YUYA? SHE'S JEALOUS, YOU KNOW.
ヒュオオ…
OOH HOO HOO... I THINK I UNDER-STAND.
...
I KNOW WHY YOU LET YUYA COME WITH YOU...
YOU, WHO CAN'T STAND WOMEN!
SHE'S LIKE HER...
NOT IN LOOKS, NOTHING SO SIMPLE AS THAT.
I CAN'T PLACE MY FINGER ON IT.
BUT YUYA...
...IS MUCH LIKE SAKUYA, ISN'T SHE?
...

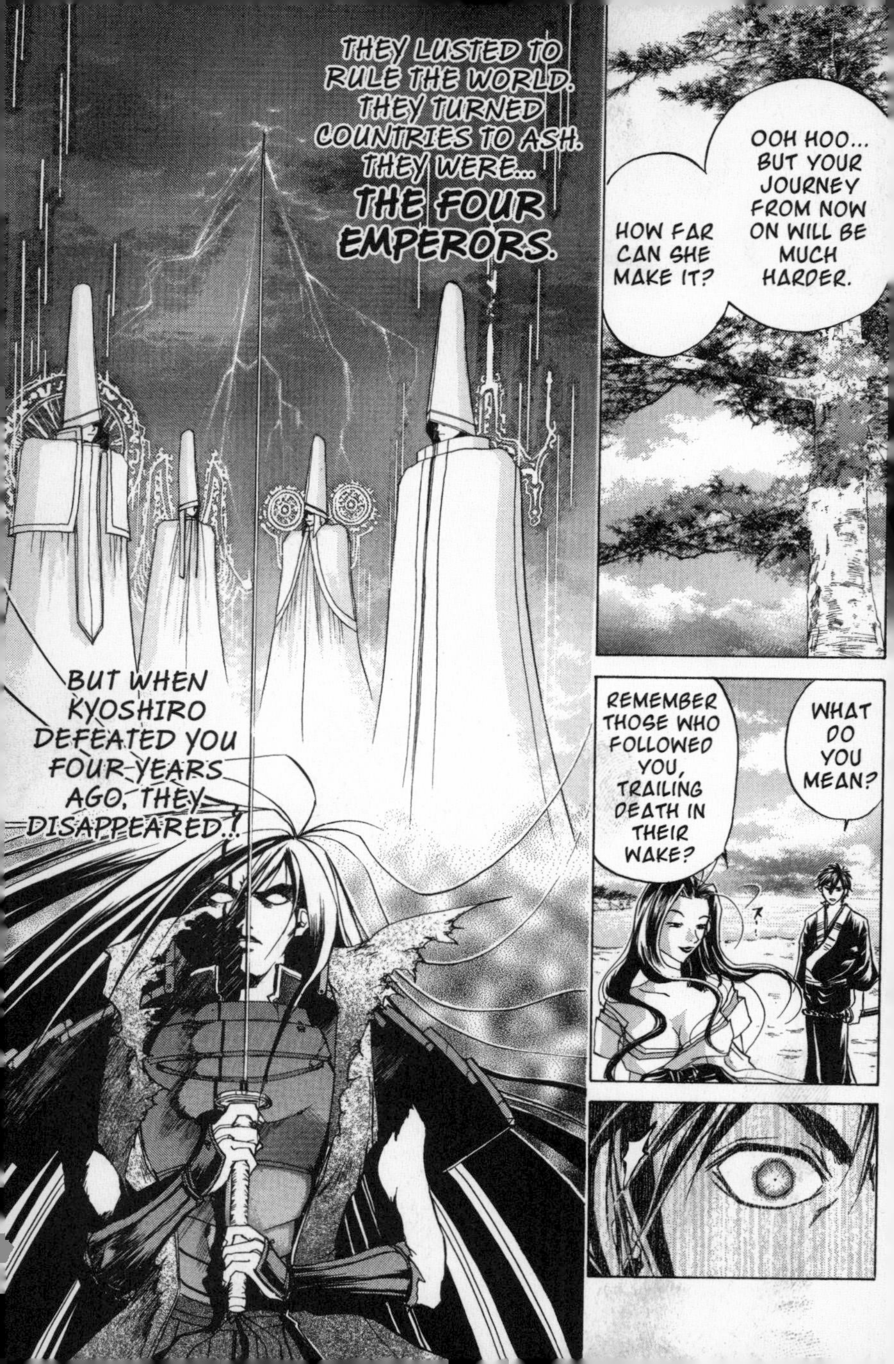
OOH HOO... BUT YOUR JOURNEY FROM NOW ON WILL BE MUCH HARDER.
HOW FAR CAN SHE MAKE IT?
WHAT DO YOU MEAN?
REMEMBER THOSE WHO FOLLOWED YOU, TRAILING DEATH IN THEIR WAKE?
THEY LUSTED TO RULE THE WORLD. THEY TURNED COUNTRIES TO ASH. THEY WERE... THE FOUR EMPERORS.
BUT WHEN KYOSHIRO DEFEATED YOU FOUR YEARS AGO, THEY DISAPPEARED...

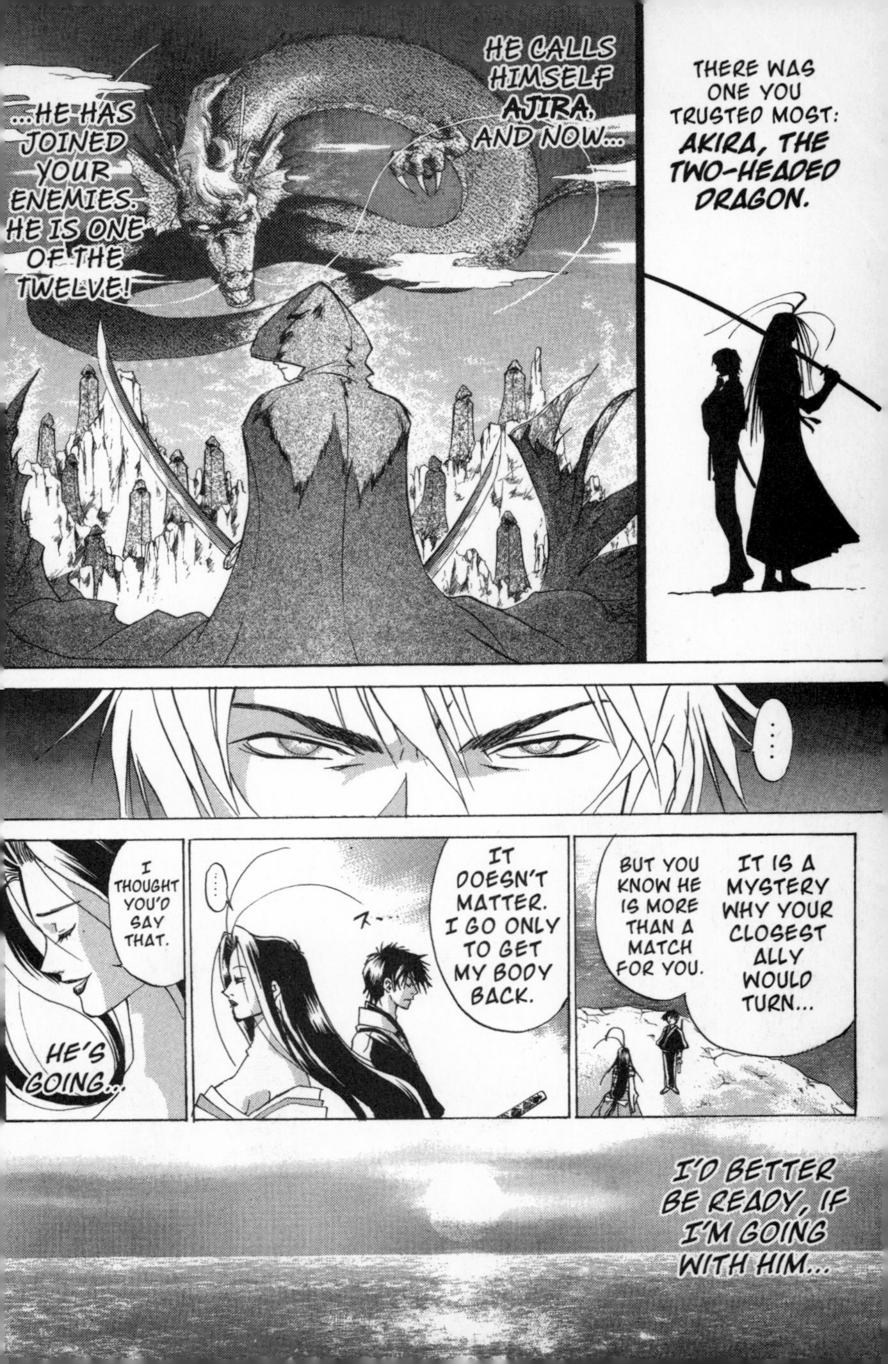
THERE WAS ONE YOU TRUSTED MOST: AKIRA, THE TWO-HEADED DRAGON.
HE CALLS HIMSELF AJIRA, AND NOW...
...HE HAS JOINED YOUR ENEMIES. HE IS ONE OF THE TWELVE!
....
IT IS A MYSTERY WHY YOUR CLOSEST ALLY WOULD TURN...
BUT YOU KNOW HE IS MORE THAN A MATCH FOR YOU.
IT DOESN'T MATTER. I GO ONLY TO GET MY BODY BACK.
....
ス-
I THOUGHT YOU'D SAY THAT.
HE'S GOING...
I'D BETTER BE READY, IF I'M GOING WITH HIM...

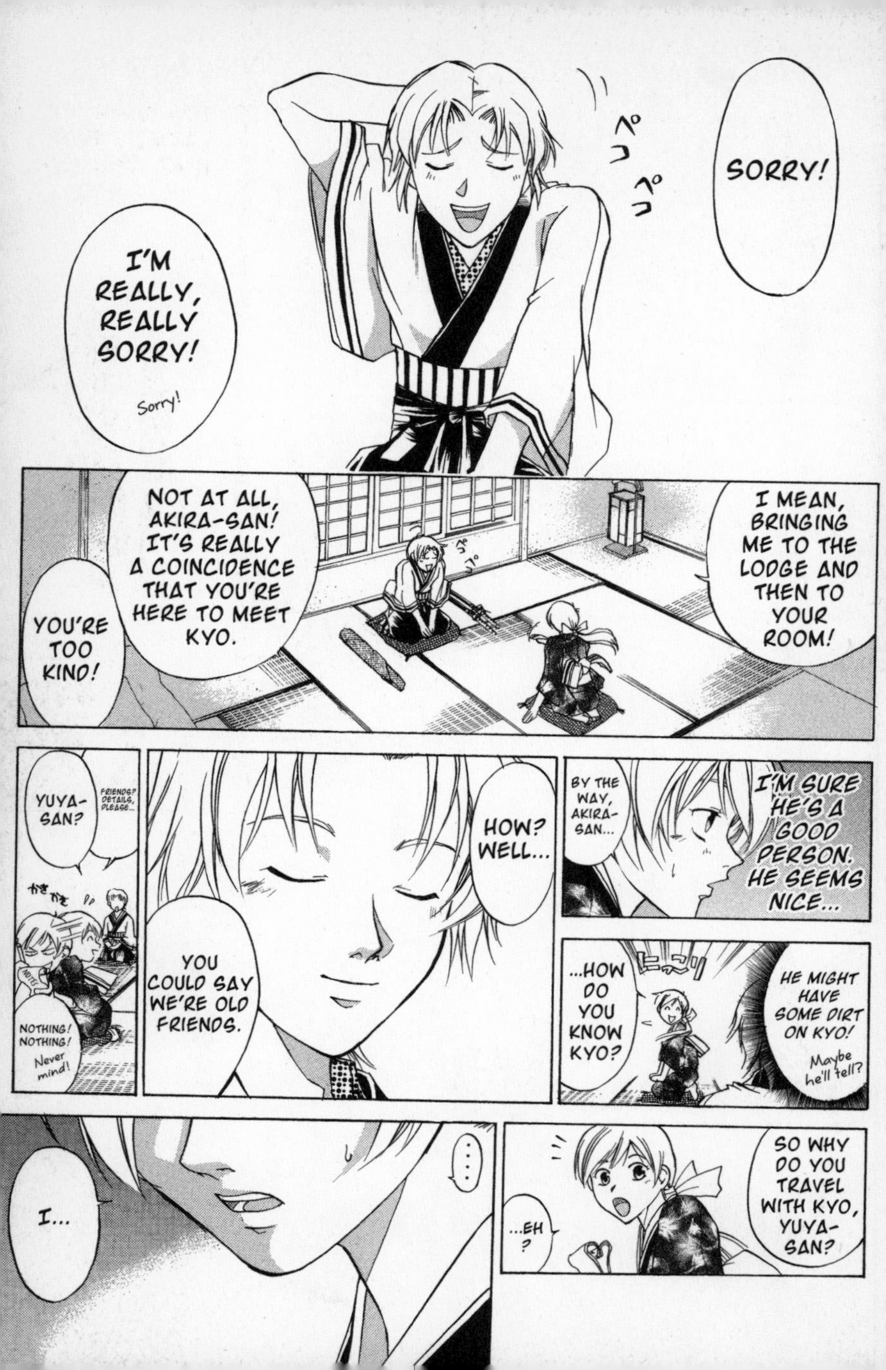
SORRY!
ペコ ペコ
I'M REALLY, REALLY SORRY!
Sorry!
I MEAN, BRINGING ME TO THE LODGE AND THEN TO YOUR ROOM!
NOT AT ALL, AKIRA-SAN! IT'S REALLY A COINCIDENCE THAT YOU'RE HERE TO MEET KYO.
YOU'RE TOO KIND!
I'M SURE HE'S A GOOD PERSON. HE SEEMS NICE...
BY THE WAY, AKIRA-SAN...
HE MIGHT HAVE SOME DIRT ON KYO!
Maybe he'll tell?
...HOW DO YOU KNOW KYO?
HOW? WELL...
YOU COULD SAY WE'RE OLD FRIENDS.
FRIENDS? DETAILS, PLEASE...
YUYA-SAN?
かきかき
NOTES
NOTHING! NOTHING!
Never mind!
SO WHY DO YOU TRAVEL WITH KYO, YUYA-SAN?
...EH?
...
I...

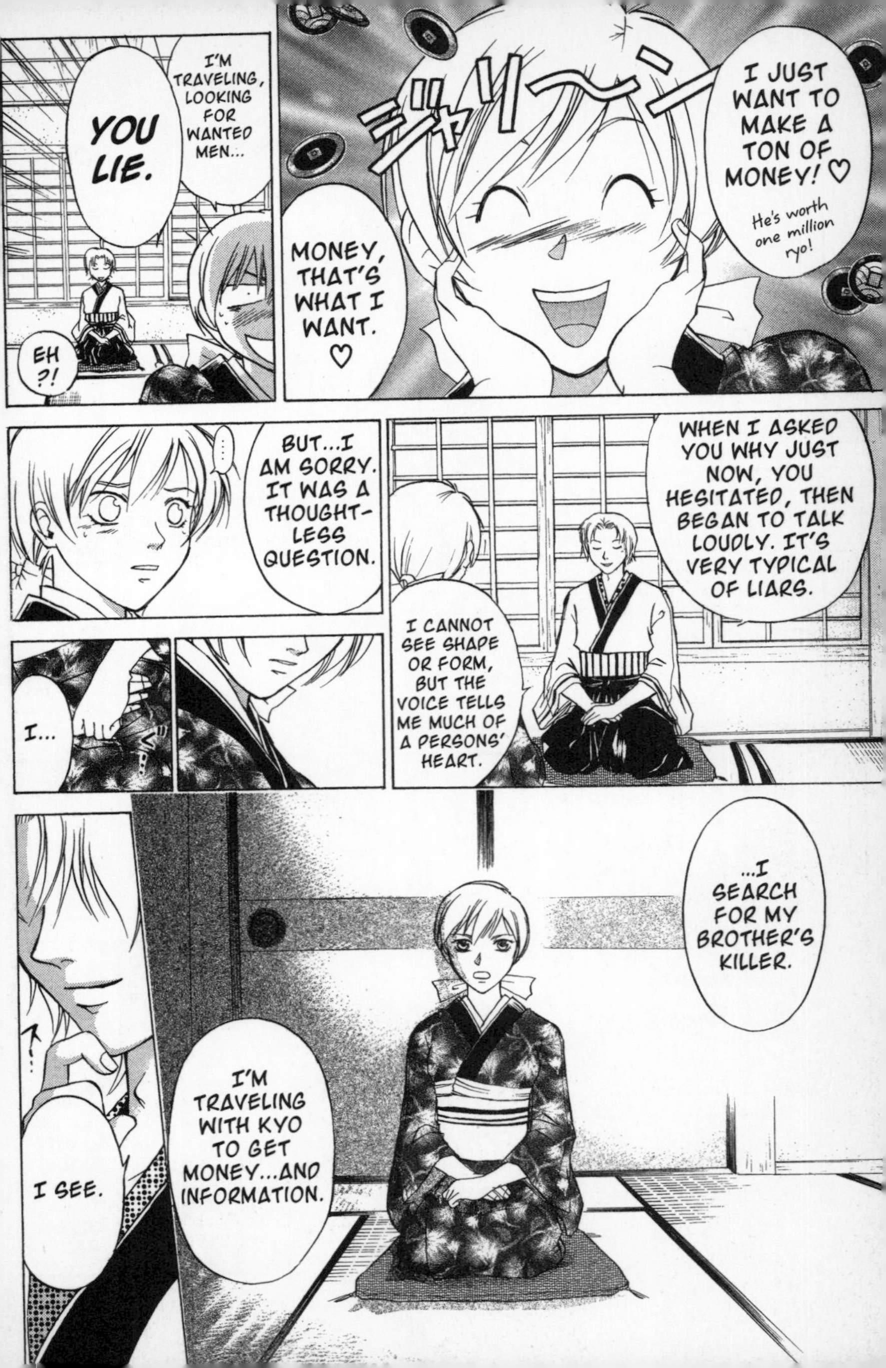

ジャリ〜ン
I JUST WANT TO MAKE A TON OF MONEY! ♡
He's worth one million ryo!
MONEY, THAT'S WHAT I WANT. ♡
I'M TRAVELING, LOOKING FOR WANTED MEN...
YOU LIE.
EH ?!
WHEN I ASKED YOU WHY JUST NOW, YOU HESITATED, THEN BEGAN TO TALK LOUDLY. IT'S VERY TYPICAL OF LIARS.
I CANNOT SEE SHAPE OR FORM, BUT THE VOICE TELLS ME MUCH OF A PERSONS' HEART.
BUT...I AM SORRY. IT WAS A THOUGHTLESS QUESTION.
...
I...
...I SEARCH FOR MY BROTHER'S KILLER.
I'M TRAVELING WITH KYO TO GET MONEY...AND INFORMATION.
I SEE.

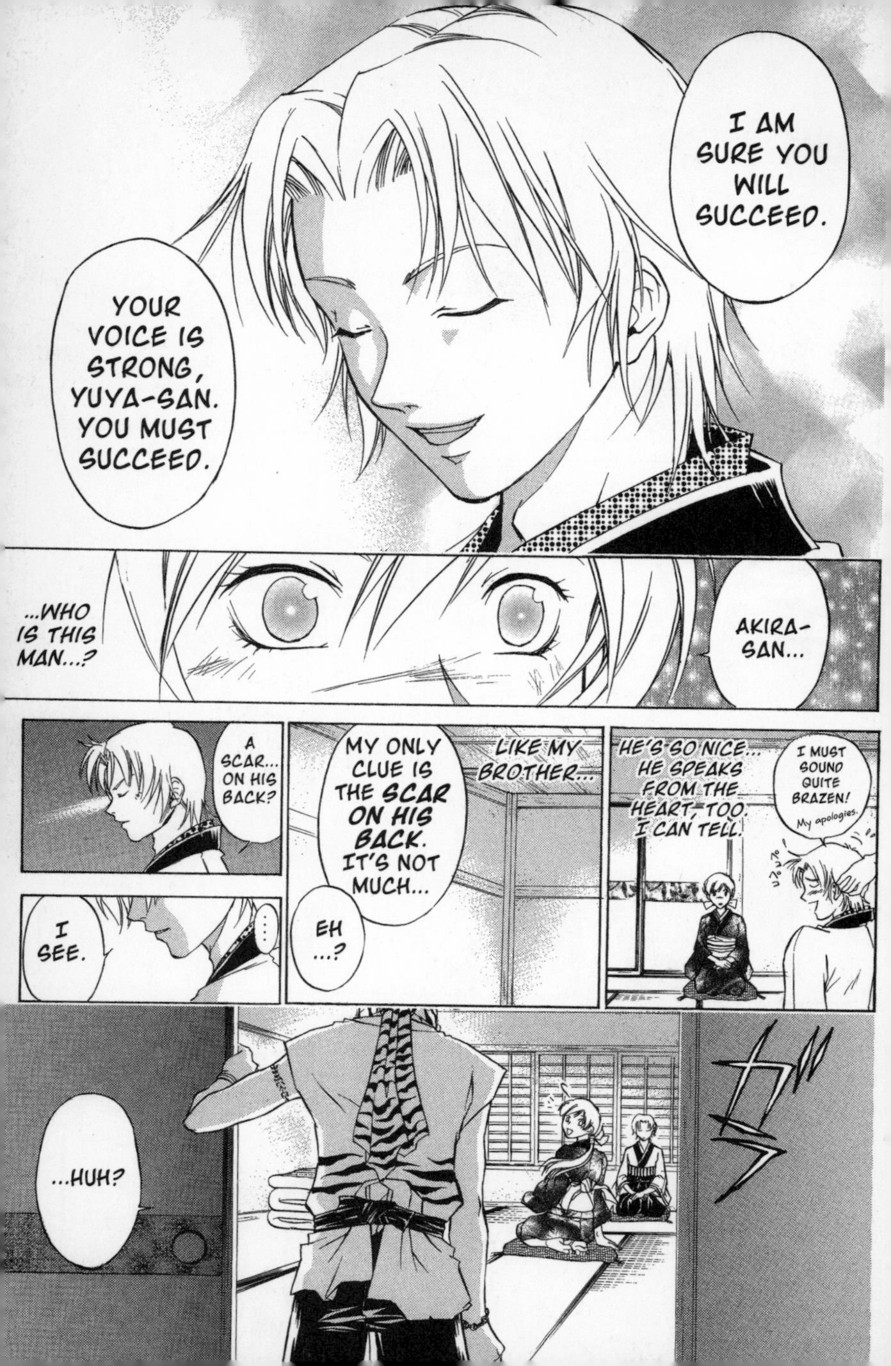
I AM SURE YOU WILL SUCCEED.
YOUR VOICE IS STRONG, YUYA-SAN. YOU MUST SUCCEED.
AKIRA-SAN...
...WHO IS THIS MAN...?
I MUST SOUND QUITE BRAZEN!
My apologies.
HE'S SO NICE... HE SPEAKS FROM THE HEART, TOO. I CAN TELL.
LIKE MY BROTHER...
MY ONLY CLUE IS THE SCAR ON HIS BACK. IT'S NOT MUCH...
EH ...?
A SCAR... ON HIS BACK?
...
I SEE.
...HUH?

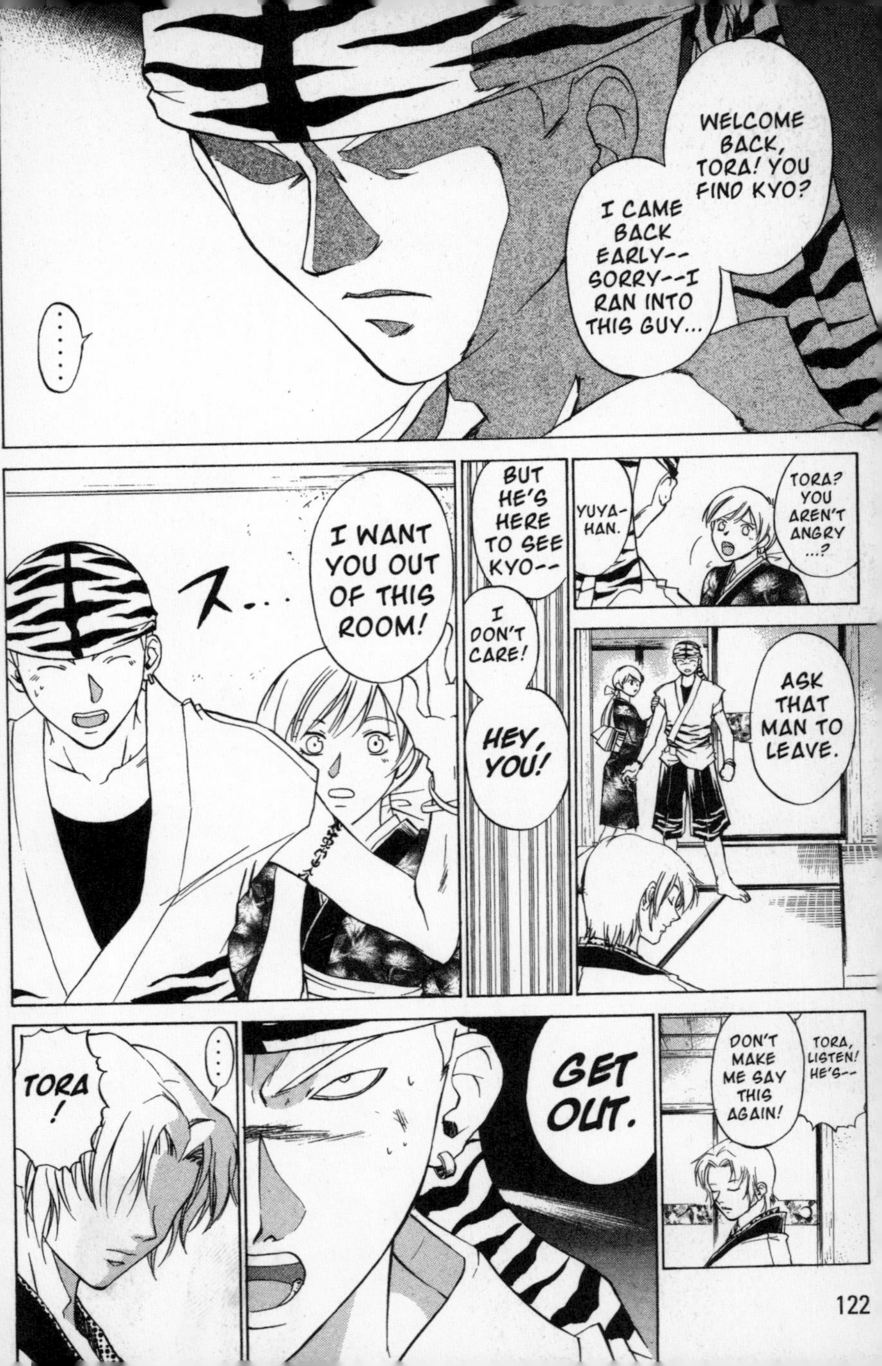
WELCOME BACK, TORA! YOU FIND KYO?
I CAME BACK EARLY--SORRY--I RAN INTO THIS GUY...
......
TORA? YOU AREN'T ANGRY...?
YUYA-HAN.
ASK THAT MAN TO LEAVE.
BUT HE'S HERE TO SEE KYO--
I DON'T CARE!
HEY, YOU!
I WANT YOU OUT OF THIS ROOM!
ス...
TORA, LISTEN! HE'S--
DON'T MAKE ME SAY THIS AGAIN!
GET OUT.
...
TORA!

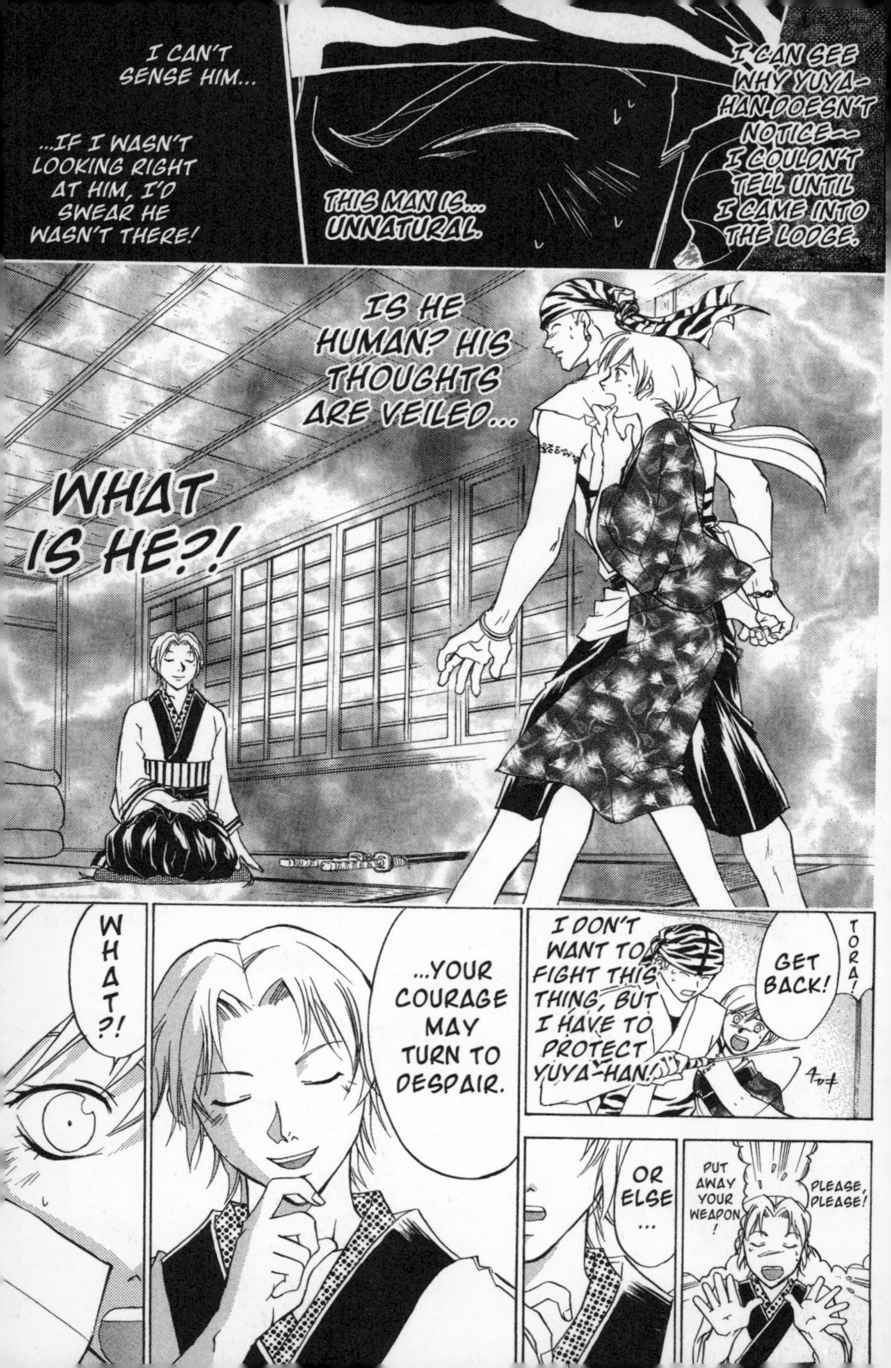
I CAN SEE WHY YUYA-HAN DOESN'T NOTICE-- I COULDN'T TELL UNTIL I CAME INTO THE LODGE.
THIS MAN IS... UNNATURAL.
I CAN'T SENSE HIM...
...IF I WASN'T LOOKING RIGHT AT HIM, I'D SWEAR HE WASN'T THERE!
IS HE HUMAN? HIS THOUGHTS ARE VEILED...
WHAT IS HE?!
TORA!
GET BACK!
I DON'T WANT TO FIGHT THIS THING, BUT I HAVE TO PROTECT YUYA-HAN!
チャキ
PLEASE, PLEASE!
PUT AWAY YOUR WEAPON!
OR ELSE ...
...YOUR COURAGE MAY TURN TO DESPAIR.
WHAT?!

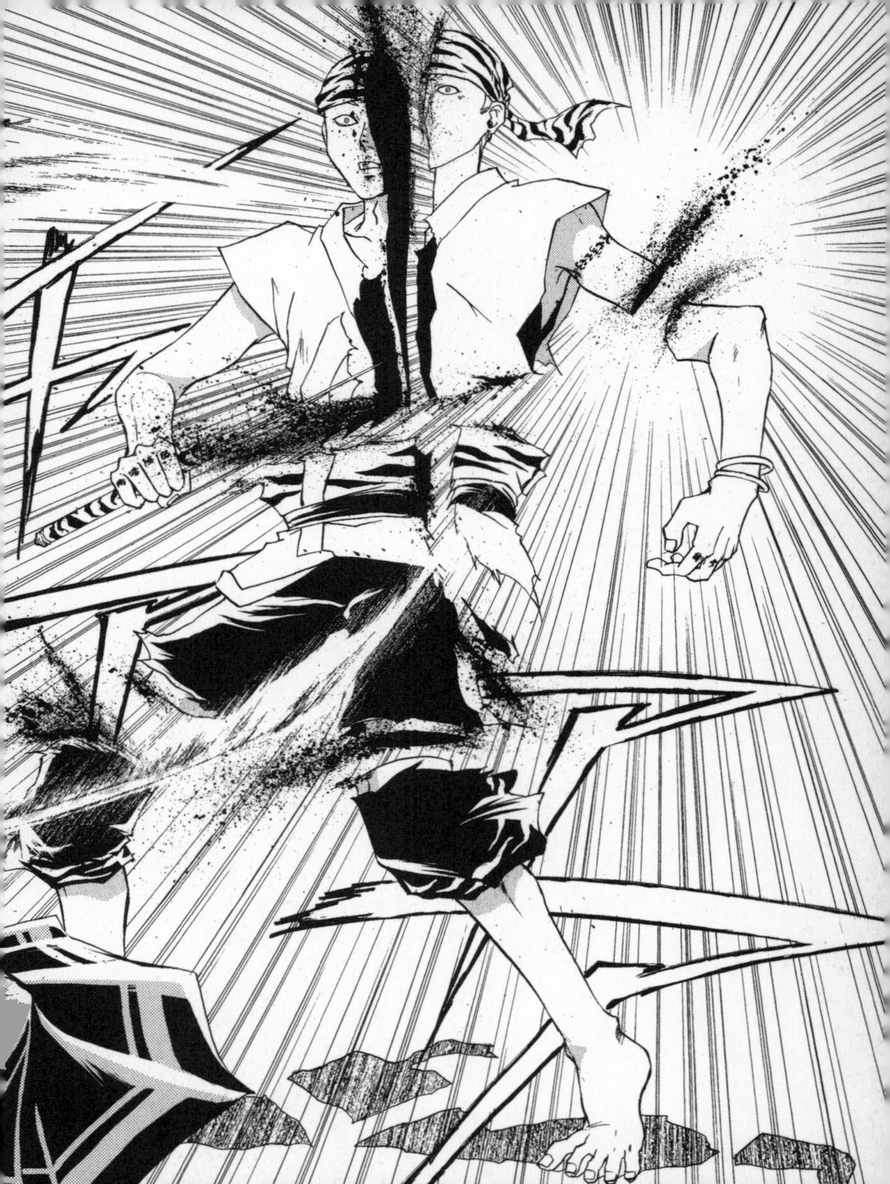

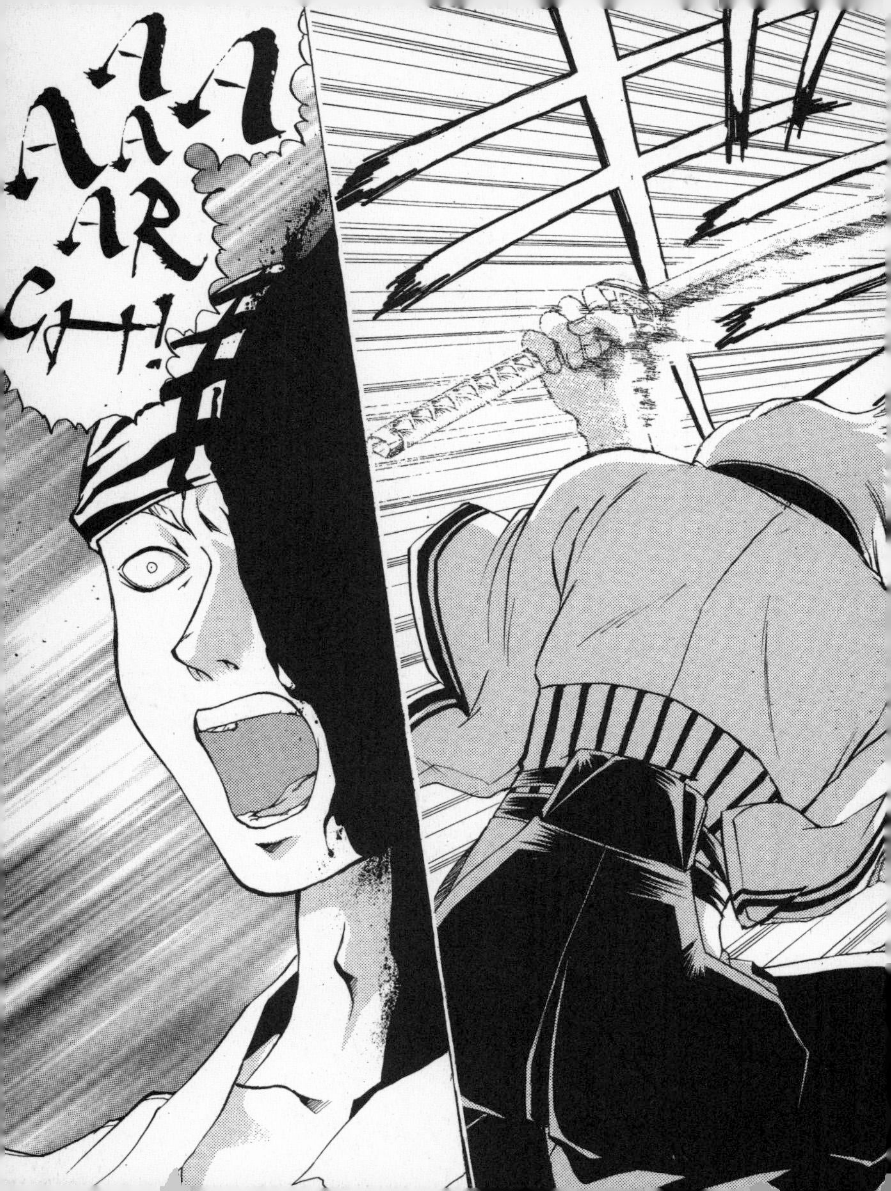
AAAAARGH!

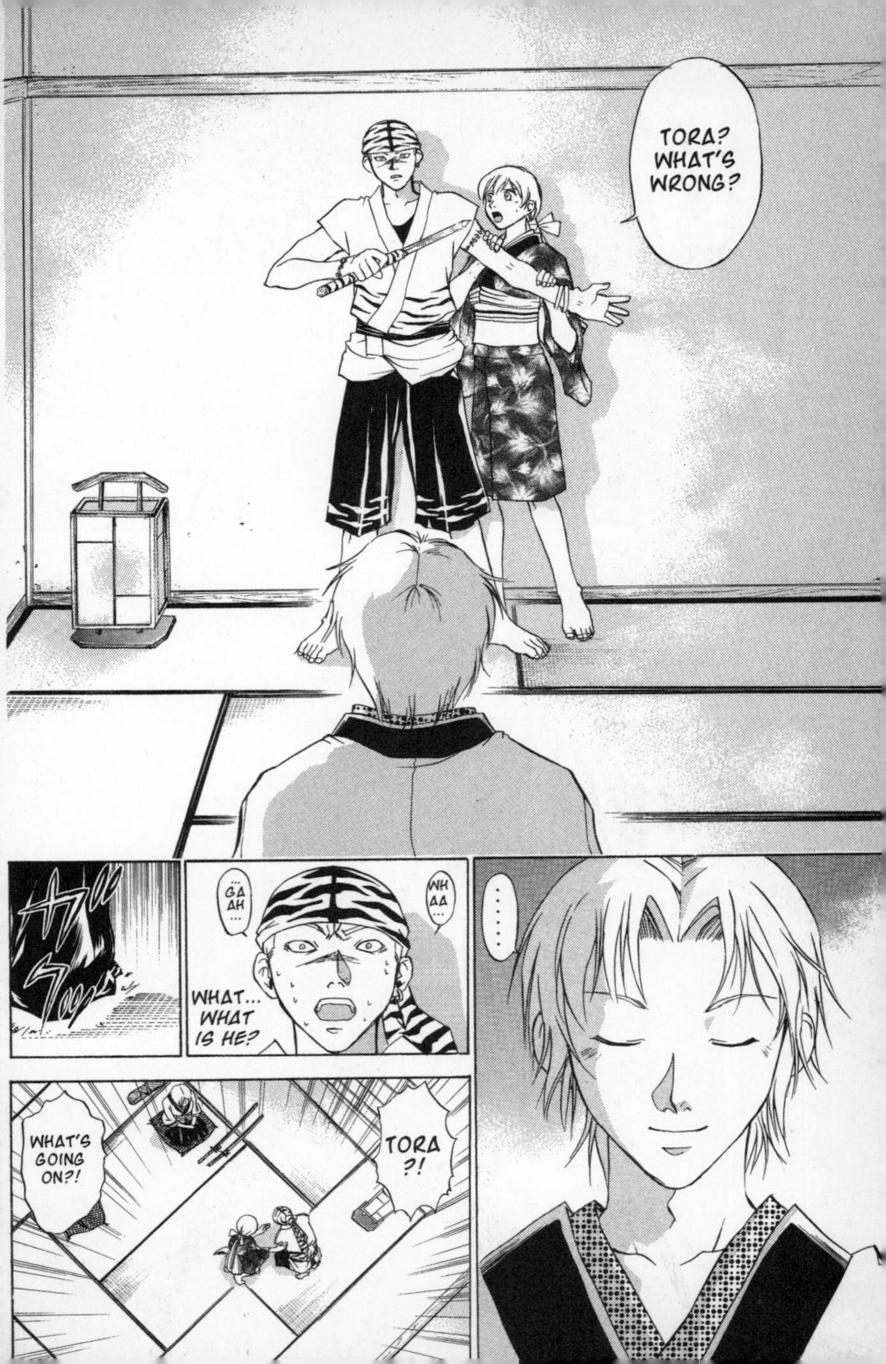
TORA? WHAT'S WRONG?
......
WHAA...
...GAAH...
WHAT... WHAT IS HE?
TORA?!
WHAT'S GOING ON?!

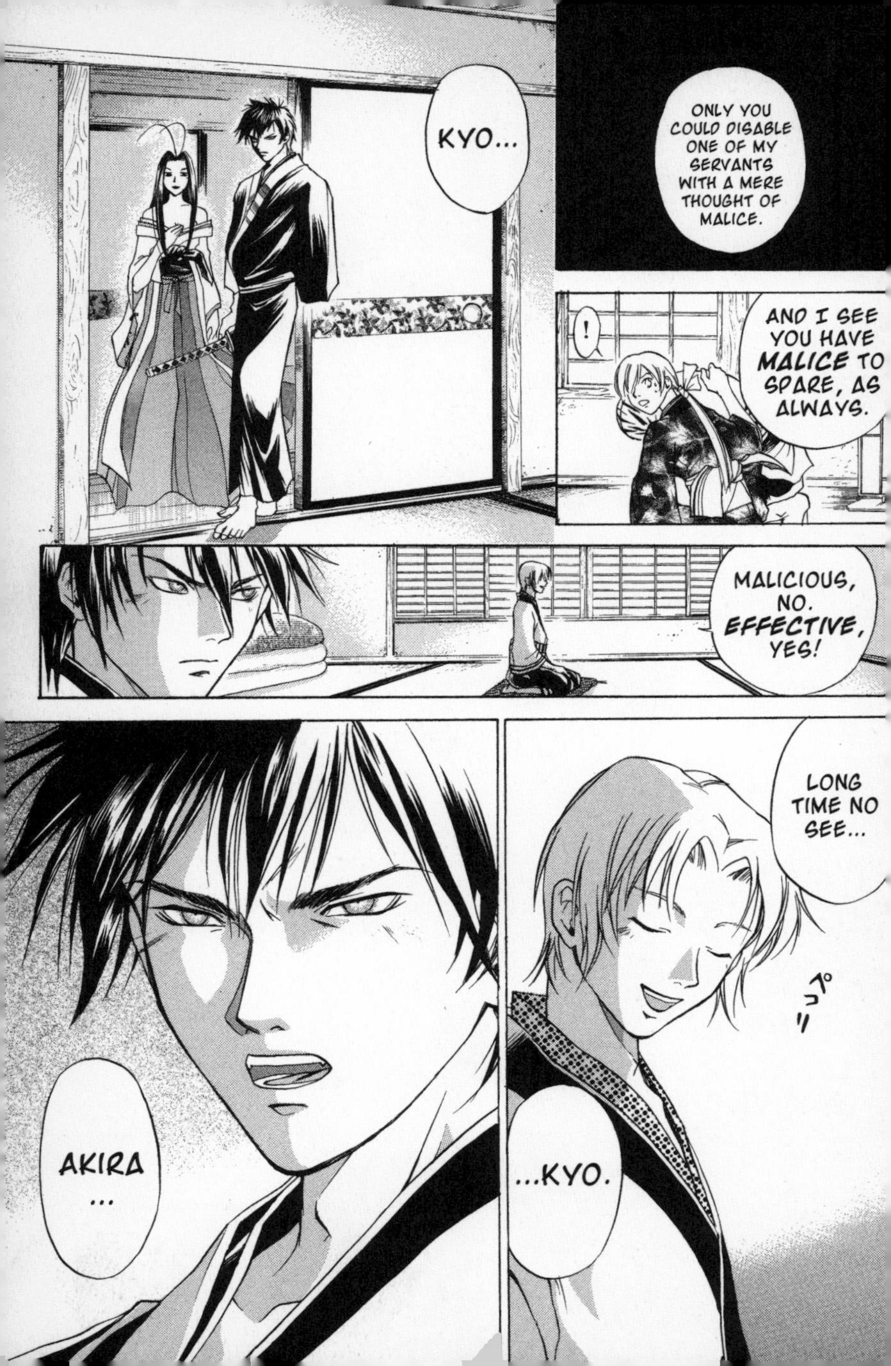
ONLY YOU COULD DISABLE ONE OF MY SERVANTS WITH A MERE THOUGHT OF MALICE.
!
AND I SEE YOU HAVE MALICE TO SPARE, AS ALWAYS.
KYO...
MALICIOUS, NO. EFFECTIVE, YES!
LONG TIME NO SEE...
...KYO.
AKIRA ...

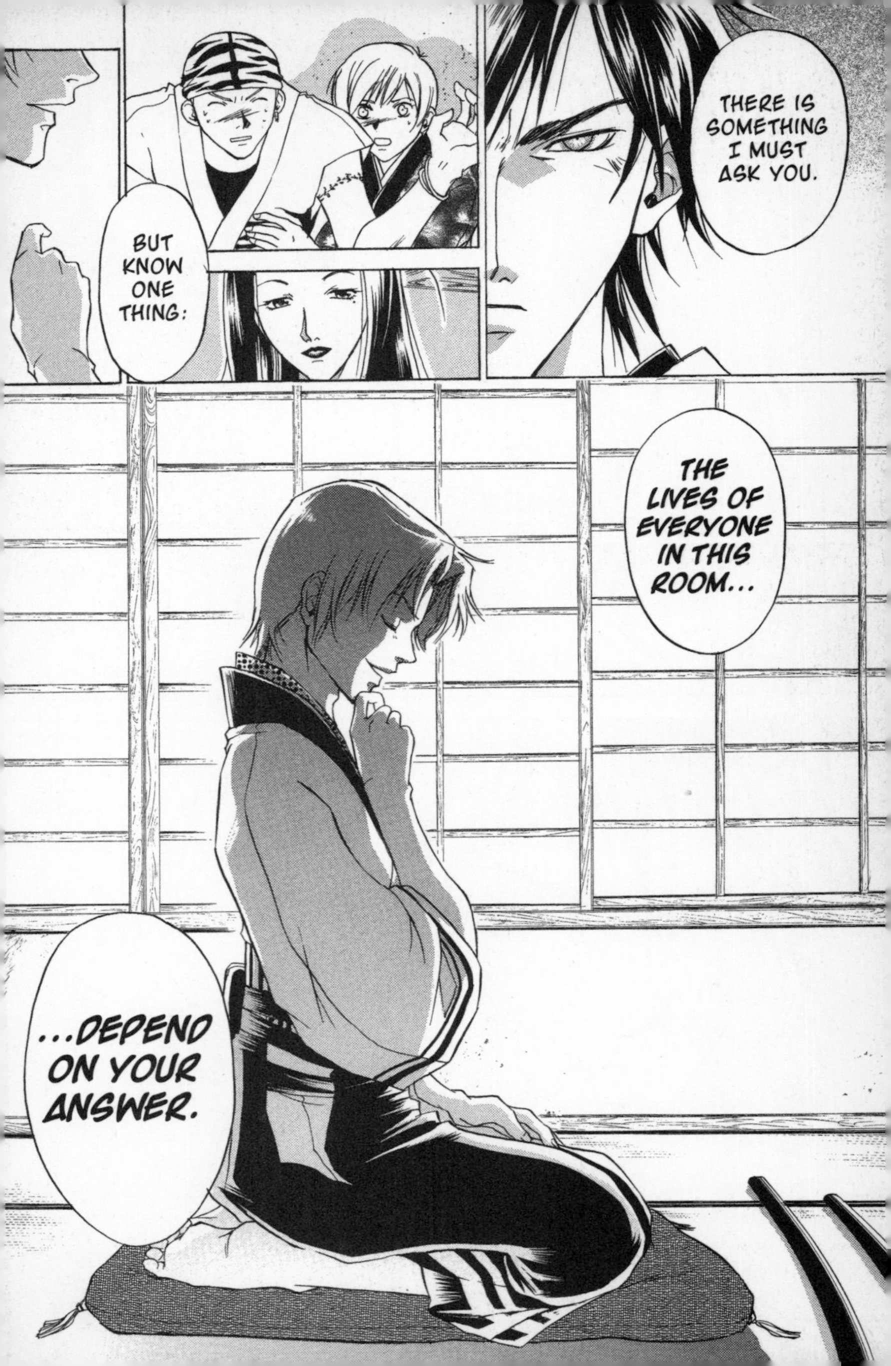
THERE IS SOMETHING I MUST ASK YOU.
BUT KNOW ONE THING:
THE LIVES OF EVERYONE IN THIS ROOM...
...DEPEND ON YOUR ANSWER.

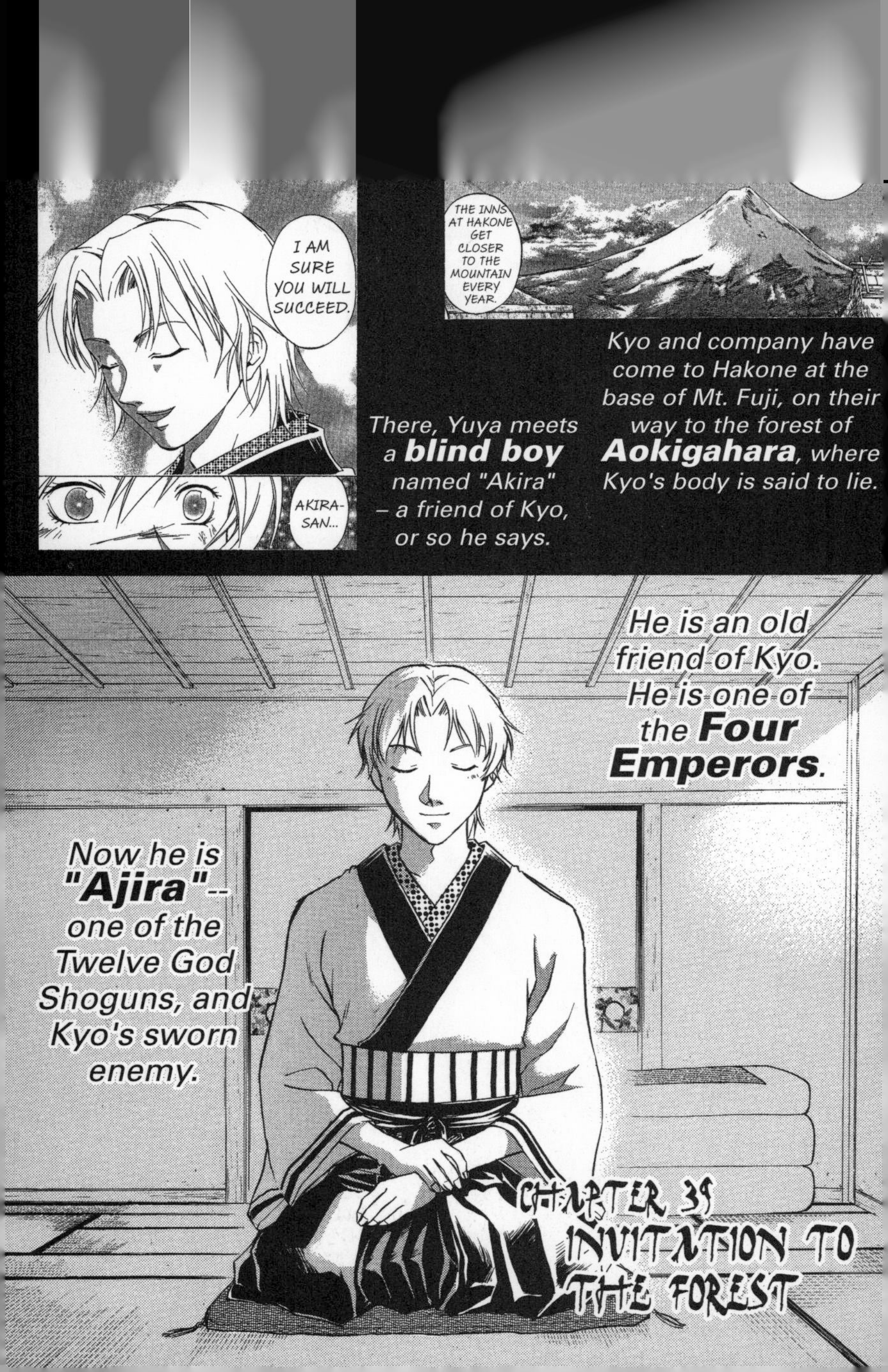
THE INNS AT HAKONE GET CLOSER TO THE MOUNTAIN EVERY YEAR.
Kyo and company have come to Hakone at the base of Mt. Fuji, on their way to the forest of Aokigahara, where Kyo's body is said to lie.
There, Yuya meets a blind boy named "Akira" – a friend of Kyo, or so he says.
I AM SURE YOU WILL SUCCEED.
AKIRA-SAN...
He is an old friend of Kyo. He is one of the Four Emperors.
Now he is "Ajira"-- one of the Twelve God Shoguns, and Kyo's sworn enemy.
CHAPTER 39
INVITATION TO THE FOREST

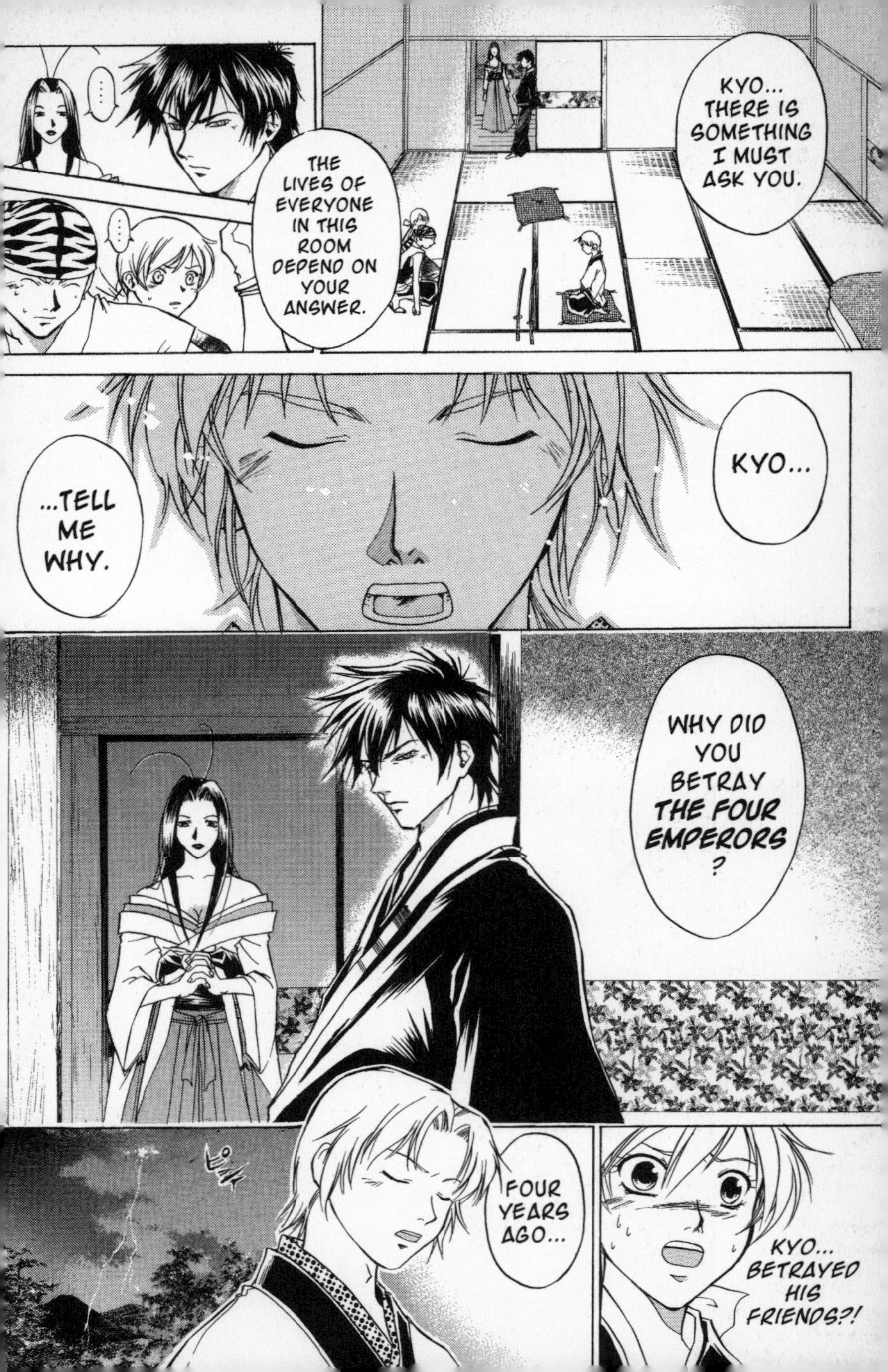
KYO... THERE IS SOMETHING I MUST ASK YOU.
THE LIVES OF EVERYONE IN THIS ROOM DEPEND ON YOUR ANSWER.
....
....
KYO...
...TELL ME WHY.
WHY DID YOU BETRAY **THE FOUR EMPERORS**?
KYO... BETRAYED HIS FRIENDS?!
FOUR YEARS AGO...
ピクッ

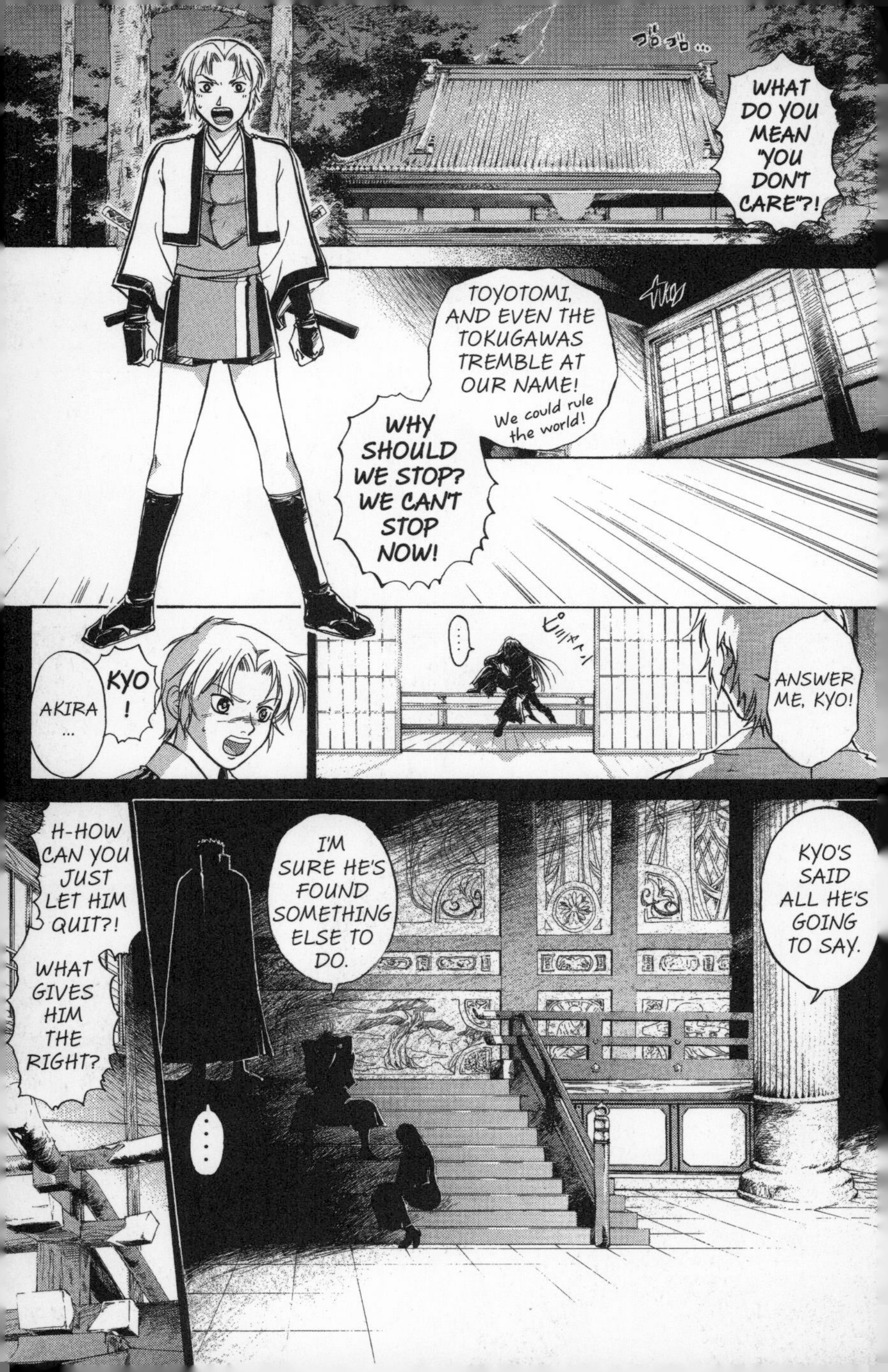
WHAT DO YOU MEAN "YOU DON'T CARE"?!
TOYOTOMI, AND EVEN THE TOKUGAWAS TREMBLE AT OUR NAME!
We could rule the world!
WHY SHOULD WE STOP? WE CAN'T STOP NOW!
ANSWER ME, KYO!
...
KYO!
AKIRA...
KYO'S SAID ALL HE'S GOING TO SAY.
I'M SURE HE'S FOUND SOMETHING ELSE TO DO.
H-HOW CAN YOU JUST LET HIM QUIT?!
WHAT GIVES HIM THE RIGHT?
...

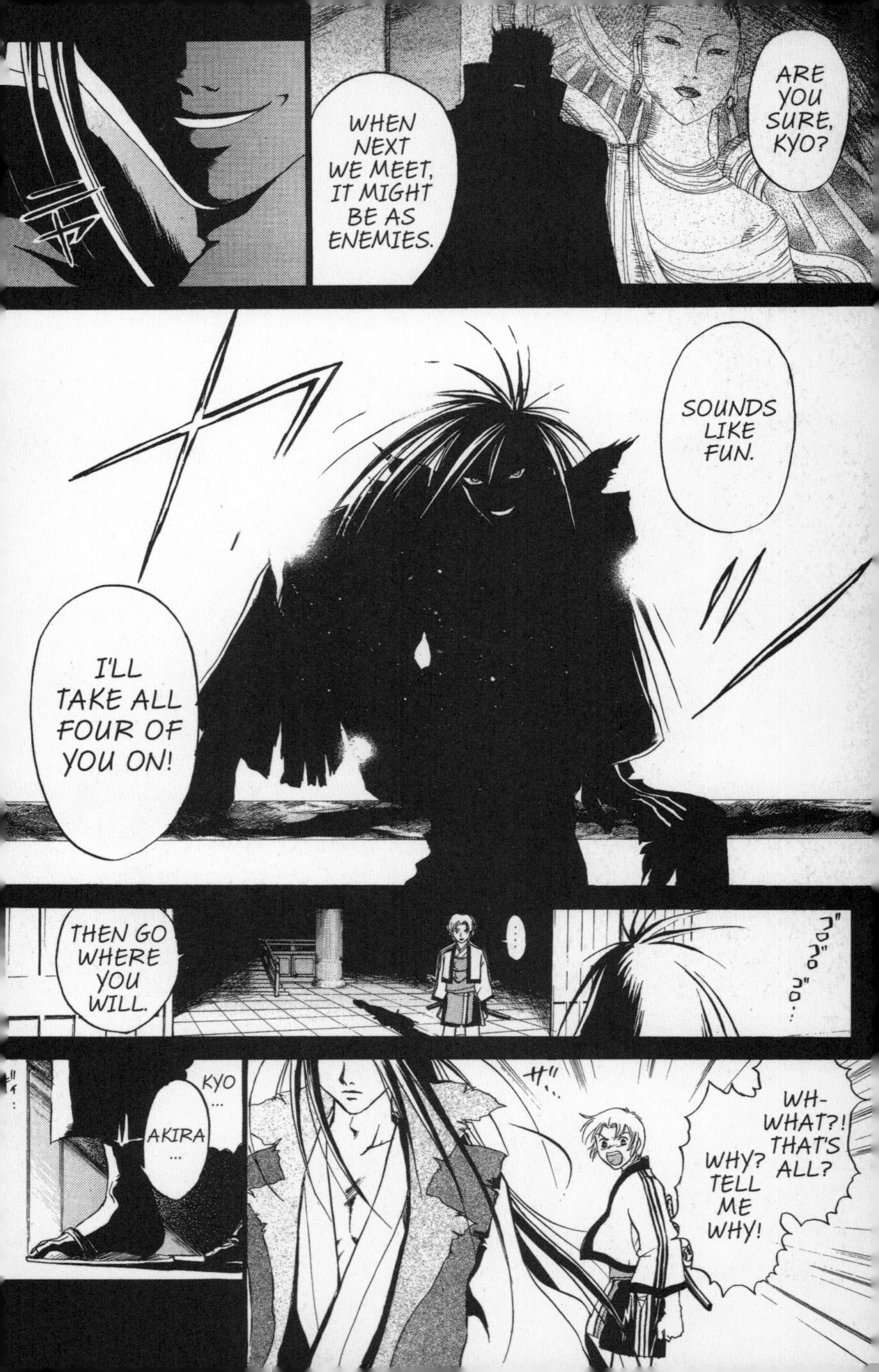
ARE YOU SURE, KYO?
WHEN NEXT WE MEET, IT MIGHT BE AS ENEMIES.
SOUNDS LIKE FUN.
I'LL TAKE ALL FOUR OF YOU ON!
...
THEN GO WHERE YOU WILL.
WH- WHAT?! THAT'S ALL?
WHY? TELL ME WHY!
KYO ...
AKIRA ...

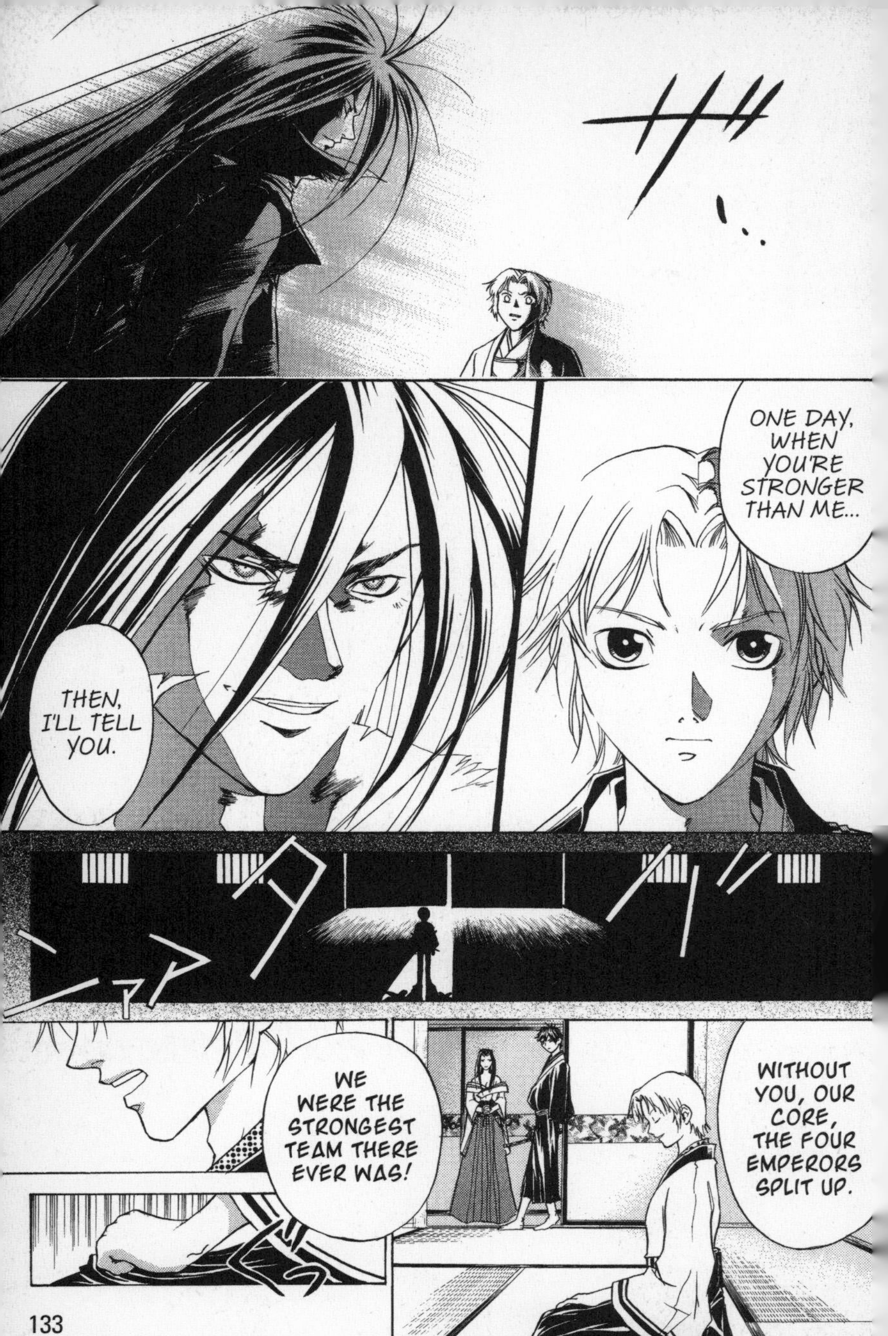
ONE DAY, WHEN YOU'RE STRONGER THAN ME...
THEN, I'LL TELL YOU.
WITHOUT YOU, OUR CORE, THE FOUR EMPERORS SPLIT UP.
WE WERE THE STRONGEST TEAM THERE EVER WAS!

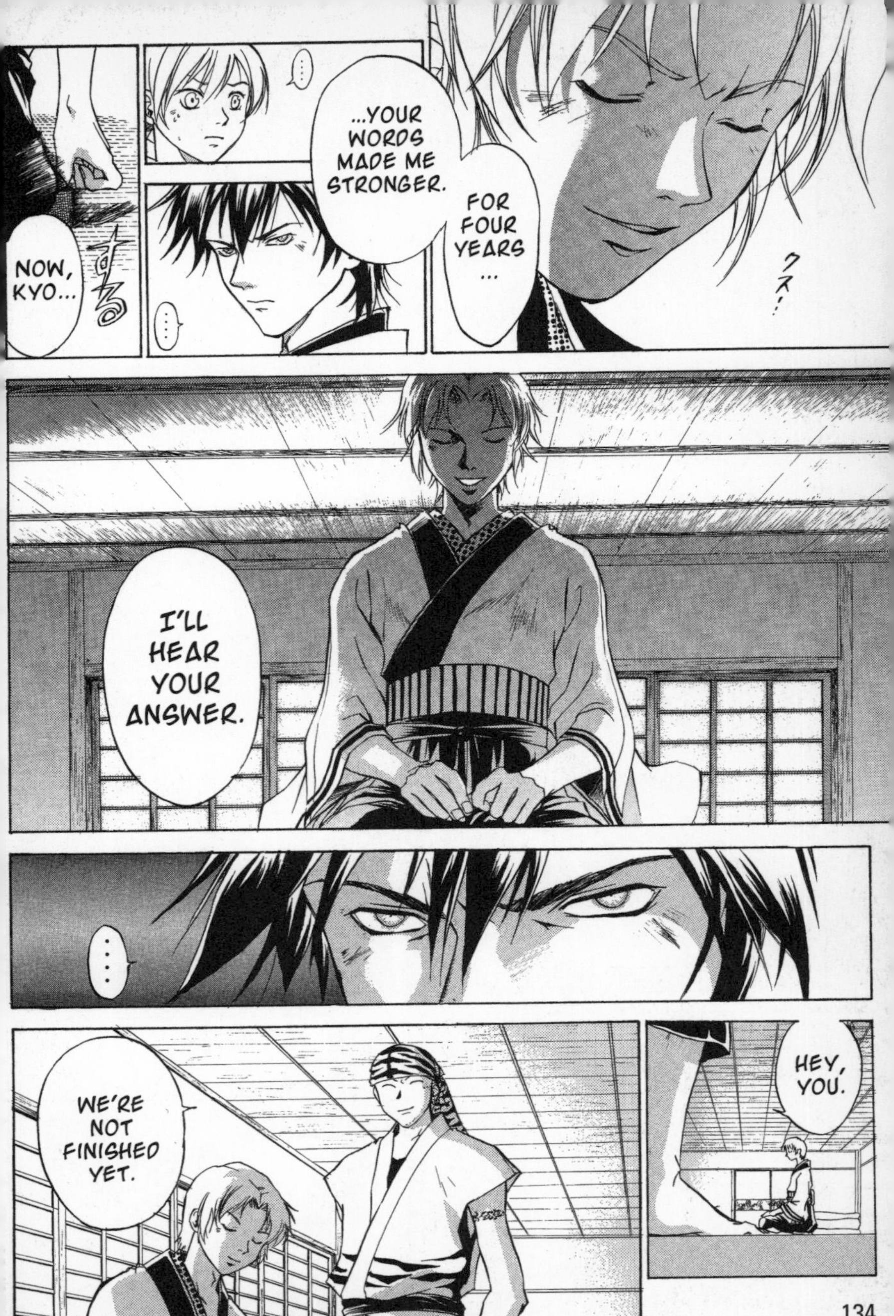
FOR FOUR YEARS...
...YOUR WORDS MADE ME STRONGER.
クス…
...
...
NOW, KYO...
するる
I'LL HEAR YOUR ANSWER.
...
HEY, YOU.
WE'RE NOT FINISHED YET.

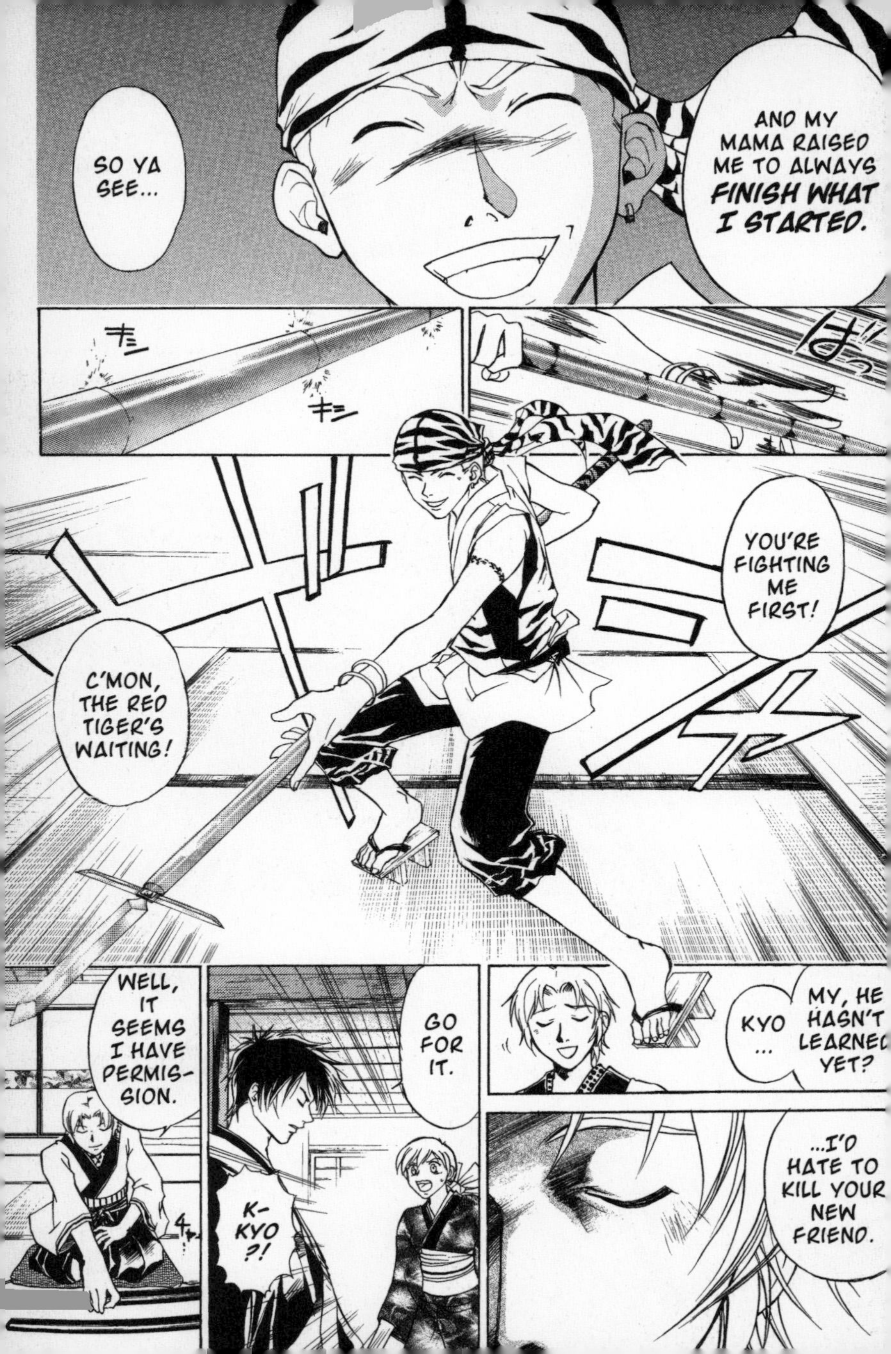
AND MY MAMA RAISED ME TO ALWAYS FINISH WHAT I STARTED.
SO YA SEE...
YOU'RE FIGHTING ME FIRST!
C'MON, THE RED TIGER'S WAITING!
MY, HE HASN'T LEARNED YET?
KYO ...
...I'D HATE TO KILL YOUR NEW FRIEND.
GO FOR IT.
K-KYO ?!
WELL, IT SEEMS I HAVE PERMIS-SION.

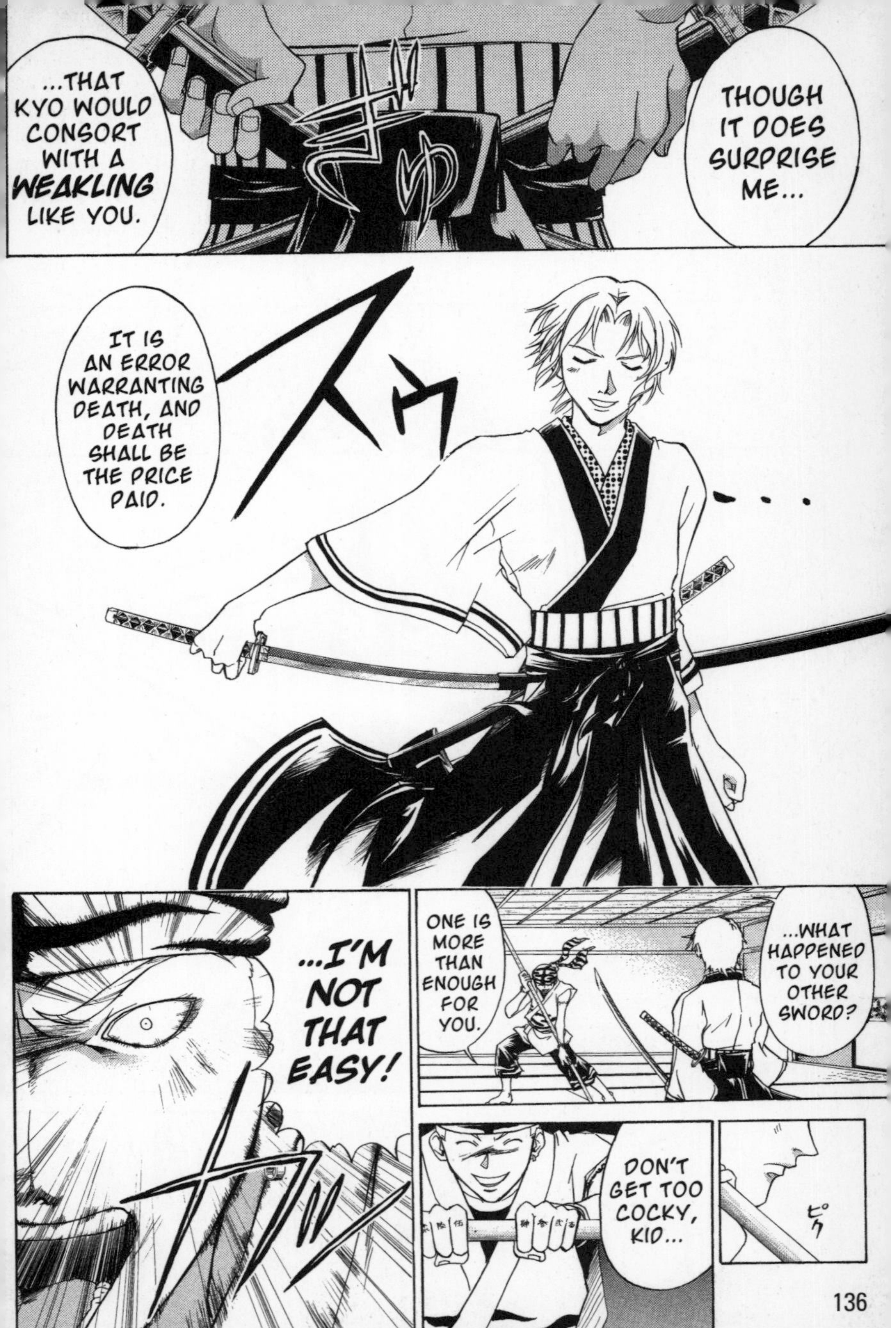
THOUGH IT DOES SURPRISE ME...
...THAT KYO WOULD CONSORT WITH A WEAKLING LIKE YOU.
IT IS AN ERROR WARRANTING DEATH, AND DEATH SHALL BE THE PRICE PAID.
...
...WHAT HAPPENED TO YOUR OTHER SWORD?
ONE IS MORE THAN ENOUGH FOR YOU.
ピク
DON'T GET TOO COCKY, KID...
...I'M NOT THAT EASY!

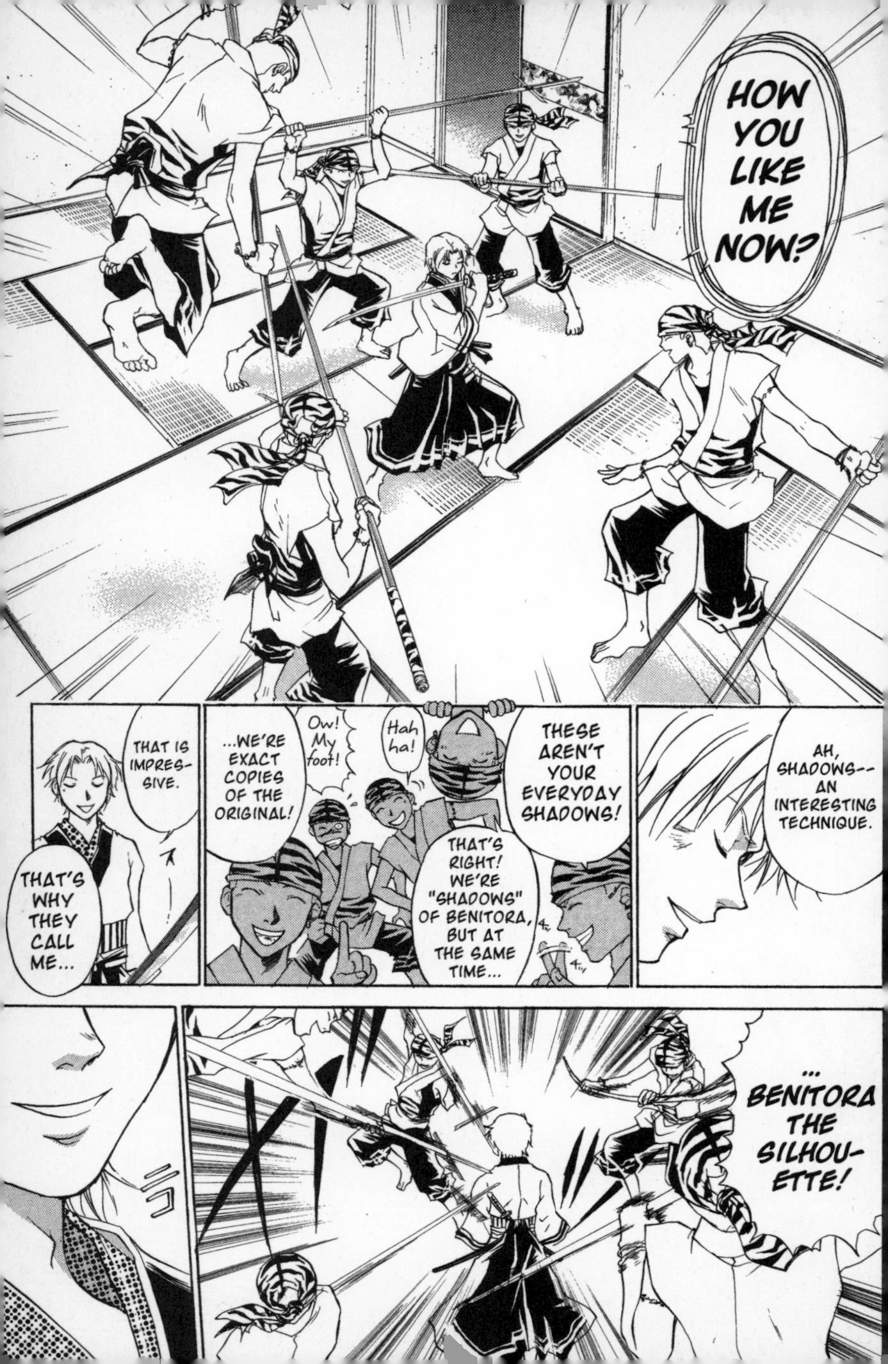
HOW YOU LIKE ME NOW?
AH, SHADOWS--AN INTERESTING TECHNIQUE.
THESE AREN'T YOUR EVERYDAY SHADOWS!
Hah ha!
Ow! My foot!
THAT'S RIGHT! WE'RE "SHADOWS" OF BENITORA, BUT AT THE SAME TIME...
...WE'RE EXACT COPIES OF THE ORIGINAL!
THAT IS IMPRESSIVE.
THAT'S WHY THEY CALL ME...
...BENITORA THE SILHOUETTE!
ニコ

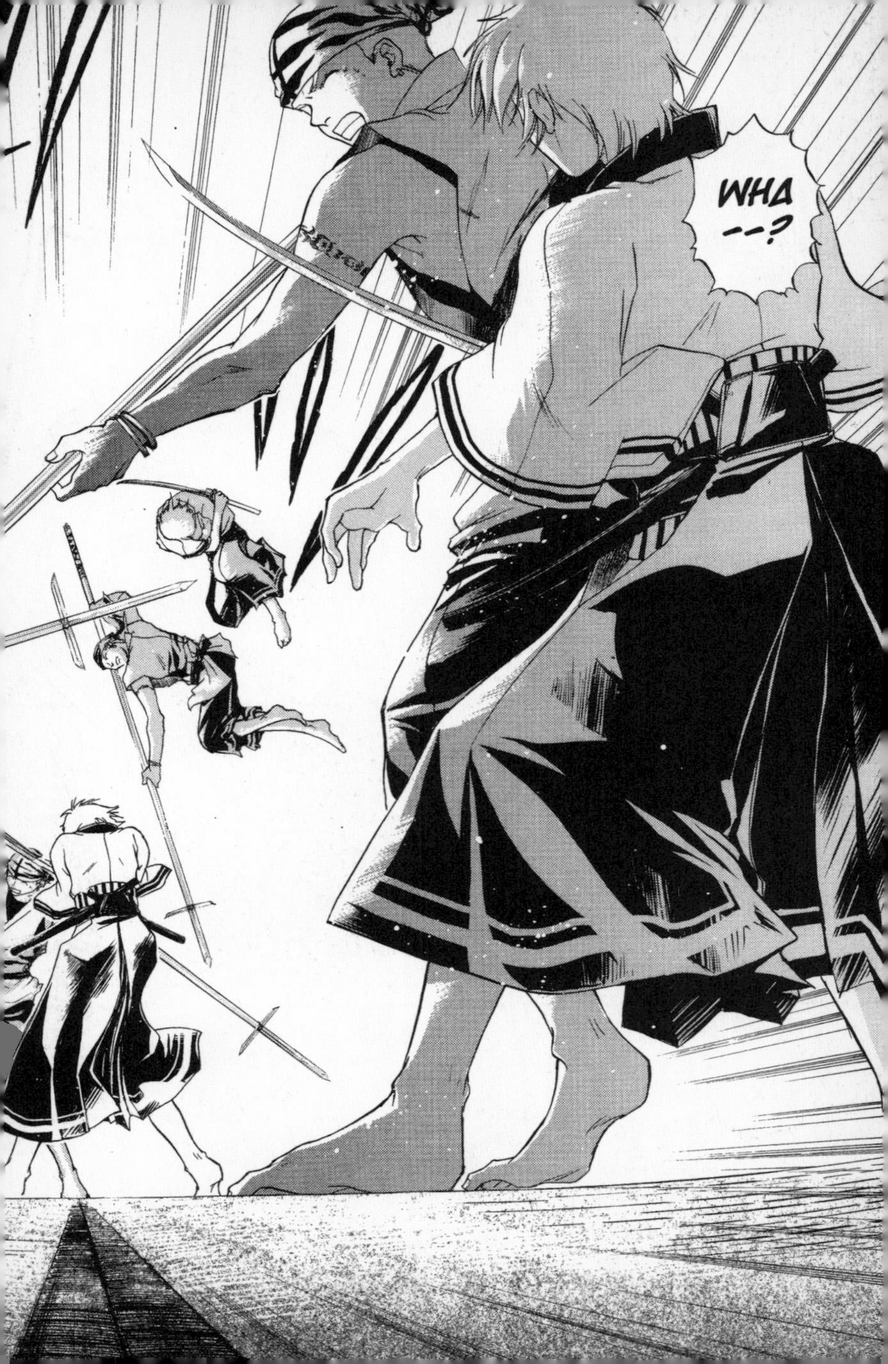
WHA--?

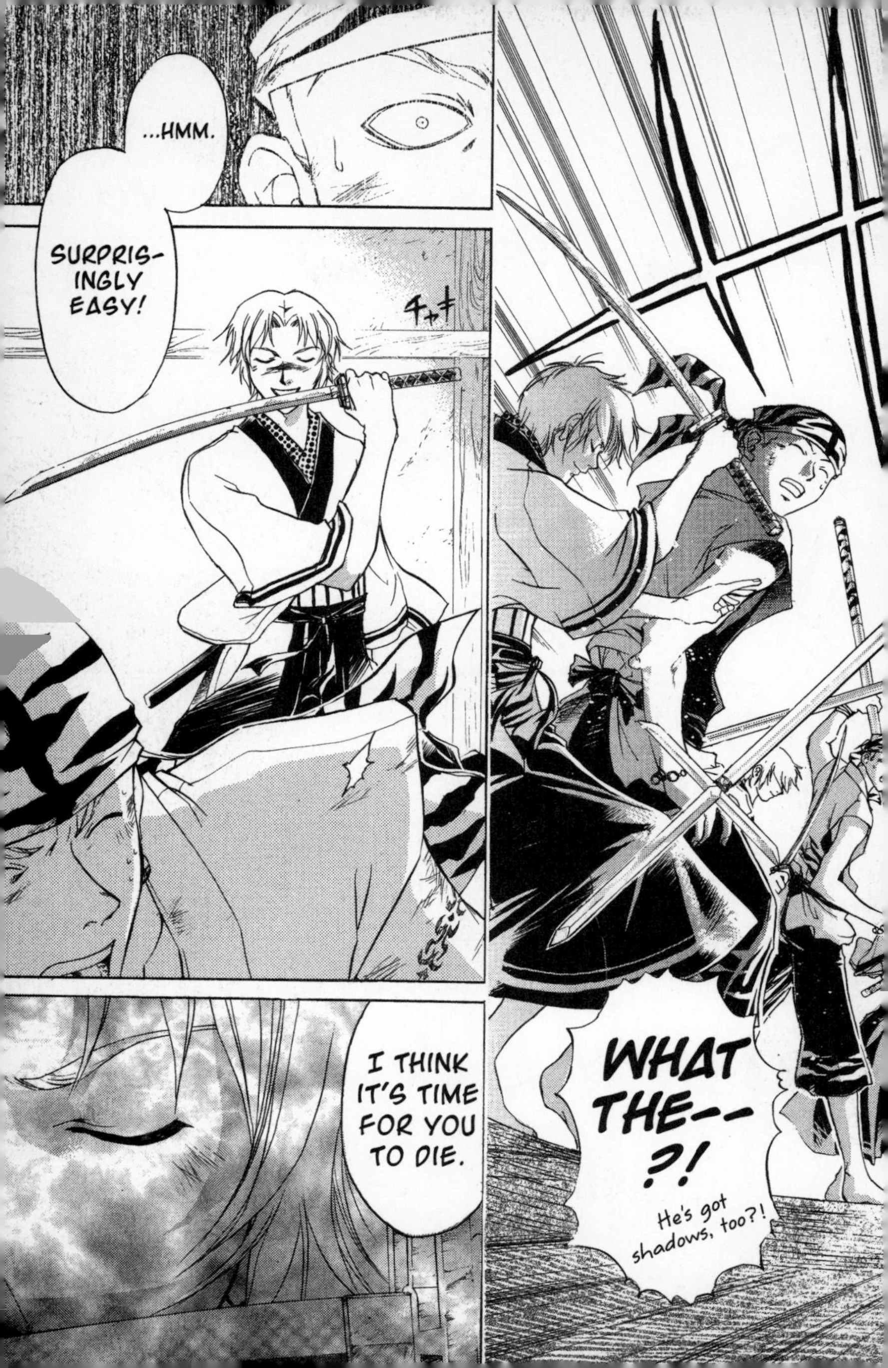
WHAT THE--?!
He's got shadows, too?!
...HMM.
SURPRIS-INGLY EASY!
チャキ
I THINK IT'S TIME FOR YOU TO DIE.

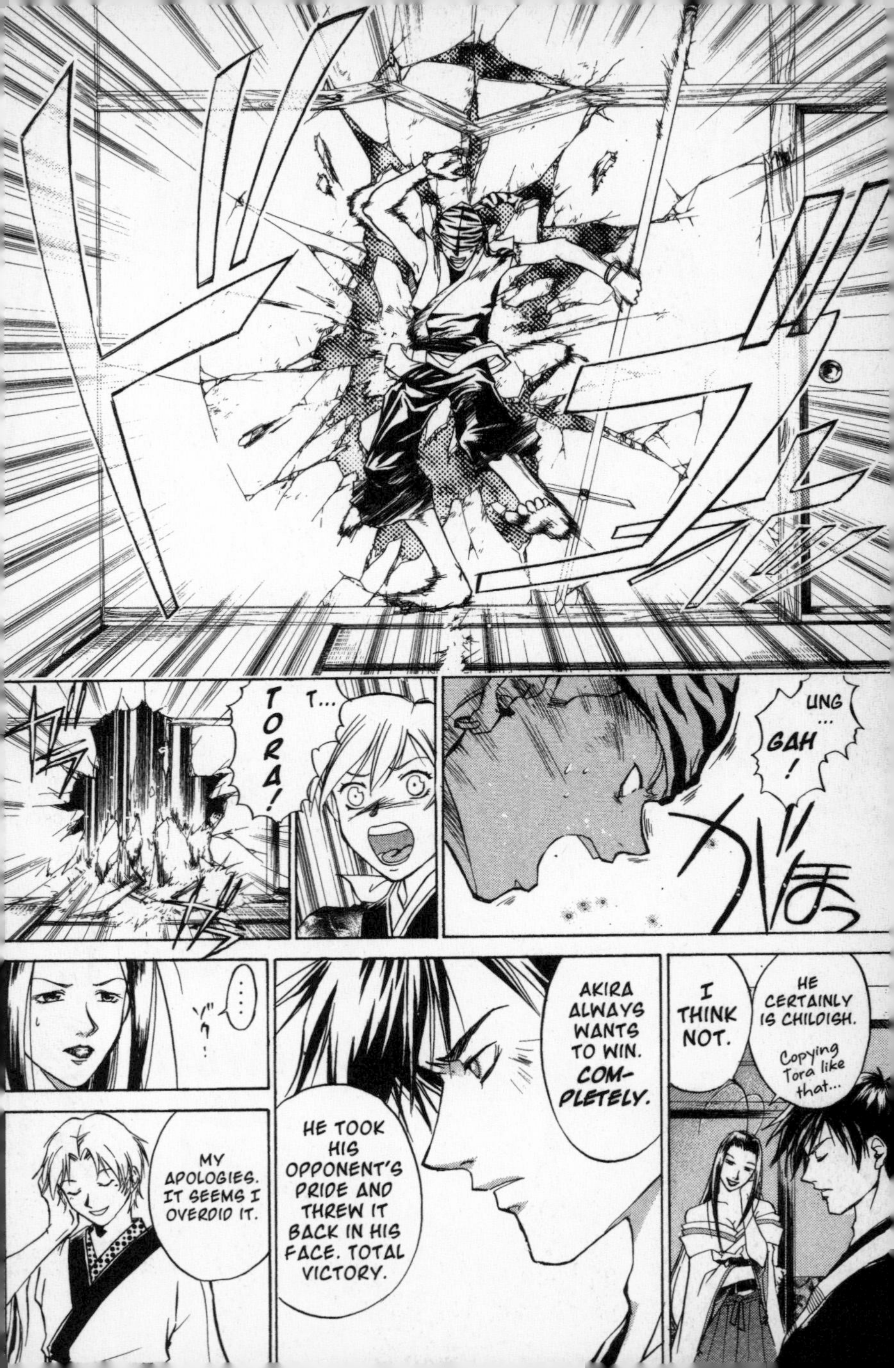
UNG ... GAH!
T...
TORA!
HE CERTAINLY IS CHILDISH.
Copying Tora like that...
I THINK NOT.
AKIRA ALWAYS WANTS TO WIN. COMPLETELY.
HE TOOK HIS OPPONENT'S PRIDE AND THREW IT BACK IN HIS FACE. TOTAL VICTORY.
....
MY APOLOGIES. IT SEEMS I OVERDID IT.

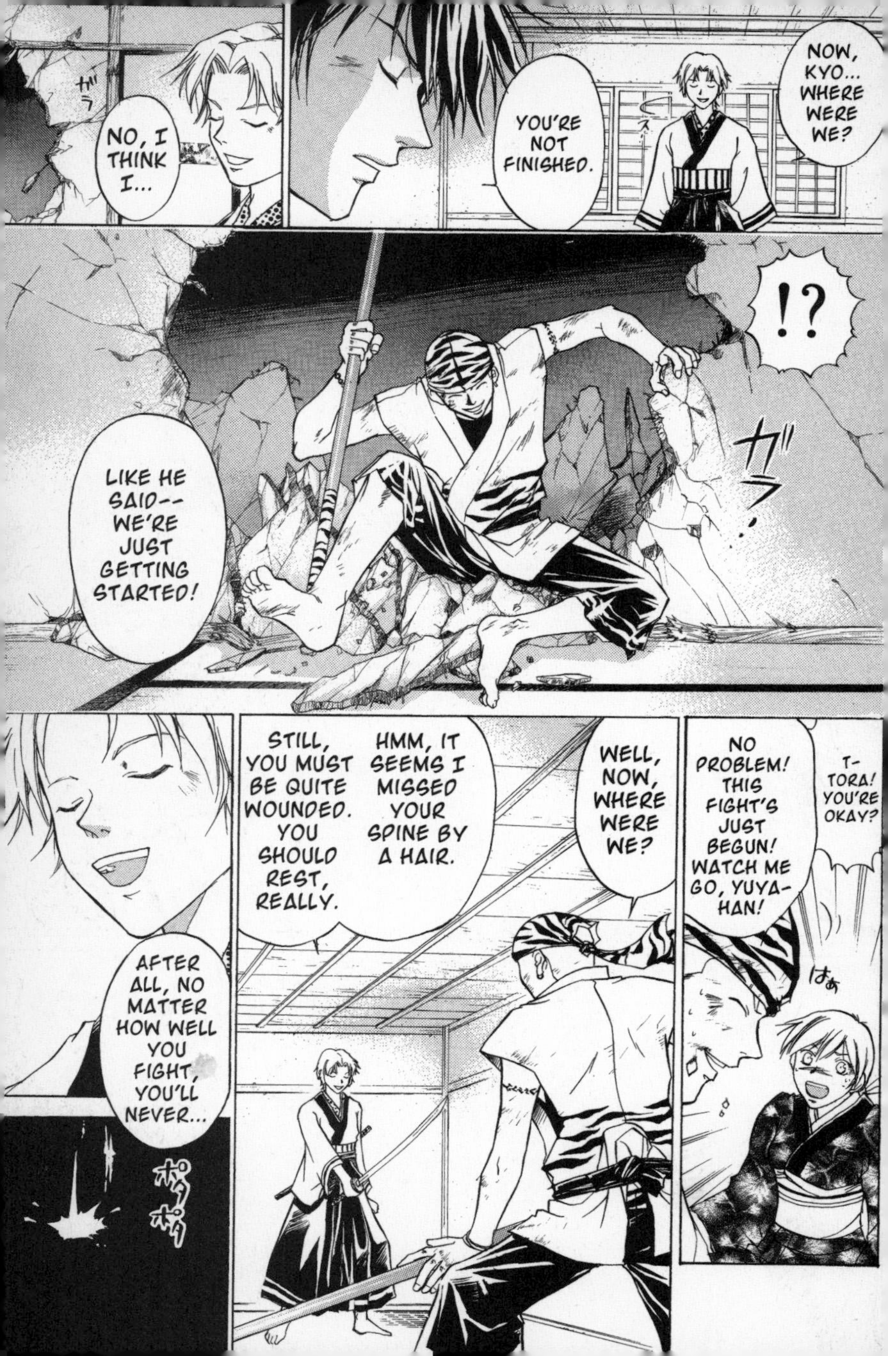
NOW, KYO... WHERE WERE WE?
YOU'RE NOT FINISHED.
ガラ
NO, I THINK I...
!?
ガラ
LIKE HE SAID-- WE'RE JUST GETTING STARTED!
T-TORA! YOU'RE OKAY?
NO PROBLEM! THIS FIGHT'S JUST BEGUN! WATCH ME GO, YUYA-HAN!
はぁ
WELL, NOW, WHERE WERE WE?
HMM, IT SEEMS I MISSED YOUR SPINE BY A HAIR.
STILL, YOU MUST BE QUITE WOUNDED. YOU SHOULD REST, REALLY.
AFTER ALL, NO MATTER HOW WELL YOU FIGHT, YOU'LL NEVER...
ポタポタ

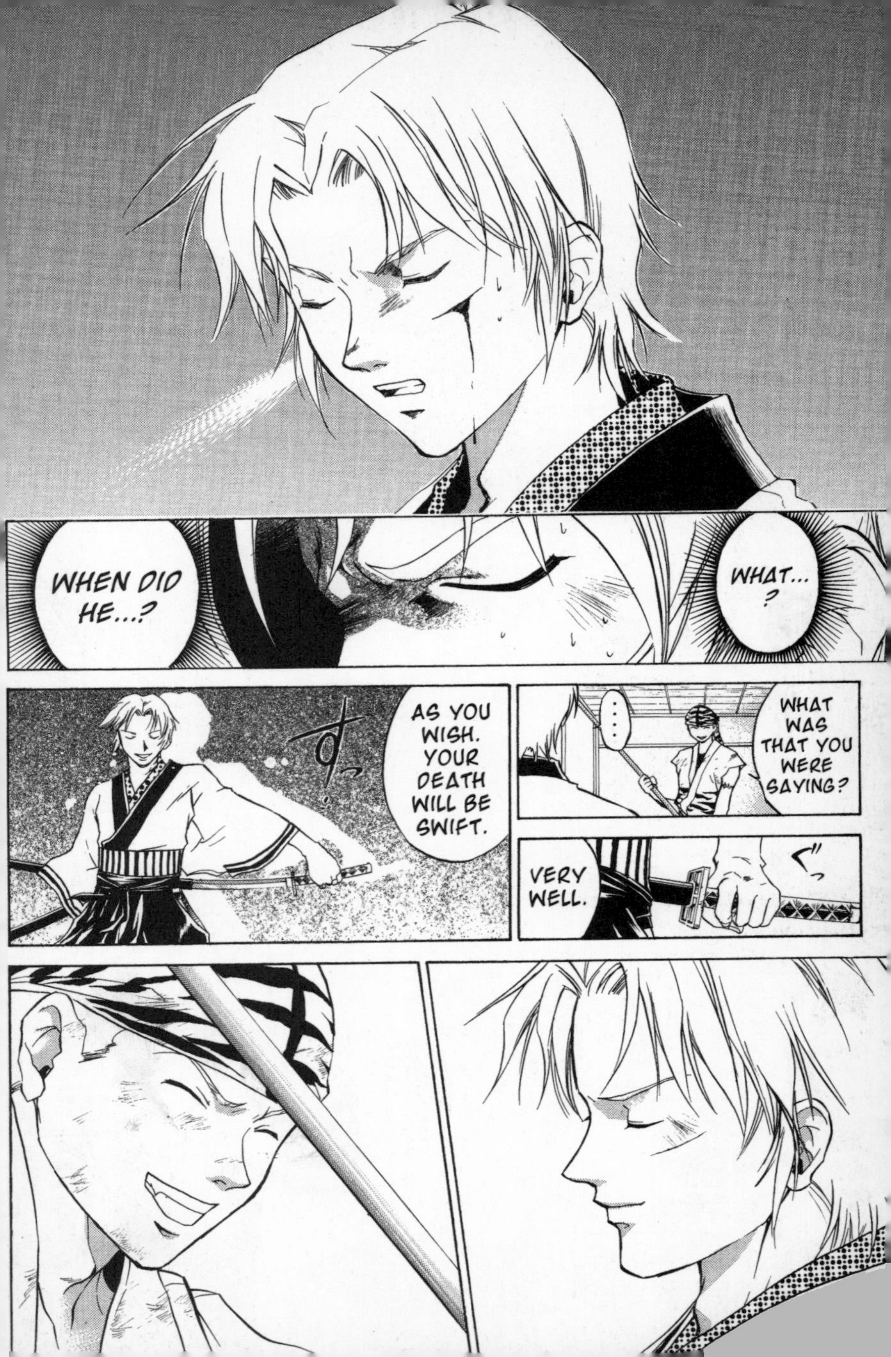
WHAT...?
WHEN DID HE...?
WHAT WAS THAT YOU WERE SAYING?
....
VERY WELL.
ぐっ
AS YOU WISH. YOUR DEATH WILL BE SWIFT.
すっ

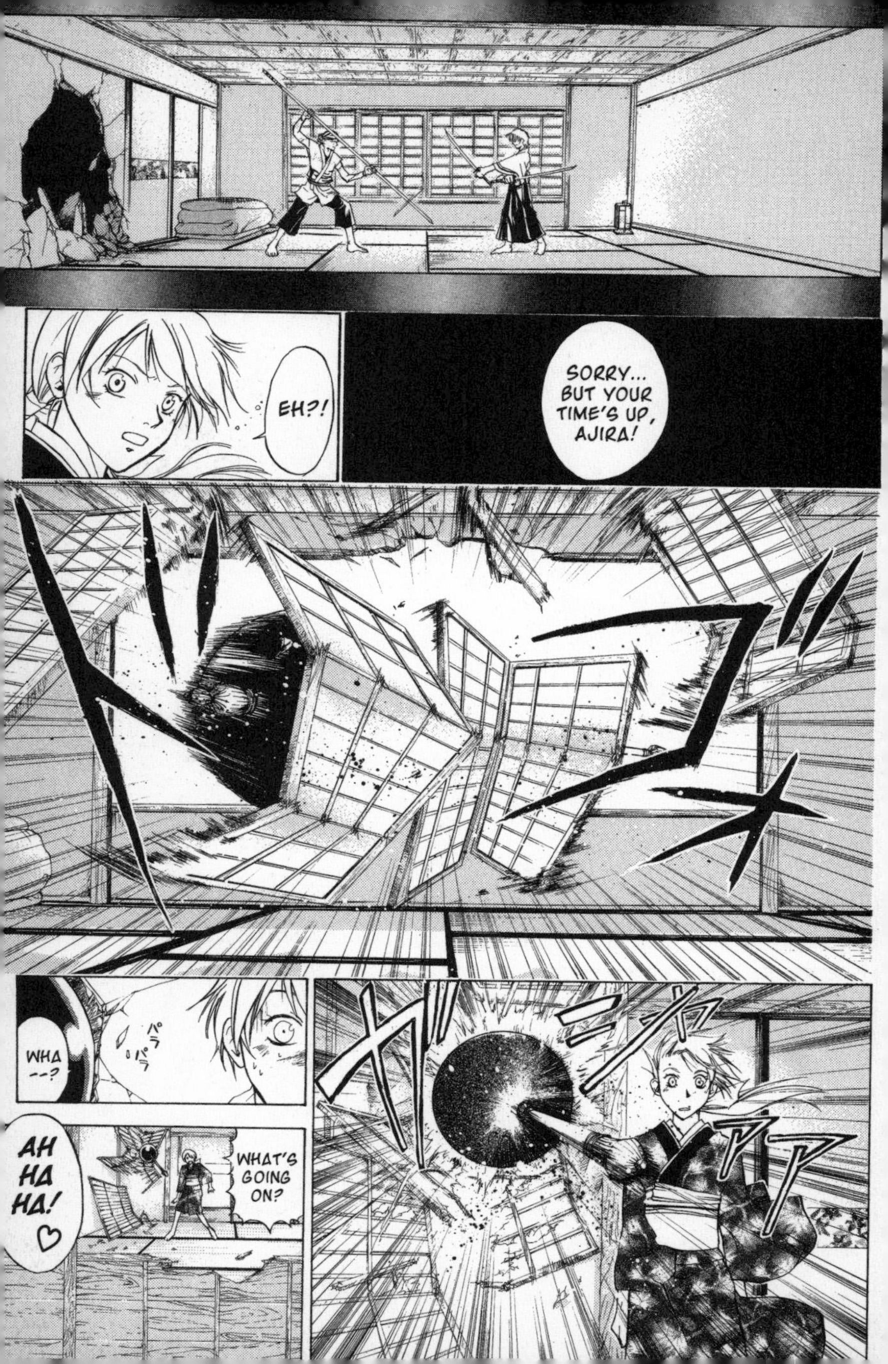
SORRY... BUT YOUR TIME'S UP, AJIRA!
EH?!
WHA--?
WHAT'S GOING ON?
AH HA HA! ♡

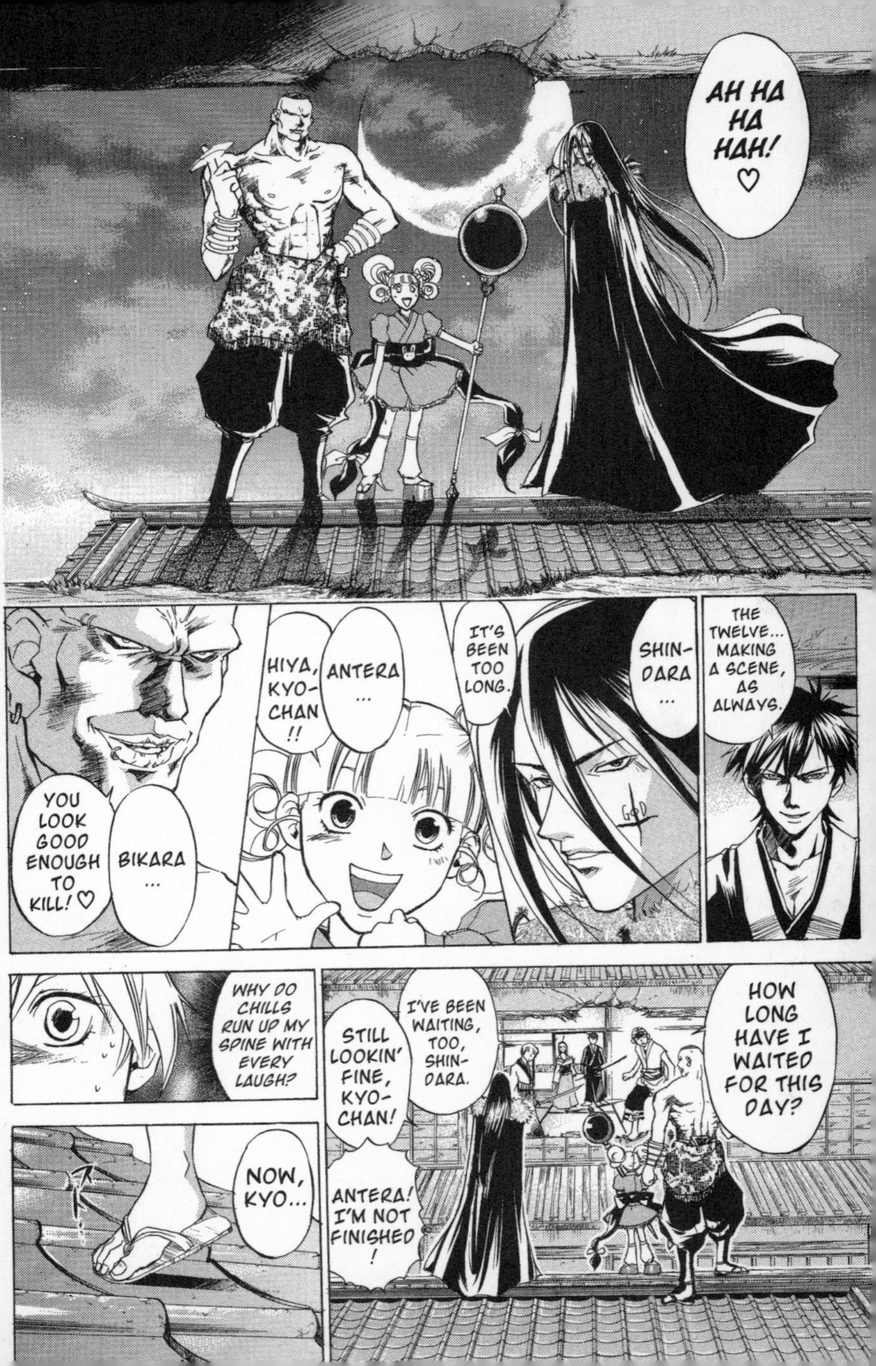
AH HA HA HA HAH! ♡
THE TWELVE... MAKING A SCENE, AS ALWAYS.
SHIN-DARA ...
IT'S BEEN TOO LONG.
ANTERA ...
HIYA, KYO-CHAN !!
BIKARA ...
YOU LOOK GOOD ENOUGH TO KILL! ♡
HOW LONG HAVE I WAITED FOR THIS DAY?
I'VE BEEN WAITING, TOO, SHIN-DARA.
STILL LOOKIN' FINE, KYO-CHAN!
ANTERA! I'M NOT FINISHED!
WHY DO CHILLS RUN UP MY SPINE WITH EVERY LAUGH?
NOW, KYO...

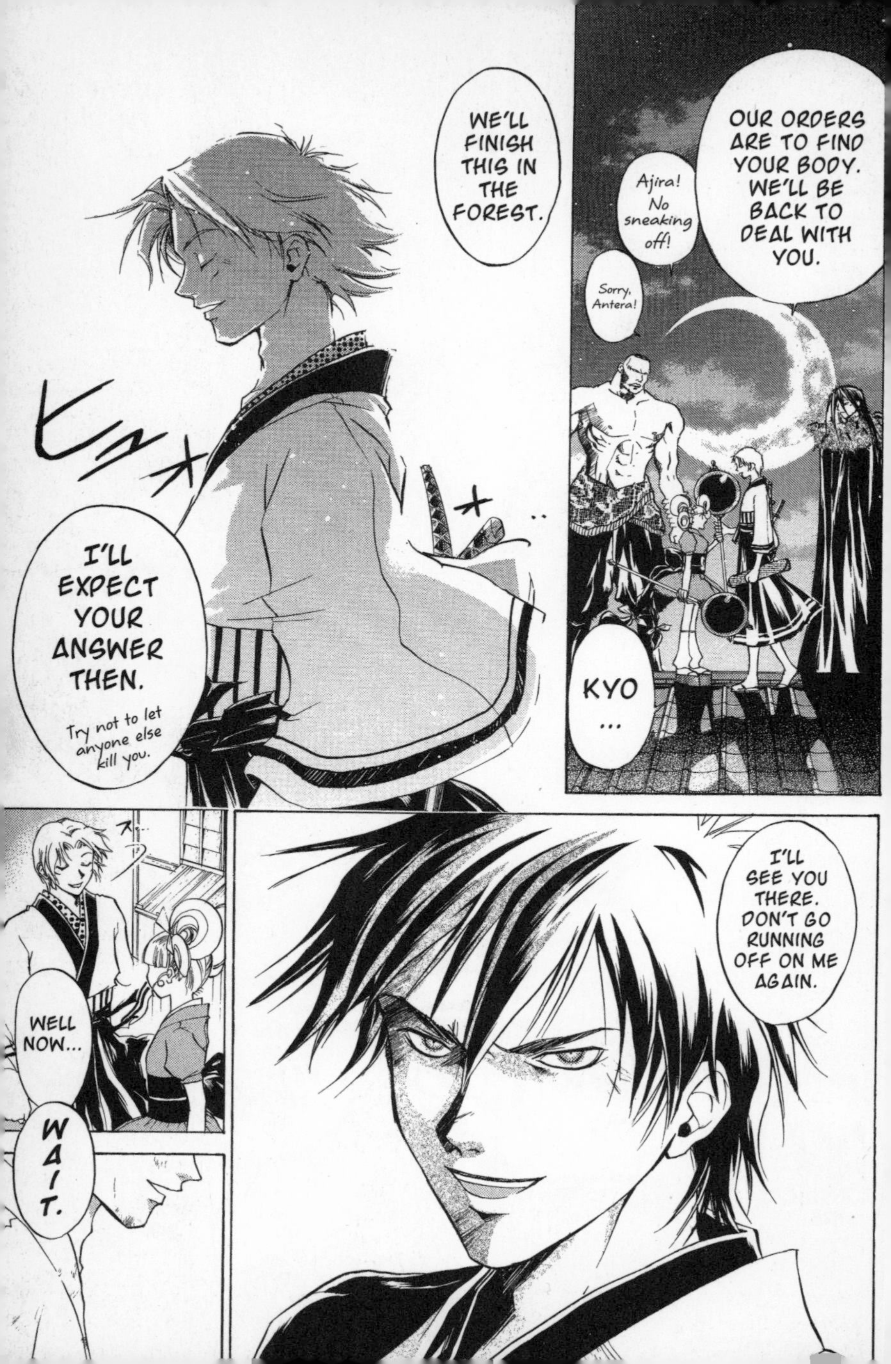
OUR ORDERS ARE TO FIND YOUR BODY. WE'LL BE BACK TO DEAL WITH YOU.
Ajira! No sneaking off!
Sorry, Antera!
KYO ...
WE'LL FINISH THIS IN THE FOREST.
I'LL EXPECT YOUR ANSWER THEN.
Try not to let anyone else kill you.
I'LL SEE YOU THERE. DON'T GO RUNNING OFF ON ME AGAIN.
WELL NOW...
WAIT.

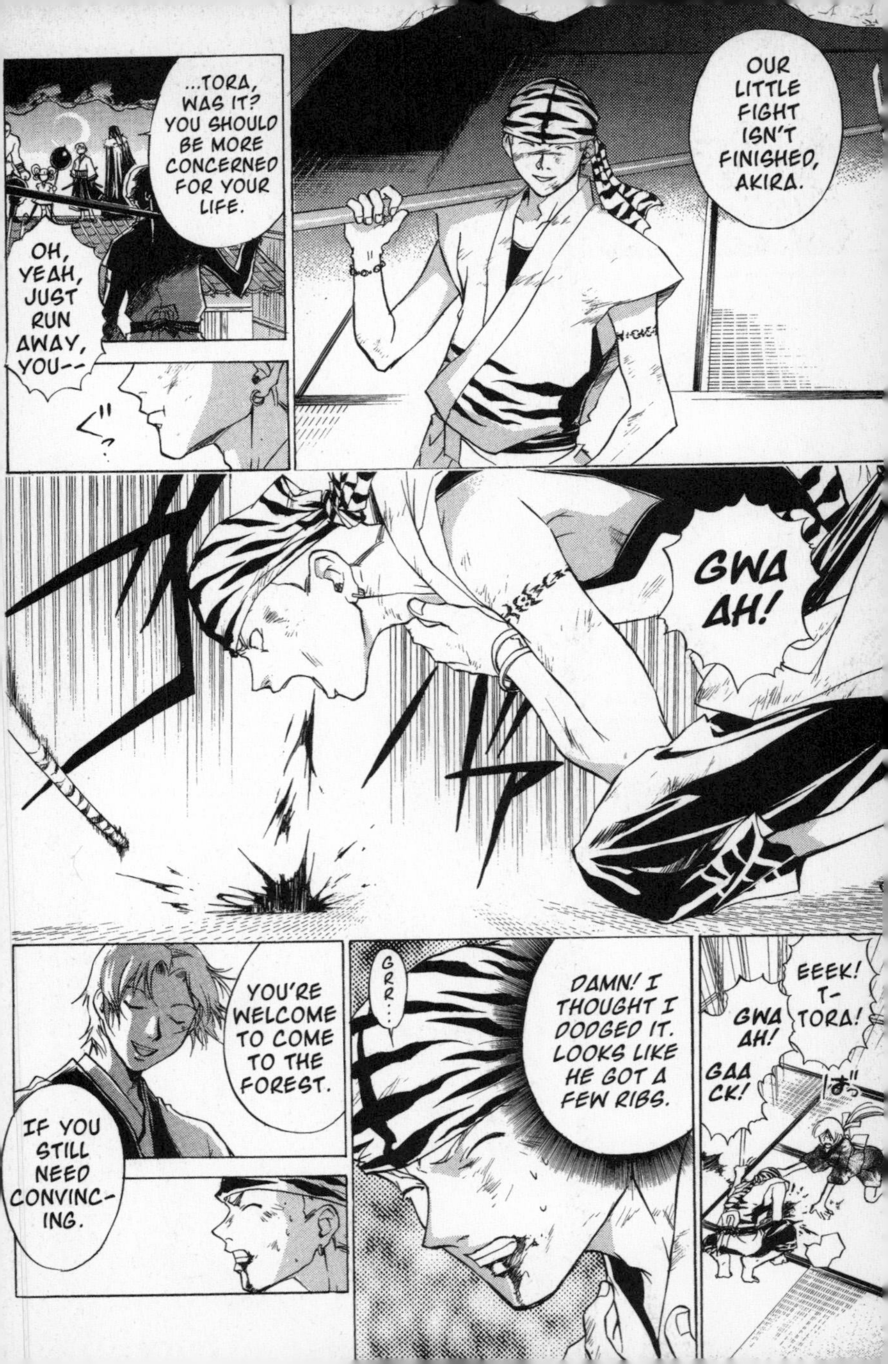
OUR LITTLE FIGHT ISN'T FINISHED, AKIRA.
...TORA, WAS IT? YOU SHOULD BE MORE CONCERNED FOR YOUR LIFE.
OH, YEAH, JUST RUN AWAY, YOU--
GWA AH!
EEEK! T-TORA!
GWA AH!
GAA CK!
GRR...
DAMN! I THOUGHT I DODGED IT. LOOKS LIKE HE GOT A FEW RIBS.
YOU'RE WELCOME TO COME TO THE FOREST.
IF YOU STILL NEED CONVINC-ING.

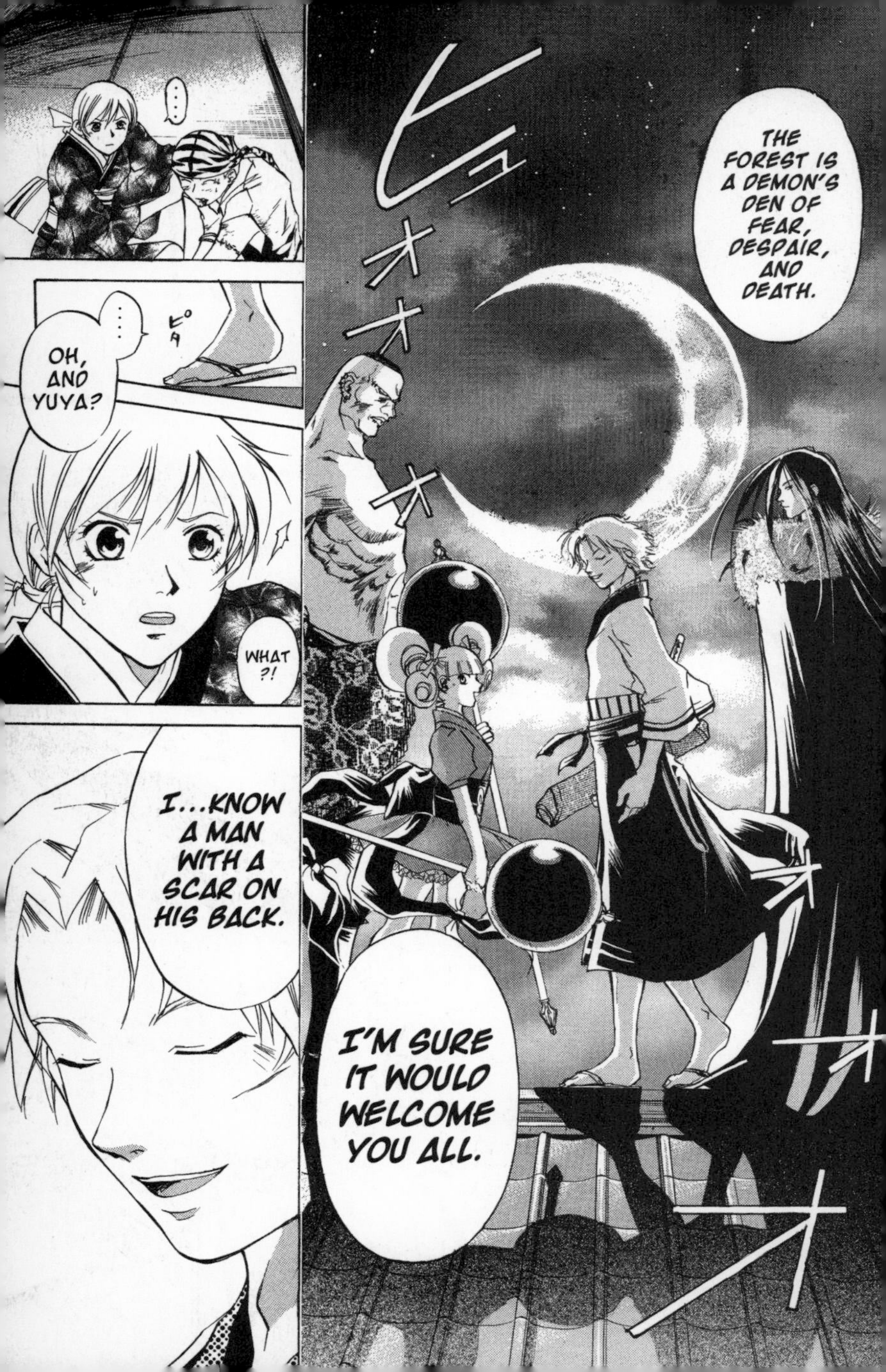
ヒュオオオ
THE FOREST IS A DEMON'S DEN OF FEAR, DESPAIR, AND DEATH.
I'M SURE IT WOULD WELCOME YOU ALL.
...
...
ピタ
OH, AND YUYA?
WHAT?!
I...KNOW A MAN WITH A SCAR ON HIS BACK.

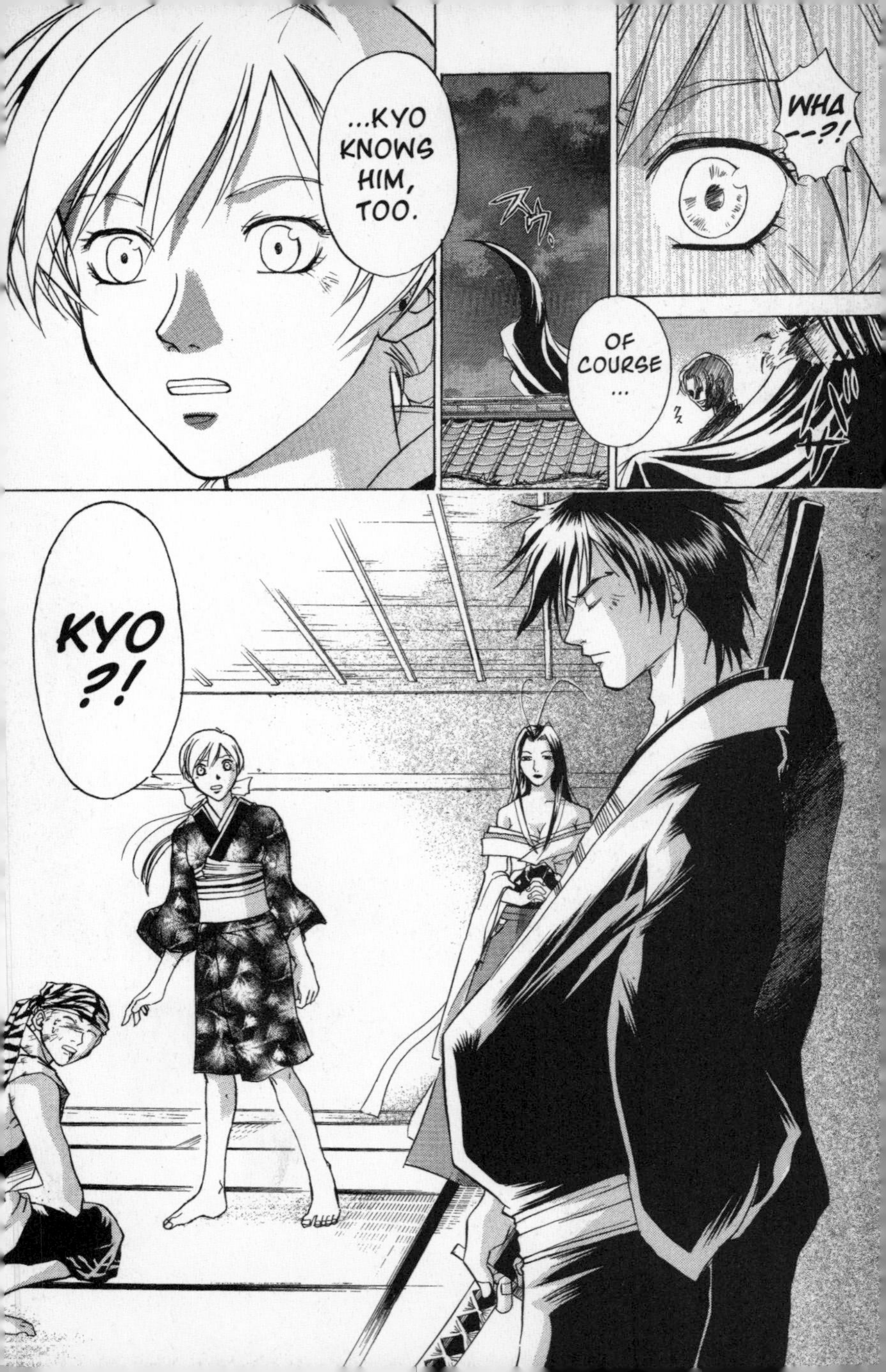
WHA--?!
OF COURSE...
...KYO KNOWS HIM, TOO.
KYO?!

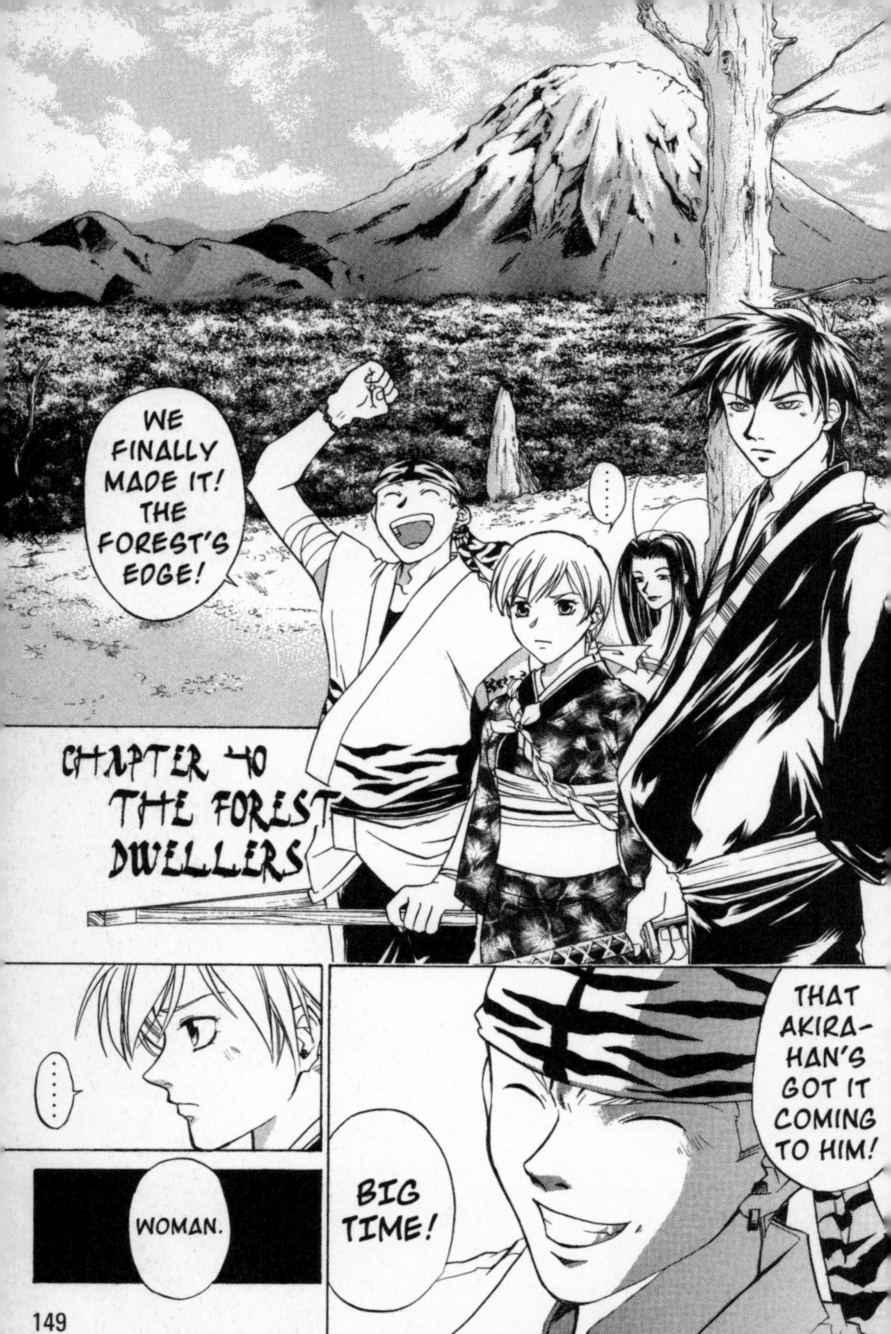
WE FINALLY MADE IT! THE FOREST'S EDGE!
......
CHAPTER 40
THE FOREST DWELLERS
THAT AKIRA-HAN'S GOT IT COMING TO HIM!
BIG TIME!
......
WOMAN.

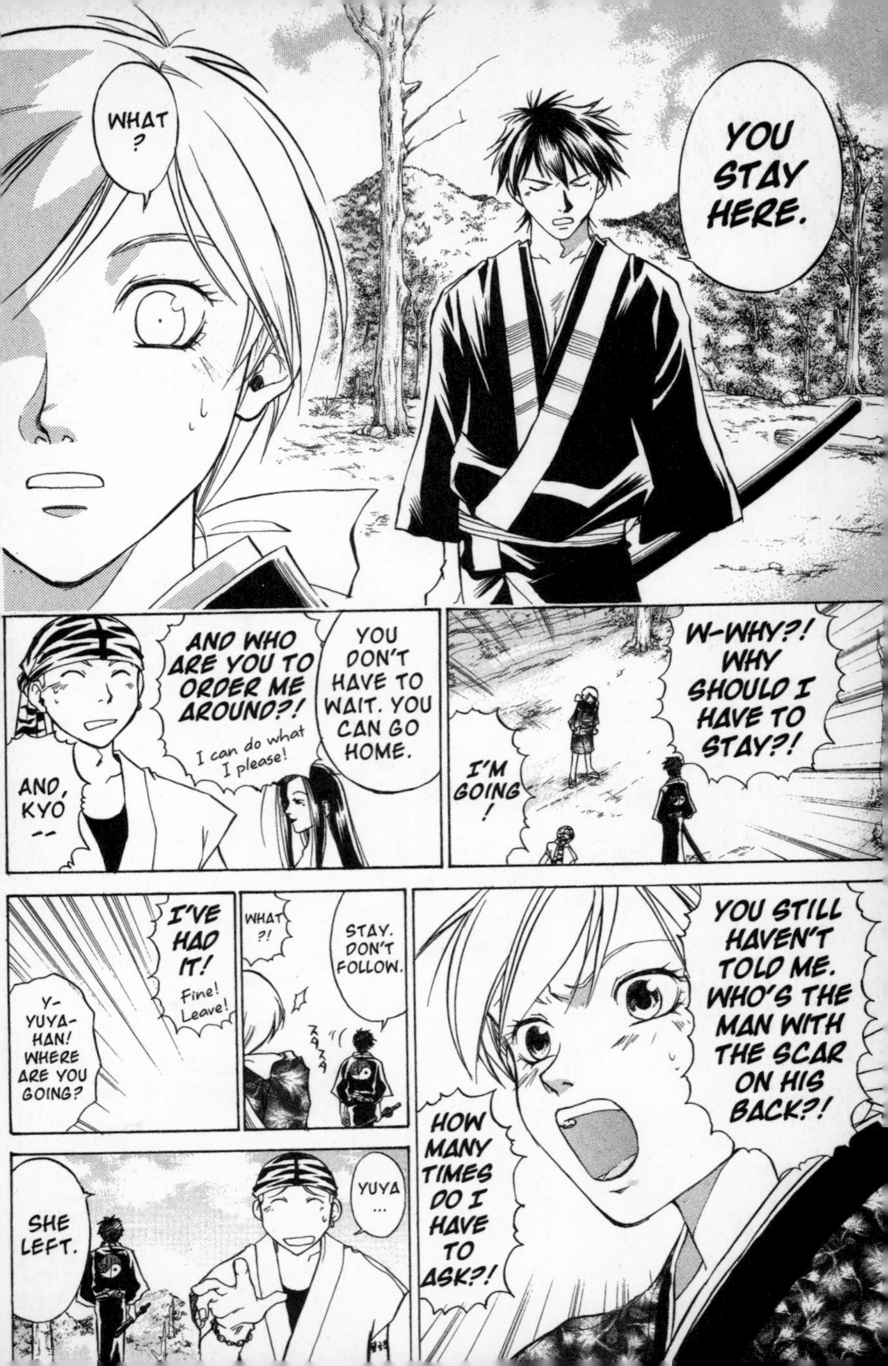
YOU STAY HERE.
WHAT?
W-WHY?! WHY SHOULD I HAVE TO STAY?!
I'M GOING!
YOU DON'T HAVE TO WAIT. YOU CAN GO HOME.
AND WHO ARE YOU TO ORDER ME AROUND?!
I can do what I please!
AND, KYO --
YOU STILL HAVEN'T TOLD ME. WHO'S THE MAN WITH THE SCAR ON HIS BACK?!
HOW MANY TIMES DO I HAVE TO ASK?!
STAY. DON'T FOLLOW.
WHAT?!
スタスタ
I'VE HAD IT!
Fine! Leave!
Y-YUYA-HAN! WHERE ARE YOU GOING?
YUYA...
SHE LEFT.

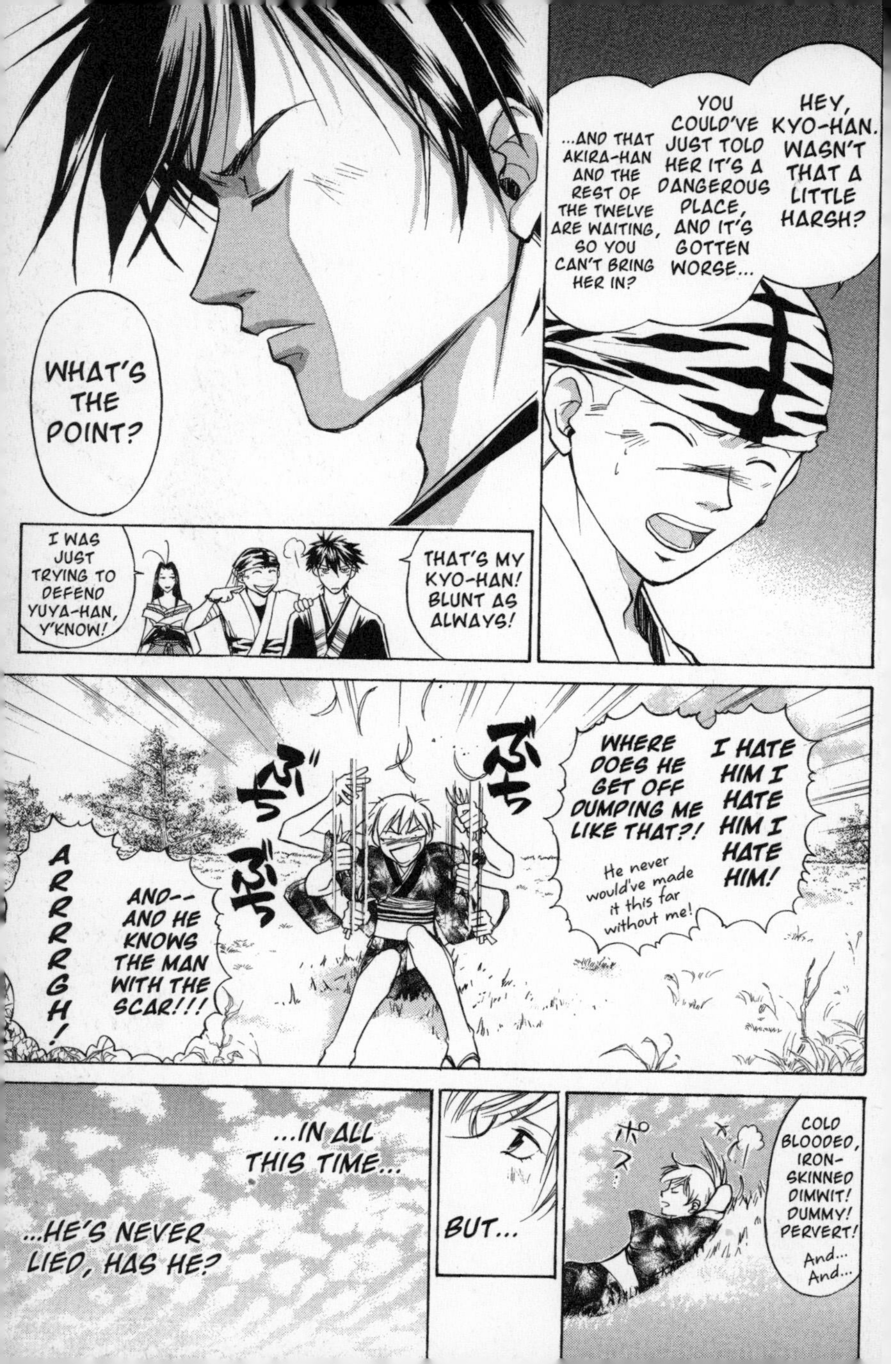
HEY, KYO-HAN. WASN'T THAT A LITTLE HARSH?
YOU COULD'VE JUST TOLD HER IT'S A DANGEROUS PLACE, AND IT'S GOTTEN WORSE...
...AND THAT AKIRA-HAN AND THE REST OF THE TWELVE ARE WAITING, SO YOU CAN'T BRING HER IN?
WHAT'S THE POINT?
THAT'S MY KYO-HAN! BLUNT AS ALWAYS!
I WAS JUST TRYING TO DEFEND YUYA-HAN, Y'KNOW!
I HATE HIM I HATE HIM I HATE HIM I HATE HIM!
WHERE DOES HE GET OFF DUMPING ME LIKE THAT?!
He never would've made it this far without me!
ぶち
ぶち
ぶち
AND-- AND HE KNOWS THE MAN WITH THE SCAR!!!
ARRRRGH!
COLD BLOODED, IRON-SKINNED DIMWIT! DUMMY! PERVERT! And... And...
ポス...
BUT...
...IN ALL THIS TIME...
...HE'S NEVER LIED, HAS HE?

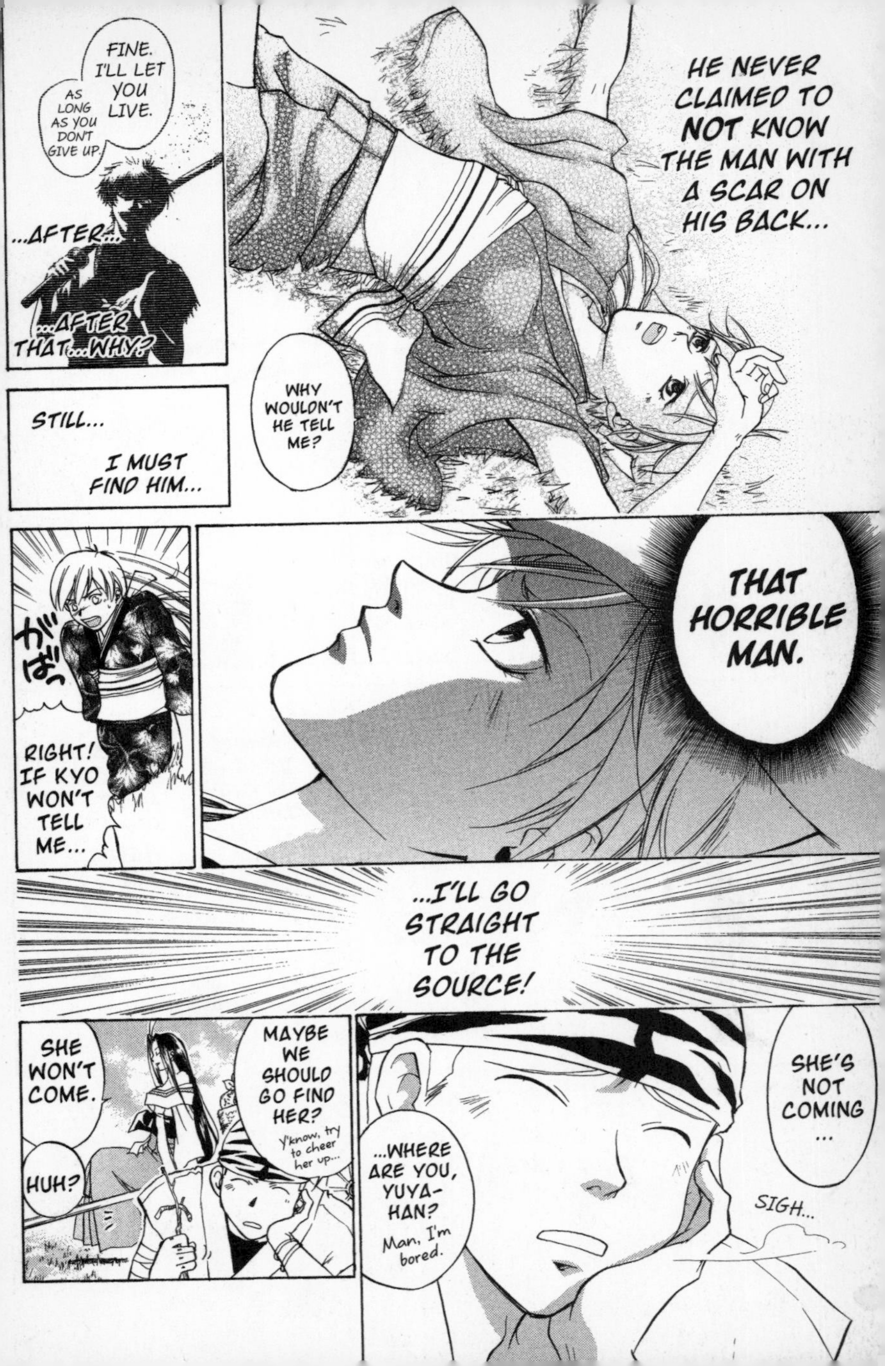
HE NEVER CLAIMED TO NOT KNOW THE MAN WITH A SCAR ON HIS BACK...
WHY WOULDN'T HE TELL ME?
FINE. I'LL LET YOU LIVE.
AS LONG AS YOU DONT GIVE UP.
...AFTER...
...AFTER THAT...WHY?
STILL...
I MUST FIND HIM...
THAT HORRIBLE MAN.
がばっ
RIGHT! IF KYO WON'T TELL ME...
...I'LL GO STRAIGHT TO THE SOURCE!
SHE'S NOT COMING...
SIGH...
MAYBE WE SHOULD GO FIND HER?
Y'know, try to cheer her up...
...WHERE ARE YOU, YUYA-HAN?
Man, I'm bored.
SHE WON'T COME.
HUH?

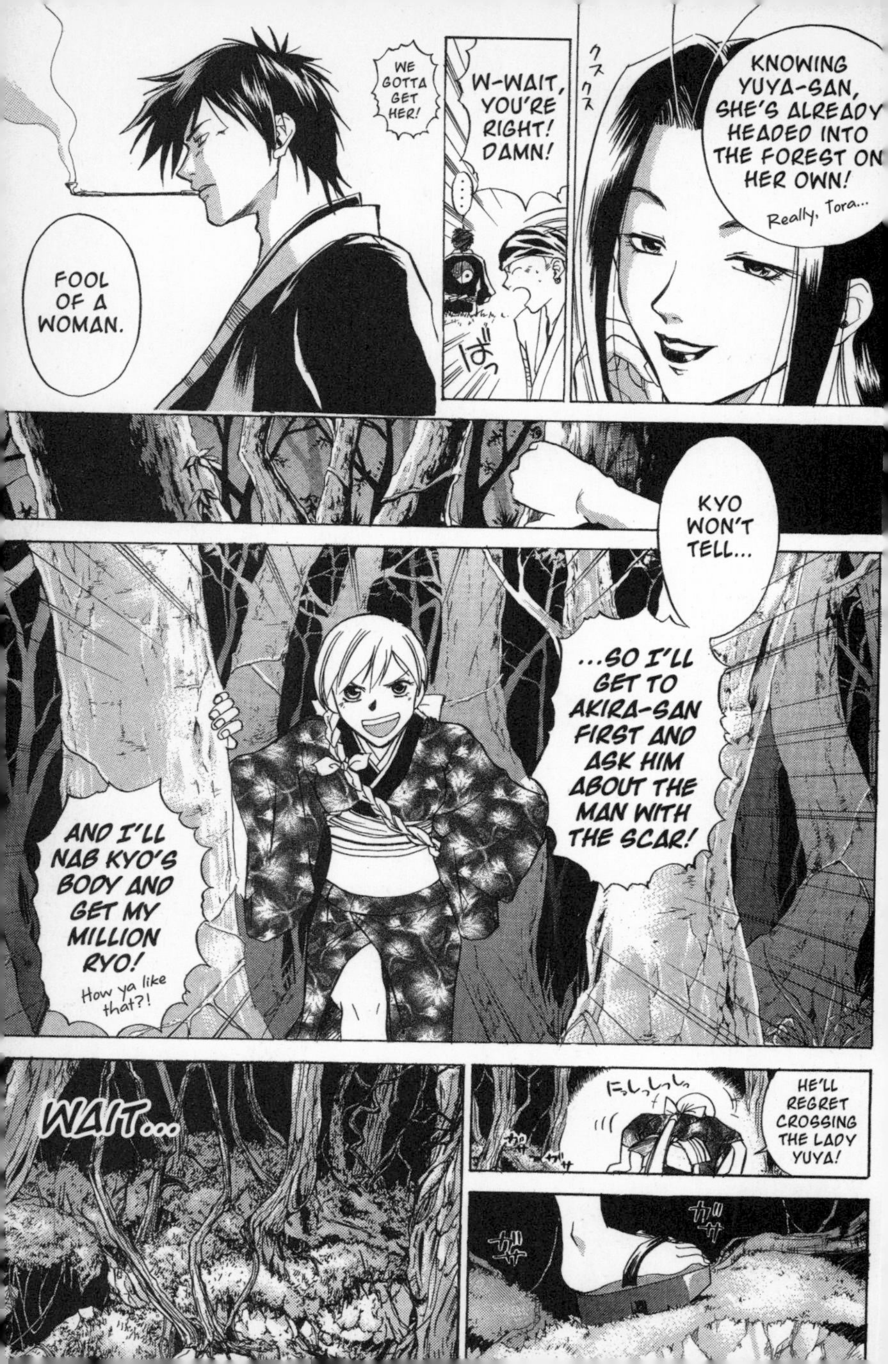

KNOWING YUYA-SAN, SHE'S ALREADY HEADED INTO THE FOREST ON HER OWN!
Really, Tora...
クスクス
W-WAIT, YOU'RE RIGHT! DAMN!
WE GOTTA GET HER!
...
ばっ
FOOL OF A WOMAN.
KYO WON'T TELL...
...SO I'LL GET TO AKIRA-SAN FIRST AND ASK HIM ABOUT THE MAN WITH THE SCAR!
AND I'LL NAB KYO'S BODY AND GET MY MILLION RYO!
How ya like that?!
HE'LL REGRET CROSSING THE LADY YUYA!
にっしっしっし
WAIT...

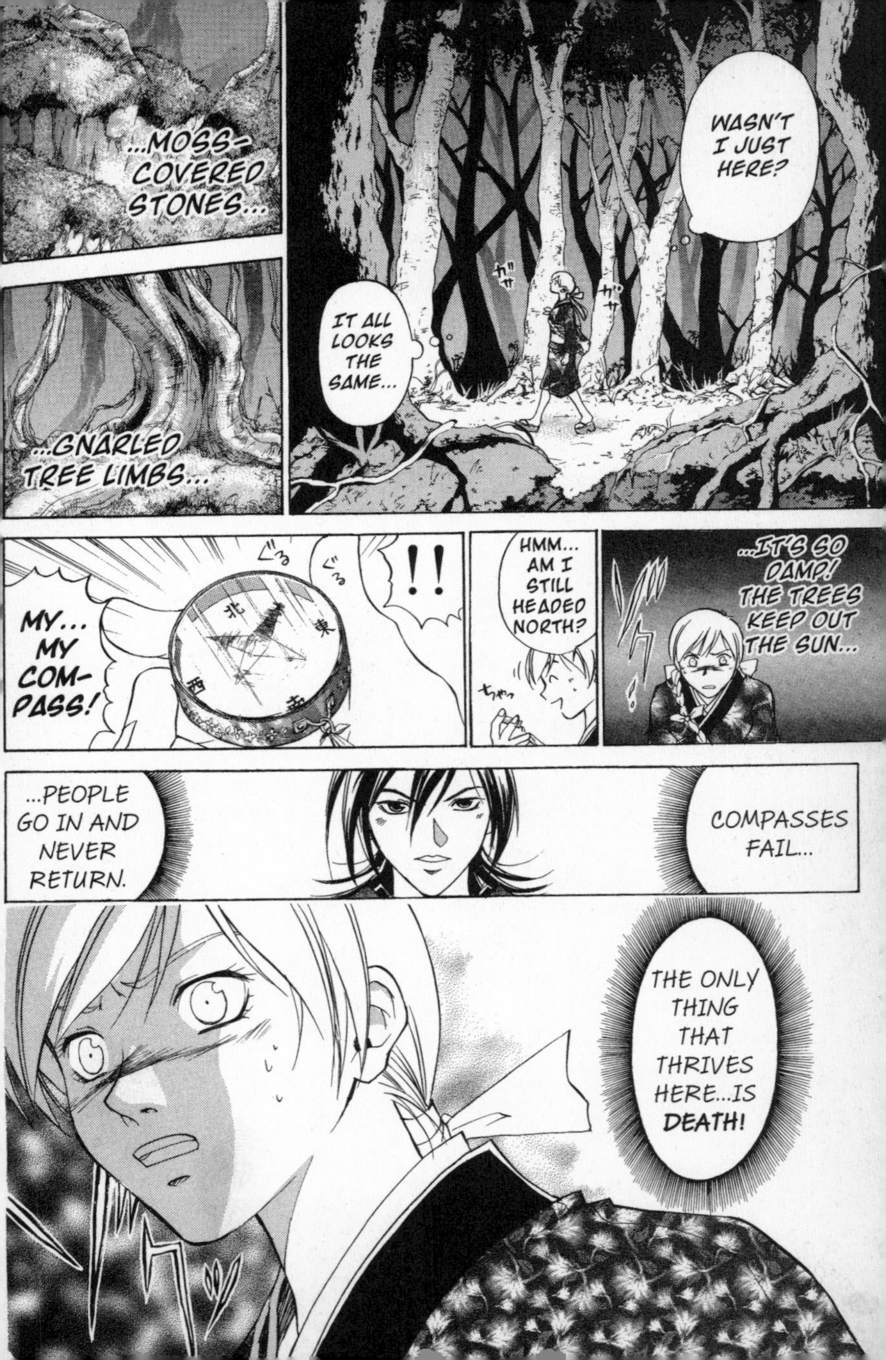
WASN'T I JUST HERE?
IT ALL LOOKS THE SAME...
...MOSS-COVERED STONES...
...GNARLED TREE LIMBS...
...IT'S SO DAMP! THE TREES KEEP OUT THE SUN...
HMM... AM I STILL HEADED NORTH?
!!
MY... MY COMPASS!
COMPASSES FAIL...
...PEOPLE GO IN AND NEVER RETURN.
THE ONLY THING THAT THRIVES HERE...IS DEATH!

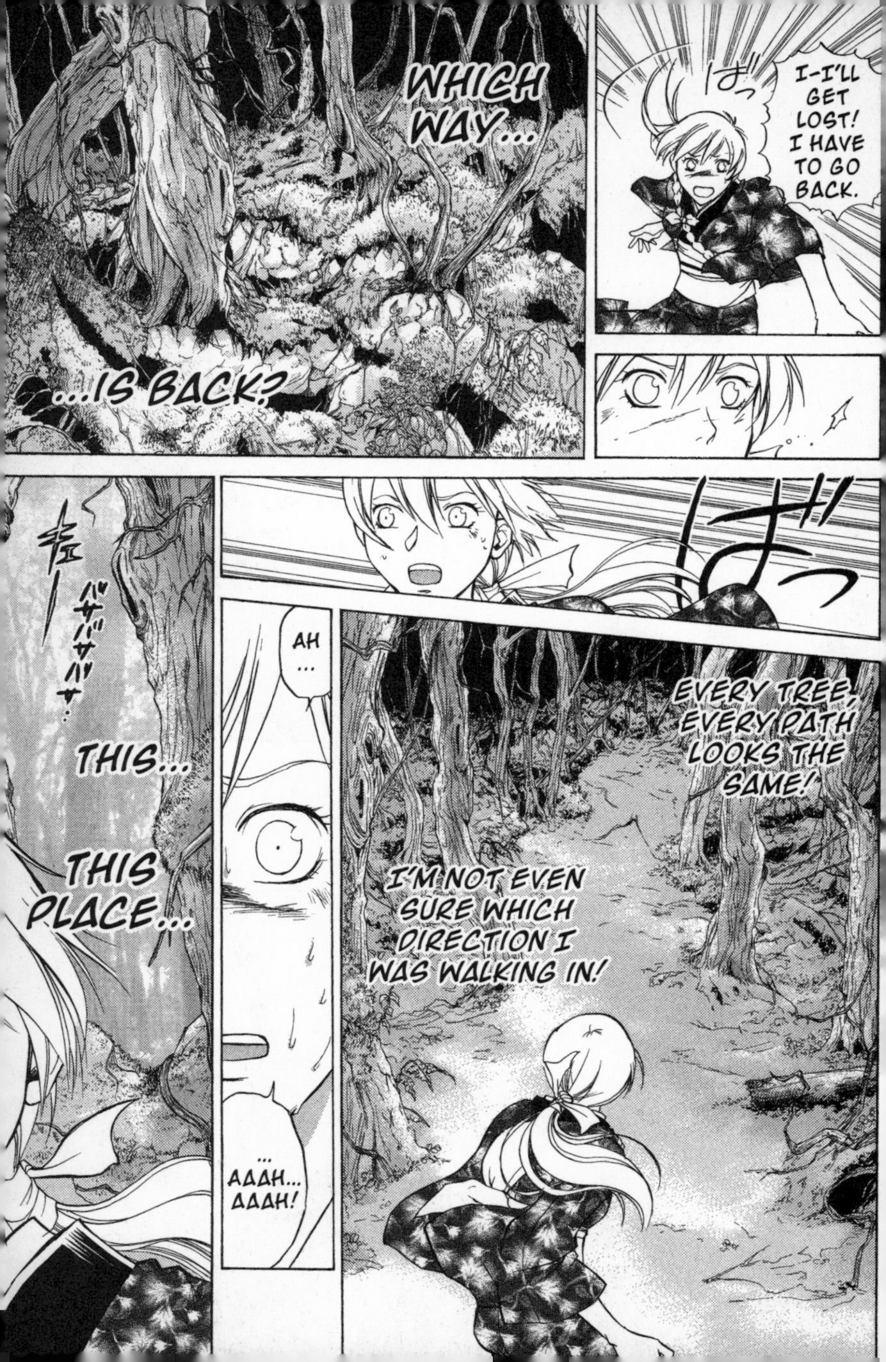
ばっ
I-I'LL GET LOST! I HAVE TO GO BACK.
WHICH WAY...
...IS BACK?
ばっ
EVERY TREE, EVERY PATH LOOKS THE SAME!
I'M NOT EVEN SURE WHICH DIRECTION I WAS WALKING IN!
AH ...
... AAAH... AAAH!
バサバサバサ・・
THIS...
THIS PLACE...

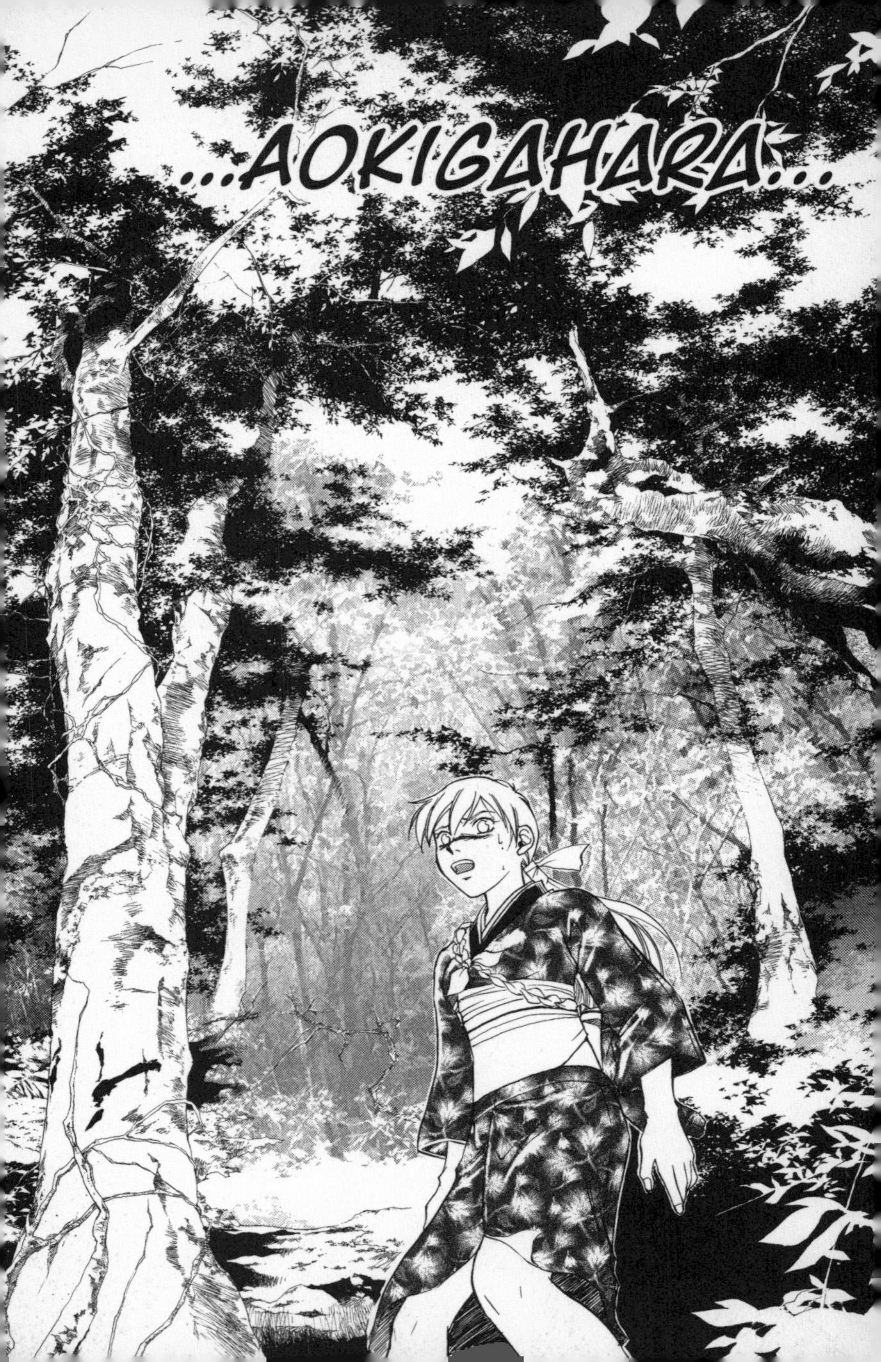
...AOKIGAHARA...

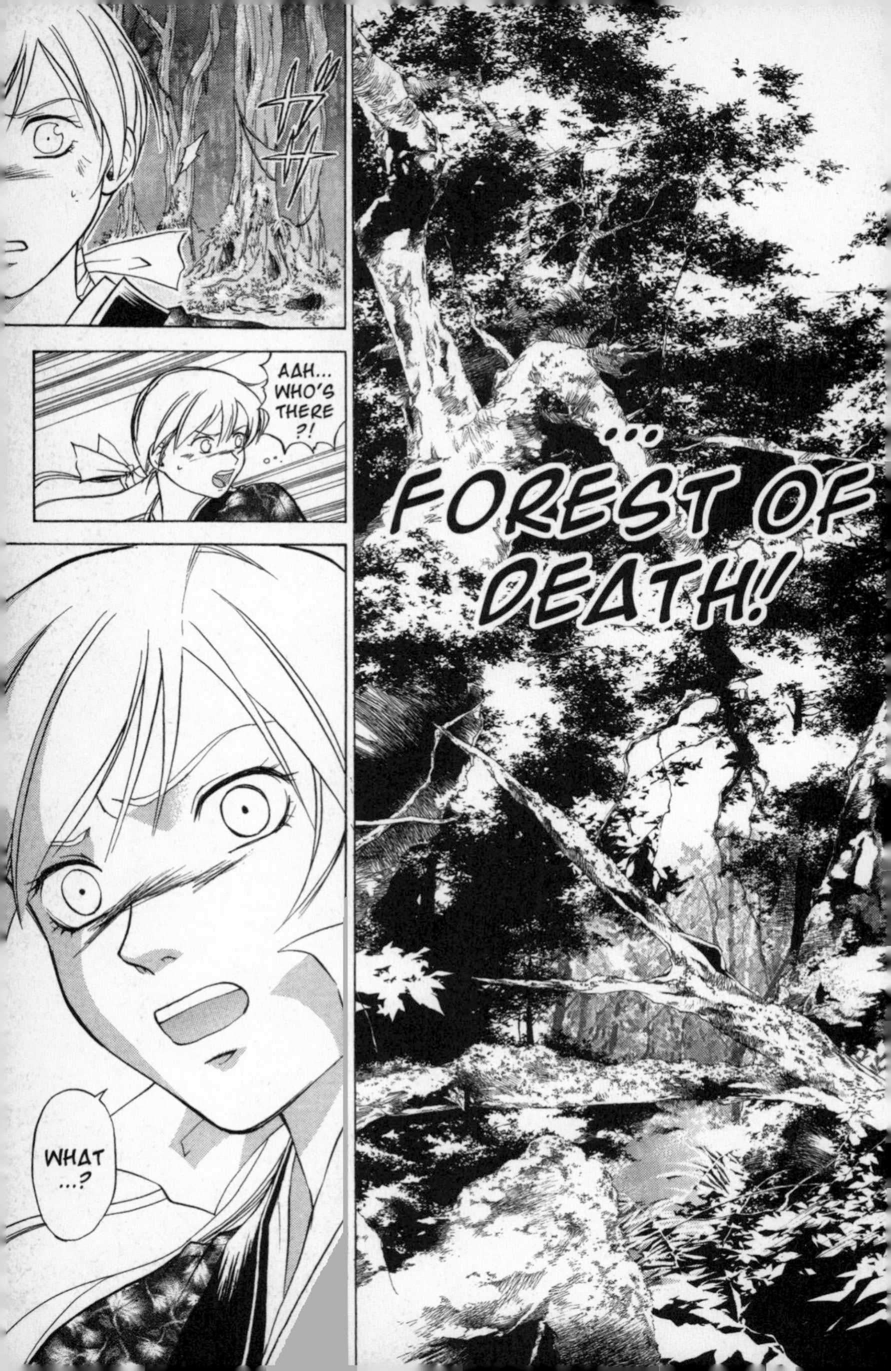

...FOREST OF DEATH!
AAH... WHO'S THERE ?!
WHAT ...?

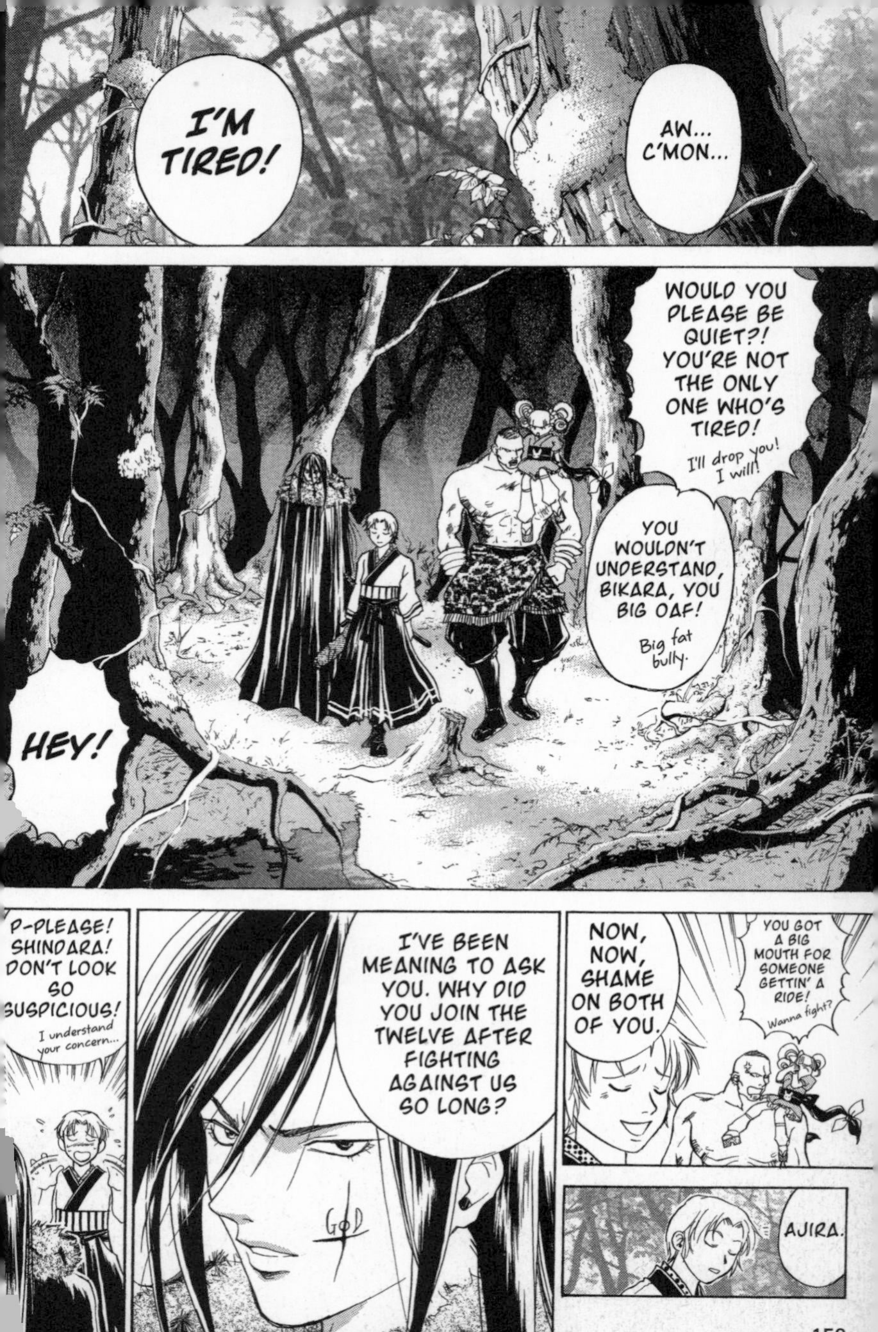
AW... C'MON...
I'M TIRED!
WOULD YOU PLEASE BE QUIET?! YOU'RE NOT THE ONLY ONE WHO'S TIRED!
I'll drop you! I will!
YOU WOULDN'T UNDERSTAND, BIKARA, YOU BIG OAF!
Big fat bully.
HEY!
YOU GOT A BIG MOUTH FOR SOMEONE GETTIN' A RIDE!
Wanna fight?
NOW, NOW, SHAME ON BOTH OF YOU.
AJIRA.
I'VE BEEN MEANING TO ASK YOU. WHY DID YOU JOIN THE TWELVE AFTER FIGHTING AGAINST US SO LONG?
GOD
P-PLEASE! SHINDARA! DON'T LOOK SO SUSPICIOUS!
I understand your concern...

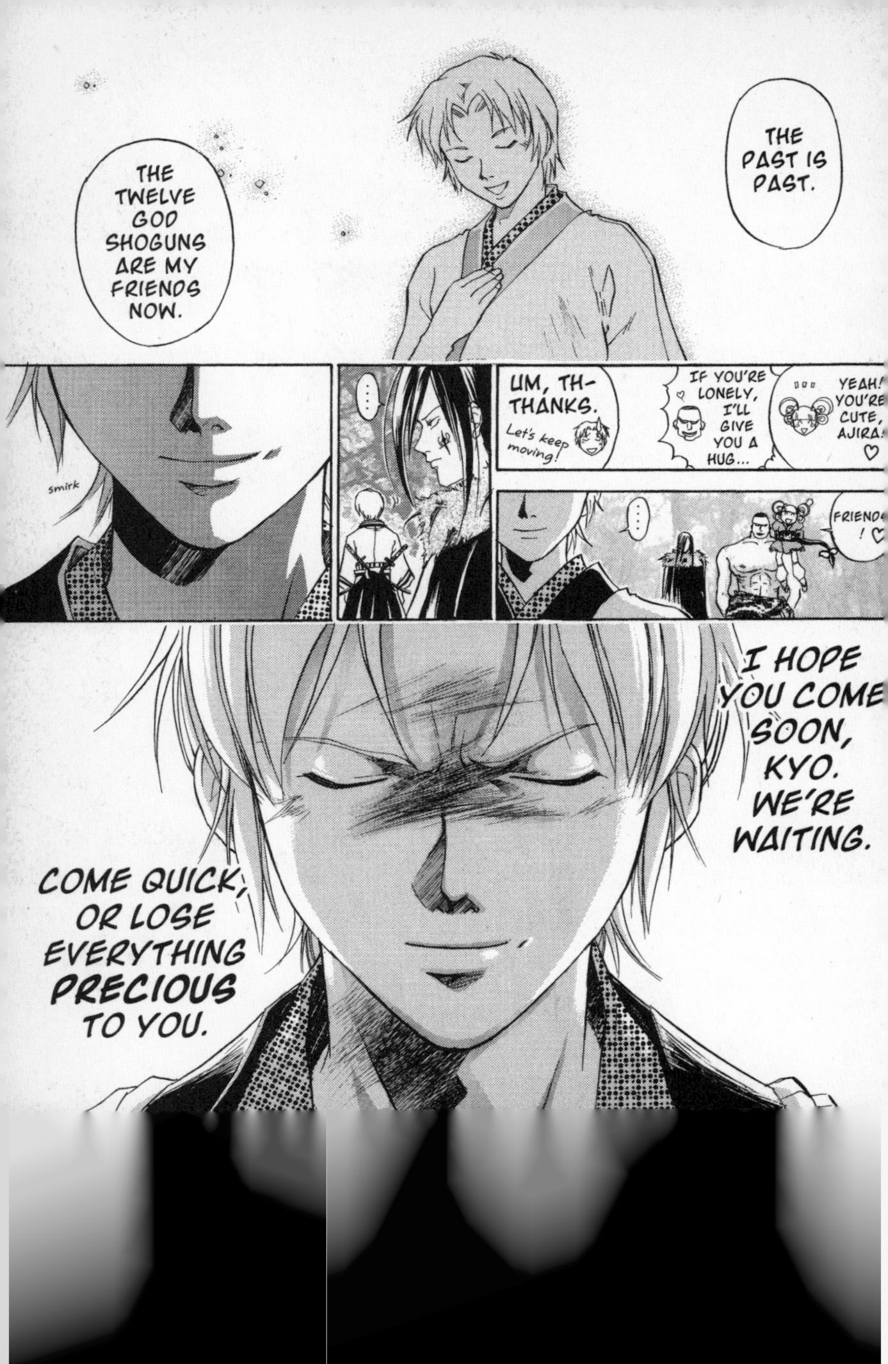
THE PAST IS PAST.
THE TWELVE GOD SHOGUNS ARE MY FRIENDS NOW.
YEAH! YOU'RE CUTE, AJIRA! ♡
IF YOU'RE LONELY, I'LL GIVE YOU A HUG...
UM, TH-THANKS.
Let's keep moving!
FRIENDS! ♡
...
...
smirk
I HOPE YOU COME SOON, KYO. WE'RE WAITING.
COME QUICK, OR LOSE EVERYTHING PRECIOUS TO YOU.

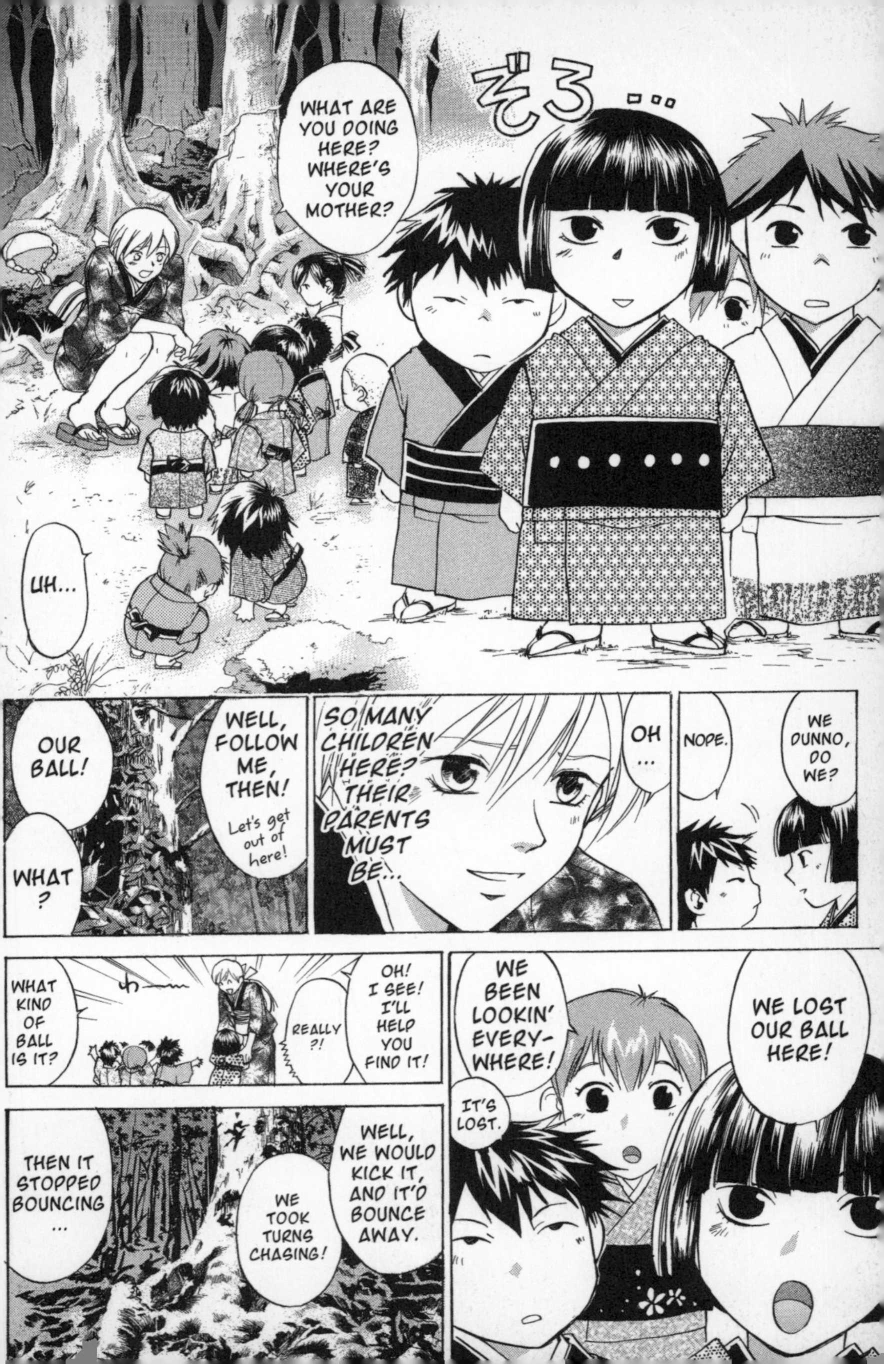
ぞろ…
WHAT ARE YOU DOING HERE? WHERE'S YOUR MOTHER?
UH...
WE DUNNO, DO WE?
NOPE.
OH ...
SO MANY CHILDREN HERE? THEIR PARENTS MUST BE...
WELL, FOLLOW ME, THEN!
Let's get out of here!
OUR BALL!
WHAT ?
WE LOST OUR BALL HERE!
WE BEEN LOOKIN' EVERY-WHERE!
IT'S LOST.
OH! I SEE! I'LL HELP YOU FIND IT!
REALLY ?!
わー
WHAT KIND OF BALL IS IT?
WELL, WE WOULD KICK IT, AND IT'D BOUNCE AWAY.
WE TOOK TURNS CHASING!
THEN IT STOPPED BOUNCING ...

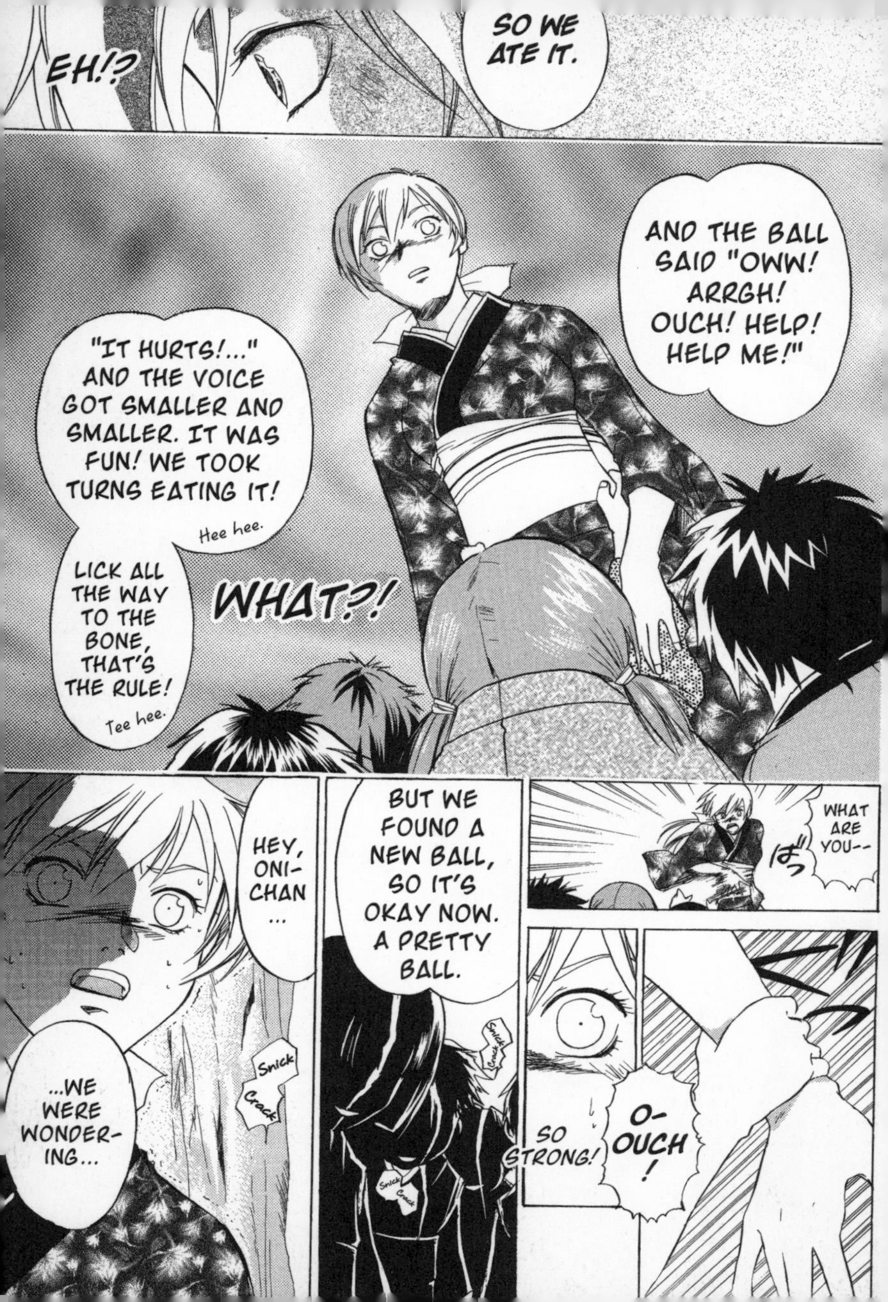
SO WE ATE IT.
EH!?
AND THE BALL SAID "OWW! ARRGH! OUCH! HELP! HELP ME!"
"IT HURTS!..." AND THE VOICE GOT SMALLER AND SMALLER. IT WAS FUN! WE TOOK TURNS EATING IT!
Hee hee.
WHAT?!
LICK ALL THE WAY TO THE BONE, THAT'S THE RULE!
Tee hee.
WHAT ARE YOU--
ばっ
O-OUCH!
SO STRONG!
BUT WE FOUND A NEW BALL, SO IT'S OKAY NOW. A PRETTY BALL.
Snick
Crack
Snick
Crack
HEY, ONI-CHAN...
...WE WERE WONDER-ING...
Snick
Crack

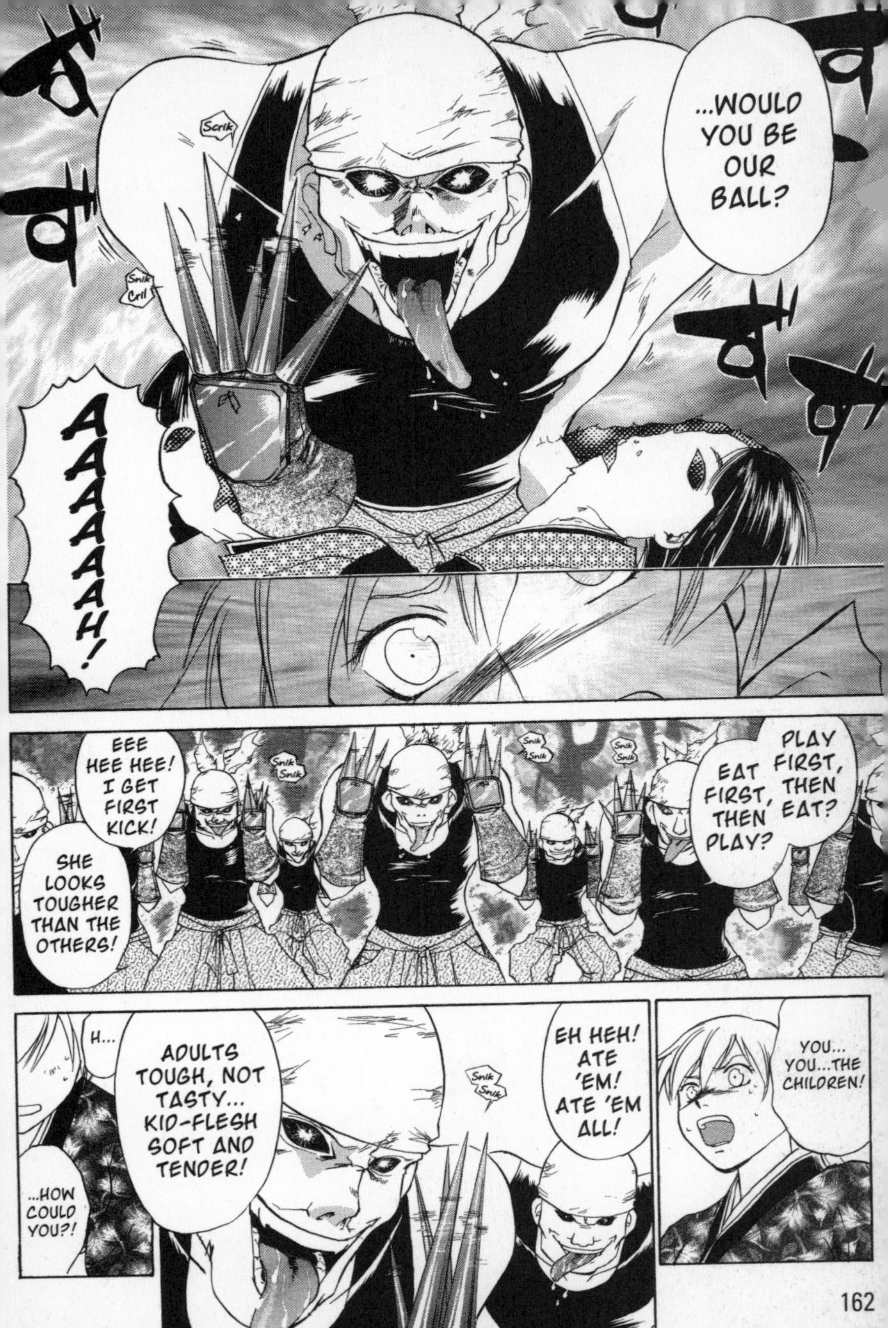
...WOULD YOU BE OUR BALL?
Scrik
Snik Cril
AAAAAAAH!
Snik Snik
Snik Snik
Snik Snik
PLAY FIRST, THEN EAT?
EAT FIRST, THEN PLAY?
EEE HEE HEE! I GET FIRST KICK!
SHE LOOKS TOUGHER THAN THE OTHERS!
YOU... YOU...THE CHILDREN!
EH HEH! ATE 'EM! ATE 'EM ALL!
Snik Snik
ADULTS TOUGH, NOT TASTY... KID-FLESH SOFT AND TENDER!
H...
...HOW COULD YOU?!

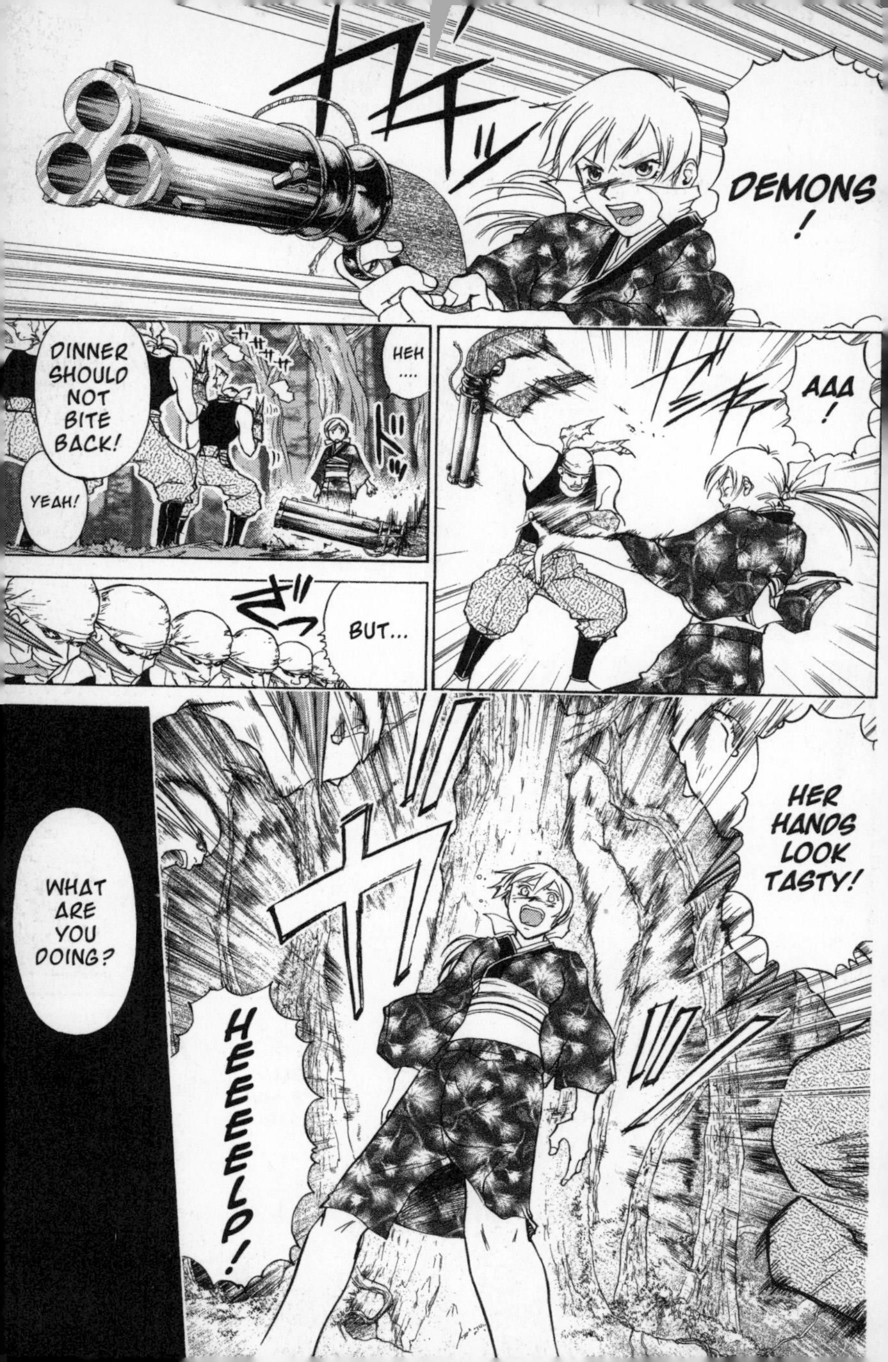
DEMONS!
AAA!
HEH ....
DINNER SHOULD NOT BITE BACK!
YEAH!
BUT...
HER HANDS LOOK TASTY!
HEEEEELP!
WHAT ARE YOU DOING?

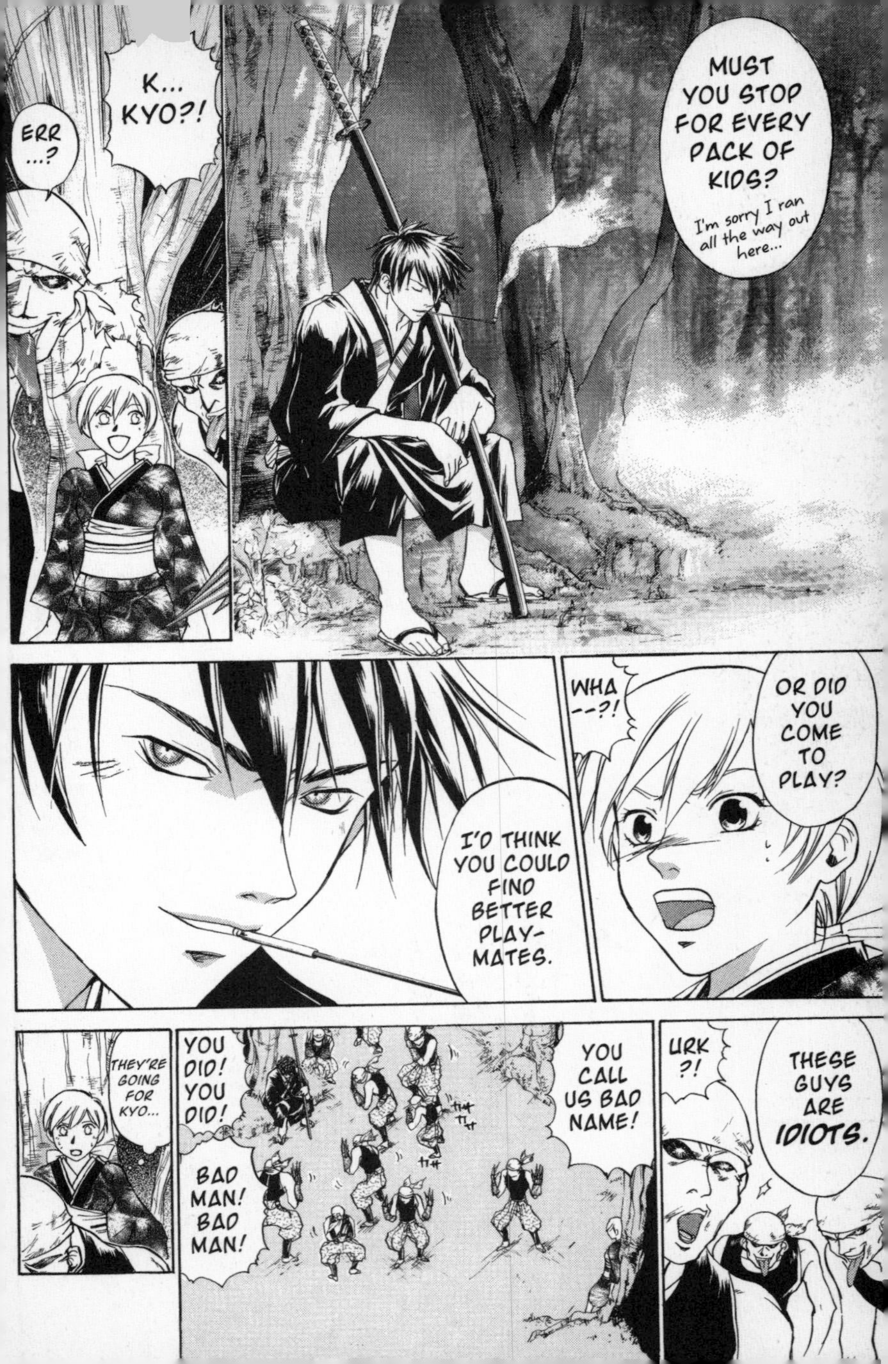
MUST YOU STOP FOR EVERY PACK OF KIDS?
I'm sorry I ran all the way out here...
K... KYO?!
ERR ...?
OR DID YOU COME TO PLAY?
WHA--?!
I'D THINK YOU COULD FIND BETTER PLAY-MATES.
THESE GUYS ARE **IDIOTS.**
URK ?!
YOU CALL US BAD NAME!
YOU DID! YOU DID!
BAD MAN! BAD MAN!
THEY'RE GOING FOR KYO...

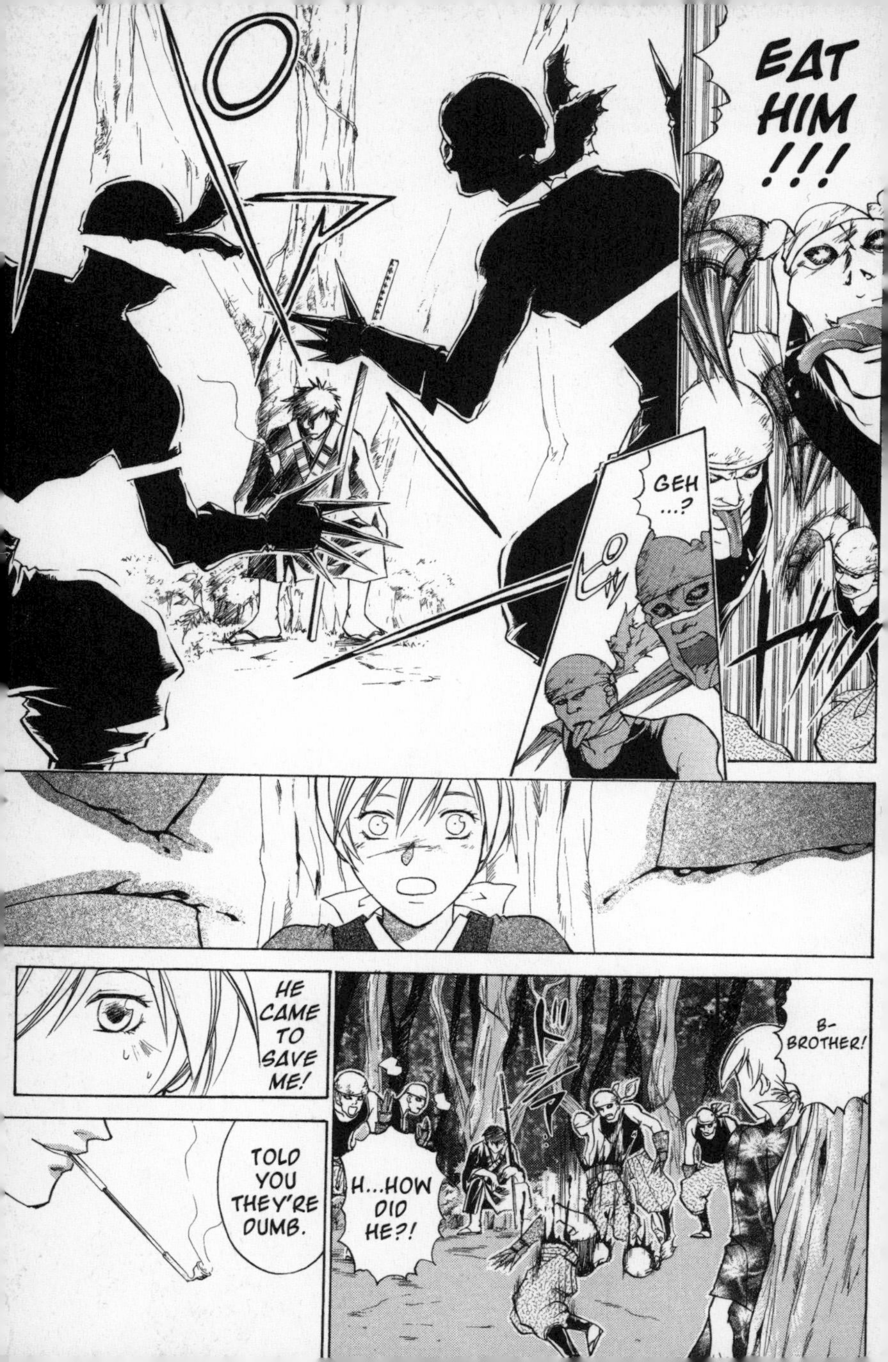
EAT HIM!!!
GEH ...?
B-BROTHER!
H...HOW DID HE?!
HE CAME TO SAVE ME!
TOLD YOU THEY'RE DUMB.

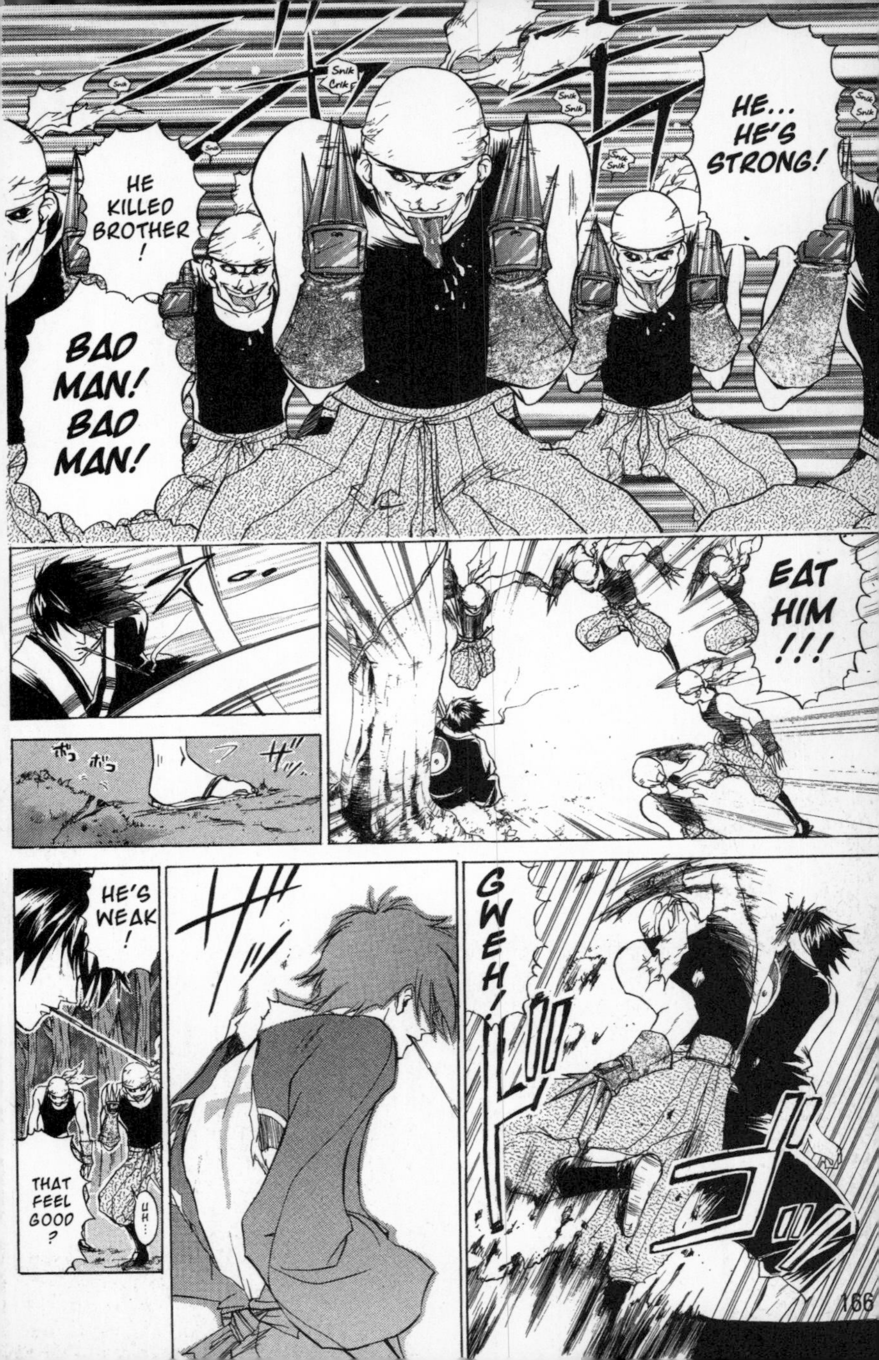
Snik
Snik Snik
Snik Snik
Snik Crik
Snik
Snik
HE... HE'S STRONG!
HE KILLED BROTHER!
BAD MAN! BAD MAN!
EAT HIM!!!
GWEH!
HE'S WEAK!
UH...
THAT FEEL GOOD?

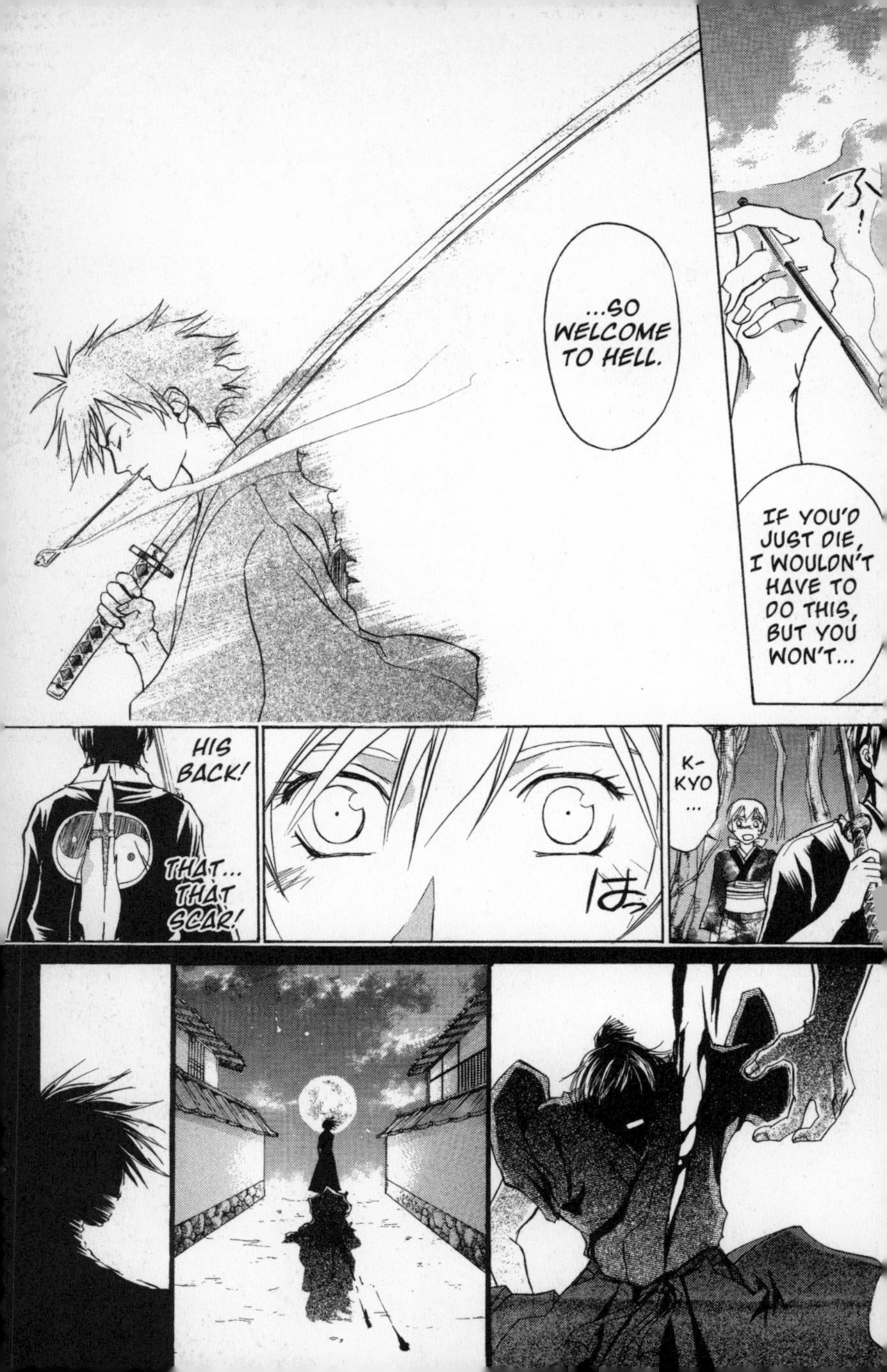
ふ!
IF YOU'D JUST DIE, I WOULDN'T HAVE TO DO THIS, BUT YOU WON'T...
...SO WELCOME TO HELL.
K-KYO ...
はっ
HIS BACK!
THAT... THAT SCAR!

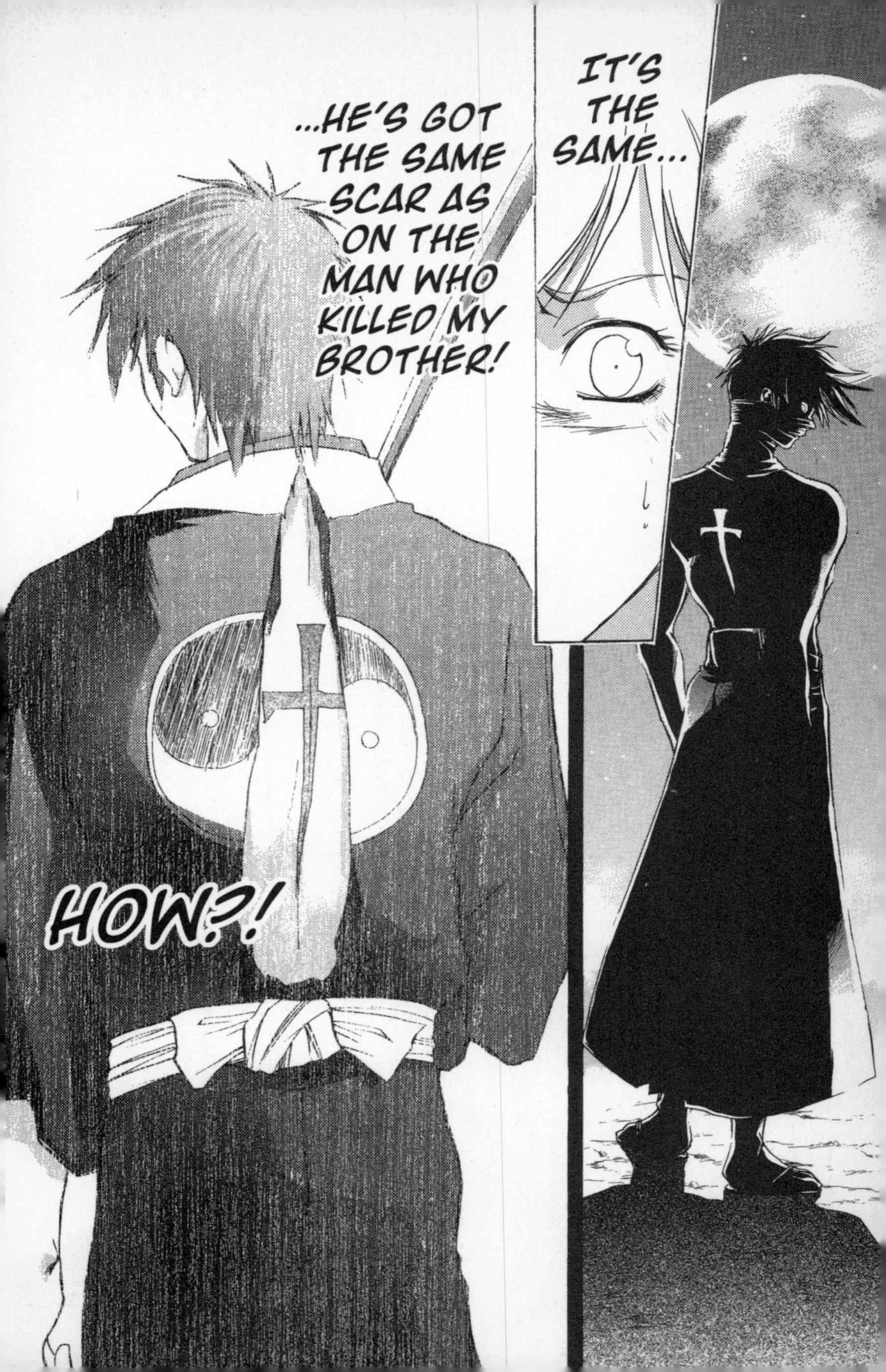
IT'S THE SAME...
...HE'S GOT THE SAME SCAR AS ON THE MAN WHO KILLED MY BROTHER!
HOW?!

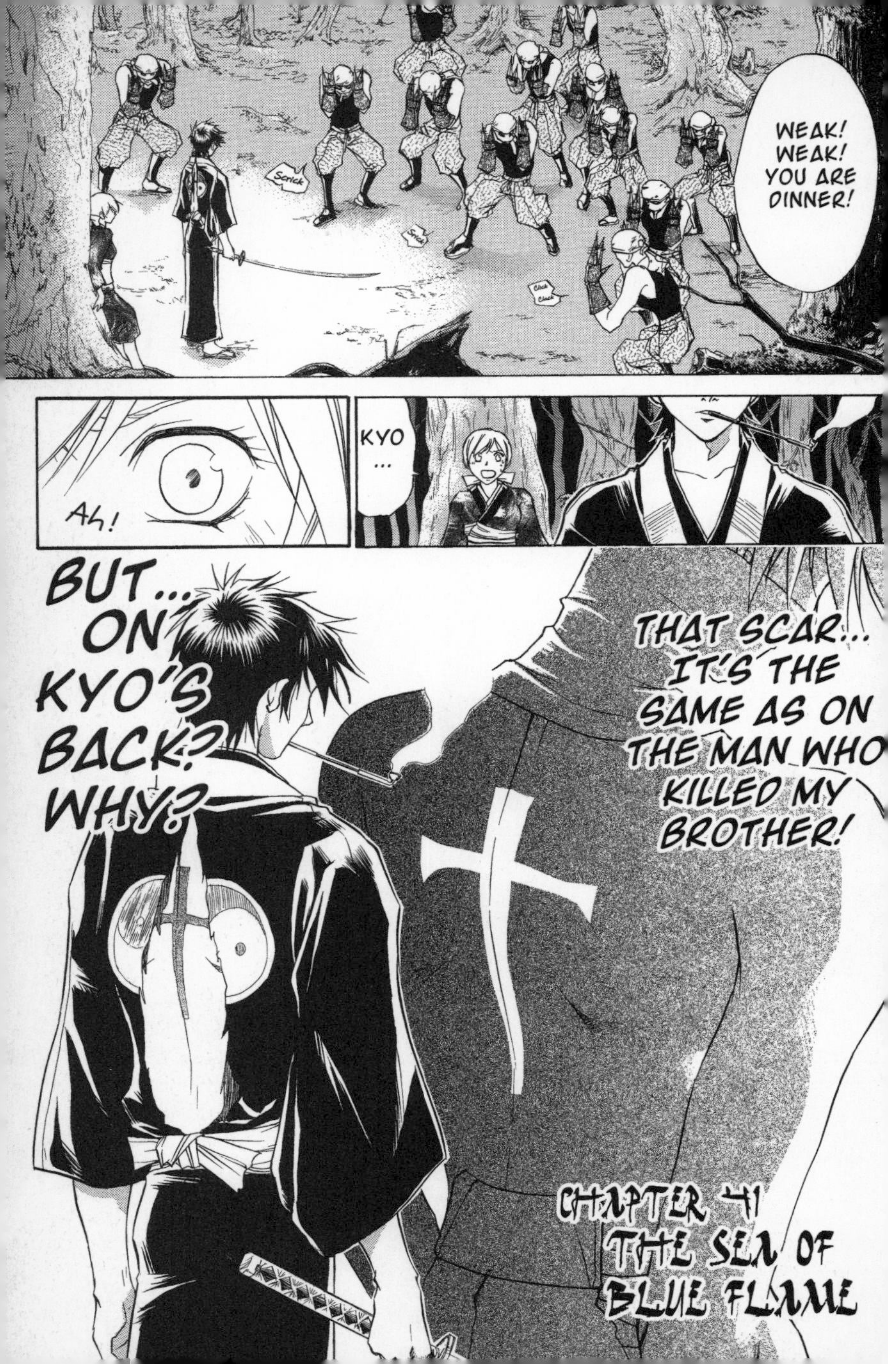
WEAK! WEAK! YOU ARE DINNER!
Scrick
Scrick
Click Clack
KYO ...
Ah!
THAT SCAR... IT'S THE SAME AS ON THE MAN WHO KILLED MY BROTHER!
BUT... ON KYO'S BACK? WHY?
CHAPTER 41
THE SEA OF BLUE FLAME

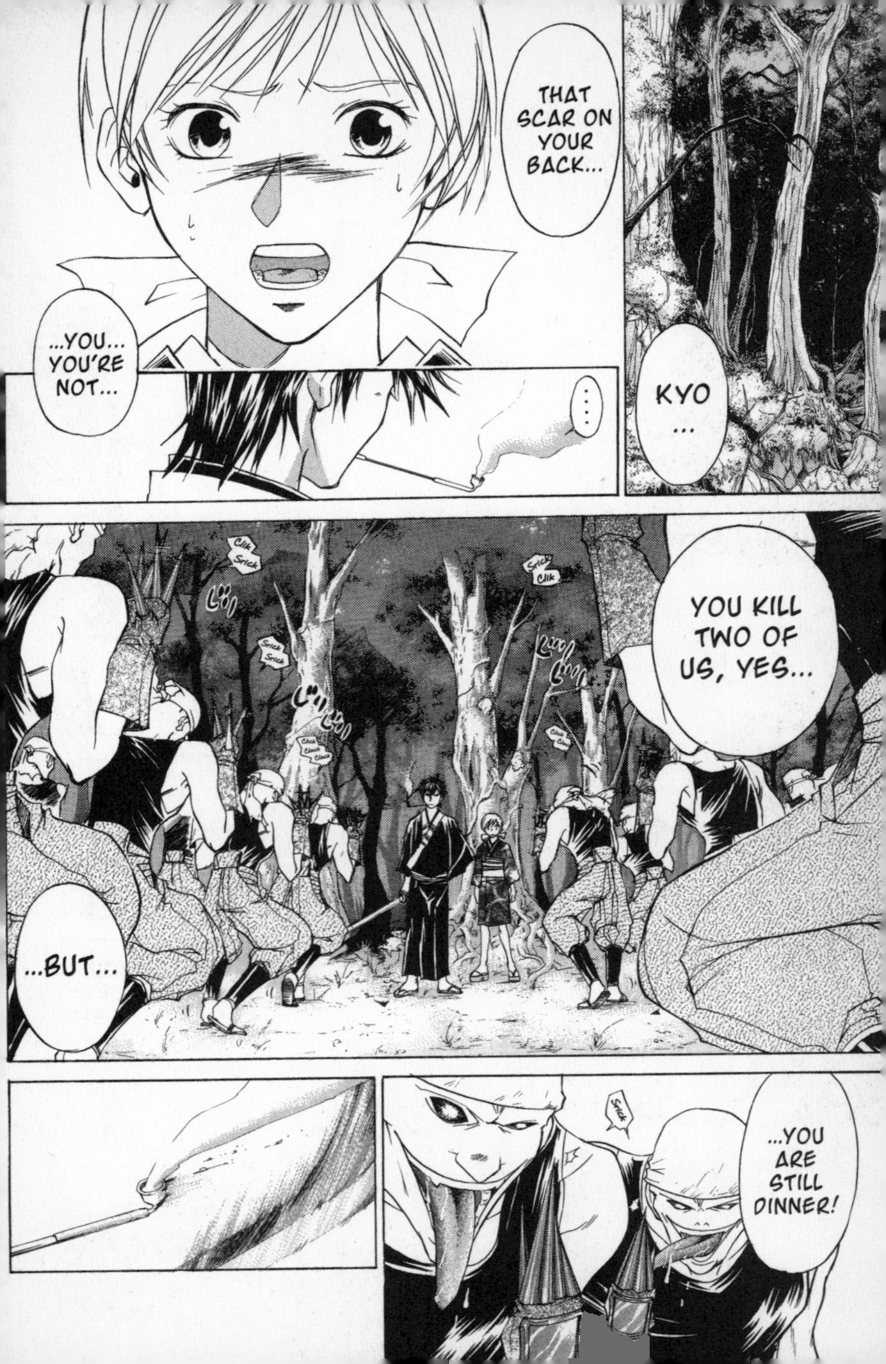
KYO ...
THAT SCAR ON YOUR BACK...
...YOU... YOU'RE NOT...
...
YOU KILL TWO OF US, YES...
...BUT...
Srick
...YOU ARE STILL DINNER!

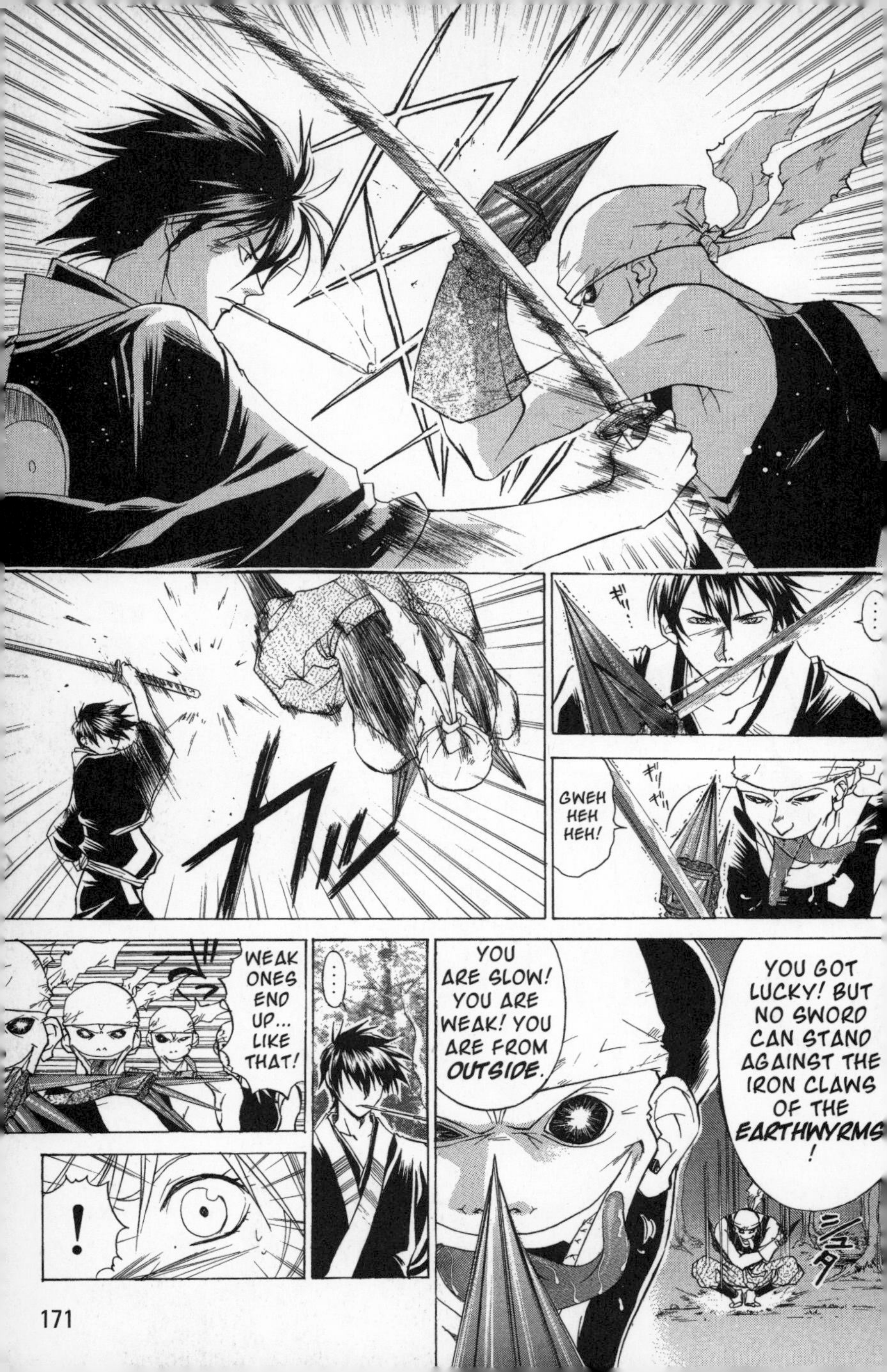

ギリ…
…
GWEH HEH HEH!
ガッ
YOU GOT LUCKY! BUT NO SWORD CAN STAND AGAINST THE IRON CLAWS OF THE EARTHWYRMS!
シュタ
YOU ARE SLOW! YOU ARE WEAK! YOU ARE FROM OUTSIDE.
…
WEAK ONES END UP... LIKE THAT!
!

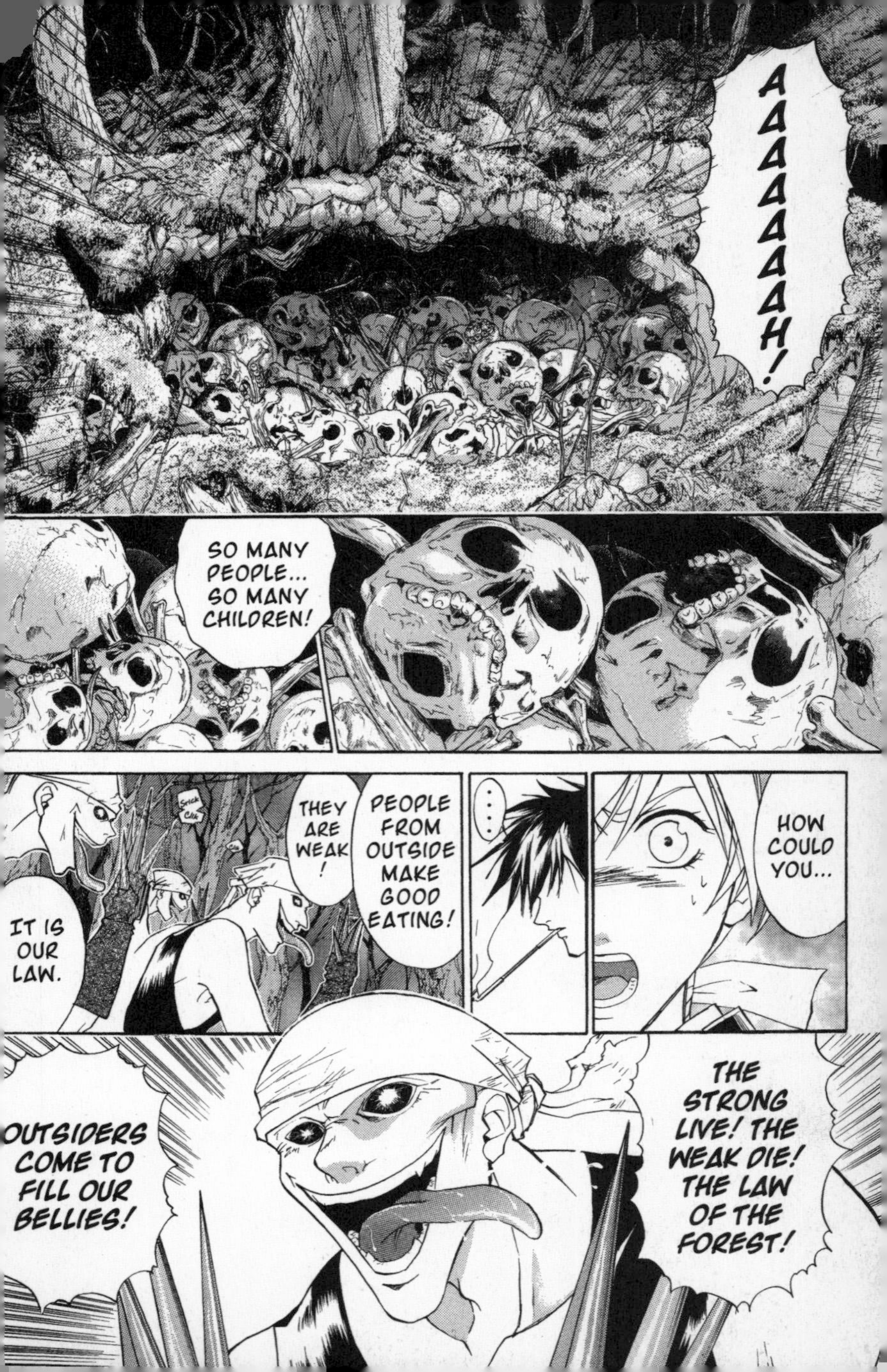
AAAAAAAH!
SO MANY PEOPLE... SO MANY CHILDREN!
HOW COULD YOU...
...
PEOPLE FROM OUTSIDE MAKE GOOD EATING!
THEY ARE WEAK!
IT IS OUR LAW.
THE STRONG LIVE! THE WEAK DIE! THE LAW OF THE FOREST!
OUTSIDERS COME TO FILL OUR BELLIES!

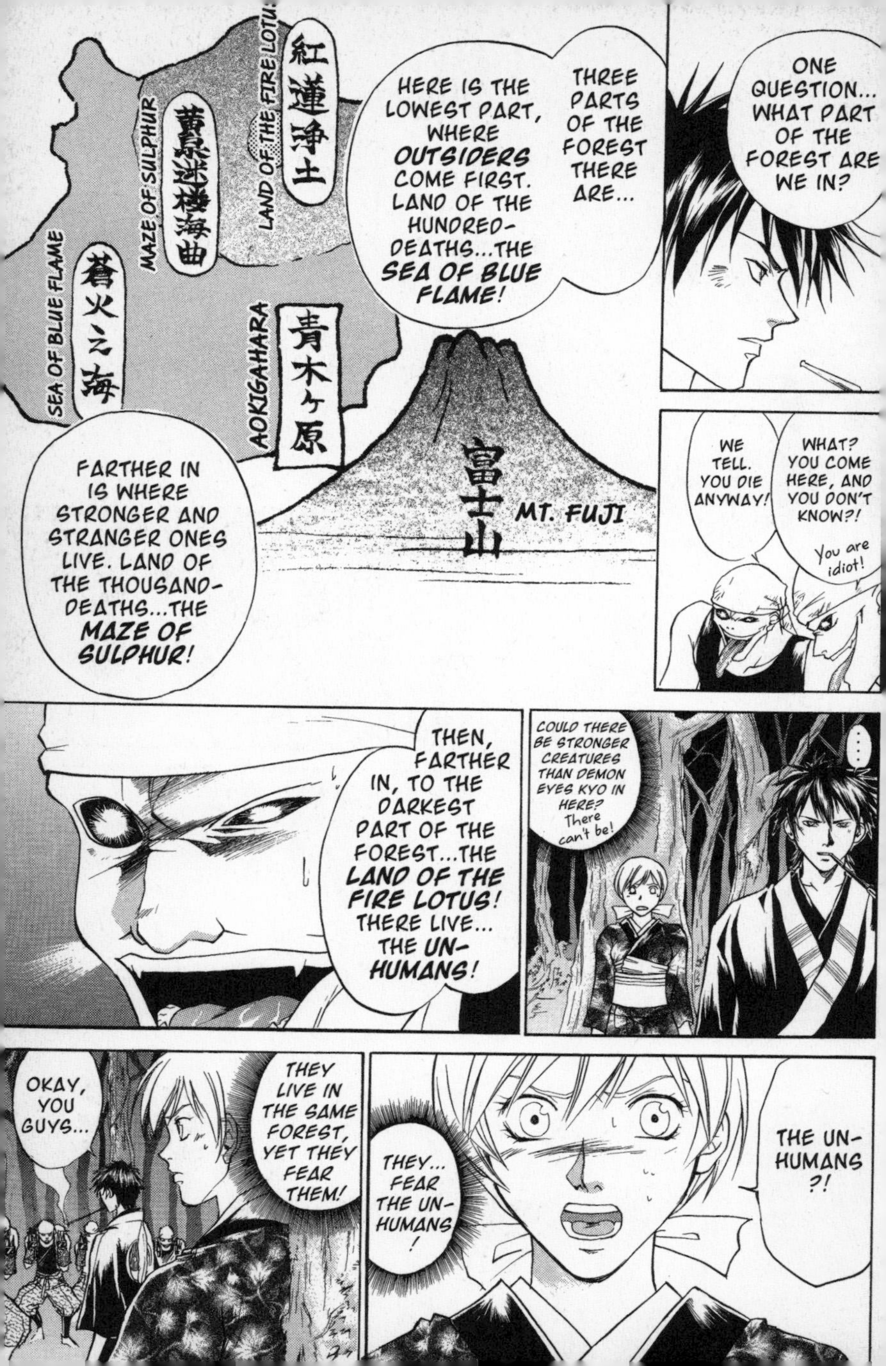

ONE QUESTION... WHAT PART OF THE FOREST ARE WE IN?
WHAT? YOU COME HERE, AND YOU DON'T KNOW?!
You are idiot!
WE TELL. YOU DIE ANYWAY!
THREE PARTS OF THE FOREST THERE ARE...
HERE IS THE LOWEST PART, WHERE OUTSIDERS COME FIRST. LAND OF THE HUNDRED-DEATHS...THE SEA OF BLUE FLAME!
紅蓮浄土
LAND OF THE FIRE LOTU
黄泉迷楼海曲
MAZE OF SULPHUR
蒼火之海
SEA OF BLUE FLAME
青木ヶ原
AOKIGAHARA
富士山
MT. FUJI
FARTHER IN IS WHERE STRONGER AND STRANGER ONES LIVE. LAND OF THE THOUSAND-DEATHS...THE MAZE OF SULPHUR!
...
COULD THERE BE STRONGER CREATURES THAN DEMON EYES KYO IN HERE? There can't be!
THEN, FARTHER IN, TO THE DARKEST PART OF THE FOREST...THE LAND OF THE FIRE LOTUS! THERE LIVE... THE UN-HUMANS!
THE UN-HUMANS?!
THEY... FEAR THE UN-HUMANS!
THEY LIVE IN THE SAME FOREST, YET THEY FEAR THEM!
OKAY, YOU GUYS...

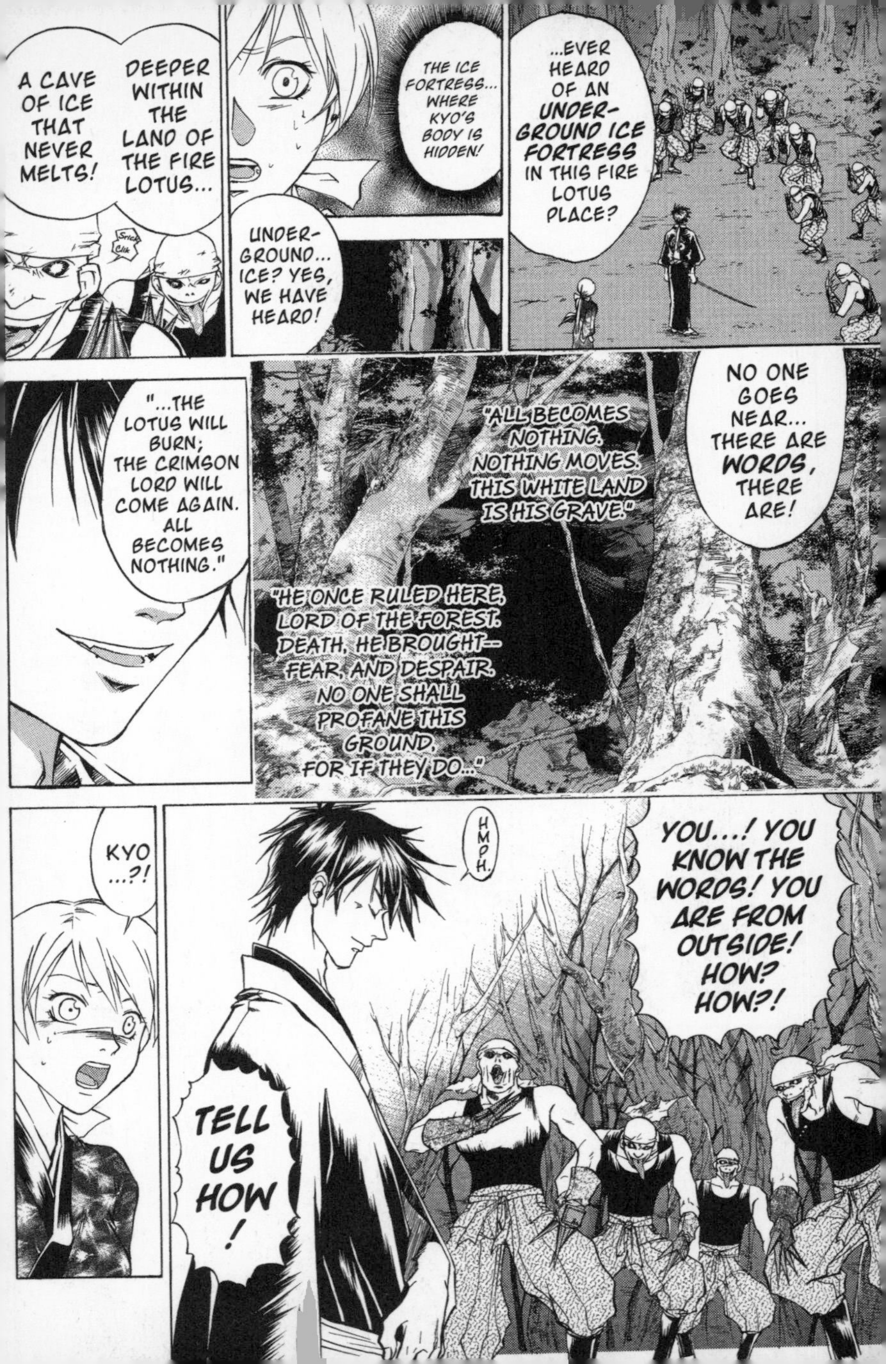
...EVER HEARD OF AN UNDERGROUND ICE FORTRESS IN THIS FIRE LOTUS PLACE?
THE ICE FORTRESS... WHERE KYO'S BODY IS HIDDEN!
UNDER-GROUND... ICE? YES, WE HAVE HEARD!
DEEPER WITHIN THE LAND OF THE FIRE LOTUS...
A CAVE OF ICE THAT NEVER MELTS!
Srick Clik
NO ONE GOES NEAR... THERE ARE WORDS, THERE ARE!
"ALL BECOMES NOTHING. NOTHING MOVES. THIS WHITE LAND IS HIS GRAVE."
"HE ONCE RULED HERE, LORD OF THE FOREST. DEATH, HE BROUGHT-- FEAR, AND DESPAIR. NO ONE SHALL PROFANE THIS GROUND, FOR IF THEY DO..."
"...THE LOTUS WILL BURN; THE CRIMSON LORD WILL COME AGAIN. ALL BECOMES NOTHING."
YOU...! YOU KNOW THE WORDS! YOU ARE FROM OUTSIDE! HOW? HOW?!
HMPH.
TELL US HOW!
KYO ...?!

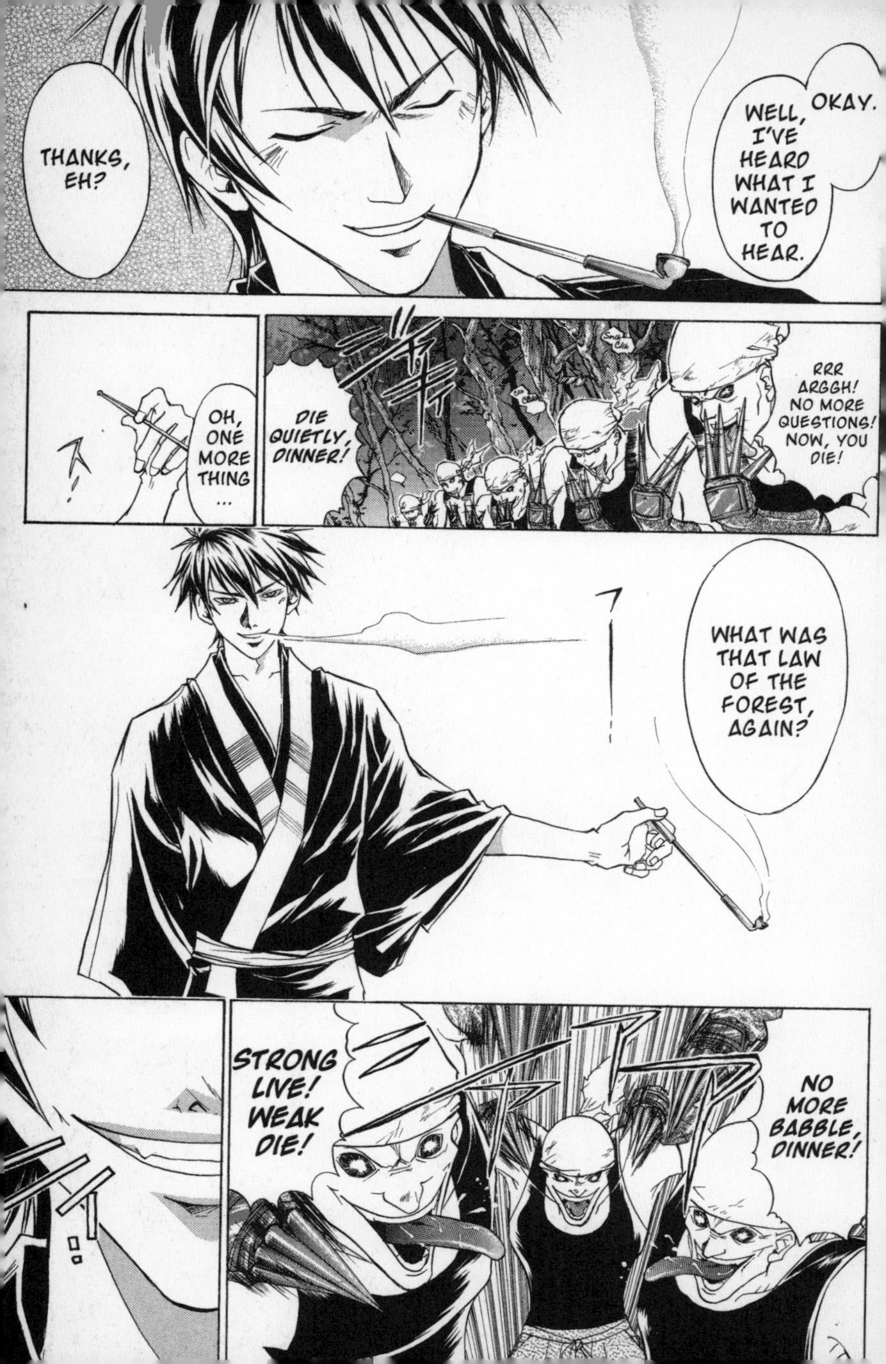
OKAY.
WELL, I'VE HEARD WHAT I WANTED TO HEAR.
THANKS, EH?
RRR ARGGH! NO MORE QUESTIONS! NOW, YOU DIE!
DIE QUIETLY, DINNER!
OH, ONE MORE THING ...
WHAT WAS THAT LAW OF THE FOREST, AGAIN?
NO MORE BABBLE, DINNER!
STRONG LIVE! WEAK DIE!

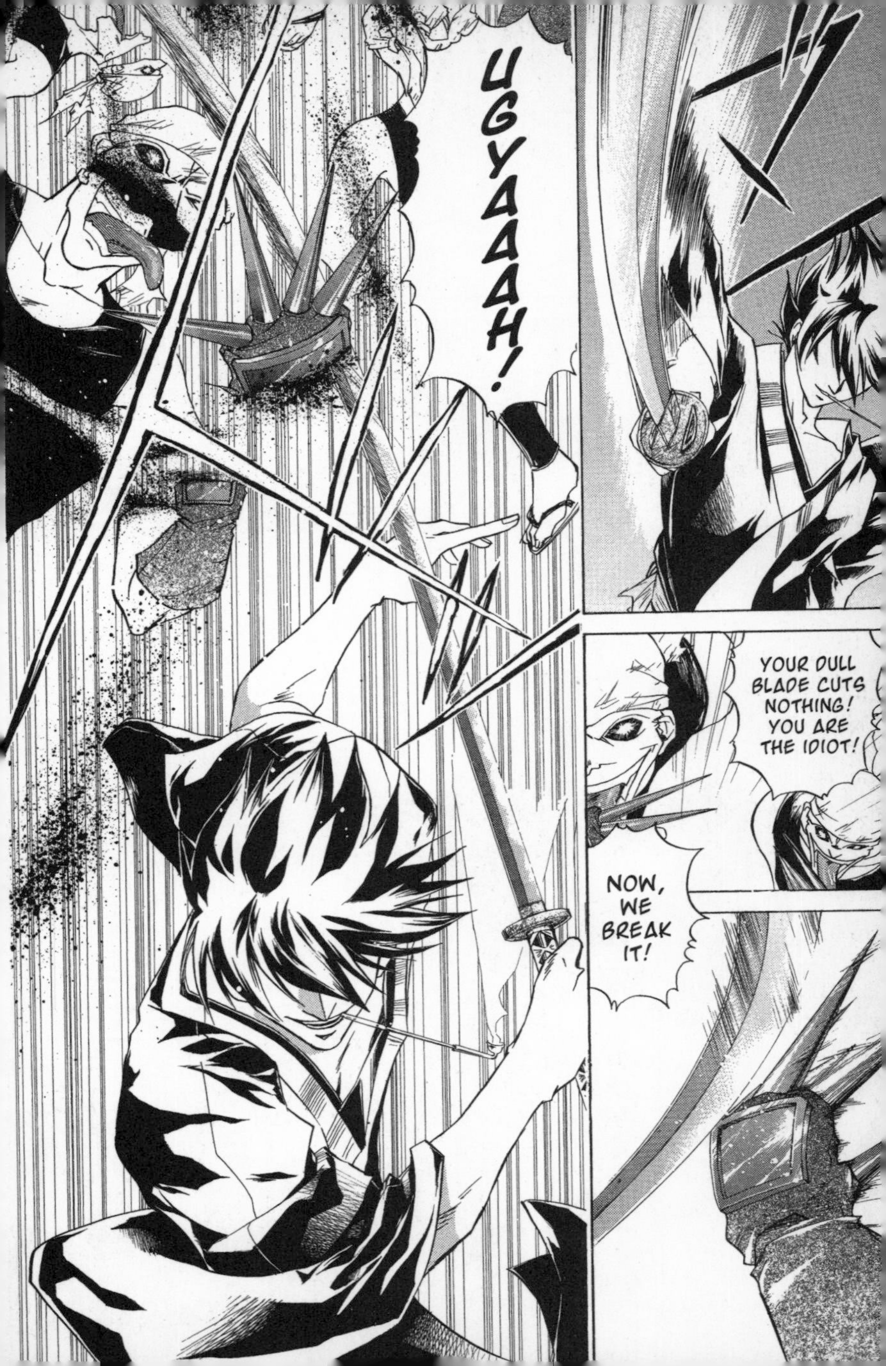
YOUR DULL BLADE CUTS NOTHING! YOU ARE THE IDIOT!
NOW, WE BREAK IT!
UGYAAAAH!

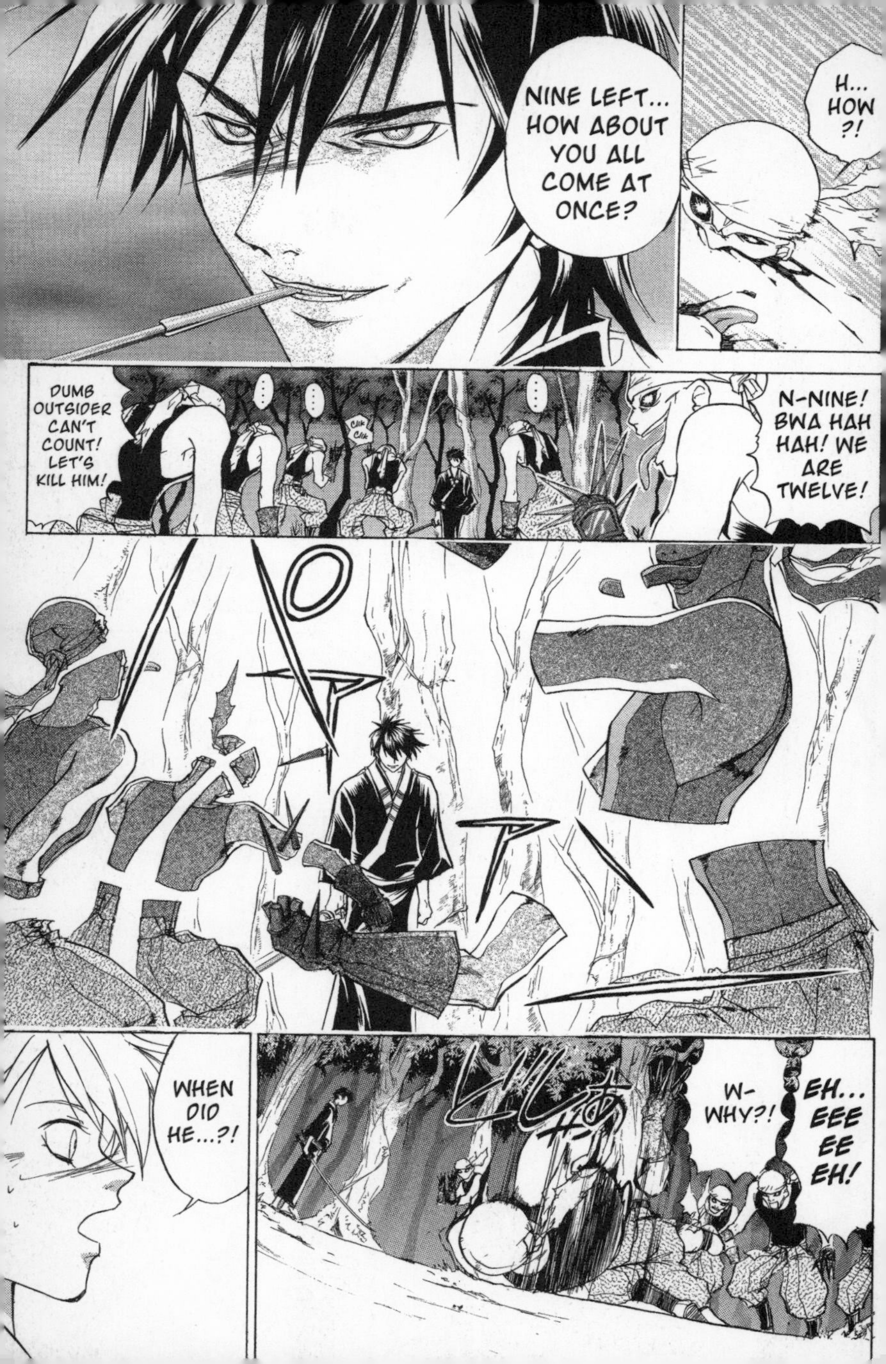
H... HOW?!
NINE LEFT... HOW ABOUT YOU ALL COME AT ONCE?
N-NINE! BWA HAH HAH! WE ARE TWELVE!
...
Clik Clik
...
...
DUMB OUTSIDER CAN'T COUNT! LET'S KILL HIM!
EH... EEE EE EH!
W-WHY?!
WHEN DID HE...?!

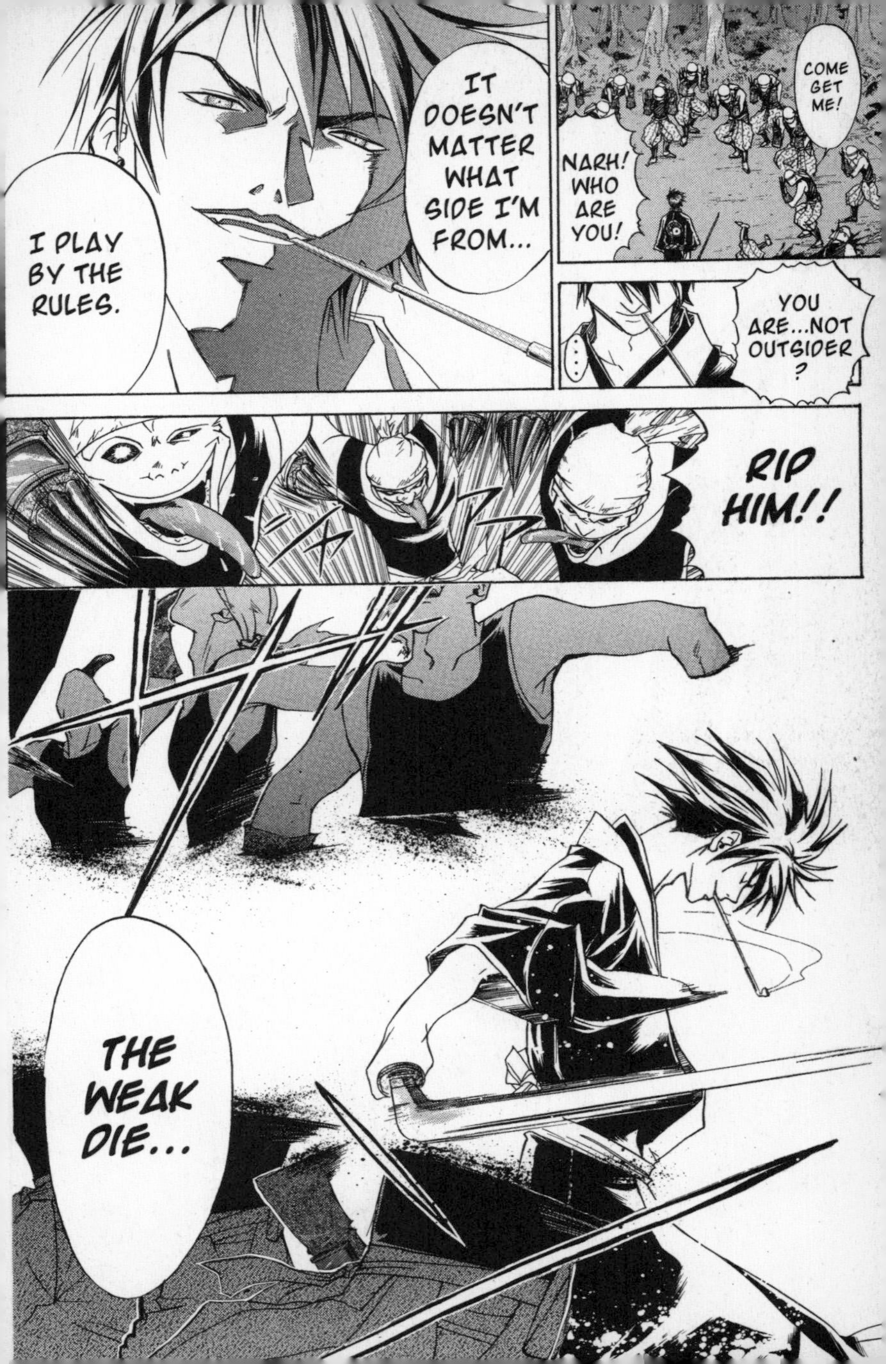
COME GET ME!
NARH! WHO ARE YOU!
YOU ARE...NOT OUTSIDER?
...
IT DOESN'T MATTER WHAT SIDE I'M FROM...
I PLAY BY THE RULES.
RIP HIM!!
THE WEAK DIE...

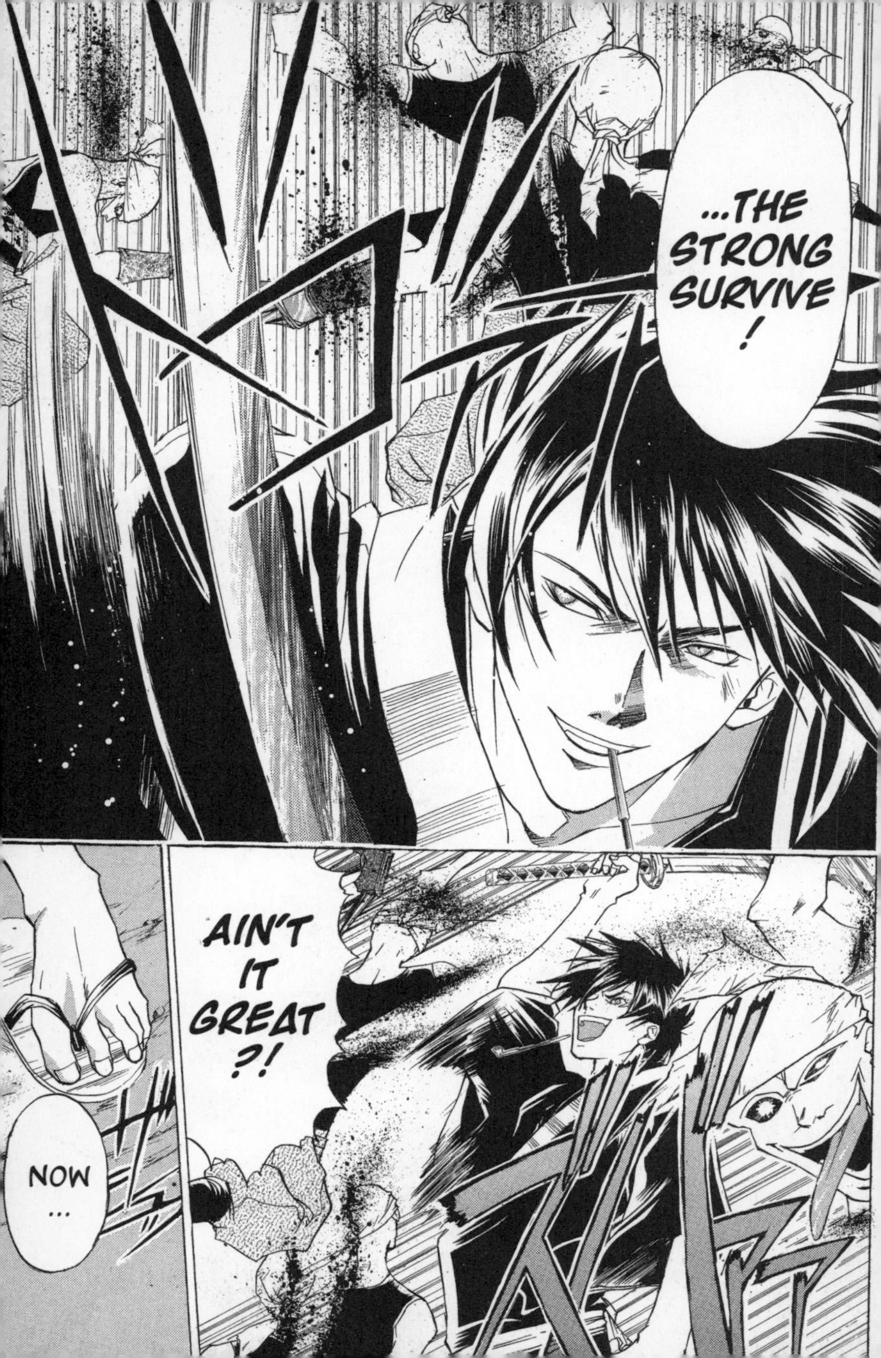
...THE STRONG SURVIVE!
AIN'T IT GREAT?!
NOW ...

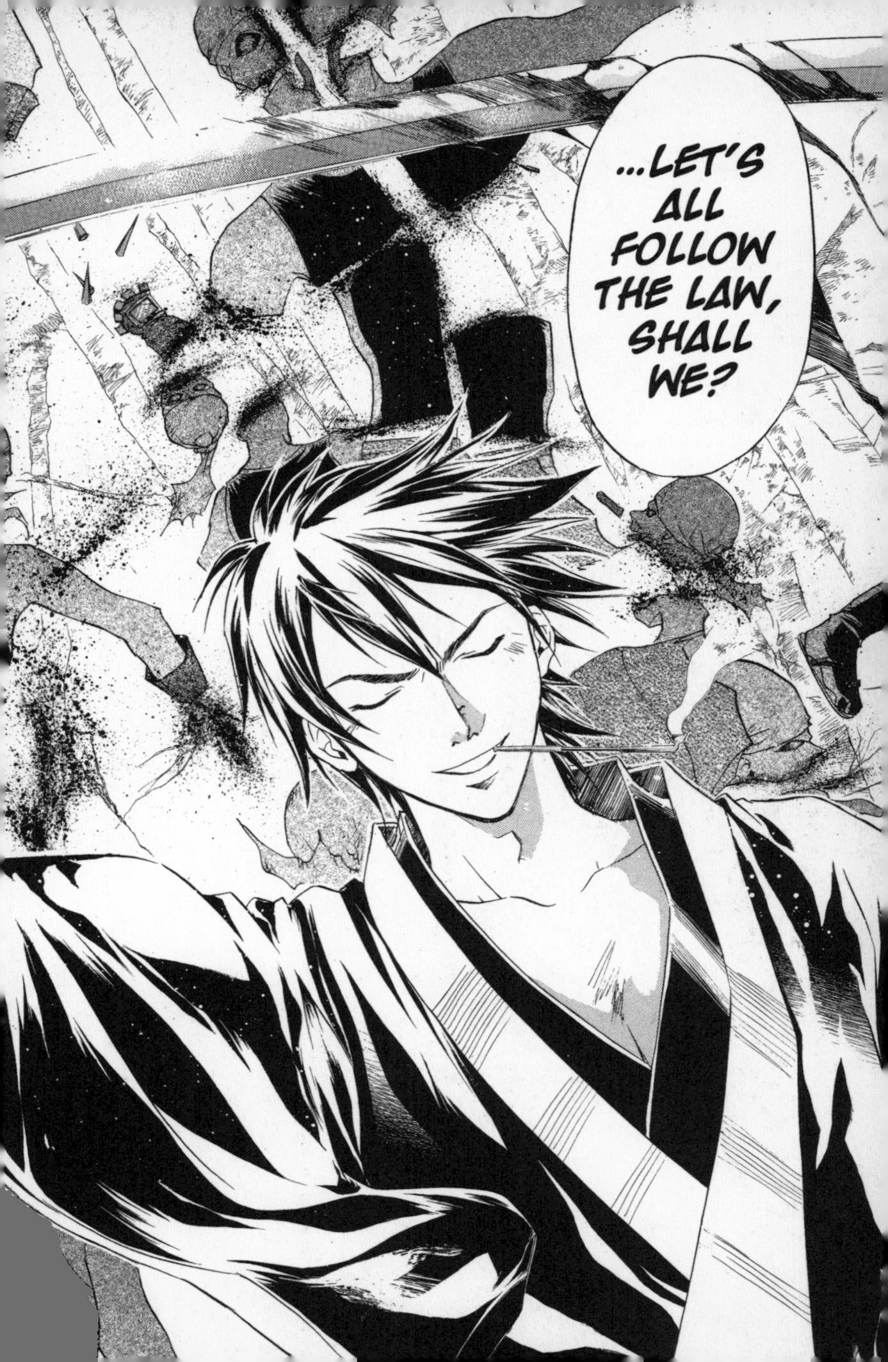
...LET'S ALL FOLLOW THE LAW, SHALL WE?

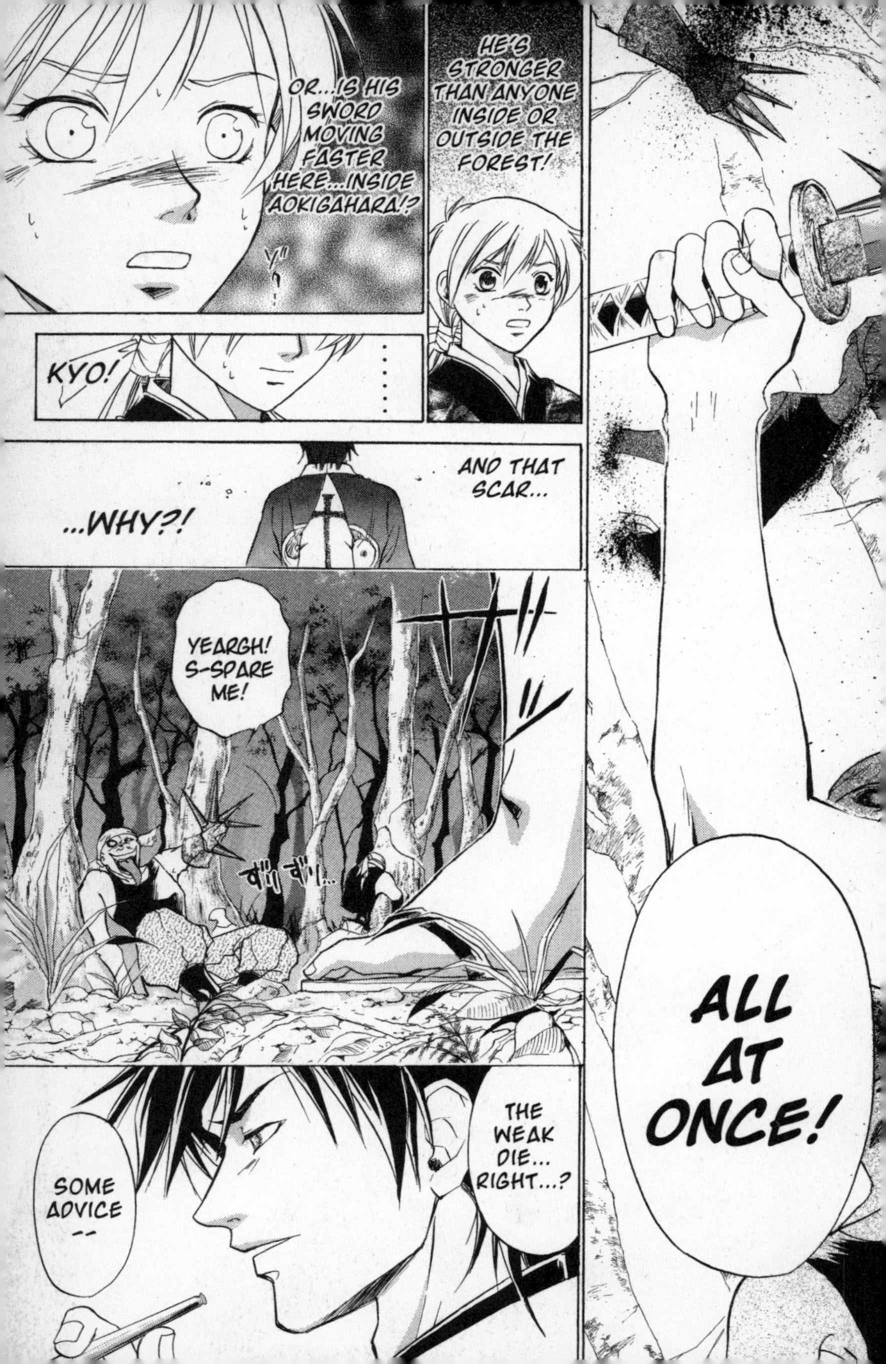
ALL AT ONCE!
HE'S STRONGER THAN ANYONE INSIDE OR OUTSIDE THE FOREST!
OR...IS HIS SWORD MOVING FASTER HERE...INSIDE AOKIGAHARA!?
KYO!
AND THAT SCAR...
...WHY?!
YEARGH! S-SPARE ME!
THE WEAK DIE... RIGHT...?
SOME ADVICE --

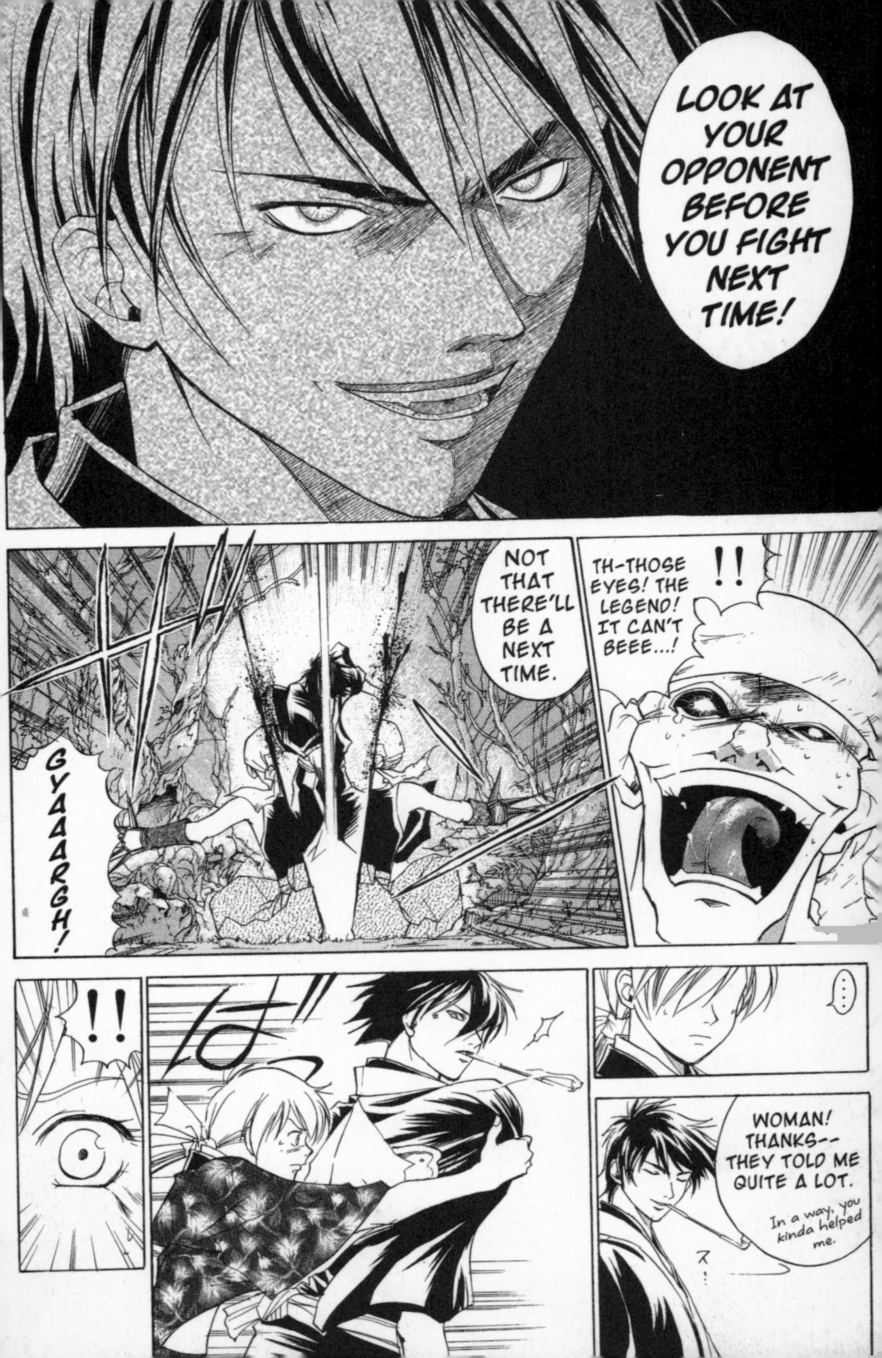
LOOK AT YOUR OPPONENT BEFORE YOU FIGHT NEXT TIME!
!!
TH-THOSE EYES! THE LEGEND! IT CAN'T BEEE...!
NOT THAT THERE'LL BE A NEXT TIME.
GYAAAARGH!
...
WOMAN! THANKS-- THEY TOLD ME QUITE A LOT.
In a way, you kinda helped me.
ス...
!!

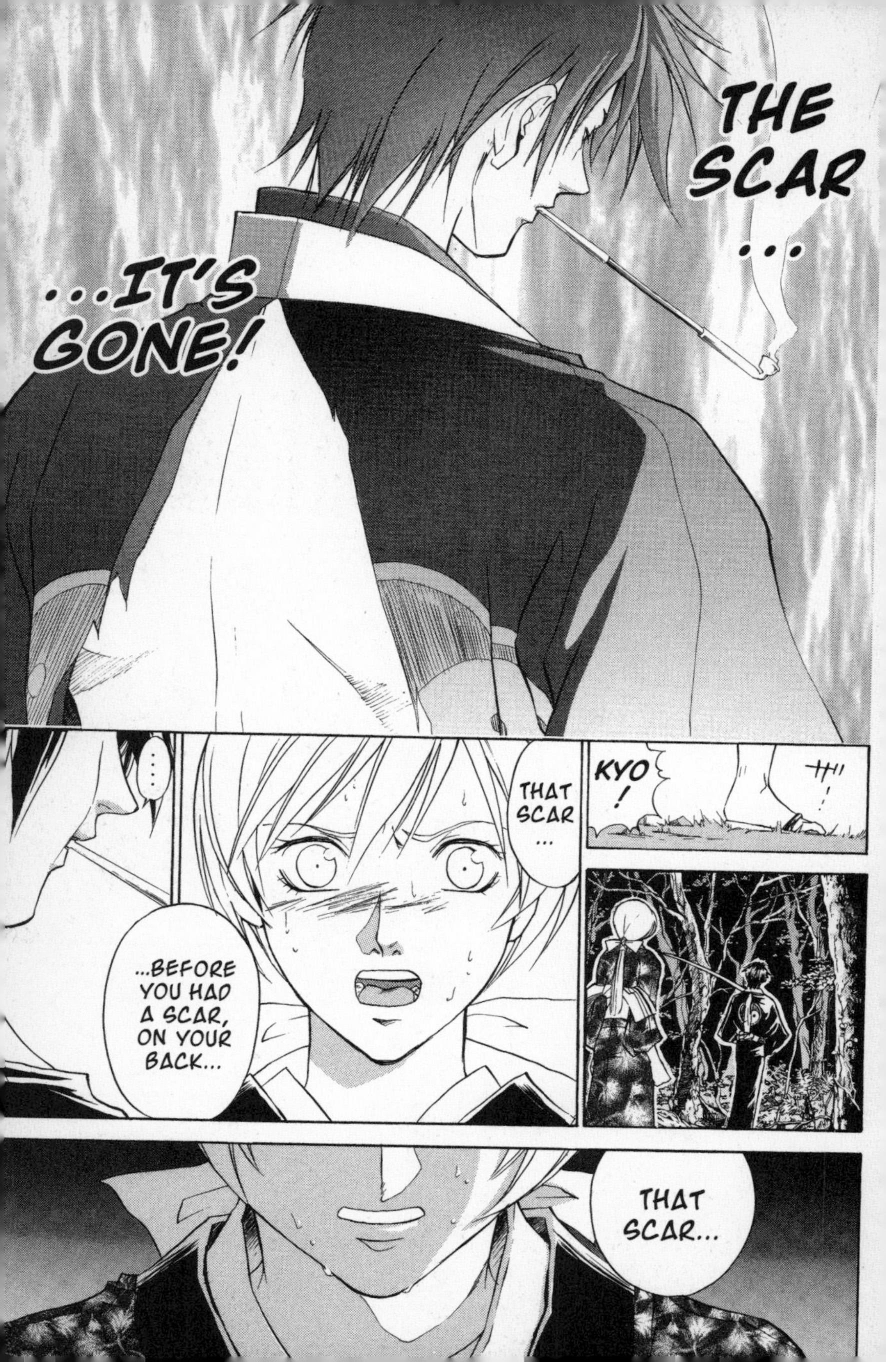
THE SCAR...
...IT'S GONE!
KYO!
THAT SCAR...
...BEFORE YOU HAD A SCAR, ON YOUR BACK...
....
THAT SCAR...

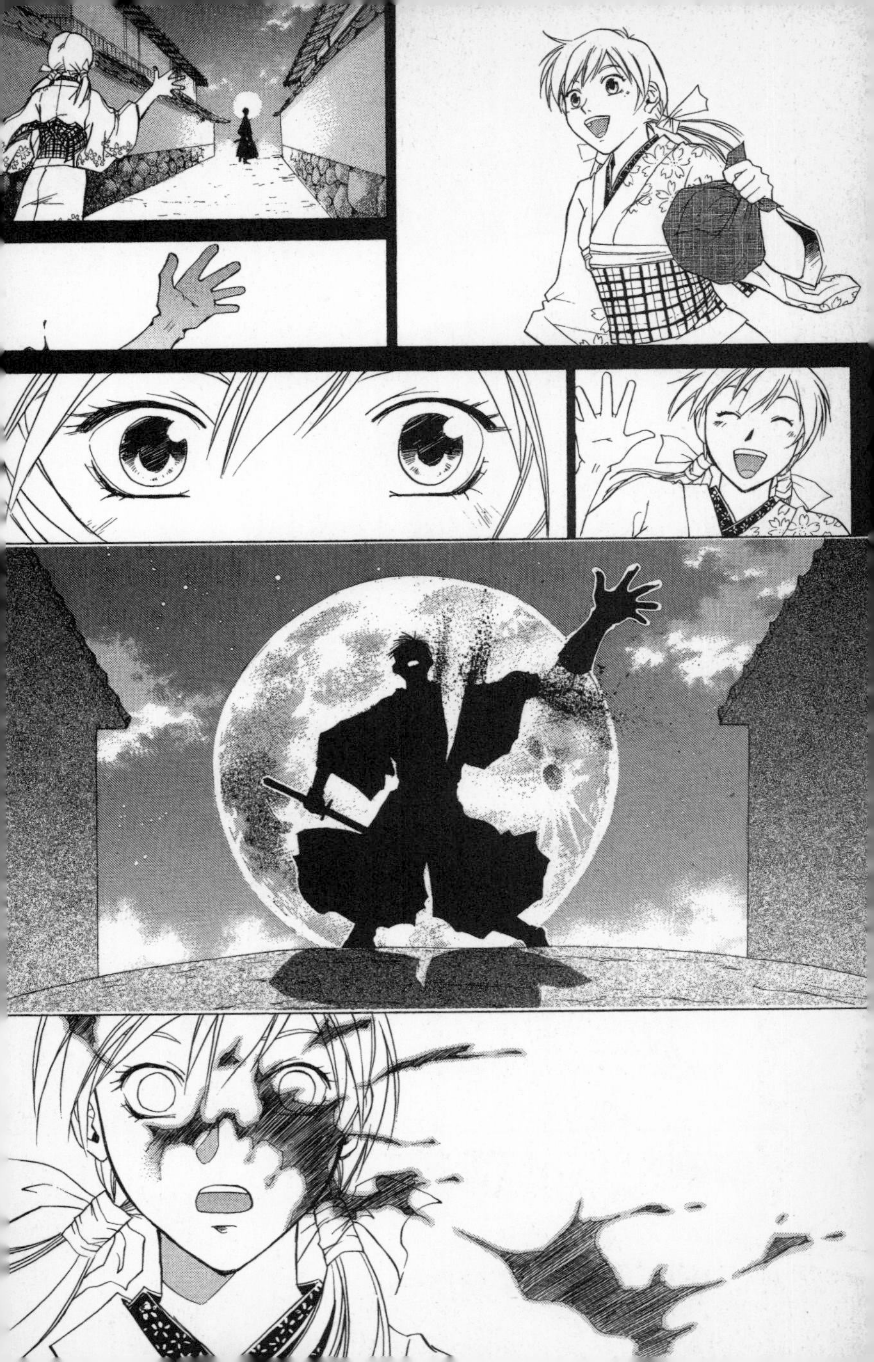

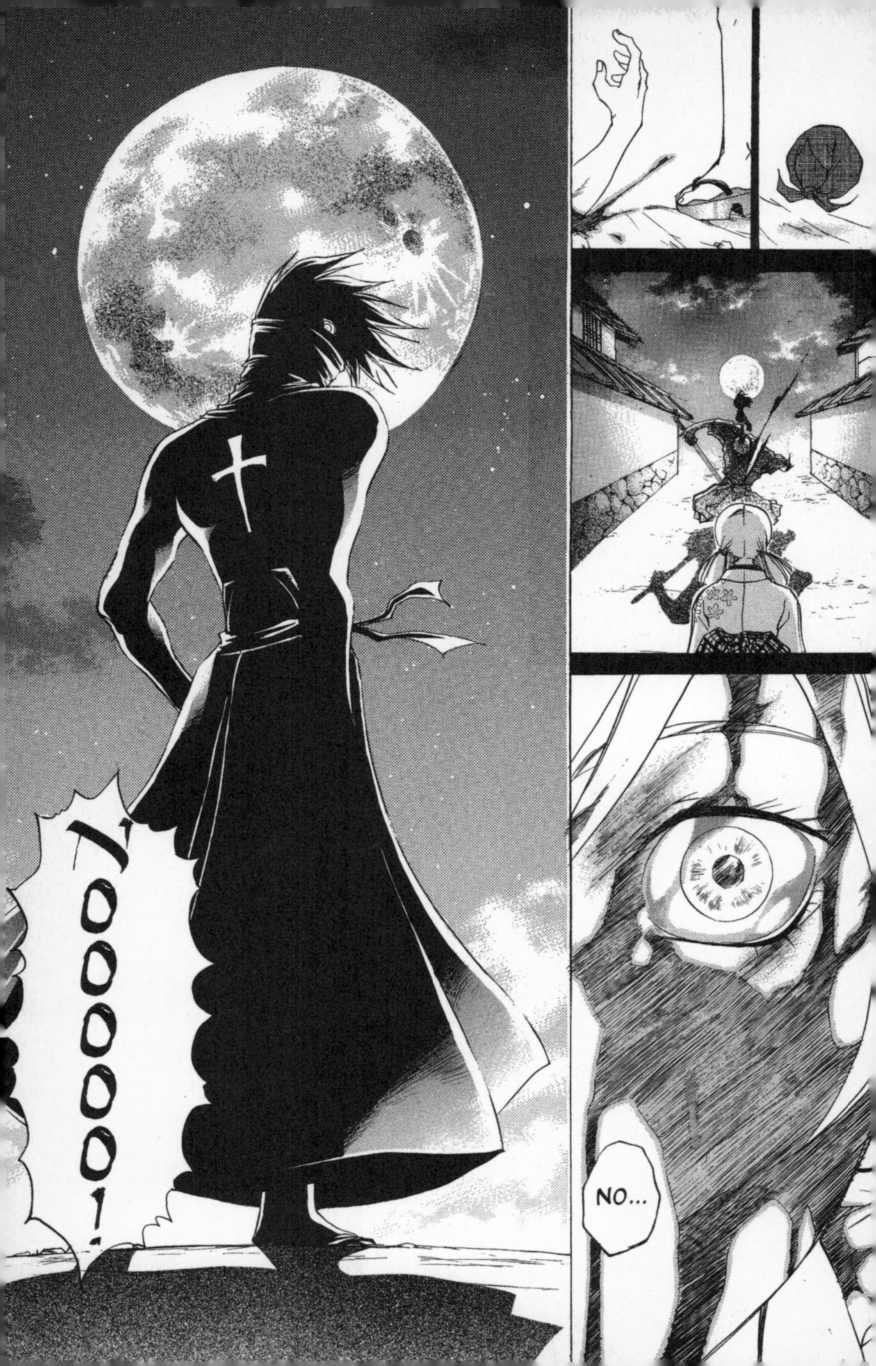
NO...
NOOOOO!

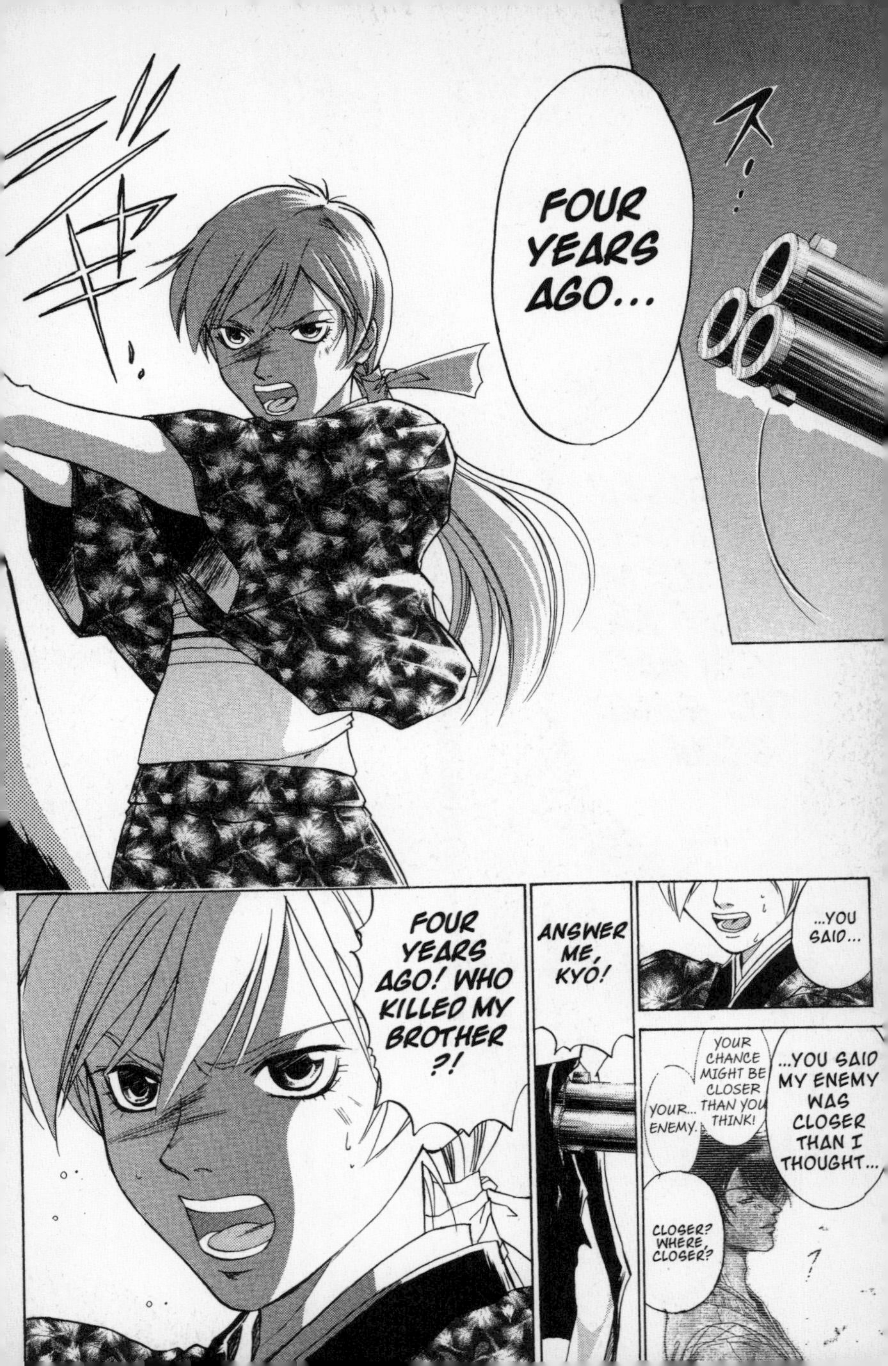

ス…
FOUR YEARS AGO...
ジャキ!
...YOU SAID...
...YOU SAID MY ENEMY WAS CLOSER THAN I THOUGHT...
YOUR CHANCE MIGHT BE CLOSER THAN YOU THINK!
YOUR... ENEMY.
CLOSER? WHERE, CLOSER?
ANSWER ME, KYO!
FOUR YEARS AGO! WHO KILLED MY BROTHER ?!

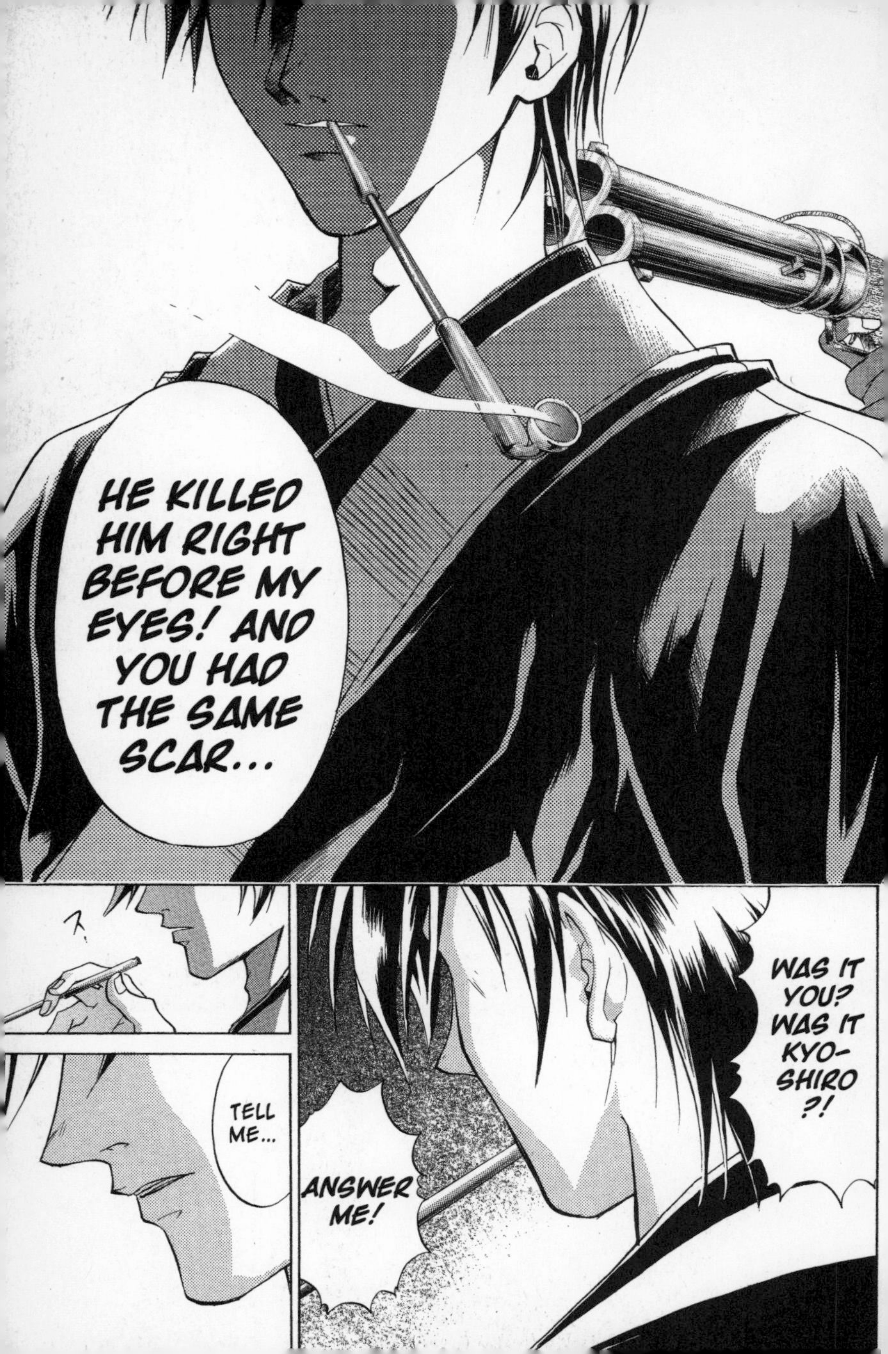
HE KILLED HIM RIGHT BEFORE MY EYES! AND YOU HAD THE SAME SCAR...
WAS IT YOU? WAS IT KYO-SHIRO?!
ANSWER ME!
TELL ME...

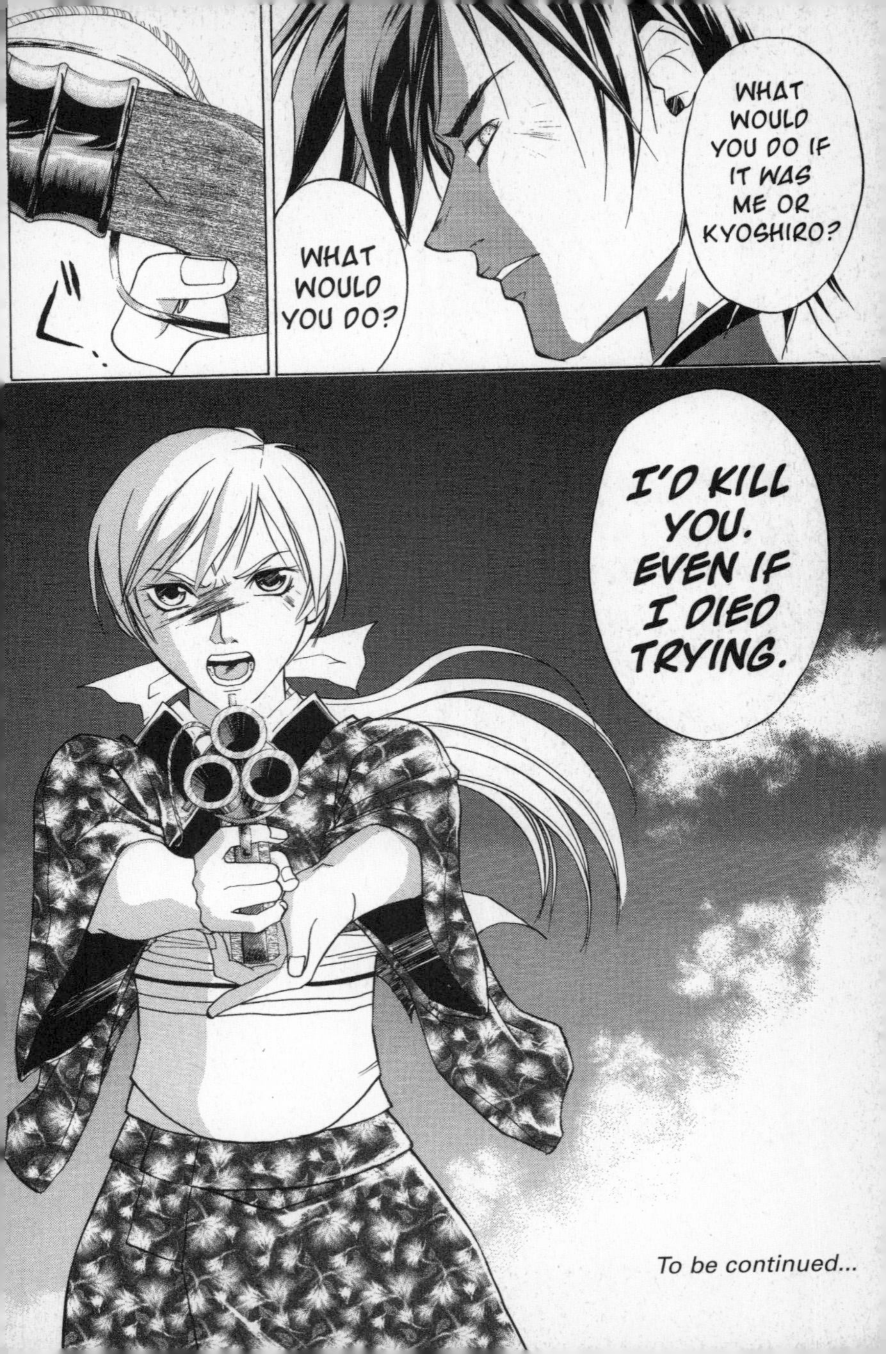
WHAT WOULD YOU DO IF IT WAS ME OR KYOSHIRO?
WHAT WOULD YOU DO?
I'D KILL YOU. EVEN IF I DIED TRYING.
To be continued...

STAFF

Yuzu Haruno
(the chief)

Hazuki Asami

Kenichi Suetake

Takaya Nagao

(*in the order they came in:)

Yuji Takada (Chapters 33, 34)

Kumiko Sasaki (Chapter 41)

CHARACTER PROFILE

Okay, let's hear it!
I'M YUYA SHIINA, FAMOUS ON THE TOKAIDO ROAD, A WOMAN,
HEIGHT 158CM, WEIGHT...THAT'S A SECRET! AND MY SIZES
ARE...B83-W58-H86! (THAT'S IN CM, BY THE WAY).

*Um...about those sizes. A certain...investigation...
shows that you're actually B82-W59-H83...?*
EH? WH-WHAT?! YOU WANNA GET SHOT?!

*Ack! Okay, okay, we'll call it 82-59-83 + a woman's
charm.*
GET ON TO THE NEXT QUESTION ALREADY!

*Okay! What are your likes, dislikes, hobbies, and
favorite meals, and what scares you?*
I JUST LOVE MONEY! (HEART) TEE HEE! (HEART) HOBBIES:
BALANCING MY ACCOUNTS AND TAKING BATHS IN THE
MORNING. I LIKE SWEETS, AND I DISLIKE WASTE OF ANY
KIND. AND...I FEAR NOTHING!

*I see... That's our Yuya, tough as always! Your kind are
always the loneliest, of course.*
WHAT?! N-NOT ME!

*I was just saying in general, you know, in general. (grin)
So, what kind of guy is your type?*
SOMEONE LIKE MY BROTHER, I THINK... AND I DON'T LIKE
BLOODTHIRSTY KILLERS.

*(Um... No one was talking about Kyo last I
checked...) Anything else?*
KYO BETTER PAY ME BACK FOR ALL THE MONEY I'VE SPENT ON
THIS TRIP!

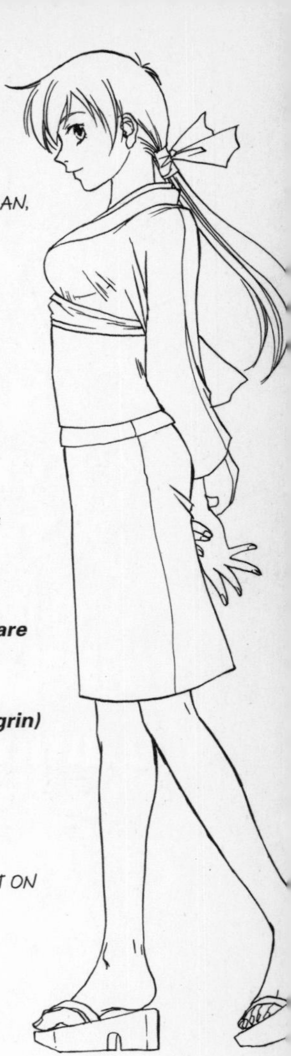

椎名 ゆや

SHIINA YUYA

CHARACTER PROFILE

Kamijyo: Okay, it's profile time!
I'M 25, MALE, HEIGHT 172CM, WEIGHT 64KG, BLOOD TYPE
O, JOB TITLE: BENITORA THE SHADOW MAN!

Wow, Tora, you're older than I thought...
SO WHAT?! I'M ALWAYS YOUNG AT HEART!

**Ah, well put. (That explains a lot...) So, what
are your hobbies and skills?**
I'M ARTISTIC, SO I FIND GREAT PLEASURE IN MAKING
FASHION ACCESSORIES OUT OF ROCKS AND SCRAPS
OF METAL I COME ACROSS. THEY ROCK!

**Yeah, I've been meaning to talk to you about
that tattoo...Doesn't that brand you as a
criminal in Edo Japan?**
HUNH? SEZ WHO?

(Moving on...) Got a favorite food?
I LIKE MY FOOD WAY SPICY! ENOUGH TO GIVE YA
HEARTBURN!

**Okay, how about your likes, your--well, we
know your type, so how about your dislikes
and your fears?**
NO, ASK ME ABOUT MY TYPE! I'M YUYA'S MAN, ALL THE
WAY! DISLIKES: POLITICS. FEARS? HMM...IF I HAD TO
PICK SOMETHING, I GUESS I FEAR MYSELF.

**Er...right. By the way, Yuya's nine years
younger than you! You dog! (grin)**
EH? REALLY?! HUNH, I WONDER IF SHE'S THE TYPE TO
WORRY ABOUT THAT KINDA THING. WHAT SHOULD I DO
GOT ANY IDEAS?

Don't look at me! Any last words?
HEY, EVERYBODY! LET'S PARTY!!!

影法師の紅虎
BENITORA, THE SILHOUETTE

GLOSSARY

Aokigahara-This is a real forest near the base of Mt. Fuji. In medieval times it was said to be home to spirits and demons and was the source of many myths. The dark legend lives on even today with Aokigahara being the site of record numbers of suicides.

-chan-An honorific which indicates friendly familiarity.

Daimyo-A feudal lord.

Edo-Present day Tokyo. After Sekigahara, Edo became the new capital of Japan and home to the Shogun.

Edo Era-(1603-1868) Japan's "golden era" of political and economic stability following the civil wars of the Sengoku Era. *Samurai Deeper Kyo* takes place at the start of the Edo Era.

Hanzo Hattori-A historical figure; leader of the Iga ninjas and ally to Ieyasu Tokugawa. His story passed into legend and became synonymous with ninja master. His presence is found in everything from the anime *Ninja Scroll*, to the video game *Samurai Showdown.*

Ieyasu Tokugawa-The first shogun who ruled over a united Japan following Sekigahara. The Tokugawa family held power in Japan until 1868 when Imperial rule was reinstated.

Kagemusha-A political or military leader's body double.

Koku-A unit of measurement based on how much rice a piece of land can produce. 1koku=180L of rice. In Feudal Japan, wealth and land holdings were measured in koku. A daimyo would control a minimum of 10,000 koku.

Ryo-A small gold coin.

-san-An honorific equivalent to Mr. or Mrs. It can be used with first or last names.

Sekigahara-The greatest battle in Japanese history which took place in fall of 1600 and ended the years of civil war.

Shogun-The supreme ruler during Edo Era Japan.

SAMURAI DEEPER KYO NEXT!

Demon-God Mibu Kyoshiro... Rises Again?!

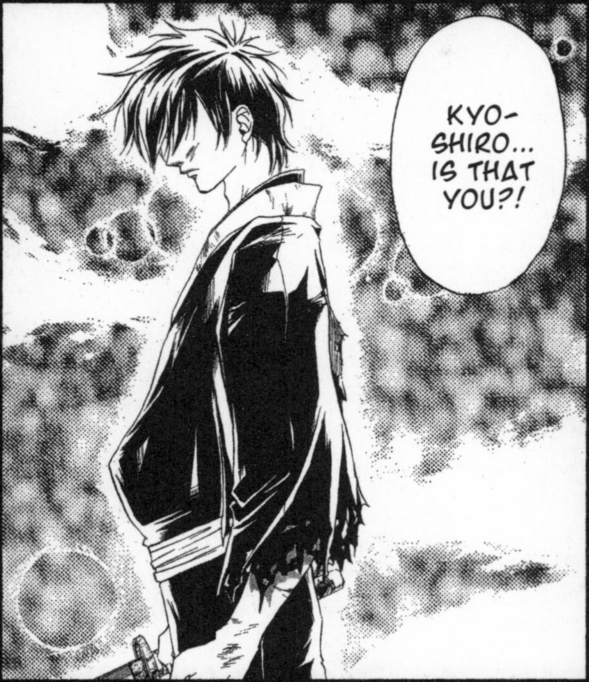
KYO-SHIRO... IS THAT YOU?!

In the next exciting Samurai Deeper Kyo! Don't miss it!!!

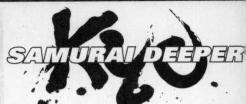

SAMURAI DEEPER KYO

FAN ART!

KYOSHIRO
KYO

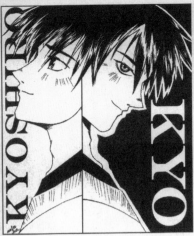

▲ Nalee H.
Eau Claire, WI

It's like the two sides of a coin!
Now, who's heads and who's tails?

Yuya!!!
Stay Away
From
my Red
Tiger

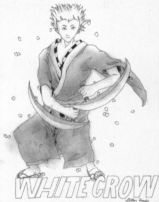

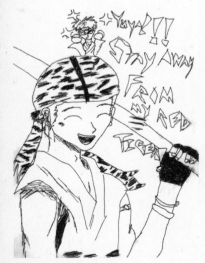

▲ Maegan W.
Conway, AR

Yay! Even number two sidekicks need love!
Thanks for the Benitora love, Maegan

WHITE CROW

▲ Dillon F.
Nashville, TN

Ah, White Crow… You may be dead,
but you still hold a place in our hearts.
Cool picture, Dillon!

Jake O.
▼ Iceland

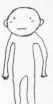

This is You. You must be
weird looking in real life.

Wow! Kamijyo-sensei has fans in Iceland!
I wonder what the manga-ka really looks like.

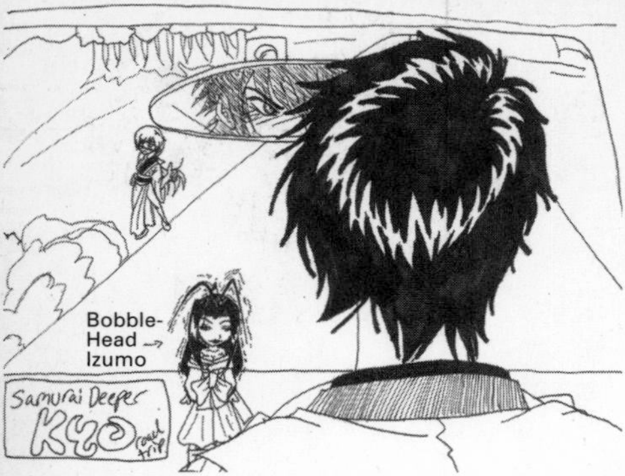
Bobble-Head Izumo
Samurai Deeper KYO

◀ Leah B.
Cedar Rapids, IA

Great concept. I wonder what kind of car Kyo would drive…?

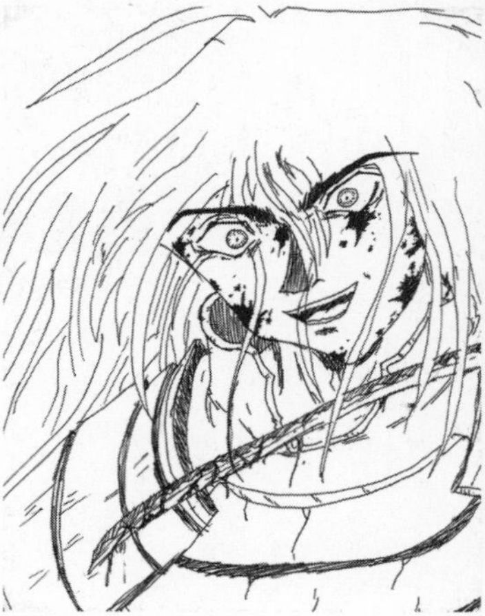

Addison M. ▶
Nashville, TN

Eep! Please, Kyo, don t hurt em! I was just starting to warm up to Kyo, but he looks awfully evil…

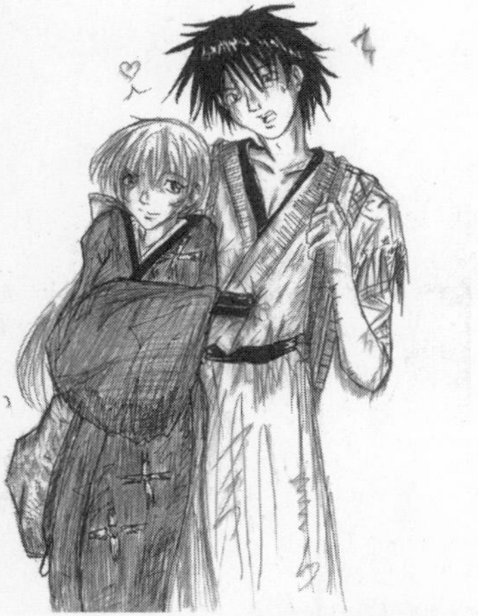

◀ Sarah W.
Concord, NC

What's this? One of Mahiro's tricks?! Surely Yuya isn't falling for Kyoshiro!

Send us your illustrations of Kyo characters! The best illustrations will be published in a future volume of Samurai Deeper Kyo.

- Send your questions and comments as well.

[Address] Samurai Deeper KYO fan mail
TOKYOPOP
5900 Wilshire Blvd., Ste 2000,
Los Angeles, CA 90036

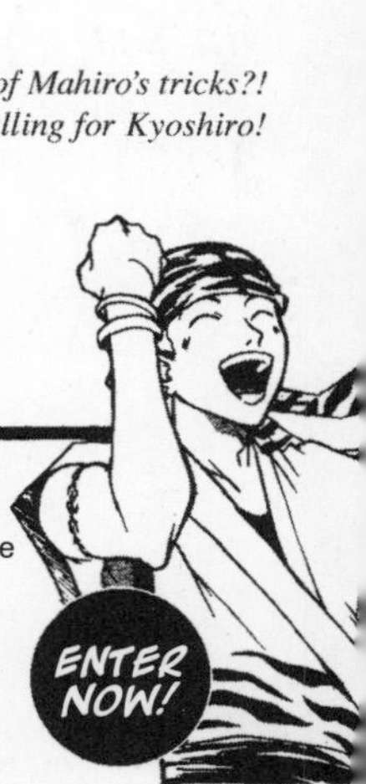
ENTER NOW!

ALSO AVAILABLE FROM ⊙TOKYOPOP®

**For more
information visit
www.TOKYOPOP.com**

11.20.03 T

ALSO AVAILABLE FROM \text{TOKYOPOP}

MANGA

.HACK//LEGEND OF THE TWILIGHT
@LARGE
A.I. LOVE YOU
AI YORI AOSHI
ANGELIC LAYER
ARM OF KANNON May 2004
BABY BIRTH
BATTLE ROYALE
BATTLE VIXENS April 2004
BRAIN POWERED
BRIGADOON
B'TX
CANDIDATE FOR GODDESS, THE April 2004
CARDCAPTOR SAKURA
CARDCAPTOR SAKURA - MASTER OF THE CLOW
CARDCAPTOR SAKURA AUTHENTIC May 2004
CHOBITS
CHRONICLES OF THE CURSED SWORD
CLAMP SCHOOL DETECTIVES
CLOVER
COMIC PARTY June 2004
CONFIDENTIAL CONFESSIONS
CORRECTOR YUI
COWBOY BEBOP
COWBOY BEBOP: SHOOTING STAR
CRESCENT MOON May 2004
CYBORG 009
DEMON DIARY
DEMON ORORON, THE April 2004
DEUS VITAE June 2004
DIGIMON
DIGIMON ZERO TWO
DIGIMON SERIES 3 April 2004
DNANGEL April 2004
DOLL - HARDCOVER May 2004
DRAGON HUNTER
DRAGON KNIGHTS
DUKLYON: CLAMP SCHOOL DEFENDERS
ERICA SAKURAZAWA WORKS
FAERIES' LANDING
FAKE
FLCL
FORBIDDEN DANCE
FRUITS BASKET
G GUNDAM
GATE KEEPERS
GETBACKERS
GHOST! March 2004
GIRL GOT GAME
GRAVITATION
GTO
GUNDAM WING

GUNDAM WING: BATTLEFIELD OF PACIFISTS
GUNDAM WING: ENDLESS WALTZ
GUNDAM WING: THE LAST OUTPOST (G-UNIT)
HAPPY MANIA
HARLEM BEAT
I.N.V.U.
IMMORTAL RAIN June 2004
INITIAL D
ISLAND
JING: KING OF BANDITS
JULINE
JUROR 13 Coming Soon
KARE KANO
KILL ME, KISS ME
KINDAICHI CASE FILES, THE
KING OF HELL
KODOCHA: SANA'S STAGE
LAMENT OF THE LAMB May 2004
LES BIJOUX
LOVE HINA
LUPIN III
MAGIC KNIGHT RAYEARTH I
MAGIC KNIGHT RAYEARTH II
MAHOROMATIC: AUTOMATIC MAIDEN May 2004
MAN OF MANY FACES
MARMALADE BOY
MARS
MINK April 2004
MIRACLE GIRLS
MIYUKI-CHAN IN WONDERLAND
MODEL May 2004
ONE April 2004
PARADISE KISS
PARASYTE
PEACH GIRL
PEACH GIRL: CHANGE OF HEART
PEACH GIRL: AUTHENTIC COLLECTORS BOX SET May 2004
PET SHOP OF HORRORS
PITA-TEN
PLANET LADDER
PLANETES
PRIEST
PSYCHIC ACADEMY March 2004
RAGNAROK
RAVE MASTER
REALITY CHECK
REBIRTH
REBOUND
REMOTE June 2004
RISING STARS OF MANGA
SABER MARIONETTE J
SAILOR MOON
SAINT TAIL

STOP!

This is the back of the book.
You wouldn't want to spoil a great ending!

This book is printed "manga-style," in the authentic Japanese right-to-left format. Since none of the artwork has been flipped or altered, readers get to experience the story just as the creator intended. You've been asking for it, so TOKYOPOP® delivered: authentic, hot-off-the-press, and far more fun!

DIRECTIONS

If this is your first time reading manga-style, here's a quick guide to help you understand how it works.

It's easy... just start in the top right panel and follow the numbers. Have fun, and look for more 100% authentic manga from TOKYOPOP®!

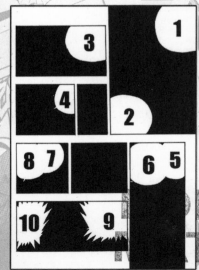